AF606060

THE *SATYRICA* OF PETRONIUS

Petronii Arbitri *Satyrica* Quae Supersunt

PHOENIX

Journal of the Classical Association of Canada
Revue de la Société canadienne des études classiques
Supplementary Volume LXIII
Tome supplémentaire LXIII

INTRODUCTION, CRITICAL TEXT, AND
TRANSLATION WITH CULTURAL NOTES BY
WADE RICHARDSON

The *Satyrica* of Petronius

Petronii Arbitri Satyrica *Quae Supersunt*

UNIVERSITY OF TORONTO PRESS
Toronto Buffalo London

Toronto Buffalo London
utorontopress.com

ISBN 978-1-4875-5071-4 (cloth) ISBN 978-1-4875-5072-1 (PDF)

Library and Archives Canada Cataloguing in Publication

Title: The Satyrica of Petronius : Petronii Arbitri Satyrica quae supersunt / introduction, critical text, and translation with cultural notes by Wade Richardson.
Names: Richardson, Wade, 1943– author, editor, translator. | Container of (work): Petronius Arbiter. Satyricon. | Container of (expression) Petronius Arbiter. Satyricon. English.
Series: Phoenix. Supplementary volume ; 63.
Description: Series statement: Phoenix. Supplementary volume ; 63 | Includes bibliographical references and index. | Text in English and Latin.
Identifiers: Canadiana (print) 20240408829 | Canadiana (ebook) 20240408888 | ISBN 9781487550714 (cloth) | ISBN 9781487550721 (PDF)
Subjects: LCSH: Petronius Arbiter. Satyricon. | LCGFT: Literary criticism.
Classification: LCC PA6559 .R53 2024 | DDC 873/.01–dc23

Cover design: John Beadle
Cover image: Main entrance façade of the Great Cipiko Palace, Trogir, Croatia: site of the *Codex Traguriensis*, which uniquely contains the *Cena Trimalchionis*, until its discovery in about 1650 (see pp. ix, xxxiv–v) (photo by author 2019).

We wish to acknowledge the land on which the University of Toronto Press operates. This land is the traditional territory of the Wendat, the Anishnaabeg, the Haudenosaunee, the Métis, and the Mississaugas of the Credit First Nation.

This book has been published with the help of a grant from the Federation for the Humanities and Social Sciences, through the Awards to Scholarly Publications Program, using funds provided by the Social Sciences and Humanities Research Council of Canada.

University of Toronto Press acknowledges the financial support of the Government of Canada, the Canada Council for the Arts, and the Ontario Arts Council, an agency of the Government of Ontario, for its publishing activities.

Canada Council for the Arts   Conseil des Arts du Canada

Funded by the Government of Canada   Financé par le gouvernement du Canada

CONTENTS

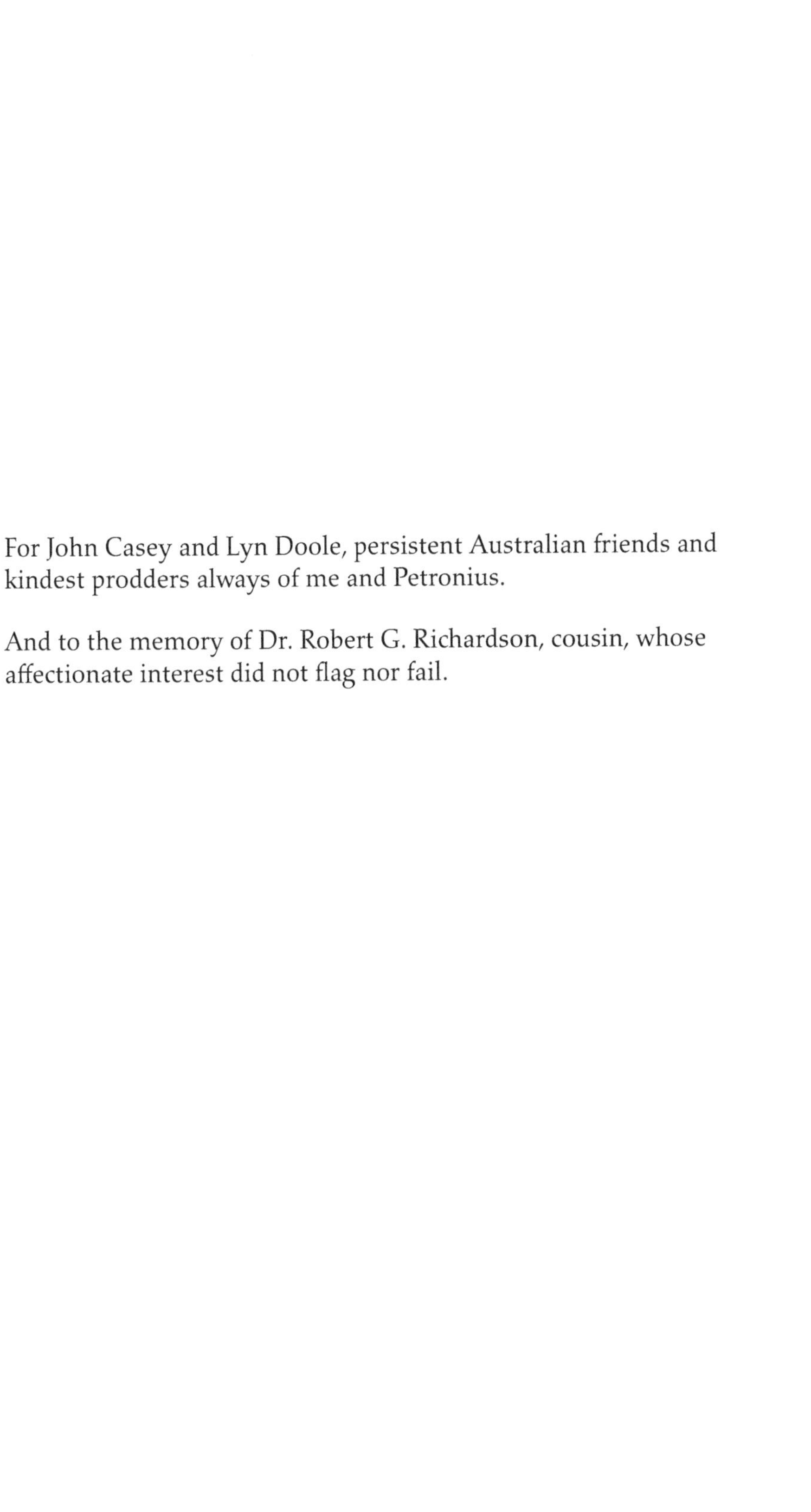

For John Casey and Lyn Doole, persistent Australian friends and kindest prodders always of me and Petronius.

And to the memory of Dr. Robert G. Richardson, cousin, whose affectionate interest did not flag nor fail.

Introduction: Petronius the (Comic) Novelist

Habent sua fata libelli, books have their destinies, a *mot* of the grammarian Terentianus Maurus (c. 200 AD), avoids triteness by ambiguity, and suits the *Satyrica* as well as any text one can think of. Our copy, the archetypal remains, was stitched together rather late, after the detective efforts of Buecheler and Beck.[1] One estimate, which I follow, is that it represents about a quarter of its original. The earliest of three principal manuscript groups, O, is anchored by the ninth-century B, seven centuries after it was written. While uncertain, the length is best gauged by book numbering, in a composite fifteenth-century manuscript, AH, found at Trogir, in modern Croatia, sequentially penned and preserved by the same hand. The former segment's exemplar (A) was late, also fifteenth century, containing the established O text. But H stood apart, unique in almost its entirety: the set-piece Dinner of Trimalchio (the *Cena*), copied from a lost exemplar of far greater age – one close to B (see Gaselee 1915, pp. 9–11; my n. 10). Yet the indications of numbers now exist in A, probably retrieved from H and repositioned to cover the supposed outside range of the full compilation.[2] From the last quartile, then, editors teased out a readable if choppy *Reiseroman* or comic road novel. The *Oxford Dictionary and Thesaurus* (1993), economically and accurately defines the novel as "a fictitious prose story

1 Buecheler 1862, xxxvi: "*Horum ego librorum [codicum] auxilio adiutus principalem satirarum formam studui redintegrare*"; C. Beck 1863 (see n. 8). And in our era meritorious are the five Heimeran/Artemis/Teubner editions of K. Mueller (d. 2015), 1961–2003.

2 O-Class A, bracketing H, has a superscript and subscript "*PETRONII ARBITRI SATYRI FRAGMENTUM EX LIBRO QUINTO DECIMO ET SEXTO DECIMO*," instead of an expected "… *EX LIBRO QUARTO, QUINTO ET SEXTO DECIMO*." An error of reading or inattentive transpolation.

of book length." Lest our *Satyrica* fall short at 150 pages (56,000 words in my translation, with notes), compare Ian McEwan's *Black Dogs* at 145 pages, Jenny Erpenbeck's *Visitation* at 145 pages, Simone de Beauvoir's *The Inseparables* at 137 pages, and so on. To Henry James, cited by G. Schmeling no doubt with the full *Satyrica* in mind, a novel is "a large, loose, baggy monster."[3] Our *Satyrica*'s size makes a more wieldy read. M. Heseltine, editor of the prior Loeb *Petronius*, compares it to Laurence Sterne's *Tristram Shandy*, itself no lightweight: "Both alternate with flashing rapidity between exhibitions of pedantry, attacks on pedants, and indecency," making it "difficult to grasp any structural outline." Heseltine's further view is that "Petronius' novel (a well-earned compliment) shares with life the quality of moving ceaselessly without knowing why."[4] Positivity (*bona mens*: see n. 16) suits the endeavour, despite Schmeling's caution that "the extant text (except for the *Cena*) is not at all a narrative but rather a collection of disjointed pieces and mutilated excerpts" – an arresting counter-blurb to dampen expectations (p. 7). Yet even a fractured continuum can bring pleasure, and a missing plot is not prejudicial.[5] Is Petronius funny? I think so. Funny enough? Yes.

1. The Author and His Date and His Work

The author's name was apparently Petronius, as some manuscripts assign, but of whether he was the Neronian Petronius of Tacitean moment or another man of the same name, *nom de plume* or heteronym, we cannot yet be certain (Tac. *Ann.* 16.17–19). It is the long-held standard view, a datum upon which believers depend for many aspects of the *Satyrica*'s interpretation and beyond. It had been losing ground, but its hermeneutic, not to say hermetic, appeal remains, and it is difficult to discard without a good alternative. In the new Loeb critical edition (Schmeling 2020, n. 3), on the first page of the Introduction, fourth line, Tacitus is given a further opportunity to strut the most admired obituary in Latin. His Petronius is assigned only one page, this time, and we are off to the races with the identification, which if incorrect would complicate Schmeling's thesis of the Neronian *Satyrica*'s seminal place in the development of the ancient novel. There are contrary indications, he concedes, but they can be confronted

3 Schmeling 2020, pp. 7–8.

4 Heseltine 1913; rev. Warmington, 1969, p. xii.

5 Main episodes post-*Cena* are of moderate length and cohesion: shipboard with Lichas at twenty pages (*Sat.* 100–15); and Croton at forty pages (*Sat.* 116–41). To Firebaugh 1922, p. xii, only the *Cena* section is not adventure-narrative but a "digression."

with the presence of another "original work in Latin" by this Petronius as the true foundation of the novel – a suggestion rising modestly at first ("it is just possible") but quick to gain altitude ("I will proceed on [that] assumption," pp. 4–5, 9–10). In the event, Schmeling is careful to keep all the options open, if the Loeb dust-jacket is as authorized as clear: "traditionally Neronian but possibly of Flavian or Trajanic date." Still, it has been remarked, and sensed by myself also, that no other era seems to fit the context so well as the Neronian in terms of social concerns and literary culture; and one could infer that the novel is staged in that era by an archaizing later writer, carefully excluding the major "subsequent" events such as the eruption of Mount Vesuvius. Also, there is a natural conservatism in Roman society which makes the dating of cultural phenomena conjectural.

Objectively, the issue of when the *Satyrica* was composed, compromised by the state of the text, has little bearing upon impact and enjoyment. We resolve an impasse by obviating it, without risk of frustrating the learned scholar and the engaged reader. All must rest on the formidable skills at the author's disposal in recounting his novel and on our less solidly founded skills in parsing them. The choices of procedure are familiar: either the I-narrative, or a controlled third-person account, or perhaps an inventive amalgam of the two. The former, front-loading authority onto the character, benefits from two points of view, although it brings with it the suspicion of artificial autofiction. In the combined Loebs, linked statements serve to cover the perspectives: 1) Encolpius is the mouthpiece of the author (Heseltine 1913, p. xiii); and 2) the narrator is an older, wiser Encolpius looking back upon the episodes in his earlier life (Schmeling 2020, p. 6), making of our text a sort of *Nacherzaehlung*. The problem here is that what we may perceive as a novel author's "cathartic satisfaction in killing off his alter egos" may be the prelude to another round of inscrutable (Petronian) self-satire.[6] The only two Encolpiuses we may infer are the confident sexual Achilles of the concluded past (see *Sat.* 129), and the depressed, ensorcelled one of the story.

6 The "confessions" of Encolpius has much served for the past fifty years as a template of the author's literary plan, from Beck 1972–9, to Schmeling 1994/5 and 2018.The clever phrase in quotes is from Alex Ross, music critic for the *New Yorker*, relating to Thomas Mann's parody of his character's quest for mastery in *Death in Venice*, 1912. It was missed by readers and had to be cleared up by Mann in his next book, *Reflections*, 1918. Also Ross: "The narrator Aschenbach's grandiloquence overshoots the mark and becomes ludicrous" (*New Yorker*, 24 January 2022). Correspondence to Encolpius is too close not to warn of such in Petronius.

2. The Manuscript Transmission and the Making of LOH in the Text

Around 800 AD, there was a manuscript, or codex – the archetype – residing in France. All the major deficits of text (principally before and after the surviving portion) were now reflected by their absence, and no more manuscript text would be added. A monastery scholar at Fleury, near Orleans, not knowing how much was missing, or where the surviving codex belonged within a putative whole, nevertheless saw the value of taking the text in hand for repair to a state of readability. Thus he copied his archetype, did some excerpting, and added asterisks to signal gaps or cruces. This rather dynamic product approximates to a descendant, which I have called *L. It became the basis for L, "the longer extracts" (so called by association with l, a handwritten apograph edition made from it and other sources by Joseph Scaliger in 1571); possibly together with the exemplar of H. Thence arrived the first text including our "full" L class: full in context but not in text, for it shows abbreviation when compared to a fuller – indeed full – version of its chapters 27.1 to 37.5, found also in H, the *Cena* (cf. p. xiii n.). We think the Fleury monk paused his obscure excerpting process here, in order to copy the *Cena* separately in full, and continue later; though three aphorisms shared by H, at 55.6, 59.2, and 75.1, caught his fancy. In this early epoch, L was subjected to another key abridgment, resulting in O – possibly at the adjacent monastery of Auxerre, some 120 kilometres to the east; or else that copyist came to Fleury – with the clearer goal of expurgation of unsuitable sexual material from *L. As we see by comparing O to L, the expurgation is broad and uniform enough to identify the target as homosexuality – from romance to behaviour (assessed below and in sections 4 and 5).

That abridged reproduction of the archetype, O, survives today in two antique pieces of B (*Sat.* 80.10–109.10 is missing), two manuscripts from the twelfth century, R and P (close to B but not directly from it); and fifteen manuscipts of the Italian Renaissance, a very useful one being A, as seen (n. 2). These O manuscript sources were employed to share readings promiscuously with the earliest printed editions (1482–1565), creating an indifferent text, until the balance was redressed by the unabridged content of L that came to light in the manuscripts and manuscript-based editions ldmrtp, from the 1560s to the 1560s. We can now see how passages, perhaps carrying variants, intersected L and O to create the LO presence; while H, with its unique text and exemplar, having disappeared from the fifteenth to the mid-seventeenth centuries, escaped the fate of being contaminated by contemporary printed editions. That way, the characters of L and O emerge jointly and individually for exact scrutiny as to the nature of the latter's abridgment. We may confirm that homosexual romance has been excised from O, but not all, and not with a high degree of care. Heterosexual sexual incident was usually retained, but "mistakes" were made.

3. Register of Shared or Singular Text Content in the LOH Manuscript Classes

1–9.5	LO	School, brothel
9.6–15.9	L	Inn, market, cloak
14.2	LO	Quid faciunt leges
16.1–19.1	"	Quartilla party, the sin
19.2–24.4	L	Quartilla, Psyche
24.5–26.6	LO	Quartilla, Pannychis
26.7–27.1	H	*Cena*: First sights
27.1–27.4	HL	Menelaus
27.4–27.5	H	"
27.5–28.3	HL	Ball game
28.3	H	A toast
28.4–28.6	HL	The pet boy
28.6–28.7	H	100 lashes
28.8–29.9	HL	The wall-painting
29.9–30.1	H	Laenas

30.1–30.4	HL	The dining-room sign
30.5–30.6	H	Dextro pede
30.7–34.4	HL	Seated, drinks, Mezes
34.4	H	Aethiopian slave, Porron
34.5–34.7	HL	Falernian wine
34.7	H	Tangomenas
34.7–34.10	HL	Memento mori
35.1–35.5	HL	Zodiac signs
35.4–37.5	HL	Food, Fortunata
37.6–54.5	H	*Cena* uniquely in H
55.1–55.6	HLO	"Publilius Syrus"
56–75.1	H/HL	56.6/59.2 HL
75.1	HL	Nemo non peccat
75.2–78.8	H	Last gasps of unique *Cena*
79.1–80.8	L	Inn spats over Giton: He goes

L, O, and H are the symbols of the three manuscript groupings in which the text of the surviving *Satyrica* is written, since Burman 1709, into 141 chapters. Note the exclusion here of the Petronius in the *Florilegium Gallicum* and the fragments, the one derivative of the earlier LOH sources (see Courtney 1991; and the other from the *Anthologia Latina*, which contains false attributions. This is not entirely desirable, but one benefit is to give the LOH interface unrivalled clarity; Warmington 1969 excludes also. In our groupings, the LO linkage is the most typical (with *Sat.* 55 uniquely in all three). Variants offer choices on the basis of age, condition, and pedigree. Significantly, the commencing ten chapters of H (*Sat.* 27.1–37.5) are present in L, in what looks like sequential abbreviation. The O class is the carrier of the oldest and best of the surviving manuscipts BRP. L is the longest grouping, a composite edition, organized in the sixteenth century by J. Scaliger, from lost medieval manuscripts and the earliest printed editions. H, a class of its own, is a manuscript written in the fifteenth century from a lost exemplar of equivalent age to our earliest ones close to the archetype, containing unique material, and not examined by scholars, including Scaliger, until the later seventeenth century.

80.9	LO	Nomen amicitiae	128.7–129.2	L	Giton sums up, secrecy
81.2–83.9	L	Blame, soldier, gallery	129.3–130.6	LO	Circe's letter, reply
83.10–84.3	LO	Eumolpus' first poem	130.7–131.7	L	Second try, Proselenos
85.1–87.10	L	The Pergamene ephebe	131.8–131.11	LO	Second tryst
88.1–89v65	LO	Art class, the Sack of Troy	132.1–132.6	L	Circe in a rage
90.1–93.9	L	Eumolpus booed, Giton found	132.7–132.10	LO	Encolpius self-harms
94.1–94.6	LO	Eumolpus courts Giton	132.10–132.11	L	Speak up, "Dido"!
94.7–94.15	L	Quarrels, Mimica Mors	132.11–132.13	LO	Body-shame precedents
95.1–96.4	LO	Innkeeper intervenes, a fight	132.13–132.14	L	More precedents
96.4	L	Encolpius gloats	132.15	LO	The Sphragis
96.4–96.6	LO	Bargates backs Encolpius	132.16	L	Aphorism on sanctimony
96.7–99.6	L	Incidents before boarding	133.1–133.3	LO	Giton and no violence
100.1–108.11	"	Lichas, Tryphaena in pursuit	133.3	"	Prayer to Priapus
108.12–109.4	LO	Peace parley	133.3v14	O	The billy-goat (in B only)
109.4–109.6	L	Kiss, make up	133.4	LO	Proselenos again
109.6–110.4	LO	Reconciling in pairs	134.1–134.2	L	Proselenos scolds
110.4–110.5	L	Giton's looks restored	134.3–134.7	LO	A sexual thrashing
110.6–113.5	LO	The Widow of Ephesus	134.7	O	Etiam lugentes rident
113.6–117.13	L	Wreck, pyre, Croton, plan	134.8	LO	Proselenos explains
118.1–124.3	LO	Lit. class and the Civil War	134.9	L	Lorum in Aqua
124.3–126.11	L	Wealth, Chrysis' proposition	134.9	LO	A slight on Circe
126.12–127.10	LO	Circe and lovemaking	134.10–134.11	L	I can fix this (Oenothea)
128.1–128.5	L	Circe mortified	134.12–135.2	LO	Scary magic arts, kiss
128.6	LO	Nocte soporifera	135.3–135.4	L	Basic rituals

135.4	LO	A kettle and beans
135.4	L	Chipped hog-jowl
135.5–136.2	LO	Dignity of simple rite
136.2	L	A burnt elbow
136.2	LO	An ash-covered face
136.3	L	Fresh kindling needed
136.4	LO	Three geese advance
136.4	L	For their rations
136.4–136.6	LO	Attack leader slain
136.7–136.13	L	Oenothea back, offer
136.13–137.3	LO	Scelerate!
137.4–137.8	L	Ostrich. All forgiven
137.9	LO	Quisquis habet nummos
137.10–141.11	L	More rough measures A phallus Escape Pursuit Chrysis returns Philomela The cure Impatience The codicil

4. Plot and Characterization

In the above chart, there are some ninety alternations of the text coverage by class as the story proceeds. The division bounds are not always precise, but they do succeed in demarcating and illustrating where and how the three classes distribute and treat their material, perversely profiling the miscellany of subject matter and enhancing by chance our narrative's frenetic feel. The chart's purpose is also more specific: to demonstrate the content exclusions and inclusions by the maker of the O class abridgment, as now clearly depicted from the best versions of our oldest manuscripts, BRP (ninth to twelfth centuries). Homosexuality has long been suspected as the low-hanging fruit, and it cannot just be shaken off. Removal of the discreet actual sex scenes and fade-outs, of Encolpius with Giton, *Sat.* 11.1 *fruorque votis usque ad invidiam*, and *Sat.* 95.7 *et cella utor et nocte*; of Ascyltus with Giton, *Sat.* 9.4 *coepitque mihi velle pudorem extorquere*; and even of Encolpius and Ascyltus together, *Sat.* 9.10, presents little problem, but the *Satyrica* rests upon an entire culture of emotional quasi-pederasty among the young male protagonists inhabiting a *Graeca urbs* of the day. It is as indispensable as ineradicable. And it is prone to metastasizing into elderly iterations, such as we see in Eumolpus, a *senex canus* (*Sat.* 83.7), who in a pinch can fancy Encolpius (*Sat.* 140.5) but shows no interest in women (see section 5).

Among notable exclusions in O are Encolpius' private ruminations in *Sat.* 81 on the vicious sexuality of his partners, but that excision deprived readers of the *Satyrica* for centuries of the most supremely valuable, unique source for Encolpius' own criminal history.[7] Then the deft and humorous accosting by the soldier disappears, its fate sealed by too-close proximity to the picture gallery visit (*Sat.* 83), where Encolpius has eyes excessively for art depicting beautiful boys snapped up by lucky gods and shameless nymphs. Even the ensuing remarkable entrance of Eumolpus loses out, together with his very polished Milesian-type tale of the Pergamene Ephebe (*Sat.* 85–7). Then the chaotic pre-boarding Donnybrook between Encolpius, Ascyltus, Giton, and Eumolpus apparently displeased (*Sat.* 96–9), taking with it the bulk of the on-board romantic skirmishing over Giton (*Sat.* 100–9). On the other hand, after Chrysis' toothsome Milesian instruction on the sexual-partner preferences of women went begging (*Sat.* 126 *init.*), the abridger saved the rest of the tryst, *Sat.* 126.12 ff. plus 127 – the failure with Circe – prompting a snippy quip from Charles Beck: "It is to be noticed that the filthiest passages [in P, a medieval O manuscript], as 126 and 127, are most correctly and carefully copied."[8] What of the Dido parody? Gone. What of Eumolpus with Philomela and her children? Gone. Excision, though determined, was not always consistent. The first three-quarters of the *Satyrica* had early fallen into its own black hole, of course, and the surviving manuscript tradition is of little use in speculatively recovering that part.[9] It is time to consider it a write-off, in the vein of Catullus' *quod vides perisse perditum ducas* (8.2). Gone means gone.

But within our last quadrant, at Books 14 to 16, shadowy reminiscences still operate, unwitnessed *in situ*. We can treat the absent linked material as proximate; close in time and place to current events (earlier in Book 14); and relevant to a cause-effect relationship as the story now continues. For the sake of space I shall raise here only one good example: Lichas, Tryphaena, and the shipboard adventure, which in fifteen intricately crafted chapters once struck me as an overplayed farce; but now I value it for furthering

7 See annexe at the end of section 5 (p. xxii), the one discussing the sex. One of the earliest references to sexual redaction is from B. de Montfaucon, acquirer in 1703 of the Trau manuscript for the King of France, who commented that in A, a manuscript of the O class, as in the others, "*obscaena et paiderastian spectantia omnia sublata fuerint.*"

8 C. Beck 1863, p. 5; see n. 1.

9 Ascyltus' complaint of being thrown over for Giton in a sexual role hints at a different Encolpius (*Sat.* 9.10).

plot and character, and for its rhetorical virtuosity. All those seductions and intended seductions enhance the present dangers, deemed the romantic consequence of "off-screen" dalliance: Hedyle, Lichas the ship-captain's wife, had run off with Encolpius (*Sat.* 110.7), angering him and his present mistress, Tryphaena, a travelling courtesan; but this is forgiven as Lichas himself now fancies Encolpius more, an old flame; and Tryphaena, also once seduced by Encolpius, transfers her passion to Giton. Musical deck-chairs.

To return to the effective beginning of our story: A trio of footloose, morally insufficient young men have stopped on the shores of the Bay of Naples, the perfect venue for melting into its populous, fun towns, for a goodish period of recuperation, chiselling, and romantic bickering. One Encolpius is the founding partner, a plausible, self-absorbed aesthete of student age, smart, well educated, and ready to hustle any adventure. This is in fact the story of him: *The Encolpiad*. He'd acquired a lover at some point, Giton, a dreamy youth of sixteen, and, like all who encountered him, became besotted. The pair join forces and invite along Ascyltus, of Encolpius' age, also good-looking, but rough-edged, not a waster of words, of a pragmatism that could come in handy for just such an adventure, whose main aims were the pursuit of sex and cash, effectuated by the seducing of other men's wives, violence and temple robbing, and hawking of the proceeds as stolen goods. This was a recipe for a heap of trouble, which soon found them. In fact, at a time before our opening pages, a lone Encolpius had been caught and sentenced to the arena, but pulled off a lucky escape in the confusion of collapsed stands, possibly from an earthquake. Also at around this time he inauspiciously stole some sacral items from a temple of Priapus, which prompted a fitting plot-altering, plot-long curse of sexual impotence, robbing him of his swagger and self-possession, and leaving him as damaged goods (see *Sat.* 81, p. xii, for the first source; then *Sat.* 130, a letter to Circe; there are questions of veracity). From now on, from our *Satyrica*'s opening to its closing scenes, Encolpius' sex life with Ascyltus, Giton, and all those women (cf. *Sat.* 129.1 "... *Achilles eram*") was in tatters. Just as worryingly, if the trio had managed to stay clear of the law, their continuing criminal imperatives had put a target on their backs, first as fugitives and then as outlaws at constant risk of being turned in. For their very public brand of living and loving on and off the streets and dossing down in bug-infested inns exposed them to ready recognition and apprehension. The fear of discovery, plus the prejudice of others to their lifestyle, are running features of the plot, given voice to by Ascyltus at *Sat.* 10.5 and 14.1, and Encolpius at *Sat.* 91.3 and 93.3.

Next in importance in the *Satyrica* are the aging poet (*senex canus*) Eumolpus and the equally aging (*senex calvus*) freedman supremo, Trimalchio, major figures both, though to the side of the operatic melodrama. Eumolpus, from *Sat*. 83 a dominant personality with a large influence over the later culture of the work (in the broad sense), will get his introduction in section 5, fittingly the one to do with sex. And Trimalchio will be covered at his dinner, in section 6, in the company of his fellow freedmen.

5. The Sex: via *Libido* and *Libidinosus*, *-a*, by Speaker and Gender Target (M/W)

Datur enim concessu omnium huic aliqui ludus aetati,
et ipsa natura profundit adulescentiae cupiditates. Cicero Cael. 28

For everyone agrees in allowing the young a few love-affairs,
and nature herself pours forth the yearnings of youth

10.7	*divisionem libido faciebat*, Encolpius of himself (M)
24.7	*in promulside libidinis nostrae*, Quartilla of herself (W)
26.2	*iocantium libidine accensa*, narrator/Encolpius of Quartilla (W)
26.4	*libidinosa speculabatur diligentia*, narrator/Encolpius of Quartilla (W)
53.1	*saltationis libidinem*, narrator/Encolpius of Fortunata (W)
74.9	*qui non contineret libidinem suam*, Fortunata of Trimalchio (M)
81.4	*adulescens omni libidine impurus*, Encolpius of Ascyltus (M)
81.5	*libidinis suae solum vertit*, Encolpius of Giton (M)
81.6	*mutuis libidinibus attriti*, Encolpius of Ascyltus and Giton (M)
87.1	*cetera quae libido distenta dictat*, Eumolpus of himself (M)
94.5	*iracundus sum et tu libidinosus*, Encolpius of Eumolpus (M)
108.8	*rabies libidine perditorum collecta*, navigator of his passengers (MW)
110.7	*peregrina libidine*, Eumolpus of Widow of Ephesus (W)
113.3	*libidinosa migratione*, narrator/Encolpius of Hedyle (W)
113.7	*omnes blanditiae quascumque mulier libidinosa fingebat*, Encolpius of Tryphaena (W)
119.60	*ferroque excita libido*, Eumolpus of soldiers (M)
126.5	*nec libidinem concitant nisi*, Chrysis of Circe (W)
126.11	*tam discordem libidinem*, narrator/Encolpius via Chrysis of Circe (W)
129.4	*si libidinosa essem*, Circe of herself (W)
138.3	*aniculae solutae mero ac libidine*, Encolpius of old women (W)

Above is a list of the twenty instances in the *Satyrica* of the Latin word, in its setting, that approximates in range and sense to "sex" in English, for which the Latin *sexus* has no use. Nominally, its central meaning is sexual lust, and adjectivally, wanting sex or available for sex. "Lustful" would fit most examples, though for variety one can reach for appropriate local nuance, as at *Sat.* 129.4, "were I oversexed," and Hedyle ("sweetie" in Greek), at *Sat.* 113.3, "running off with another man." The *Satyrica* has a reputation as a formational homoerotic classic, which of course it is. Yet tallying up these windows onto *libido,* and mindful of the reach of satire and misogyny in male-mediated texts, one finds it bracing that the fictitious women in the common imagination of the day can surpass the men in lustful industry by a count of eleven to eight (one affects both). Leaving aside whether this is a high number or a low, a trove of libidinous activity per se or suspicion or accusation of it is found throughout, and the list will serve, if partially, as a sexual usage guide and place keeper as the narrative proceeds.

We commence our review of the *libido* examples by noting the numerical predominance of women by this metric, remarkable considering how Encolpius, in a few moments, can rack up three complaints of the faithless, licentious behaviour of his two male sex partners (*Sat.* 81.4–6). To this add his rumination early on (*Sat.* 10.7) that it was "lust, pure and simple, that precipitated the separation," and we have a concise verbal record of homoerotic misbehaviour, though on multiple further occasions we shall see it in play. Do these fraught moments from the romantic homoerotic playbook entitle us to think of the trio as idiopathic natural sensualists, nonbinary *avant la lettre,* in that the sexual engagement is not restricted to males? The study of the phenomenology versus ontology of homosexuality is a very complex one, and well outside my competence, though I am comfortable with seeing how, through Petronius, a gay affair, gay sex, and gay love can be grasped as real and of teachable substance. In essence, is the Encolpius of T.P. Arbiter the gay equivalent to the Maurice of E.M. Forster, or is he typologically different?

Homosexualized sex addicts of the classical period would risk perhaps a shake of the head, not a jail term, and the era is notorious for its forgiving tolerance of the strongly erotic (that is to say, inguinal, sanguinal) charge of youthful physical beauty wherever encountered; and perennially justified in romancing, eroticizing, sensualizing, and acting upon it more or less indiscriminately. After all, the gods stood as its enduring archetype, though unconventional excess in men could raise eyebrows and was not always greatly approved, as the tagging of the deceased freedman Chrysanthus with *pullarius* (or *puellarius*) indicates (*Sat.* 43.8).[10] Either would be *outré*, for there were obviously ethical, social, and familial restraints and well-appreciated downsides to underage sexual engagement, with its potential for emotional and physical abuse. Shades of Aurelius in Catullus 15, with his *penis infestus pueris bonis malisque*; and one notes the vain efforts by his parents to keep pedagogic predators away from their son, the "Pergamene Ephebe" (see *Sat.* 87.1 in the *libido* list), whose beauty would be the ultimate provocation – a topos throughout classical culture, from Jupiter to Juvenal. Even Trimalchio, lord in his manor, could not escape a tongue-lashing from his Fortunata (*libido* list 74.9, for a lingering buss of a moderately attractive boy slave. Greek and Roman solicitude over sin and guilt had a trigger set stiffer than ours, but in this case Fortunata had none of of it, certainly not the stock excuse of an affectionate kiss for a frugal boy (*Sat.* 75.4).

Fortunata was great friends with Scintilla, wife of the late-arriving Habinnas, who insisted that she come and take her place, sliding onto the same couch. The new, married, couple at dinner were social equals, to judge from the bonhomie between the men, and Scintilla's uninhibited remarks and behaviour, like the mutual showing off of jewellery. As the drinks went down and the evening wore on, the women got into a full on the mouth smooching session (*Sat.* 67.11 *iunxerunt oscula … dumque sic cohaerent*), to which Habinnas firmly put an end with a grab and back-flip of Fortunata's ankles over the couch. This being today, the question arises, can the women's absorption in each other be sign of a lesbian affect? Why not? Habinnas' boorish horseplay seems vengeful and cruelly disruptive, with a point to make; but no further guidance is supplied.

One person clearly warming to his work at the expiation ceremony and party of the priestess Quartilla (*libido* list *Sat.* 24.7, 26.2, 26.4) was the *cinaedus*, an invited male drag performer called Toddy (*Sat.* 21–4), let loose to fellate vigorously the horrified Encolpius as punishment for his Priapeian sacrilege – a scene of high comedy, as Petronius signals by having Giton "nearly bust a gut laughing" (*Sat.* 24.5 *dissolvebat ilia sua*). The *cinaedi*

10 The present reading of H, *puellarius* – girl-mad – is apparently unexpected enough to cause it to have been emended by Burman to *pullarius*, pursuer of little boys. In H the spacing of the -el- is unkerned, i.e., very cramped, suggestive of an insertion or adjustment in the copyist's hand, although there is no doubt of the reading now. The question is whether Burman leapfrogged over it to land upon *pullarius* as the original reading of Petronius. Yes. See for convenience Gaselee 1915, p. 212, l. 2. Gaselee is interesting for evaluating the copyist's "mistakes" as indicators of the exemplar's age (p. 11). See section 8.

were a recognized class (not even subject to constraints upon *libido; hors de combat*), often castrati, of men inclined to gravitate to camp, sexualized entertaining, of little use to women and vice versa (cf. *Sat.* 23.3, a poem by Toddy summoning the brotherhood). It is no surprise that *Sat.* 18.7 to 24.5 forms an especially obscure and mangled episode, with plentiful lacunae and reassembled short passages, some in the wrong place, excluded from O and pointedly resuming at Giton and the little girl Pannychis' mock wedding (*Sat.* 24.5–26.5). The child-play fades, as this chapter crosses mid-path into the staider cosmos of H and the dinner with Trimalchio.

Eumolpus, the resilient, old, but still randy poet (*Sat.* 94.5 *libidinosus*), appearing on the scene half-way through the novel in *Sat.* 83, makes the *libido* honour roll with four mentions, the result of an intact sex-drive with a preference for good-looking boys and very young men. He has little time for women also, but his "homosexuality" is more complicated. Young and/or sexually active women would have had little time for him back, and for an old man with his drive the search for sex was all about playing the percentages and backing the odds. In the culture of the road, boys were an easier mark. He knew them better for having been one. I imagine him as a role model for Encolpius and Ascyltus should they get to live that long. We might call him a homosexual of convenience, contingency, and temperament. Now he recognizes instantly in the unhappy Encolpius a boy-smitten fellow-traveller, and he has just the prescription in a story of a homoerotic adventure he had as a young man, like Encolpius.[11] The seduction of the Pergamene Ephebe (*Sat.* 85–7) has the status of a Milesian classic. A comment in my translation section *ad locum* notes the striking use of *ephebe* (adolescent) five times in rapid succession, a rare word found only once elsewhere in Petronius, for Philomela's boy in a like context (*Sat.* 140.5). To counter reproach of age-inappropriate pederasty? Admittedly, *puer* (boy) occurs five times too.

Fortunata earns dishonourable mention on the *libido* watchlist for her dancing (*Sat.* 53.1), making it now a good time to mention the many

11 The illustrator Norman Lindsay, noted father of Jack Lindsay, known for a distinctive Satyricon translation (1944), oddly sketches Eumolpus in Pergamum on the quaestor's payroll (*Sat.* 85.1 *stipendio eductus*) as bald, elderly, and sizing up a boy of no more than ten and well short of ephebe stature (ad p. 80, ill. 3). Jack may have misled his dad with a translation, rendering *Sat.* 85.2 *de usu formosorum* as "on the proper use of little pretty boys" (p. 67). Both men were prolific authors and utopian Marxists. From this point on, with such an account, Encolpius was on notice to watch out after Giton, *Sat.* 94.5 *"tu libidinosus!"* and himself: *Sat.* 140.5 *tam frugi erat ut illi etiam ego puer viderer.* "[Eumolpus] was so adaptable that even I was like a boy to him." His last act was a feel of Encolpius' genitals to vet personally his recovery (*Sat.* 140.13).

lusty women who see to it that they outnumber the men in their quest for default heterosexual satisfaction, often under limitations forced by age and poverty. In text order: Quartilla, thrice libidinous, including a self-mention (*Sat.* 24.7–26.4); Psyche (*Sat.* 20.2 ff, unlisted but earned); the Widow of Ephesus (*Sat.* 110.7); Hedyle (*Sat.* 113.3); Tryphaena (*Sat.* 113.7); Chrysis (*Sat.* 126.5), herself a late convert to Encolpius; Circe (*Sat.* 126.11); Proselenos and Oenothea, the drunk old women giving chase (*Sat.* 138.3); Philomela (*Sat.* 140.1 ff, unlisted but a contender). And one should not miss the lowly Proselenos' so-accurate nutshell characterization of the breakdown of Encolpius' bifunctionality: *Sat.* 134.8 *neque puero neque puellae bona sua vendere potest*; "he can't make a sale to boy or girl." The pick of the pack is Circe, who happens to like it rough (*Sat.* 126.7); Encolpius, slave-impostor, has let her down, and is overmatched for "sex with a real woman"; cf. *Sat.* 9.8 (Ascyltus to Encolpius, prophetically): *ne tum quidem, cum fortiter faceres, cum pura muliere pugnasti*. This is a perceptively staged, utterly alluring performance: elegant, sardonic, furious in disappointment, as the lush, lyrical setting turns into a wasteland of shame. Though not on the list, recall the passionate greeting exchanged by Fortunata and her old girlfriend Scintilla (*Sat.* 67.4–14; see p. 12, above) and its consequence.

Annexe. Encolpius' ruminations upon desertion (*Sat.* 81; not present in the O-class):

> I sadly gathered up my things and rented a quiet place by the sea. There I holed up for three days' worth of brooding upon my loneliness and humiliation. I racked my wounded soul with many a wail, and amid the profoundest groans proclaimed over and over, "And why couldn't I have been buried in that landslide? Or drowned in the sea, which takes it out even on the innocent? Did I evade the law, cheat the amphitheatre, kill my host, only to languish in defiance of my bold record a penniless, friendless exile in some Greektown rooming house? And who made me an outcast? A young dude polluted by every vice and deserving of exile even by his own admission, not only free but freeborn, thus doubly degenerate – who sold his tender youth for a throw of the dice to someone thinking he was buying a man but got a pseudo girl instead." As for the other one, on the very day for celebrating his manhood he put on a dress – when his own mother convinced him he was no man – and worked a prison farm like a woman. Then his money ran out, and he found new grounds for lust, abandoning the tie of a stable relationship and like a kept woman – for very shame! – sold out on the strength of a one-night stand. As I speak the lovers lie entwined the night long, and spent

from their mutual lusts are doubtless mocking my loneliness. But they will pay. If I'm the man, the free man I think I am, I'll redress my wrong with their guilty blood!"[12]

6. The Freedmen and Their Table Talk and Trimalchio [Spellings after Ernout]

Since Republican times, freedmen – freed slaves eligible for citizenship, as their description implies (*liberti*) – were a working class of artisans, masons, traders, shopkeepers, copyists, bailiffs, secretaries, and teachers, often carrying on the professions and lives they led before manumission. They became attached as clients to their former owners, who were "patrons," in a connection that offered social and political protections and advantages to both sides. A few attained wealth and influence, attracting hostility in literature for vulgarity and ostentation. Trimalchio is one. Yet they used their wealth generously, as benefactors to the town where they lived, spending on public works and holding local civic office, like Habinnas, who also "made good," and may have become a Roman citizen.

To the character Trimalchio we owe the survival of our archetype – of which his famed dinner is the centrepiece, as the ambient plot is the accidental frame. The author's commitment to him is a comprehensive labour of love, which embraces and draws out not only the cenatory and human details, but the evaluation of them, and all else, from the points of view of four social perspectives and talents: new, educated, but unfamiliar and cash-poor young guests, ready, for all that, with snobbish opinions well beyond their ken; that of a near-dozen close-knit regular invitees from the class to which their host belongs; that of Trimalchio himself; and, finally, the perspectives of Petronius, from his curation of the interplay of the above. The host's most significant verbal foray begins with a ghost story, is refreshed by the arrival of his friend and equal Habinnas, sidetracks to his wife Fortunata, coasts along with his interactions with his slaves, and comes to rest with the reading of his will. But then, later (*Sat.* 74, early a.m.), he makes a move on a slave boy, and hell breaks loose for him and Fortunata; but even this has the grace to conclude with his autobiography, and an account of the mingled careers of man and wife, providing invaluable data of social biography – to conclude in a Wodehousian ending with the turning up of the fire brigade (*Sat.* 75–8).

---

12 The reader of today cannot judge these charges, presented as private, heartfelt ruminations brought against a Giton presented elsewhere as the soul of compassion and intelligence. Are they fantastical fancies? The contrary evidence is everywhere. He was a young sixteen, as Quartilla takes pains to remark, still with a novice pecker (24.7 *vasculum tam rude*).

The Eleven Freedmen at Dinner in Order of Appearance, by Name, or Ascribed Name […]

37.1–38.16	[Hermeros]	–	Ranking, articulate, well-informed informant of Encolpius who takes angry offence at Ascyltus, below, for laughter and perceived air of superiority.
38.7–38.10	[Diogenes]	–	According to Hermeros, newly freed, smart enough to quickly acquire wealth. A non-speaker.
38.11–38.16	[Proculus]	–	According to Hermeros, acquired great wealth and sophistication but got swindled into bankruptcy by his business colleagues. A non-speaker.
41.10–41.12	Dama	–	A simple, listless soul, fond of drink. (*Trimalchio goes to the washroom*.)
42.1–42.7	Seleucus	–	Was at Chrysanthus' funeral so couldn't bathe. Air of melancholy from this. A funny, useful contribution on what killed his friend. Ungrateful wife.
43.1–43.8	Phileros	–	Sympathy for Chrysanthus ill placed. Corrects the record: a harsh man who fought with his family, overspent an inheritance; a long, lecherous life.
44.1–44.18	Ganymedes	–	Useful passage. Hard times, high food prices, incompetent officials, not like the old days when they were friendly. Aediles all crooks. Things gone to hell.
45.1–46.8	Echion	–	Valuable passage: substance, humour, optimism, gladiating. A small son doing well in study; had to kill his birds. Lawbooks. (*Trimalchio is back*.)
57.1–57.11	Hermeros	–	Ascyltus a muttonhead (*vervex*). A lovely passage full of colourful invective. Biography. A slave forty years. Kept out of trouble.
61.3–62.14	Niceros	–	Prompted by Trimalchio. A night walk to Melissa. Soldier guard turns into werewolf. It pays Melissa a visit. Is speared. No wolf, sick soldier.
64.3–64.5	Plocamus	–	Trimalchio tries to coax him to cheer up: "Oh the sweet figs of yesteryear!" Plocamus talks of his decline, in age; ends with a snatch of a Greek song.
65.1–67.3	Habinnas	–	A full-blown treatment of his entrance with wife, tipsy from another party; Urged to recite menu – which he does at length. Call for Fortunata to join.

7. The Latin and the Translation

The Latin

If Trimalchio gave us the *Satyrica*, Petronius gave us Vulgar Latin, and by this I acknowledge, to a point, the judgment by Donald C. Swanson that the *Satyrica* "is a Vulgar Latin document, but an artificial one," and arguably the most consolidated and important such text we have, despite its limitations, for appraising colloquial, conversational Latin style as a discipline of study.[13] Vulgar Latin comprises many characteristic, interlocking elements, and has several ways of being categorized: *sermo cotidianus, sermo urbanus, sermo plebeius*, even *sermo campanus* and *sermo Africus*, sharing the common features of colloquiality, if not much else. Further, despite our tendency to find intuitively an adversarial distinction between "educated" and "uneducated" converse, Swanson insisted that informal speech, as practised by both sets of "classes," carries into common speech its inherent nature: "all speakers use conversational style, i.e. Vulgar Latin"; and that most exceptions arise either out of Petronius' inconsistencies of usage, or uncertainties of manuscript spelling as conveyed in the H text. This entry-level view, that everyone engaged in conversation is employing a form of Vulgar Latin, falls well short of accounting for the situational linguistic dexterity on display in the *Satyrica*, and it took Hubert Petersmann's thorough analysis of the language to bring this out – best consulted verbatim in his cleverly titled *Petrons Urbane Prosa*, a testimony to the elegance and elevation of many speakers of their Latin within the register of conversational but still structured speech. I should like to conclude this Introduction, however, with an informal short critique of Petronius' remarkable portrayal of the mostly informal vocabulary and diction, best typified by participants in the *Cena Trimalchionis*, freedmen and free, based more on my own observational inferences than on a quantitative "ticking-of-the boxes" for the double Rubik's Cube of elements that might support or refute linguistic claims.[14]

These interlocking elements – archaisms, Graecisms, metaphors, proverbs, riddles, obscenities, vulgarities, superstitions, folktale, Milesian-tale, ghost-tale, and werewolf-tale sallies, must skew their nonce-pronouncers in the direction of "more vulgarity" than less (I am thinking of Dama's water

13 Swanson 1963, p. xxiii.

14 Swanson 1963, pp. xxiv, xxxi. For him Vulgar Latin was never fixed in time but an evolving, dynamic retreat since before Plautus from formal written style in response to Greek literature's incursion, creating a "diglossy" out of Latin. Consult extensively, via the indexes, Petersmann 1977.

with teeth; he sounds drunk; and Niceros' werewolf account): the more of them, the stronger the flavour; whereas the Latin of the more verbally at ease freedmen, like Ganymedes, Echion, Hermeros, Niceros, Habinnas, and especially Trimalchio, bids fair, by clarity and persuasiveness, to put them among the guests of confirmed education, like Agamemnon and Encolpius. The former's Latin, however, may be influenced by the requirement for haste: half of the freedmen, from Dama to Echion, had to get out their piece in the time of Trimalchio's bathroom visit. Coincidence or not, their public comments are where the true interest lies: graphic bursts of declarative statement, lively and vivid, including even the bios of Trimalchio and Fortunata to the ear of Encolpius. Perhaps also their brevity bespeaks a hesitancy at both ends of the addresses: the speakers' own syntactic control and their friends' presumed impatience with wordiness. For all that, in the skilled hands of Petronius, these are vivid, convincing, confident men and women, equally adept in the conversational art; and it is a pleasure – a banquet withal – climaxed by Trimalchio's autobiography.

The Translation

Critical editions of the *Satyrica* with English translation have been few: none before the twentieth century, with that century yielding up M. Heseltine's 1913 Loeb Classical Library translation of a text supplied by Buecheler, revised by E.H. Warmington and reprinted in 1969.[15] In our century, it was deservedly finally decommissioned for the freshly edited and translated 2020 Loeb of G. Schmeling; and that is it. New text editions have an accepted precedence, and stand-alone translations are not uncommon. Uniting them, though, is its own unique pleasure. In the past century, the English of most Loebs was valued for services as a no-frills educational tool, eschewing literary inanimation. French is served by Ernout's fluid bilingual edition of 1950^{3}, with some scholars more attracted to it than to the Latin text (Buecheler's was a hard act to follow). And German has W. Ehlers to accompany K. Mueller's 1983 text. One envies the fecundity of translators of modern European languages, and imagines their hard-earned ease as a model for Petronius, free from scholarly paraphernalia warning of a want of liveliness to come. Notes and indexes like a mini-gazetteer complete the picture of a translation primarily for study, not for reading aloud every

15 The Latin edition by Sage, 1929, is the only such by a native English speaker, to then and since.

page of the way.[16] For the translator must seek out the tempo of the *Satyrica*, and the tiptoe resilience of its characters – as they cope with fun, loss, sensuality, and connection – first noted in my affectatious teenage years at boarding school and carried more confidently into a classics career.[17] Except by the few remaining specialists, I do not think another magisterial classical conspectus must vie with theirs.[18] It is enough to find pleasure and humour in the characters, situations, and especially writing and dialogue – for their relatability in the hands of a peerless Latin stylist, a Roman Joyce, Nabokov, Mann, Proust, Borges, Eliot, Woolf, and Walcott. In the matter of sustained efforts to convey the language of the freedmen at the *Cena* in some sort of modern English vernacular equivalent, I'm agin it. Every dialect comes with its very own allusive echoes, and the *sui generis* content of the *Cena* leads to embarrassing artificiality. In moderation there will be occasion to impart a little analogous grammatical slippage. Conversely, and through the genius of Petronius, I am impelled to embrace Encolpius and friends as *paenissime nostri*, within a hair of us, finding familiarity in their diction and life-perspectives in the way Graves in the 1930s so shamelessly reclaimed them for Claudius as the pitch-perfect Englishman. John Sullivan ensnares them too, in his gifted Penguin Classics translations. Here clearly is someone else who put his all into Petronius, an unusual all with more to give, had he the time.[19]

16 I see my notes as side-bones to the narrative, cultural contemplations in the spirit of *bona mens* (seven times in *Sat.*).

17 This was the era of W. Arrowsmith's (d. 1992) Mentor PB translation (New York, 1960), a grenade toss into the curriculum and a scholar's vindication of a world of classical romance to unite reverie with calling. Robert Graves (d. 1985) was on side with his Penguin *The Golden Ass of Apuleius* (London, 1950). New editors M. Grant (1990) and E.J. Kenney (1998) are "more accurate," at a cost, and given to dated locutions and class-defined errors: "Oh God, that's torn it" (Kenney at 3.24, Fotis' "*occisa sum misera*"). Graves made a better Lucius; and like him I find it just as important to seek the rhythm, tone, and context of the phrasing as its accuracy.

18 I mention that my earlier study of the manuscript transmission, *Reading and Variant in Petronius* (1993), "is intended as a prolegomenon [extended introduction] to a critical edition (p. 4)," a Volume I of sorts. Twelve citations from it in Mueller 1995 and fourteen in Schmeling 2020 stake a claim for a place in the text-transmission canon. After a long interval, not without precedent in the study of our author, which I was fortunate enough to see out, the present work might be taken as Volume II of that edition.

19 Sullivan 1986, with a number of textual changes. Penguin Books published the first edition in 1965 (without Seneca); then seven reprints.

8. The Stemmata of the Manuscripts and the Earliest Editions

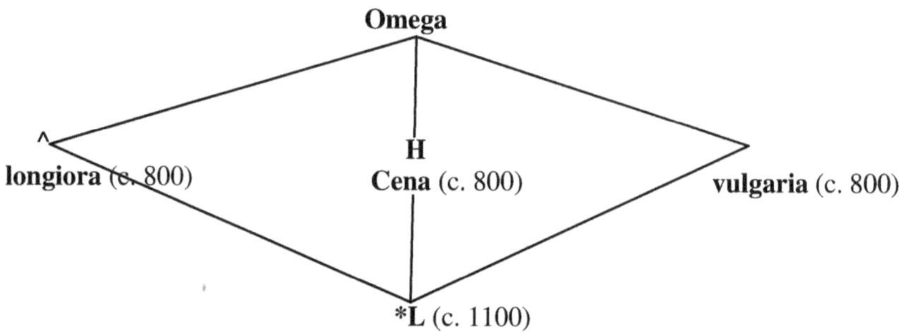

Figure 1. Stemma Omega to *L

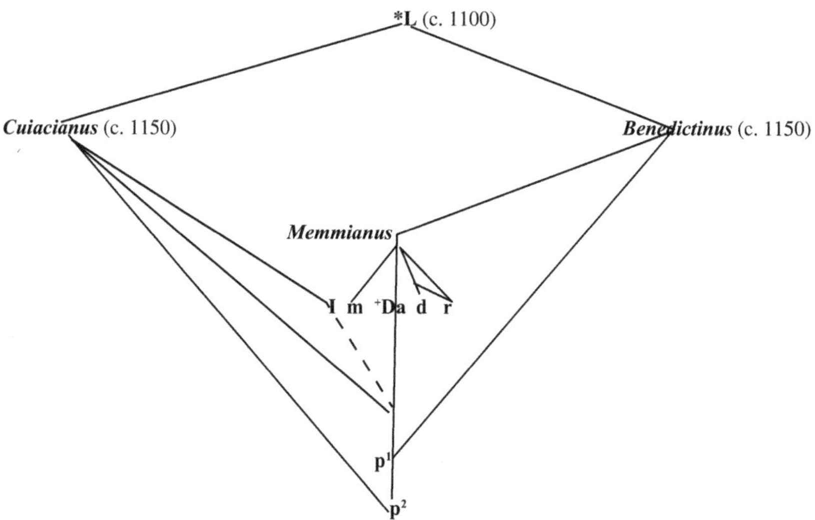

Figure 2. Stemma *L to p^2

The Renaissance Manuscripts and Editions

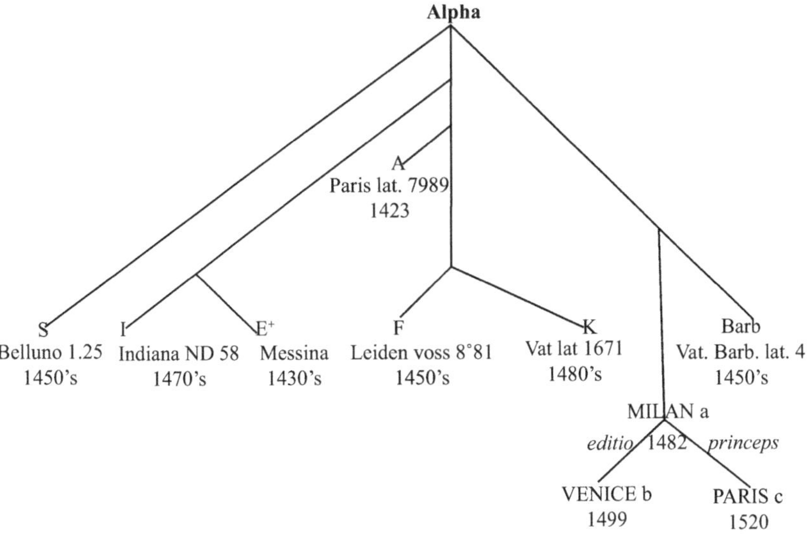

Figure 3a.

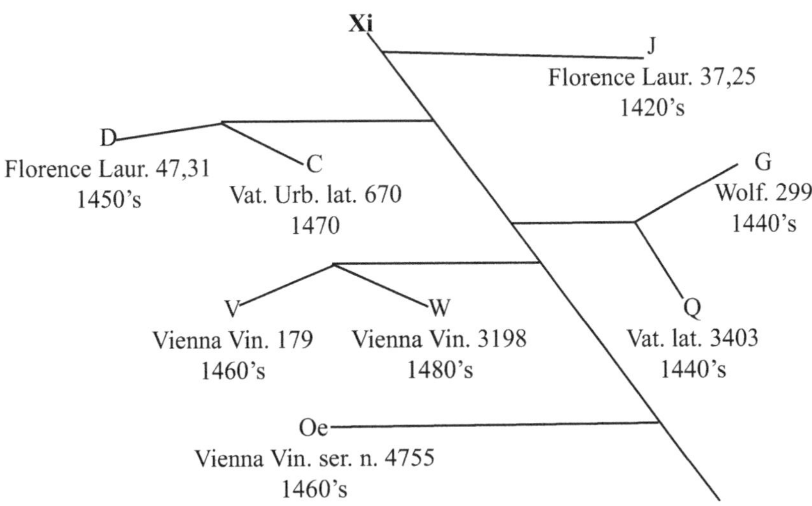

Figure 3b.

9. The Sigla of the Manuscripts and Editions for the Apparatus Criticus[20]

Omega	*Satyrica* archetype, consensus of ***L**, **O**, and ***Cena***.
Lambda	Hypothesized manuscript of "longer excerpts," written around 800 AD from the archetype, source of ***L**
***L**	Hypothesized manuscript, conflation of **Lambda** and **O**, parent of the lost manuscripts **Cuiacianus** and **Benedictinus**.
l	Leiden, Universiteitsbibliotheek, **Scaligeranus 61**, edition in the hand of J. Scaliger, written around **1571**, derived from manuscripts **Cuiacianus** and **P**, and from printed editions **c** and **s** (*q.v.*) of the **O** class.
d	Bern, Stadt- and Universitaetsbibliothek, **Bong. IV. 665. (10)**, transcription in the hand of P. Daniel, written around **1564**, of an excerpt (the *fragmentum veteris libri Cuiacii*?) from the **Memmianus**, containing c. 1–15.4.
Da	**Dalecampianus**, lost sixteenth-century manuscript transcribed from the **Memmianus**, used only by de Tournes in constructing **t**. An intermediary, *Beta*, is posited by Mueller[3] (396–405), accepted by Schmeling 2020, p. 45, to account for errors shared by **m r t**. Unnecessary: all derive from **Memmianus** either way; evidence is scant from gaps in **d m** and possible "correction" in **t**.
m	Città del Vaticano, Biblioteca Apostolica Vaticana, **Vaticanus lat. 11428**, owned by M.-A. de Muret, a handwritten edition up to c. 80.9, made around **1565**, conflating the **Memmianus** with **s** (*q.v.*).
r	London, Lambeth Palace Library, **Lambethanus 693**, owned by D. Rogers, a transcription of the **Memmianus**, made around **1570**, collated in c. 1–15.4 with a *fragmentum veteris libri Cuiacii*, which is source or sibling of **d** (*q.v.*).
r^{comm}	Portion of **Lambethanus 693** (ff. 51–52v) which contains a transcription of the *Notae* of F. Daniel, written around **1570**, which was first published from the original by Goldast 1610.
r^{m}, **r**^{c}	In **Lambethanus 693** the marginalia and corrections, many in the hand of Rogers.
t	Printed edition of de Tournes, Lyon **1575**, with the status of *editio princeps* of the **LO** material; derived mainly from **Cuiacianus** and **Dalecampianus** (the former after c. 112.4); the first French editions of **O** (**c** and **s**; *q.v.*); and Scaliger **1572**.
t^{v}	From de Tournes' edition (**t**) the *variae lectiones ex collatione v.c.*, selected variants from the **Cuiacianus** not available for consideration for his text, extending up to c. 112.4.
p^{1}	First printed edition of Pierre Pithou, Paris **1577**, derived mainly from the lost **Benedictinus**, **B** (**Autissiodurensis**), **P** (**Bituricus**), and **t**.

20 This Table of Sigla had its first appearance with a wider aim as "Symbols for Manuscripts and Editions" in Richardson 1993, pp. xxi–xxiv. It is now modified to accommodate the ensuing Latin text and apparatus.

p^2	Revised edition by Pithou of **p^1**, Paris, **1587**, employing the same sources, and the addition of **Cuiacianus**, called "*Thol.*" by Pithou.
p	Readings shared by the two editions of Pithou.
p^{1v}, p^{2v}	In the two editions of Pithou the *varietas lectionum*, lists of lemmata together with rejected variants and manuscript attribution (**p^{2v}** ***"Thol."* = *Cuiacianus***).
p^v	Readings shared in the *varietas* of Pithou.
Benedictinus	Lost manuscript, dating to about 1150, of the editors used by Pithou alone, from which the **Memmianus** was copied.
Cuiacianus	Lost manuscript, dating to about 1150, derived from ***L**, first owned by J. Cujas, used by F. Daniel, Scaliger, de Tournes, and Pithou.
Memmianus	Lost manuscript, copied in the sixteenth century, after writing, from the **Benedictinus**, cited by Turnebe, the source of **d Da m r** (*q.v.*).
Tholosanus	Manuscript so designated in p^{2v} as "*Thol.*" which is the lost Cuiacianus (from Toulouse).
O	Hypothesized manuscript, the consensus of **B R P**, which do not descend directly from each other, between the ninth and the twelfth centuries, reflecting the best of the **O** tradition and spawning the fifteen Renaissance manuscripts.
B	Bern, Buergerbibliothek, **Bernensis** 357 + Leiden, Universiteitsbibliotheek, **Vossianus lat. Q. 30** ff. 58, 57 (c. 81–109 missing), ninth century, **O** class, known as the *"Autis,"* or *"Aut,"* (**Autissiodurensis**) to Pithou, who alone used it extensively, though P. Dupuy cited readings from **Vossianus** only.
R	Paris, Bibliothèque Nationale, **Parisinus lat. 6842 D**, twelfth century, **O** class, not known to the French scholars of the sixteenth century.
P	Paris, Bibliothèque Nationale, **Parisinus lat. 8049**, twelfth century, **O** class, used by Scaliger and Pithou for their editions, wherein cited as *Bit.*, *Brit.*, *Bitur.*, *Biturig.*, i.e., **Bituricus**.
a	The *editio princeps* of the **O**-based text [Milan 1482], unknown to the sixteenth-century French scholars.
b	A reprinting of **a**, with changes [Venice 1499], unknown to the sixteenth-century French scholars.
c	The *editio Chalderiana*, second reprinting of **a**, with further changes, [Paris 1520], widely (if not wisely) used by scholars of the sixteenth century, in their first acquaintance with Petronius, for their edited texts.
s	The *editio Sambuci* [Antwerp 1565], another influential **O** text and the final one, published even as the ***L** texts were making their first informal appearance; founded on **c** but corrected on a manuscript with a better text, Vienna, Oesterreichische Nationalbibliothek, **Vin. 3198**.
Cena	The lost **codex Coloniensis** of Poggio's, a ninth-century copy of c. 26.7–78 from **Omega**, itself transcribed to form the now lost exemplar of **H**.
H	Paris, Bibliothèque Nationale, **Parisinus lat. 7989**, the part containing a copy, made in the fifteenth century, of the above **Cena** text, plus an **O** text, **A** (*q.v*), made by the same scribe.

10. The Scholars Cited in the Apparatus Criticus

Anton	(1781)	*Gevaerts*	(Burman)
Birt	(1924)	*Giardina-Melloni*	(1995)
Bluemner	(1920)	*Gifanius*	(1725)
Bodel	(1989)	*Goesius*	(Burman)
Bongars	(Burman)	*Goldast*	(1621)
Bouhier	(1737)	*Gonsalius*	(Burman)
Brassicanus	(Burman)	*Gronovius I.F.*	(Burman)
Braswell	(1981)	*Gronovius J.*	(Burman)
Broukhusius	(Burman)	*Gruter*	(Burman)
Buecheler	(1862 et sqq.)	*Gulielmus*	(Burman)
Burman	(1709, 1743)	*Haase*	(Buecheler 1862)
Bursian	(Buecheler)	*Hadrianides*	(1669)
Busche	(1911)	*Haley*	(1892)
Butrica	(2007)	*Haupt*	(1876)
Canterus	(1793)	*Heinze*	(Burman)
Cholodniak	(1909)	*Heraeus*	(1912 et sqq.)
Colladonius	(Buecheler)	*Hofmann*	(1951)
Conte	(1992)	*Jacobs*	(Buecheler)
Corbett	(1967 et sqq.)	*Jahn*	(Buecheler)
Cornelissen	(Buecheler)	*Jungermann*	(Burman)
Courtney	(1970 et sqq.)	*Junius*	(Burman)
Crusius	(Buecheler)	*Kaibel*	(Mueller)
Cueva	(Buecheler)	*Keller*	(1861)
Cuperus	(Burman)	*Kelly*	(Buecheler)
F. & P Daniel	(Goldast 1621)	*Kraffert*	(1888)
Delz	(1961 et sqq.)	*Krohn*	(1887)
Dousa	(Burman)	*Lachmann*	(1892)
Ehlers	(Mueller 1983)	*Leo*	(Mueller)
Faber	(Goldast 1621)	*Lipsius*	(Burman)
Fraenkel	(Mueller 1961)	*Martindale*	(1976)
Friedlaender	(1891 et sqq.)	*Mentel*	(Burman)
Fuchs	(1938 et sqq.)	*Meyer*	(Buecheler)
Gaselee	(1944)	*Moessler*	(Buecheler)
George	(1967)	*Morgan*	(1978)
Gessner	(Buecheler)	*Mueller L.*	(1866)

Mueller K.	(1961 et sqq.)	*Rutgers*	(Burman)
Muncker	(Burman)	*Salmasius*	(Burman)
Nisbet	(1962)	*Salonius*	(1926)
Novak	(Buecheler)	*Scheffer*	(Burman)
Öberg	(1999)	*Schioppius*	(Burman)
Oevering	(Burman)	*Schrader*	(1867)
Orelli	(1836)	*Segebade*	(1880)
Orioli	(1836)	*Shackleton-Bailey*	(1980)
Oudendorp	(1824)	*Simon*	(1975)
Palmer	(Buecheler)	*Smith*	(1975)
Passerat	(Burman)	*Stagni de Palmerio*	(1580)
Pellegrino	(1980)	*Strelitz*	(1879)
Petersmann	(1977)	*Sullivan*	(1986)
Pickard	(Buecheler)	*Suringar*	(Buecheler)
Pius	(Buecheler)	*Thielmann*	(1884)
Putschius	(Goldast 1621)	*Thomas*	(1893)
Reeve	(1971)	*Triller*	(Buecheler)
Reinersius	(Burman)	*van Thiel*	(1971)
Reiske	(Burman)	*Vossius*	(1684)
Ribbeck	(Burman)	*Watt*	(1986)
Richard	(Buecheler)	*Wehle*	(1861)
Richardson	(2023)	*Whittick*	(1986)
Rohde	(1879)	*Winterbottom*	(1972)
Rose	(1968)	*Zinn*	(1961)

Context and Analysis of the List

The design of this list, and its drawbacks, will be familiar, but it is still a useful medium for coping with the panoply of scholars and lemmata of a larger apparatus criticus. It is the invention of K. Mueller, beginning with Mueller^{2} (1965), and the staple for his editions until the last of 2003$^{4\,c}$. It has been reproduced *mutatis mutandis* by editors who have chosen an abundance of *adnotationes*, notably J.C. Giardina and R.C. Melloni, J. Öberg, and now myself. It was of Mueller's devising to mark with an asterisk (*; retired in my case) the names of past and present scholars appearing in a number of guises for the exhaustive 1709 Petronius edition of Pieter Burman, taken up by his son Gaspard in 1743. A. Ernout (1950)[3], xxxvi, comments soberly on the undertaking, but not unfairly: "La part personelle de [P.] Burman y est médiocre, mais l'édition est commode par l'abondance des opinions reproduites." Vacuumed up among the many was N. Heinze, who has stood out for me. He was about to publish an edition under his own name when death took him. And the rather fewer, later scholars assembled compendiously for Goldast 1610 and 1621 were given a *circulus*. My wish here is to ensure that merit among the pre-modern scholars be spread about, even as one scholar as easily might have one hundred lemmata as one. Looming always behind the Mueller list is its rendering of the text contribution of F. Buecheler in his six editions from 1863 to 1922, which Mueller needed to acknowledge with a prominent part. Ironically, that came by default. In the Swiss scholar's *Verzeichnis der im Apparat Genannten Gelehrten* (1965[2], p. 421) a blank against a name, i.e., no asterisk or circlet and listed without data, meant use somewhere in Buecheler's texts: "Alle uebrige Angaben stammen, soweit hier nicht die Fundstelle genannt ist, aus Buechelers grosser Ausgabe (Berlin 1862) oder aus den Editiones minores (zuletzt … 1922)." In other words, Mueller's *docti* were to be looked for scattered about (no index supplied) in those editions. Another complication is that Buecheler is prone privately to trading readings among W. Wehle, O. Jahn, and F. Jacobs, his scholar associates, in person or in correspondence, with only the name given. One is put in mind of J. Mentel, J. Scheffer, and M. Hadrianides, who after the discovery of H at Trogir in about 1650 (Buecheler p. xvi) had the similar luck to be in the right place at the right time, to emend, to their own specifications, a clean, lightly corrected but unedited manuscript exemplar of obvious viral interest. Buecheler's challenging operational methods declined in importance as Petronian scholarship moved through mid-century and into the gravitational orbit of Konrad Mueller himself, and the many scholars for whom his editions from 1961 to 2003 were such individual boons and milestones. On the subject of Mueller, the Buecheler/Jacobs/Jahn/Wehle alliance had one more analogue left: himself and E. Fraenkel. At Oxford in 1959, as Mueller was preparing what would be his first Petronius edition of 1961, he fell in with the retired but still majestic Fraenkel, and together they mapped out a basis, and the examples to go with it, of a comprehensive theory of interpolations in the vulnerable Petronius text. This possibility had been inchoate since the time of Wehle and Jacobs, and was much furthered by H. Fuchs in 1938 and 1959. Mueller now allowed himself to be persuaded by Fraenkel of their ubiquity, only to be faced in 1965, after respectfully sceptical reviews of Mueller[1], with having to retract a good percentage of Fraenkel's while saving the principle for his own. The number of scholars cited in my list above is well over a hundred, representing more than five hundred years of textual activity. Though sounding a lot, it pales in comparison against the several hundred lemmata they represent. As to whether that many *adnotationes* make a positive or a negative contribution to a new edition, I see spareness or abundance as false choices, for they express the two separate but complementary goals of editing: 1) recovery of the proper text; and 2) dissemination of transmissional knowledge. It is not difficult to detect how surges in lemma clusters appear to coincide with major text-historical incidents. Some of these would be the publication of an *editio princeps*, or of the fuller *variorum* editions of the 1570s and 1580s, indicating acquisition of or access to new manuscripts. The discovery of the *codex Traguriensis* and H is a significant case in point. With no other manuscipt for comparision, and for around a score of years before the *editio princeps* appeared in print, scholars could go *mano a mano* with a virgin exemplar – an easier task than expected because H is well if hurriedly written (*culpa velocitatis*), and words repaying quick emending stand out from gibberish. But the gibberish too earns a laugh, showing up unfamiliarity with tricky divisions, types of corruption, and strange new words. In the Introduction, for handiness and proximity to the text, I have produced only an outline of contributors to the apparatus. Reference credit is found in the Aggregate Bibliography at the end.

SATYRICA

Note for the English translation

One asterisk (*) in the texts denotes lacunae signalled by sixteenth-century scholars from within their sources or provided by themselves in their source-rich editions. Ellipsis points (...) denote lacunae posited by more recent scholars in their editions and endorsed by subsequent editors, without manuscript authority.

PETRONII: The Latin Text and Apparatus

1 "Num alio genere furiarum declaratores inquietantur, qui LO
clamant, 'Haec vulnera pro libertate publica except, hunc oculum
pro vobis impendi; date me [ducem] qui me ducat ad liberos meos,
2 nam succisi poplites membra non sustinent'? Haec ipsa tolerabilia
essent, si ad eloquentiam ituris viam facerent. Nunc et rerum
tumore et sententiarm vanissimo strepitu hoc tantum proficiunt,
ut cum in forum venerint, putent se in alium orbem terrarum
3 delatos. Et ideo adulescentulos in scholis stultissimos fieri,
quia nihil ex his quae in usu habemus aut audiunt aut vident,
sed piratas cum catenis in litore stantes, sed tyrannos edicta
scribentes quibus imperent filiis ut patrum suorum capita
praecidant, sed responsa in pestilentiam data ut virgines tres
aut plures immolentur, sed mellitos verborum globulos et omnia
dicta factaque quasi papavere et sesamo sparsa.

L (= ldmrtp), O (= BRP)
PETRONII ARBITRI SATYRICON (SATIRICON Bd) rtp, *titulo a Mario Victorino* GL 6. 153.33 *sumpto, ut videtur*: INCIPIUNT EXCERTA PETRONII SATIRICI R: Petronii arbitri satirarum (P.A. affranii Satirici Pl^m) liber INCIPIT P: P.A. Satyri fragmenta ex libro quinto decimo et sexto decimo A, *numeris a scriba nimirum in codice Coloniensi repertis*

---

1 num] cum RP declamatores *del. putant Giardina et Melloni del. Jacobs* 3 sed tyrannos slt: et tyrannos

I
At The School of Rhetoric

"'These wounds I took for the common freedom! This eye I gave for you! Find me someone to lead me to my children, for my legs are hamstrung and carry me no more!'

So cry the professors of declamation in their ravings. Even this stuff might be overlooked if it set people on the path to eloquence, but no: with this mix of bombast and dinning cliché the one thing these teachers accomplish is to make us suspect, as we face the courts for the first time, that we have been dropped off on another planet. It's in school, then, I believe, that we are turned into young ninnies, since we never get to hear or watch anything of practical value. Instead, it's pirates shaking chains as they stand on the beach, or tyrants scribbling orders for sons to cut off their own fathers' heads, or oracles in time of plague calling for the sacrifice of a virgin or three: so many words, phrases, gestures, honey-glopped and dredged in sesame and poppyseed.

The Encolpiad. The speaker of the opening lines of the surviving portion of the comic novel of Petronius, perhaps the last quarter of the full peripatetic adventure, is Encolpius, an intelligent, articulate, serious-minded, neurasthenic college-age sometime student of rhetoric. He is the constant presence of the entire story, as it proceeds in a mixture of observed situation and recounted narrative and dialogue, in prose and in poetry. His point now is that the Greek classical canon of prose and poetry is seriously out of fashion and now abandoned in exchange for facile predicamental drills and melodramatic fictitious tropes, with predictably pernicious results: the dumbing-down of the student mind. His professor Agamemnon's earnest response is that he can only teach what parents sanction and students come to hear and pay for. Ironies abound from the start. Encolpius the student is espousing a conservative, challenging curriculum appropriate to his teacher and out of step with his less serious colleagues. And the good sense he recognizes in that education has had small effect on raising his his own life and prospects, outside his skills. The humour of our comedy comes in fact from the counter-irony of his failings, as he and his partner Ascyltus, now also present in the classroom, abandon the high ground of aesthetic literateness for living off the avails of emotions and petty crime – an *otium* that has got him into serious trouble with the law and the humiliating collapse of his romantic life. He is not, like his partner Ascyltus, a strong, assertive young man. Sensitivity and sentiment are his stock in trade. Here now he is on his turf, and continuing into *Sat.* 2, he has the wind at his back, as never afterwards. His points are sound and his grasp of the curriculum has paid off, to a point, with the presence of fifteen sallies of poetic impovisation throughout. In *Sat.* 3 and 4 his teacher addresses his points seriatim, courteously and with respect. The *Satyrica* therefore opens in a spirit of calm, constructive discussion, displaying for the first time, as applied to Encolpius by Agamemnon (*Sat.* 3.1), the virtue of *bona mens*, good sense, which appears in our text seven times across cultural levels as a kind of catch-phrase or axiom (cont'd).

2 Qui inter haec nutriuntur non magis sapere possunt quam
2 bene olere qui in coriaria habitant. Pace vestra liceat dixisse,
primi omnium eloquentiam perdidistis. Levibus atque inanibus
sonis ludibria quaedam excitando effecistis ut corpus orationis
3 enervaretur et caderet. Nondum iuvenes declamationibus
continebantur, cum Sophocles aut Euripides invenerunt verba
4 quibus deberent loqui. Nondum umbraticus doctor ingenia
deleverat, cum Pindarus novemque lyrici Homericis versibus canere
5 <non> timuerunt. Et ne poetas [quidem] ad testimonium citem,
certe neque Platona neque Demosthenen ad hoc genus exercitationis
6 accessisse video. Grandis et ut ita dicam pudica oratio non
est maculosa nec turgida, sed naturali pulchritudine exsurgit.
7 Nuper ventosa ista et enormis loquacitas Athenas ex Asia
commigravit animosque iuvenum ad magna surgentes veluti
pestilenti quodam sidere afflavit, semelque corrupta eloquentiae
8 regula ... stetit et obmutuit. Quis postea ad summam Thucydidis,

---

L (= ldmrtp), O (= BRP)

2 coriaria *Salmasius ex* coria B: culina L Ioan. 2 omnium *Poggio,* s: omnem 3 *post* quibus *lac. signant Giardina et Melloni* deberent] deberemus *Cuiac., non Bern. 276 (perperam laud. Daniel)* 4 *suppleverunt Giardina et Melloni*: invenerunt r 5 *del. Buecheler* video *Turnebus*: et ideo 6 ut] velut O 7 eloquentiae regula] regula eloquentia *Haase; lac. indic Fuchs, quam* ars *implendam coni. Mueller in quarta*

2 People put on a diet of this stuff have about as much chance of learning something as of smelling good in a tannery. If you'll let me speak frankly, it's you teachers first and foremost who have destroyed the gift of speech. You strive for tricky effects with sound and smoothness, only to produce a gutless piece that collapses from lack of substance. There were no declamatory exercises yet to handicap students in the days when Sophocles and Euripides found the right words for them. When Pindar and the nine lyric poets turned away from Homeric verse, there was no ivory-tower professor yet to snuff out young talents. Let me go beyond the evidence of the poets: I certainly see no evidence of this kind of exercise in Plato and Demosthenes. Their style of speech is grand but also somehow chaste, because it attains to elevation not from spotty sallies and bombast but from an inner beauty of language. The present preoccupation with windy, hulking verbiage is a recent one: an import from Asia into Athens, it infected the minds of the young and ambitious with a kind of plague-ridden contagion; and, once perverted, the norm of eloquence ended and fell into silence. After their time, was there anyone to scale the heights of Thucydides or achieve the fame of Hyperides?

(cont'd) It is true that the conservative perspective may not be original, but that is the point: Encolpius is not that kind of thinker or character; but I accept his critique as sound and in earnest, and not mere posturing. The early chapters express sincere commitment to his intellectual program, and he is genuinely indignant at the short shrift given by Ascyltus to the debate. In the current uncertainty over when Petronius lived or set his novel, we cannot go about our critical business as usual on the topic of what may or may not be hackneyed. And in a work of creative imagination and comic fantasy throughout, it is a waste of time even to raise the question of whether or not Encolpius is expressing the author's views as some kind of alter ego. Petronius, like P.G. Wodehouse, is no doubt close to his favourite comedogenic character, and would relish the competent true novelist's privilege of floating free from him in the exercise of ironic distance (see Introduction, n. 6). Only at *Sat.* 107.7, and then at *Sat.* 132.15, am I tempted to argue an irresistible use of authorial *sphragis* as the work draws near to its close. Ernout's citation of Sen. *Controv.* 3. Pref. (1950[3], ad loc. p. I), refers to *declamatores* who step away from their shady colonnades and lose it in the Senate or law court (*vix se inveniunt*), and Petronius seems to have Encolpius echo this by making *declamatores* the implied subject of *cum in forum venerint*. The first victims of their own idiocies. Perhaps the young graduates are styled *declamatores* now; though more effective is to regard the teacher-rhetorician as spreading the bad results of his syllabi far and wide.

quis Hyperidis ad famam processit? Ac ne carmen quidem sani
coloris enituit, sed omnia quasi eodem cibo pasta non potuerunt
9 usque ad senectutem canescere. Pictura quoque non alium exitum
fecit, postquam Aegyptiorum audacia tam magnae artis
compendiariam invenit."

3 Non est passus Agamemnon me diutius declamare in porticu
quam ipse in schola sudaverat, sed "Adulescens," inquit, "quoniam
sermonem habes non publici saporis et, quod rarissimum est,
2 amas bonam mentem, non fraudebo te arte secreta. Nimirum in
his exercitationibus doctores peccant, qui necesse habent cum
insanientibus furere. Nam nisi dixerint quae adulescentuli
3 probent ut ait Cicero, 'soli in scholis relinquentur.' Sicut
ficti adulatores cum cenas divitum captant nihil prius meditantur
quam id quod putant gratissimum auditoribus fore (nec enim
aliter impetrabunt quod petunt nisi quasdam insidias auribus
4 fecerint) sic eloquentiae magister, nisi tamquam piscator eam
imposuerit hamis escam, quam scierit appetituros esse
4 pisciculos, sine spe praedae moratur in scopulo. Quid ergo
est? Parentes obiurgatione digni sunt, qui nolunt liberos
2 suos severa lege proficere. Primum enim sic ut omnia, spes

L (= ldmrtp), O (= BRP)
3 2 nimirum] nil mirum si *Leo* Cicero] *pro Caelio* 41
3 ficti: *i.q. fallaces, reduntanter certe; cf.* 83.10.3
vilis adulator cenas] cenam O **4** pisculos] discipulos B
praedae spe BR moritur B

With all genres fed the same pap, even poetry failed to shine forth in ruddy health and lost its ability to ripen us with age. And when the Egyptians devised a technique of shameless mass production, the great art of painting met a like fate."

3 Agamemnon was not about to let me speechify out in the colonnade for a second longer than he had sweated in the classroom behind. "Young man," he said, "your speech shows uncommon good taste and you also value good sense (a much rarer gift), so I won't short-change you with tricks of the trade. There is little question that the instructors are at fault for setting these drills, but they feel the need to rant along with the madmen. If they don't prescribe what their young pupils want, 'they will be left alone in their schools,' as Cicero says. Like dissembling flatterers who cadge meals at rich men's tables, their first concern is for what they deem to be most pleasing to the ears of their audience, for which they set a kind of trap to achieve their goal. Similarly the declamation teacher must be like a fisherman who attaches to his hook the type of bait he knows will get a nibble from his prey, unless he intends to sit on his rock empty handed.

4 What is to be done, then? Parents must carry the reproach, for not wanting their children to be challenged by the strictest standards.

quoque suas ambitioni donant. Deinde cum ad vota properant,
cruda adhuc studia in forum [im]pellunt et eloquentiam, qua
nihil esse maius confitentur, pueris induunt adhuc
3 nascentibus. Quod si paterentur laborum gradus fieri,
ut studiosi [iuvenes] lectione severa irrigarentur, ut
sapientiae praeceptis animos componerent, ut verba exacto
stilo effoderent, ut quod vellent imitari diu audirent,
<si persuaderent> sibi nihil esse magnificum quod pueris
placeret, iam illa grandis oratio haberet maiestatis suae
4 pondus. Nunc pueri in scholis ludunt, iuvenes ridentur in
foro, et quod utroque turpius est, quod quisque perperam
5 didicit, in senectute confiteri non vult. Sed ne me
putes improbasse schedium Lucilianae humilitatis, quod
sentio et ipse carmine effingam:

L (= ldmrtp), O (= BRP)

4 2 ambitioni a: ambitione impellunt] propellunt dmrtp ex *Benedictino: corr. Buecheler* maius] magis O 3 delendum; *adiunctionem vide* exacto *scripsi, cf.* 5.1.3: Attico *Mueller*: acri Giardina: atroci LO *add. Winterbottom praeeunte Haupt* esse *Buecheler*: esset L videntur d <puer> perperam *Jacobs* didicit A: discit L: dicit O confutari *Rohde* 5 schedium *corr. Pithou ex* schadium B: studium *B[m] cum ceteris* Lucilianae B: Lucianae vel Lucilianae humilitatis] improbitatis O, *quod in margine corr.* B *nescio quomodo, nisi ambo videbantur in* O

First, they conceive an ambition, to which they offer up their young aspirants and all else. Then, in their march to success, they propel these fledgling intellects into the courts and cram into mere babes the eloquence for which they profess the highest respect. If the parents only allowed a gradual approach to the difficulties, so that the serious boy first immersed his mind in a demanding course of reading, then settled it with precepts of wisdom, then pruned his compositions with brutal severity, then listened long and hard for what he might imitate – if they only could realize that boys do not take immediately to what is truly worthwhile – then their sons' oratory would achieve a nobility from its own weight. Nowadays boys play about in school and grow up to become the laughing-stock of the courts. Worse than both those consequences, though, is that in old age no one wants to admit he learned wrong. In case you think I am ruling out modest poetic improvisation in the Lucilian mode, here is my point expressed as a poem:

This is the first of twenty-eight poems scattered about the narrative, giving this comic novel a special character of off-beat creative charm and "musicality." Most are less than ten lines long, but one is close to three hundred. The main contributors are Encolpius, in his commentator's role, with fifteen (117 lines), and Eumolpus with five (393 lines). Others with the poetic itch are Ascyltus, Quartilla, a transvestite, Trimalchio, Tryphaena, and Oenothea. This assemblage of variety and perspective serves to put to bed any thematic connection between the *Satyrica* and Menippean or other brands of satire (see below). In the short poems, the performative basis is mostly *jeu d'esprit,* adding elevation and emphasis to the discussion, as announced here in the first poem. Others celebrate, chasten, or employ comic parody. I struggle but fail to avoid evoking for overall effect Dennis Potter's musical drama "Pennies from Heaven" (BBC TV, 1978), with its grim plot realities poignantly suspended momentarily by song-and-dance fantasy acts. The *Satyrica* employs even the shortest poems by the sketchiest of denizens similarly, to adjust kinetically, for a moment, the imaginative narrative temperature. Of one thing I am convinced: their main intent is the provision of enjoyment; and even some respect, as in the case of the impressively long *Civil War.* We know little of the reception of such an effort, though it is there to be examined alongside the *Pharsalia* of Lucan, and, despite the responses communicated via self-regarding students, we should not necessarily take them to be telegraphing deserved scorn at its size, hallucinatory lushness, or tedious bombast. The point is the generation gap: Eumolpus is old and the poem is miles out of fashion, in the manner of Tennyson, Swinburne, or Longfellow today, but could come back. Meanwhile, one finds much to enjoy in the use of language, imagery, and sentiment, even as it parodies Eumolpus himself. It should be noted, in regard to the choice of the Menippean format, that Petronius was no perfunctory poetaster, pointlessly working in an obscure rhythm: he deploys eight different metres (of which many reside in the *Fragmenta,* here omitted). See the *Index Metrorum* in Ernout 1950^3, pp. 211–13.

5 Artis severae si quis ambit effectus
Mentemque magnis applicat, prius mores
Frugalitatis lege poliat exacta.
Nec curet alto regiam trucem vultu
Cliensque cenas impotentium captet,
Nec perditis addictus obruat vino
Mentis calorem, neve plausor in scenam
Sedeat redemptus histrionis ad rictus

Sed sive armigerae rident Tritonidis arces
Seu Lacedomonio tellus habitata colono
Sirenumve domus, det primos versibus annos
Maeoniumque bibat felici pectore fontem.
Mox et Socratico plenus grege mittat habenas
Liber et ingentis quatiat Demosthenis arma
Hinc Romana manus circumfluat et modo Graio
Exonerata sono mutet suffusa saporem.
Grandiaque indomiti Ciceronis verba minentur,

L (= ldmrtp), O (= BRP)
5 ambit t^m: amat: hamat l^m *cum* "non" 2 mores BR: more 3 poliat *Heinze* palleat: *Cuiac.*: polleat exactae *probat Mueller, in Sen. Dial.* 10.18.4 frugalitatis exactae homines *inventis* 8 redimitus *Cuiac.* histrionis *Turnebus*: histrioni ad rictus *Ribbeck*: addictus 9 crinigerae *Cuiac.*
11 Sirenumve *Buecheler*: sirenumque 16 exonerata *vix sanum; hic post v. 16 transp. v. 20 Burman*

5 He who takes the challenge of a testing skill,
And sets his mind on great things, will
Hone with care his habit first of thrift, and ought
For no high outlook'd frowning palace make his thought.
At dinners of the grand as humble guest he will not eat,
Nor will o'erwhelm with wine in evil crowd his heat
Of mind, nor will he sit before the stage,
Bought claqueur of the actor's rage.

Whether citadel of armed Tritonis upon you smiles,
Whether the land be inhabited by Spartan farmer,
Whether home of the Sirens, give to poetry early years,
And with happy heart drink deep of the Maeonian spring.
Then, gorged on the circle of Socrates, set reins
Free and brandish the mighty weapons of Demosthenes.
Then, lifted by Roman arms, do you change your note
Full sated of Greek measures and now unburdened,
And let noble words of brave Cicero sound warning.

Interdum subducta foro det pagina cursum 17
Et fortuna sonet celeri distincta meatu;
Dent epulas et bella truci memorata canore. 19
His animum succinge bonis: sic flumine largo 21
Plenus Pierio defundes pectore verba." 22

6 Dum hunc diligentius audio, non notavi mihi
Ascylti fugam … et dum in hoc dictorum aestu motus
incedo, ingens scholasticorum in porticum venit, ut
apparebat,ab extemporali declamatione nescio cuius,
2 qui Agamemnonis suasoriam exceperat. Dum ergo iuvenes
sententias rident ordinemque totus dictionis infamant,
opportune subduxi me et cursim Ascylton persequi coepi.
3 nec viam diligenter tenebam [quia] nec quo <loco>
4 stabulum esset sciebam. Itaque quocumque ieram, eodem
revertebar, donec et cursu fatigatus et sudore iam madens
7 accedo aniculam quandam, quae agreste holus vendebat, et
"Rogo," inquam, "mater, numquid scis ubi ego habitem?"
Delectata est illa urbanitate tam stulta et, "Quidni
sciam?" inquit, consurrexitque et coepit me praecedere.

L (= ldmrtp), O (= BRP)
5 17 versum *Heinze* **6** 1–2 *locus mancus ab interpolatore resartus; frustra corrigimus* hunc] haec L [in] hoc *del. Daniel* mutus *Delz et Nisbet*: motus: totus incendor *Heinze, adsumunt Giardina et Melloni* 3 viam *ad locum quia transp. Giardina et Melloni om. Goldast add. Dousa; cf.* 8.2: [quia] nec quod *Buecheler* **7** est B: *om. cett.*

From time to time let page desert the courts,
To sound out Fortune adorned by rapid beat,
And recount feasts and wars with fierce blast.
With these treasures gird up your minds. Thus bursting
You will pour forth from your heart the Pierian flood."

2
Habits of The Heart, I

6 Agamemnon captured my full attention, and as I was pacing to and fro, caught up in the flood tide of his words, I failed to notice that Ascyltus had slipped away and that the large crowd of students had filed out into the colonnade, evidently after an impromptu declamation delivered by someone following Agamemnon's pleading exercise. So while these youths were joking over the speaker's epigrams and trashing the composition from beginning to end, I took the moment to steal away and head after Ascyltus at the double. But I paid little attention to where I was going and didn't know the right direction to our lodgings, with the result that no matter where I set off for I always returned to the same spot. Eventually, tired by all the running about and dripping with sweat, I approached a tiny old woman selling farm produce.

7 "Good lady," I asked, "do you happen to know where I live?" This weak joke caught her fancy. "Of course I do," she replied, as she got up and began to lead the way.

2 Divinam ego putabam et … subinde ut in locum
secretiorem venimus, centonem anus urban reiecit et,
3 "Hic," inquit, "debes habitare." Cum ego negarem me
agnoscere domum, video quosdam inter titulos nudasque
4 meretrices furtim spatiantes. Tarde, immo iam sero
intellexi me in fornicem esse deductum. Execratus itaque
aniculae insidias operuique caput et per medium lupanar
fugere coepi in alteram partem, cum ecce in ipso aditu
occurrit mihi aeque lassus ac moriens Ascyltus; putares
5 ab eadem anicula esse deductum. Itaque ut ridens eum
consalutavi, quid in loco tam deformi faceret quaesivi.
8 Sudorem ille manibus detersit et, "Si scires," inquit,
2 quae mihi acciderunt." "Quid novi?" inquam ego. At ille
deficiens, "Cum errarem," inquit, "per totam civitatem
nec invenirem quo loco stabulum reliquissem, accessit
ad me pater familiae et ducem se itineris humanissime
3 promisit. Per anfractus deinde obscuratissimos egressus
in hunc locum me perduxit prolatoque peculio coepit
4 rogare stuprum. / Iam pro cella meretrix assem exegerat, L
/iam ille mihi iniecerat manum, et nisi valentior LO
fuissem, dedissem poenas" *

L (= ldmrtp), O (= BRP)
7 2 *pauca excidisse per haplographiam statuit Buecheler, qui* subsequi coepit *conatur implere* 3 ego L: ergo O agnoscere O: cognoscere L titulos] viculos a: vetulas *Sullivan* 4 in alteram …. aditu: *lupanaris schema non in aperto est* alteram O: aliam L *hic primum testimonium scribae* O *contra vitiositatem in* L

I took her for a psychic and … before long we arrived in a rather out of the way locale. The kind old lady threw back a curtain. "This is your house," she announced. As I was denying it I caught sight of men inside, furtively circling naked whores carrying placards, and knew all too late I'd been brought to a brothel. I cursed the old dame for her trick, concealed my face, and dashed through to the far end, where at the back whom should I meet but Ascyltus, no less wiped out and for all the world the old woman's victim too. Laughing, I greeted him and asked what he was doing in a dump like this.

8 "If you only knew what I've been through!" he replied, wiping away the sweat with both hands. "What?" I asked. "I was wandering about all over the town," he said wearily, "trying to find where I lived, when a gent came up and very kindly offered to show me the way. After taking me through a maze of twists and turns he ended up in this place, whereupon he pulled out his wallet and demanded sex. By now the madam had her fee for the room and his hand was on me, and had I not been the stronger of the two I'd have been for it, no question! …

The manuscript tradition had opened with the stable text and genteel content of the visit to the school of rhetoric; but from *Sat.* 6 the story reverts to the lurid ups and downs of a far from sexually exclusive homoromantic triangle, consisting of Encolpius, Ascyltus, and the newly (re)appeared Giton (*Sat.* 9), a sixteen-year-old for whose familiarities and affections the two older youths had been vying in the good many days and miles of meandering south on foot and by ship to their present location of coastal Campania. From the forthcoming references to earlier contacts we discern that their all-too-typical adventures have left them broke, sexually overstretched, wanted by the authorities, and needing to proceed with a furtive discretion they find difficult to maintain. At the same time, as if to order, starting between *Sat.* 8 and 9, the text exhibits a gappiness and dislocation of content that contribute unintentionally, but somehow in an appropriate and satisfying way, to the murky, louche atmosphere. What I mean by this is that an off-kilter collage of snippets and swatches will not detract excessively from the strengths of a sufficient comic novel as a "whole" to continue to read well. The Quartilla narrative, *Sat.* 16–26, is a test case: the ordeal takes place amid one of the most disrupted sections available, giving the whole a nightmarish, not unpleasing episodic ambiance that, if anything, is encouraged and even enhanced by the textual uncertainties. Certainly in the translation, if not in the Latin text, one may exercise the discretion of punctuation and page design to make dislocations less obtrusive; and it is not very concerning for readers of the novel in English that a short sentence ending up in *Sat.* 8 actually belongs in *Sat.* 20 at Quartilla's party.

/ Adeo ubique mihi videbantur satyrion bibisse * L
iunctis viribus molestem contempsimus *
9 Quasi per caliginem vidi Gitona in crepidine semitae
stantem et in eundem locum me conieci …
Cum quaererem numquid nobis in prandium frater
parasset, consedit puer super lectum et manantes lacrimas
3 pollice extersit. Perturbatus ego habitu fratris quid
accidisset quaesivi. At ille tarde quidem et invitus, sed
4 postquam precibus etiam iracundiam miscui, "Tuus," inquit,
"iste frater seu comes paulo ante in conductum accucurrit
5 coepitque mihi velle pudorem extorquere. / Cum ego LO
proclamarem, gladium strinxit et, 'Si Lucretia es,'
inquit, 'Tarquinium invenisti.'"
6 / Quibus ego auditis intentavi in oculos Ascylti L
manus et, "Quid dicis," inquam, "muliebris patientiae
7 scortum, cuius ne spiritus <quidem> purus est?" Inhorrescere
se finxit Ascyltus, mox sublatis fortius manibus longe maiore
8 nisu clamavit: "Non taces," inquit, "gladiator obscene, quem
9 de harena ruina dimisit? Non taces, nocturne percussor,
qui ne tum quidem, cum fortiter faceres, cum pura muliere

L (= ldmrtp), O (= BRP)
8 4 *post* bibisse *et* contempsimus *et in seqq. signum* * *apponunt saecli XVI edd., lacunas indicantes; ab edd.recc. itemque signatas sic … declaro* **9** *lac.ind. Hadr.*
2 extersit *Fr. Pithou*: expressit 3 habitu fratris *suspicor* etiam l: et dmtp, r[m]; *om.* R 6 *add. Buecheler* 8 harena ruina *transp. Schioppius*

... In fact everywhere I looked people seemed to have been drinking aphrodisiac *

we joined forces together and fended off the troublesome fellow *

9 As if through a mist I caught sight of Giton standing at the edge of a lane and I hurried over to him ... When I asked the dear boy whether he had made anything for our lunch he sat down on the bed and stuck a thumb in his eyes to wipe away the coursing tears. I was shaken by his appearance and asked what had happened. It took entreaties and even threats, but the story came out, slowly and unwillingly. "That partner and best friend of yours just now came running into this room and tried to take me by force! When I cried out in protest he just drew his sword and proclaimed that if I wanted to play Lucretia he would be my Tarquin!"

At this news I shook my fists in Ascyltus' face: "Explain yourself, whore bitch!" I yelled: "Your breath stinks!" He first pretended to be horrified, then brandished his own fists even more aggressively and gave far more than he'd got: "Shut up, you dirty criminal!" he cried, "It took a collapsed stand to save your skin! Shut up, you stab-in-the-dark! Even at peak of performance you never took on a real woman!

Sat. 9 and 10 are a major source for the sexual dynamics of the trio. Playing the sexual field leaves Encolpius and Ascyltus open to the full range of intimate insults. Giton, sharp as always to give a good ac count of himself, is using terms confirming the (former) relationship between Encolpius and Ascyltus as sexual ("partner and best friend" translate back to Latin as *frater* but more than a brother, and *comes* but more than a comrade). Giton himself is still of the age and looks to be a pretty boy, so Ascyltus refers to him as Lucretia. It deteriorates. Encolpius, mixing things up, tasks Ascyltus with "playing the female part," i.e., "going down on men" (*Sat. 9.6 scortum muliebris patientiae cuius ne spiritus quidem purus est*). Ascyltus' riposte is equally damaging – Encolpius the escaped desperado who has lost his touch with women.

In respect of age-and-appearance-suitedness for the role of sexualized romantic object to which Giton is assigned, one may peek ahead to his "Wanted" proclamation: "Age about sixteen, hair curly, boyish, nice-looking" (*Sat.* 97). This conforms with the expectations of Petronius' readership, and it applies exactly to the other cuspidal youths later pressed into sexual service: the Pergamene ephebe/boy, and the son of Philomela, also described as an ephebe/boy. On all occasions the author is careful to indicate to his audience, via his characters' descriptions that (1), the youth is of an age to "take it," and (2), this is routine, met with physical indfference and sang-froid. From this we infer from Petronius that opportunities for abuse abounded.

10 pugnasti, cuius eadem ratione in viridario frater fui qua
nunc in deversorio puer est?" "Subduxisti te," inquam, "a
10 praeceptoris colloquio." "Quid ego, homo stultissime, facere
debui, cum fame morerer? An videlict audirem sententias,
id est vitrea fracta et somniorum interpretamenta?
2 Multo me turpior es tu hercule, qui ut foris cenares
3 poetam laudasti." Itaque ex turpissime lite in risum
diffusi pacatius ad reliqua successimus *
4 Rursus in memoriam revocatus iniuriae, "Ascylte," inquam,
"intellego nobis convenire non posse. Itaque communes
sarcinas partiamur ac paupertatem nostram privatis
5 quaestibus temptemus expellere. Et tu litteras scis et ego.
Ne quaestibus tuis obstem, aliquid aliud promittam; alioqui
mille causae nos quotidie collident et per totam urbem
6 rumoribus different." Non recusavit Ascyltos et, "Hodie,"
inquit, "quia tamquam scholastici ad cenam promisimus,
non perdamus noctem. Cras autem, quia hoc libet, et
<aliam> habitationem mihi prospiciam, et [aliquem] fratrem."
7 "Tardum est," inquam, "differre quod placet" *

L (= ldmrtp)
9 10 inquam pt: inquit lt^{v}., *id est Cuac.*: *cett. de Bened.*
10 ego lrp: ergo dmr^{m} vitrea fracta $l^{m}m^{c}$.: vitream fractam
2 mehercules turpior es tu *"fortasse" Buecheler* 3 *lac. prop. Buecheler*
6 *sic scripsi; adiunctionem videas*: [aliquem] alium *Buecheler*

And in the park wasn't I your lover in the same role as this boy now is in our digs?" "But why did you sneak away from our discussion with the teacher?" I replied.

10 "What was I supposed to do, you dope!" he countered. "I was dying of starvation. Maybe I should have dined on aphorisms instead – all tinkling glass and dream mongering! Your behaviour is sleazier than mine by far – cozying up to a hack to get a free dinner!" ... The squalid dispute soon melted into laughter as we turned peaceably to other matters *

But later on the memory of Ascyltus' treachery returned. "Ascyltus," I said, "I have decided we can't get along. Let's divvy up the stuff we share and try to make ends meet by our own personal efforts. We are well matched in education, you and I, and I don't want to stand in the way of your earnings, so I'll try something else for myself. Otherwise there'll be a thousand excuses for a daily collision and we'll be the talk of the town." Ascyltus had no objection. "But today," he said, "we have a dinner engagement as visiting scholars, so let's not throw away the evening. Tomorrow I'll look for another place to stay and another boyfriend, if that's what you want." "When the mind is made up all delay is a waste of time," was my reply *

In *Sat.* 10 the reference is to Encolpius' excessive attendance upon his professor, Agamemnon. This bit of jealousy from Ascyltus is unfair, since Encolpius was temperamentally invested in the debate on education, whereas it never meant a thing to Ascyltus from the beginning. Other tidbits of interest here: *"et tu litteras scis et ego,"* the matching quality of their education and an air of competent confidence in it, borne out by some of the later discussion; the dinner engagement to come, to provide content as visiting scholars: *"tamquam scholastici."* A further item of interest is Ascyltus' warning that quarrelling risks giving away the trio's identity, a worry felt throughout the story.

7 Hanc tam praecipitem divisionem libido faciebat;
iam dudum enim amoliri cupiebam custodem molestum,
ut veterem cum Gitone meo rationem reducerem *

11 Postquam lustravi oculis totam urbem, in cellulam
redii osculisque tandem bona fide exactis alligo
artissimis complexibus puerum fruor votis usque ad
2 invidiam felicibus. Nec adhuc quidem omnia erant facta,
cum Ascyltos furtim se foribus admovit discussisque
fortissime claustris invenit me cum fratre ludentem.
Risu itaque plausuque cellulam implevit, opertam me
3 amiculo evolvit et, "Quid agebas," inquit, "frater
4 sanctissime, qui vesticontubernium facis?" Nec se solum
intra verba continuit, sed lorum de pera solvit et
me coepit non perfunctorie verberari, adiectis etiam
petulantibus dictis, "Sic dividere cum fratre nolito" *

12 Veniebamus in forum deficiente iam die, in quo
notavimus frequentiam rerum venalium, non quidem
pretiosarum sed tamen quarum fidem male ambulantem
2 obscuritas temporis facillime tegeret. Cum ergo et ipsi
raptum latrocinio pallium detulissemus, uti occasione

L (= ldmrtp)
10 7 reducerem *Buecheler*: diducerem **11** 2 cellam dmr
opertam dm, *de Memmiano fortasse* 3 qui *lego*: quid de *veste*
contubernium *Giardina*: vesticontubernium *Turnebus: verti*
contubernium **12** male vacillantem *vel* male labentem *Heinze*
2 raptum latrocinio *susp. van Thiel,* latrocinio *Mueller*

It was lust, pure and simple, that precipitated the separation. I had in fact been wanting for some time to shed my inconvenient chaperone so as to get back with my dear Giton on the old terms *

11 After making an inspection of the entire city, I returned to our little room, at last to claim Giton's sincerest kisses, hold him in tightest embrace, and achieve to distraction my dearest wish. All had not yet run its course before Ascyltus stepped quietly up to the door, dislodged the bolt with a mighty shove, and found me making out with my lover. The room rang with his laughter and clapping as he rolled me out of the cloak covering us. "What were you up to, honourable friend?" he jeered. "Boy scouting beneath the canvas, was it?" And not content with a verbal lashing, he unbagged a belt and began to lay into me in no unconvincing fashion, chanting, sarcastically, "Not the way we share with friends!" *

12 As day was ending we arrived at a flea market in the forum and took in the many items displayed for sale – none of great value, of course, and of a doubtful provenance that the fast-fading light did well to conceal; and we had brought along a stolen cloak.

Lust" (*libido, libidinosus, libidinosa*) is *the* driving mechanism of the *Satyrica*; with a significant preponderance (12: 8) in reference to oversexed women (*libidinosae*): Quartilla, Fortunata, Tryphaena, Widow, Hedyle, Matronae, Circe, Aniculae); *libidinosi* are Encolpius, Ascyltus, Giton, Trimalchio, Eumolpus, Chrysanthus (a deceased freedman). Sexual activity is given its own section (sec. 5) in the Introduction.

opportunissima coepimus atque in quodam angulo laciniam
extremam concutere, si quem forte emptorem splendor
3 vestis posset adducere. Nec diu moratus rusticus quidam
familiaris oculis meis cum muliercula comite propius
accessit ac diligentius considerare pallium coepit.
4 Invicem Ascyltus iniecit contemplationem super umeros
5 rustici emptoris ac subito exanimatus conticuit. Ac
ne ipse quidem sine aliquo motu hominem conspexi, nam
videbatur ille mihi esse qui tuniculam in solitudine
6 invenerat. Plane is ipse erat. Sed cum Ascyltos timeret
fidem oculorum, ne quid temere faceret, prius tamquam
emptor propius accessit detraxit umeris laciniam et
13 diligentius temptavit. O lusum fortunae mirabilem! Nam
adhuc ne suturae quidem attulerat rusticus curiosa manus,
sed tamquam mendici spolium etiam fastidiose venditabat.
2 Ascyltus postquam depositum esse inviolatum vidit et
personam vendentis contemptam, seduxit me paululum a
turba et, "Scis," inquit, "frater, rediisse ad nos
3 thesaurum de quo querebar? Illa est tunicula adhuc, ut
apparet, intactis aureis plena. Quid ergo facimus aut quo

L (= ldmrtp)
12 2 splendor lt^{v} *ex Cuiaciano*: splendida *ceteri ex Benedictino* 3 diligentius *om. libri, qui hic Beta secuti sunt* 4 *post* contemplationem *aliqua desiderari velut* tunicae pendenti *censuerat Buecheler; Encolpii enarratio mihi sane non concinna* emptoris *susp. Fraenkel* 5 motu *Tornaesius*: metu 6 temptavit *Burman*: tenuit

3
At The Flea Market

The idea was to take full advantage of the opportunity provided: from a convenient corner to flap about the garment's outer edge and bring in a buyer with its brilliant hue. And we did not have long to wait. A familiar-looking farm labourer, who was with a young woman, stepped up close and stared at it intently. Meanwhile Ascyltus' gaze settled on something slung over the customer's shoulder, and he promptly froze. I too surveyed the individual not without emotion, as he looked to be the very man who had found our tunic out in the bush. It was him, for sure, but Ascyltus still needed confirmation before any hasty move, so, feigning an interest in buying the tunic, he stepped forward to remove it from the man's shoulder and gave it a careful feel.

13 What an incredible stroke of luck! The labourer hadn't even put his sticky fingers to the stitching and was selling the thing with an air of disdain as if it had been lifted from some tramp. Ascyltus, after satisfying himself that our cache was intact and that the vendor was a person of no account, took me to one side. "You realize, don't you, buddy boy," he said, "that the lost treasure I was making such a fuss about has come back to us? That's our tunic, with its supply of gold pieces apparently untouched! The question is:

Just prior to the action in our manuscript tradition, an encounter with a labourer accompanied by a young woman resulted in the theft of their expensive cloak by our trio of adventurers. Coincidentally, a tunic in their possession and then lost, humble but made valuable by the insewing of gold pieces, was found by the man and his companion. At this point in the story, the parties visited a flea market and recognized each other and their own belongings. This produced a noisy tug-of-war, each side claiming the other's item as their own. A farcical imbroglio of Wodehousian proportions, it shows how Petronius links and weaves the past into the present without necessarily inflicting damage upon the current story line. And the episode has its own judicial interest, from discussion of predatory trustees, judges, and legal avenues that our heroes will have no intention of pursuing because of the now familiar and ongoing fear of official discovery and re-arrest, not to mention being cheated in the end (*Sat.* 13–15).

4 iure rem nostram vindicamus?" Exhilaratus ego non tantum
quia praedam videbam, sed quod fortuna me a turpissima
suspicione dimiserat, negavi circuitu agendum, sed plane
iure civili dimicandum, ut si nollet alienam rem domino
14 reddere, ad interdictum veniret. Contra Ascyltus leges
timebat et, "Quis," aiebat, "hoc loco nos novit aut quis
habebit dicentibus fidem? Mihi plane placet emere,
quamvis nostrum sit, quod agnoscimus, et parvo aere
recuperare potius thesaurum quam in ambiguam litem
descendere:

2 Quid faciunt leges, ubi sola pecunia regnat LO
Aut ubi paupertas vincere nulla potest?
Ipsi qui Cynica traducunt tempora pera
Non numquam nummis vendere verba solent.
Ergo iudicium nihil est nisi publica merces,
Atque eques in causa qui sedet empta probat."

3 Sed praeter unum dipondium [sicel], lupinosque quibus L
destinaveramus mercari, nihil ad manum erat.

L (= ldmrtp), O (= BRP)
13 4 domino *Cuiacianus quid si* alienam *delemus?*
14 quod agnoscimus *verba improvisa* 2 *carmen hic Anton auctore collocant edd.*: *post* veniret *in fine* **13**.4 *habet* L
2.1 faciant s 2.2 nuda B *Cuiacianus* 2.3 pera *Heinze*: cera
2.4 verba L: verba solent emere O 3 dipondium *del. Giardina et Melloni* del. *Gaselee*

what do we do now? How do we rightfully reclaim our own property?" I, overjoyed not only at seeing our loot but because fate had freed me from a pall of suspicion, argued against indirection and for contesting it head-on in the courts. "If he refuses to return lost property to its rightful owner, then we'll sue," said I.

14 Ascyltus disagreed, fearing recourse to the law. "Who knows us around here?" he said. "Who will believe our version of events? By far the best plan is to buy the tunic back, even though we know it's ours – invest a little money in recovering our cache instead of risking the uncertain outcome of litigation.

> What good is the law where cash is king?
> Where the poor man can never win?
> Even Cynics who with sack the times traduce
> For pelf will put their words to use.
> Justice is another word for public gain,
> And the jury's award will follow the coin."

But except for two bits and some lupine seeds that we had planned to use for supplies, there was no cash to hand.

4 Itaque ne interim praeda discederet, vel minoris pallium
addicere placuit et pretium maioris compendii leviorem
5 facere iacturam. Cum primum ergo explicuimus mercem,
mulier operto capite quae cum rustico steterat inspectis
diligentius signis iniecit utramque laciniae manum
6 magnaque vociferatione latrones tenere clamavit. Contra
nos perturbati, ne videremur nihil agere, et ipsi scissam
et sordidam tenere coepimus tunicam atque eadem invidia
proclamare nostra esse spolia quae illi possiderent.
7 Sed nullo genere par erat causa nostra, et cociones, qui
ad clamorem confluxerant, nostram scilicet de more ridebant
invidiam, quod pro illa parte vindica<ri vide>bant
pretiosissimam vestem, pro hac pannuciam ne centonibus
8 quidem bonis dignam. Hinc Ascyltos paene risum discussit,
15 qui silentio facto, "Videmus," inquit, "suam cuique rem
esse carissimam; reddant nobis tunicam nostram et pallium
2 suum recipiant." Etsi rustico mulierique placebat
permutatio, advocati tamen iam plani [nocturni], qui volebant
pallium lucri facere, flagitabant uti apud se utraque

L (= ldmrtp)
14 4 itaque *hic* t^{m}, *ante* vel L interim pt: viritim l
et *Buecheler*: ut facere[t] *Buecheler* 5 operto *Wouweren*:
aperto quae … steterat *del. Delz* tenere *del. Oudendorp*
7 nostra *Benedictinus*: nam l *ex Cuiaciano*: *del. Buecheler*
cociones *Buecheler post Salmasius*: conciones quae *add. Strelitz*
15 videmus *Jungermann*: videamus 2 plani *scribo*: pene *deleo*

With our prize in danger of slipping away, we opted to knock down the price on the cloak and take a small loss to secure a greater gain. No sooner had we put the goods on display than the woman at the labourer's side, who was wearing a veil, after inspecting the patterns minutely, grabbed the border with both hands and started shrieking, "Thieves! Thieves!" at the top of her voice. We were mortified and, hardly wishing to be caught at a loose end, in turn grabbed the dirty, tattered tunic, yelling with equal fervour that these people had our stolen merchandise. Our case seemed far from being a fair swap, and some dealers, attracted by the noise, stood laughing as they witnessed our strange and heated effort to pit a claim for a rag hardly good for patches against a valuable item of clothing. Ascyltus eventually managed to still their laughter, and as silence fell he spoke:

15 "We see how everybody likes their own things best. Tell them to give us back our tunic and they will get their cloak." The exchange was agreeable to labourer and woman, but crooked mediators, intent on reaping a windfall from the cloak, were now demanding that both items be deposited with them against a judge's hearing next day.

deponeretur ac postero die iudex querellam inspiceret.
3 Neque res tantum quae videretur in controversia esse,
sed longe aliud [quaeri], <quod> in utraque parte scilicet
4 latrocinii suspicio haberetur. Iam sequestri placebant,
et nescioquis ex cocionibus, calvus, tuberosissimae
frontis, qui solebat aliquando etiam causas agere,
invaserat pallium exhibiturumque crastino die affirmabat.
5 Ceterum apparebat nihil aliud quaeri nisi ut semel
deposita vestis inter praedones strangularetur et nos
metu criminis non veniremus ad constitutum … Idem plane
6 et nos volebamus. Itaque utriusque partis votum casus
7 adiuvit. Indignatus enim rusticus, quod nos centonem
exhibendum postularemus, misit in faciem Ascylti tunicam
et liberatos querella iussit pallium deponere, quod solum
litem faciebat …
8 Et recuperato, ut putabamus, thesauro in deversorium
praecipites abimus praeclusisque foribus ridere acumen non
minus cocionum quam calumniantium coepimus, quod nobis
ingenti callidate pecuniam reddidissent.

Nolo quod cupio statim tenere
Nec victoria me placet parata *

L (= ldmrtp)
15 3 *del. Fraenkel add. Tornaesius* 4 *post* frontis *desinit* d etiam ad *sive* et ad L 5 veste is l^{m}: veste lis *Fuchs lac. ind. Buecheler* 7 *lac. ind. Pithou* 8 *post distichon lacunam satis amplam intellegamus*

There was far more to this dispute than met the eye, they said, because of the risk that both parties possessed stolen property. They immediately settled on trustees, and one of the dealers, a bald man with a forehead covered in warts who pleaded cases on occasion, grabbed the cloak, claiming he would exhibit it on the following day. Thus their interest appeared confined to having this garment deposited in order to be swallowed up among these crooks, with us too afraid of prosecution to press charges. ... We obviously had no objection. Chance came to the rescue of both sides. The labourer, indignant that we should be insisting upon the exhibiting of a mere rag, threw the thing in Ascyltus' face and demanded that we (now quit of our claim!) deposit the cloak as the sole item in dispute ...

With our treasure recovered, or so we thought, we raced off to the inn, barred the door, and had a good laugh at those smart dealers and accusers alike, whose great cunning had procured the return of our money.

I decry the wish that is quickly got,
And the easy triumph pleases me not *

16 / Sed ut primum beneficio Gitonis praeparata nos LO
implevimus cena, ostium [non] satis audaci strepitu
exsonuit impulsum ...
2 Cum et ipsi ergo pallidi rogaremus quis esset,
"Aperi," inquit, "iam scies." Dumque loquimur, sera sua
sponte delapsa cecidit reclusae subito fores admiserunt
3 intrantem. Mulier autem erat operto capite [illa scilicet
quae paulo ante cum rustico steterat] et, "Me derisisse,"
inquit, "vos putabatis? Ego sum ancilla Quartillae,
4 cuius vos sacrum ante cryptam turbastis. Ecce ipsa venit
ad stabulum petitque ut vobiscum loqui liceat. Nolite
perturbari. Nec accusat errorem vestrum nec punit. Immo
potius miratur quis deus iuvenes tam urbanos in suam
17 regionem detulerit." Tacentibus adhuc nobis et ad neutram partem
assentationem flectentibus intravit ipsa, una comitata
2 virgine, sedensque super torum meum diu levit. Ac ne
tunc quidem nos ullum adiecimus verbum, sed attoniti
expectavimus lacrimas ad ostentationem doloris paratas.
3 Ut ergo tam ambitiosus detonuit imber, retexit superbum
pallio caput et manibus inter se usque ad articulorum

L (= lmrtp), O (= BRP)
16 *delendum putant Scaliger et Tornaesius,* nostrum *tempt. Buecheler bene* exsonuit impulsum lO: *transp.* L *lac. indic. Buecheler* 3 *del. Jacobs* sacrum RP: *om. B:* sacram L: sacra *Salmasius* **17** 2 doloris *an necesse?*
3 detonuit *cf. Verg. Aen. 10.809* superbum] opertum *Jacobs* pallio del. *Fuchs* interius in articulorum *Cuiacianus*

4
Quartilla's Party

16 We had barely enough time to eat our fill of the lunch that Giton had been good enough to serve before there was a loud knocking on the door …

Blanching, we asked who was there. "Open up and you'll find out," was the reply. Even as we spoke the bolt slid back on its own and fell out, the door burst open, and in came a woman with her face covered up. "Did you think you could make a fool of me?" she began. "I am the maid of Quartilla, and it was her ceremony in front of the grotto you disrupted. Now she has come to your lodging to ask in person if she may speak with you. Do not be alarmed; she is not pressing charges or seeking punishment. In fact she feels only amazement at what god could have brought such cultured young men to her neighbourhood."

17 As we stood silently, without so much as a yes or a no, Quartilla herself entered, with a little girl at her side, sat down on my bed, and cried and cried. We still hadn't found our tongues but simply watched this tearful show of grief in amazement. Eventually the mighty storm abated; she removed the shawl from an aristocratic head and wrung her hands until the knuckles cracked:

The long-anticipated dinner with Trimalchio, referred to by Ascyltus in *Sat.* 10, finds itself preceded by an afternoon episode at *Sat.* 16–26 that is a comedic high point of the entire narrative: the extraordinary exaction of a punishment of sexual humiliation, by the dominatrix Quartilla, appropriately the high priestess of Priapus, upon Encolpius and Ascyltus for a professionally compromising voyeuristic infraction of her rites. And this despite twenty gaps in the manuscript tradition, witnessed and signed off on by the sixteenth-century editors who possessed it. There was a foretaste in *Sat.* 8, a line of similar sexual content not belonging there but here: aphrodisiac drugs and uncomfortable sex. The formula is not dissimilar to that used by Dickey in *Deliverance* (1972) and Tarantino in *Pulp Fiction* (1994): homosexual rape. The signal triumph of Petronius is to keep it funny and ultimately harmless: humiliation followed by escape. Nobody died. A school of scholarship, invigorated recently by H. van Thiel (1971), has tried to reconstruct the order of the text and plot. But for our present needs this is not required. (cont'd)

4 strepitum constrictis, "Quaenam est," inquit "haec
audacia, aut ubi fabulas etiam antecessura latrocinia
didicistis? Misereor mediusfidius vestri; neque enim
5 impune quisquam quod non licuit adspexit. Utique nostra
regio tam praesentibus plena est numinibus ut facilius
6 possis deum quam hominem invenire. Ac ne me putatis
ultionis causa huc venisse, aetate magis vestra commoveor
quam iniuria mea. Imprudentes enim, ut adhuc puto,
7 admisistis inexpiabile scelus. Ipsa quidem illa nocte
vexata tam periculoso inhorrui frigore ut tertianae etiam
impetum timerem. Et ideo medicinam somnio petii iussaque
sum vos perquirere atque impetum morbi monstrata
8 subtilitate lenire. Sed de remedio non tam valde laboro;
maior enim in praecordiis dolor saevit, qui me usque ad
necessitatem mortis deducit, ne scilicet iuvenili impulsi
licentia quod in sacello Priapi vidistis vulgetis deorumque
9 consilia proferatis in populum. Protendo igitur ad genua
vestra supinas manus petoque et oro ne nocturnae religiones
iocum risumque faciatis neve traducere velis tot annorum
secreta, quae vix tres homines noverunt."

L (= lmrtp), O(= BRP)
17 4 haec om. L etiam *Cuiacianus*: et 6 aetatis magis O vestrae L 7 *aliquod post* nocte *ut* curis *vel* insomniis *suppl. putavit Buecheler* timeam O; *cf.* 18.7 somnio r: somno 8 impulsi licentia rtp *ex Benedictino*: impulsu licentiam 9 obtendo *Cuiacianus* tres *Nisbet*: mille: decem, *id est* x, *posse censent Giardina et Melloni*

"What brazenness have we here?" she began. "Where did you learn such larceny surpassing fiction? I feel sorry for you, God knows, since no one witnesses what is taboo and gets away with it – especially in these parts, where the supernatural is so common that you'd as easily run into a god as a human. Still, do not think I have come here bent on revenge; I have been impelled more by regard for your youth than slight to me. You have committed a crime beyond expiating only out of sheer ignorance, I still like to think. On that very night I suffered an attack of the shivers so bad I thought I had a bout of the tertian fever. In a dream I learned the antidote: I had to seek you out and effect my cure by a certain exquisitely elaborate means. But getting the remedy is not my worst burden: to the depths of my soul I am racked by dread, suicidal dread, that you in all youthful impulsiveness will divulge what you saw in the chapel of Priapus and make common knowledge of the gods' counsels. So I lay my hands in pleading upon your knees and beg and beseech you not to make a laughing-stock of my midnight ceremonies, nor be tempted to betray the secrets of the ages, known by scarce a handful in all the world!"

(cont'd) The episode reads all the more suspensefully, not despite the serious damage done to the manuscript, but because of it. The content implicates clumsy attempts at censorship, followed in another era by equally clumsy restoration of the remnant. The emotions and spot-on speeches of the magisterial Quartilla, her sexual aphorisms, including her thematic poem in *Sat.* 18, the colourful, extreme, drug-laced sexualized activities, the "mystification at the random change in mood" (*Sat.* 19), the laughter, the tears, the terrifying lamentations, and finally the vow of silence – all in rapid, dissociative order – create an effect that might not have been matched for sheer mayhem with the text in better condition. As ever in the *Satyrica,* we enjoy it to the full extent of what we possess.

18 Secundum hanc deprecationem lacrimas rursus effudit
gemitibusque largis concussa toto facie ac pectore torum
2 meum pressit. Ego eodem tempore et misericordia turbatus
et metu bonum animum habere eam iussi et de utroque esse
3 securam: nam neque sacra vulgaturum, et si quod praeterea
aliud remedium ad tertianam deus illi monstrasset,
adiuvaturos nos divinam prudentiam vel periculo nostro.
4 Hilarior post hanc pollicitationem facta mulier basiavit
me spissius et ex lacrimis in risum mota descendentes
5 ab aure capillos meos lenta manu duxit / et, "Facio," L
inquit, "indutias vobiscum et a constituta lite dimitto.
Quod / si non adnuissetis de hac medicina quam peto, iam LO
parata erat in crastinum turba quae et iniuriam meam
vindicaret et dignitatem:

6 Contemni turpe est, legem donare superbum
Hoc amo, quod possum qua libet ire via.
Nam sane et sapiens contemptus iurgia nectit,
Et qui non iugulat, victor abire solet" *

7 Complosis deinde manibus in tantum repente risum
effusa est ut timeremus. Idem ex altera parte et ancilla
fecit quae prior venerat, idem virguncula quae una
19 intraverat. Omnia mimico risu exsonuerant, cum interim

L (= lmrtp), O (= BRP)
18 3 providentiam rtp 4 lenta *Bongars*: temptata
5 lite <vos> *obtulit Buecheler* adiuvissetis l
6 nectit *Sambucus*: flectit et … solet obscura
lacunam indic. lmrt **19** mimico B: nimio

18 Following this entreaty she let go with more tears, and, convulsed by mighty sobs, buried face and breast in my bed. Moved simultaneously to pity and to fear, I told her to take comfort on both counts: I had no intention of divulging her secrets, and in regard to any further remedy for the tertian fever that the god had prescribed for her, why, even to our peril we would abet divine wisdom in any way we could. After these reassurances the woman cheered up, kissed me excessively, replaced tears with smiles, and languidly fondled the hair about my ears. "I propose a truce," she said, "and I'll withdraw any formal charges. But if you hadn't both agreed to participate in the cure which I am asking, tomorrow I would have had a crowd ready to avenge my wrong and restore my self-respect:

> To be despised is shame, to rule is fine:
> This I love: to go where I approve.
> Even wise man scorned devises ill,
> And who grants reprieve is victor still." *

Next she clapped her hands and promptly fell into such a fit of laughter that we cowered in fear. On the other side of the room the laughter was taken up by the maid who had preceded her, and also by the little girl, Quartilla's companion.

19 The whole place echoed with theatrical laughter, while we,

nos, quae tam repentina esset mutatio animorum facta
ignoraremus ac modo nosmet ipsos modo mulieres intueremur *
2 / "Ideo vetui hodie in hoc deversorio quemquam L
mortalium admitti, ut remedium tertianae sine ulla
3 interpellatione a vobis acciperem." Ut haec dixit
Quartilla, Ascyltus quidem paulisper obstupuit, ego
autem frigidior hieme Gallica factus nullum potui verbum
4 emittere. Sed ne quid tristius expectarem, comitatus
faciebat. Tres enim erant mulierculae, si quid vellent
conari, infirmissimae scilicet; contra nos, si nihil
aliud, virilis sexus [esset] et praecincti certe altius
5 eramus. Immo ego sic iam paria composueram, ut si
depugnandum foret, ipse cum Quartilla consisterem,
Ascyltus cum ancilla, Giton cum virgine *
Tunc vero excidit omnis constantia attonitis, et
mors non dubia miserorum oculos coepit obducere *

20 "Rogo," inquam, "domina, si quid tristius paras,
celerius confice; neque enim tam magnum facinus
admisimus ut debeamus torti perire" *
2 Ancilla quae Psyche vocabatur lodiculam in pavimento
diligenter extendit *

Sollicitavit inguina mea mille iam mortibus frigida *

L (= lmrtp)

19 1–**20** 3 *lacunae uno meo asterisco signatae in* lmrpt *asteriscis notantur* 4 scilicet; contra *distinxit Fraenkel, adverbium intellegens* nos <quibus> *Dousa* sexus esset. et *libri*: sexus sed et *Pithou*: deleo; *adiunctionem videas*

in mystification at this random change in mood, could only glance at each other and then back at the women *

"I have given instructions that not a mortal soul be admitted to this inn today, to ensure no interruption as I extract from you the cure for my tertian fever." At this utterance by Quartilla, Ascyltus gasped, whereas I, having gone colder than a winter in Gaul, failed to manage a sound. But at least, I thought, I could be assured of no worse calamity, on the basis of resources. If they wanted to try anything, they were only three women, supposedly the weaker sex; while we at least were males, and certainly more dressed for action. I had even mentally matched up pairs in the event of it coming to a fight: I'd take on Quartilla, Ascyltus the maid, and Giton the little girl *

But then in our panic all resolve collapsed, and a miserable and certain death began to close over our eyes *

20 "Mistress," I pleaded, "if you have anything worse in store please get it over with quickly; our crime was not so great that we deserve to die by torture!" *

The maid, whose name was Psyche, carefully spread the blanket upon the floor *

tried to stimulate my member, but it had died of cold a thousand times over *

3 Operuerat Ascyltus pallio caput, admonitus scilicet
periculosum esse alienis intervenire secretis *
4 Duas institas ancilla protulit de sinu alteraque
pedes nostros alligavit, altera manus *
5 Ascyltus iam deficiente fabularum contextu,
6 "Quid? Ego" inquit, "non sum dignus qui bibam?" Ancilla
risu meo prodita complosit manus et, "Apposui quidem,"
7 <inquit>. "Adulescens, solus tantum medicamentum
ebibisti?" "Ita est?" inquit Quartilla, "quicquid satyrii
fuit, Encolpius ebibit?" *
Non indecenti risu latera commovit *
8 / Ac ne Giton quidem ultimo risum tenuit, utique LO
postquam virguncula cervicem eius invasit et non
repugnanti puero innumerabilia oscula dedit *
21 / Volebamus miseri exclamare, sed nec in auxilio erat L
quisquam, et hinc Psyche acu comatoria cupienti mihi
invocare Quiritum fidem malas pungebat, illinc puella
penicillo, quod et ipsum satyrio tinxerat, Ascylton
opprimebat *
2 Ultimo cinaedus supervenit myrtea subornatus gausapa

L (= lmrtp), O (= BRP)
20 3–**21** *lacunas, quas singulas asteriscis notavi, asteriscis varie numero signant* lmrtp **20** 3 esse *Cuiacianus non Benedictinus* 6 ego] ergo l <re> risu meo prodita *suppl. Courtney* apposui *corr. Scaliger*: apposuit *lacunam post* quidem *statuerunt* mrtp, *sed verbum solum dicendi fort. desideratur* 8 ac … dedit *om.* l

Ascyltus had wrapped his head in his cloak, presumably all too conscious of the peril in witnessing rites involving another party *

The maid took two strips of cloth from her dress and tied together our feet with one and our hands with the other *

With the conversation flagging, Ascyltus interjected, "Hey, don't I get to drink any?" The maid was given away by my chuckle. She clapped her hands and replied, "I put some next to you. Encolpius, did you drink all that medication on your own?" "What's this?" inquired Quartilla. "Did he drink up the whole supply of aphrodisiac?" *

Her sides shook with laughter, quite becomingly *

At last even Giton couldn't help laughing, particularly when the little girl threw her arms about the boy's neck and landed kiss after kiss, quite without any resistance *

21 We wanted to cry out in our misery, but there was no one to help us, and at every appeal for a Citizens' Rescue Psyche gave my cheeks a poke with a hat pin, while the little girl flicked Ascyltus with a brush that she had also dipped in the aphrodisiac *

Eventually, a transvestite climbed on us, and, dressed in a shift of myrtle green

cinguloque <cerasino> succinctus, modo extortis nos clunibus
cecidit, modo basiis olidissimis inquinavit, donec
Quartilla ballaenaciam tenens virgam alteque succincta
iussit infelicibus dari missionem *
3 Uterque nostrum religiosissimis iuravit verbis inter
duos periturum esse tam horribile secretum *
4 Intraverunt palaestritae complures et nos legitimo
5 perfusos oleo refecerunt. Utcumque igitur lassitudine
abiecta cenatoria repetimus et in proximam cellam ducti
sumus, in qua tres lecti strati erant et reliquus
6 lautitiarum apparatus splendidissime expositus. Iussi
ergo discubuimus, et gustatione mirifica initiati vino
7 etiam Falerno inundamur. Ecepti etiam pluribus ferculis
cum laberemur in somnum, "Ita est?" inquit Quartilla,
"etiam dormire vobis in mente est, cum sciatis Priapi
genio pervigilim deberi?" *
22 Cum Ascyltus gravatus tot malis in somnum laberetur,
illa quae iniuria depulsa fuera ancilla totam faciem
eius fuligine pefricuit et non sentientis latera
2 umerosque sopi[ti] onibus pinxit. Iam ego etiam tot malis

L (= lmrtp)
21 2 *addidit Sullivan, renuens lacunam a Buechelero post* succinctus *signatam* 2 *et* 3 *asteriscos in libris repperimus* 4 complures *Buecheler*: quamplures 5 utcumque igitur *cf.* 87.8; nescio quo modo *significat.* 6 inundabamur *Memmianus* **22** larga *Jungermann*: longa: large *Fuchs* latera *Delz*: labra *del. Vossius, Cat.* 37.10 *adferens*

that was hitched high by a sash of cherry pink, first wrenched about and slapped our buttocks, then beslimed us with stinking kisses until Quartilla, skirts tucked up, waved a whalebone wand and commanded him to give the wretches quarter *

By all that was holy we swore that this appalling secret would die with us *

Several trainers came in and gave us a restorative massage using plenty of good-quality oil. And so somehow casting off our exhaustion we put on our dinner clothes again and were brought into an adjacent room, where three divans had been decked out and all the trappings of a splendid feast put on view. We were told to take our places, and started with a wonderful hors-d'oeuvre, followed by all the Falernian wine we could drink. Quite recovered after several courses, we were beginning to doze off when Quartilla spoke up: "What's this? Do you mean to go to sleep when you know Priapus demands an all-night vigil to honour his divinity?" *

22 Ascyltus, worn out by all his trials, slipped into unconsciousness, whereupon the maid whom he had so rudely spurned rubbed his face all over with a thick layer of lampblack and daubed his sides and shoulders with wine dregs.

fatigatus minimum veluti gustum hauseram somni; idem et
tota intra forique familia fecerat, atque alii circa
pedes discmbentium sparsi iacebant, alii parietibus
applicíti, quidam in ipso limine coniunctis marcebant
3 capitibus. Lucernae quoque umore defectae tenue et
extremum lumen spargebant, cum duo Syri expilaturi
[lagoenam] triclinium intraverunt, dumque inter argumentum
4 avidius rixantur, diductum fregerunt lagoenam. Cecidit
etiam mensa cum argento, et ancilla super torum marcenti
excussum forte altius poculum caput <paene> fregit. Ad quem
ictum exclamavit illa pariterque et fures prodidit et
5 partem ebriorum excitavit. [Syri] illi qui venerant ad
praedam postquam se deprehensos intellexeerunt, pariter
secundum lectum conciderunt, ut putares hoc convenisse,
et stertere tamquam olim dormientes coeperunt.
6 Iam et tricliniarches experrectus lucernis occidentibus
oleum infuderat, et pueri detersis paulisper oculis
redierant ad ministerium, cum intrans cymbalistria et
23 concrepans aera omnes excitavit. Refectum igitur est
convivium et rursus Quartilla ad bibendum revocavit.
Adiuvit hilaritatem comissantis cymbalistria<e cantus> *
2 Intrat cinaedus, homo omnium insulsissimus et plane

L (= lmrtp)
22 3 *del. Jahn* diductam] deiectam *Delz* 4 marcentis] marcenti *Delz, probat Mueller* <paene> caput fregit *Buecheler; immo, sed ordinem supra malo* 5 *del. Kraffert*
23 *add. Buecheler*

I too had had my share of trials and was snatching the merest sip of a sleep; inside and out the whole household was similarly engaged – some lying scattered around the feet of the guests, others propped against the walls, still others drooped on the doorstep, heads lolling together; and the very lamps were guttering and giving off their last, thin light. Suddenly two Syrian burglars entered the room, and in their greedy bickering over the silver they pulled a decanter to pieces. The table set with the silver was knocked over, and a goblet performed a high arc to smash into the head of the maid where she lay draped over the couch. Her cry upon impact served to awaken some of the drunks and give the thieves away. When the would-be robbers saw that they had been discovered they sank down in unison next to the couch, in a move that seemed rehearsed, and snored as if they had been sleeping all the time.

The maître d'hôtel woke up and refilled the dying lamps, and the slave boys, with a quick rub of their eyes, returned to their tasks; at which point a female cymbalist entered and with a clash of brass ensured that everyone was wide awake.

23 Thus was the banquet revived, and Quartilla invited all anew to drink their fill, as the cymbalist's singing did her part for the guests' enjoyment *

illa domo dignus, qui ut infractis manibus concrepuit,
eiusmodi carmina effudit:

3 "Huc, huc <cito> convenite nunc, spatalocinaedi
Pede tendite, cursum addite, convolate planta
Femore <o> facili, clune agili, [et] manu procaces,
Molles, veteres, Deliaci ferro recisi!"

4 Consumptis versibus suis immundissimo basio me conspuit.
Mox et super lectum venit atque omni vi <me> detexit recusantem.
5 Super inguina mea diu multumque frustra moluit. Perfluebant
per frontem sudantis acaciae rivi, et inter rugas malarum
tantum erat cretae, ut putares [detectum] parietum nimbo
24 laborare. Non tenui ergo diutius lacrimas, sed ad ultimam
perductus tristitiam, "Quaeso," inquam, "domina, certe
2 embasicoetan iussaras dari." Complosit illa tenerius manus
et, "O," inquit, "hominem acutum atque urbanitatis
vern<ac>ulae fontem. Quid? Tu non intellexeras cinaedum
3 embasicoetam vocari?" Deinde ut contubernali meo melius
succederet, "per fidem," inquam, [nostram] Ascyltus <noster>
4 in hoc triclinio solus feria agit?" "Ita," inquit Quartilla,
"et Ascylto embasicoetas detur." Ab hac voce equum cinaedus

L (= lmrtp)
23 2 concrepuit *Jahn: congemuit* 3.1 *add. Luc. Mueller* 3.3 *add. Fraenkel, qui del. post* l 3.4 ferro *scripsi pro manu codd. iterato; adiunct. vide* 4 *supplere placet* 5 *deleo; cf.* 23.4 detexit **24** 2 tenerius *mirum; cf.* 20.6 *add. Schoppius* 3 ut: ne *Goldast del. Buecheler: transpono; cf.* 25.1: *adiunct. videas*

A transvestite entered – the queerest fellow you could imagine and quite the fitting comment on the establishment. He gave a crack of his knuckles and came out with the following:

"Hither, jewelled eunuchs come:
On tripping feet fly to our home!
Thighs and buttocks, twitchy hand,
Delian capons, seasoned, bland!"

When he finished his poem he planted upon me the most disgusting smacker. Next, he climbed onto the bed, roughly pulled off my clothes (resistance was useless), and bent to work long and hard upon my member, without result. Streams of acacia pomade mingling with sweat poured from his forehead, and, with all the powder caking into the wrinkles on his cheeks, the effect was of a wall flaking off in a thunderstorm.

24 I could hold back the tears no more, and in my last extremity of grief, "Please, mistress," I inquired, "I could have sworn you only ordered me toddy." Quartilla clapped her hands daintily, exclaiming, "What a sharp one you are! What a fount of down-home wit! Go on! Surely you hadn't known my eunuch's name was Toddy!" Then, in an effort to "improve" my comrade's fortunes, "Dear me," I exclaimed, "is friend Ascyltus the only one in the room who gets the day off?" "No," Quartilla replied, "Ascyltus must be administered his Toddy too!" At this the eunuch dismounted,

mutavit transituque ad comitem meum facto clunibus
5 eum basiisque distrivit / Stabat inter haec Giton LO
et dissolvebat ilia sua. Itaque conspicata eum
Quartilla cuius esset puer diligentissima sciscitatione
6 quaesivit. Cum ego fratrem meum esse dixissem, "Quare
ergo," inquit, "me non basiavit?" Vocatoque [ad se] in
7 osculum <se> applicuit. Mox manum etiam demisit in sinum
et pertractato vasculo tam rudi, "Haec," inquit, "belle
cras in promulside libidinis nostrae militabit; hodie
enim post asellum diaria non sumo."

25 Cum haec diceret, ad aurem eius Psyche ridens
accessit, et cum dixisset nescio quid, "Ita, ita,"
inquit Quartilla, "bene admonuisti. Cur non, quia
bellissima occasio est, devirginatur Pannychis nostra?"
2 Continuoque producta est puella satis bella et quae non
plus quam septem annos videbatur [et ea ipsa quae primum
3 cum Quartilla in cellam venerat nostram]. Plaudentibus
ergo universis et postulantibus nuptias facerent
obstupui ego et nec Gitona, verecundissimum puerum,
sufficere huic petulantiae affirmavi, nec puellam eius
aetatis esse, ut muliebris patientiae legem posset
4 accipere, "Ita," inquit Quartilla, "minor est ista quam

L (= lmrtp), O (= BRP)
24 6 vocatumque *libri: sic tamen muto deleo suppleo* 7 etiam *Cuiacianus* haec sc. mentula; *cf. ad* 132.7 **25** haec *Poggio*: hoc 2 *del. Fraenkel* 3 facerent *Petersmann, cf.* 112.3: fecerunt

remounted, and rubbed his way into my comrade with buttocks and tongue. Amidst all stood Giton, splitting his sides with laughter. Quartilla took him in, and with a studied curiosity asked to whom the boy belonged. I said he was mine – my boyfriend; whereupon she asked why in that case had he not given her a kiss. She then called him over for his kiss. Before long she had dropped her hand into to his lap, and as she fondled that novice pecker (*vasculo tam rudi*) she pronounced, "yes, tomorrow this will do very nicely to whet my appetite; as for today, I don't eat crackers after fish."

25 As she spoke, Psyche came up and smilingly whispered something into her ear, whereat, "Yes, yes," Quartilla replied, "Good idea! This is the perfect occasion for Pannychis to lose her virginity!" Immediately a pretty little girl was led out. She seemed scarcely seven years old. As all applauded and called for a "wedding" I gasped that Giton, most bashful of boys, was hardly capable of such mayhem and that the girl was not of an age to receive her lesson in womanly submission. "Oh?" replied Quartilla,

---

Here is a rare physical confirmation of Giton's sexual status. Taken with confirming his age and Encolpius' ensuing worries about the performance of husbandly duties, he is not a fully developed male sixteen-year-old, and behind for his years. This is not to infer a lack of sexual history, as we shall encounter it later. Sotadean metre employed by the *cinaedi* in *Sat.* 23 is also known as "cinaedic" or "palindromic," and is particularly suited to the most ribald or obscene of insults. Hardly a coincidence, then, that the only other example is the vitupera-tive, self-harming attempt by Encolpius at *Sat.* 132.8: *ter corripui* ... The so-called *cinaedi* offer an awkward problem to translators of preserving neutrality and good comprehension within our less judgmental contemporary culture. The word connotes adult men moving sexually – suggestively, or invitingly. Twinkers? One used to be content with pathics or passives (though the present ones belie the term) or transvestites or drag queens. Berdaches has been tried (too obscure and indigenous), and recently two-spirit, too arch and open to objection, like most.

ego fui, cum primum virum passa sum? Iunonem meam iratam
5 habeam, si umquam me meminerim virginem fuisse. Nam et
infans cum paribus inquinata sum, et subinde prodeuntibus
annis maioribus me pueris applicui, donec ad [hanc]
6 aetatem perveni. Hinc etiam puto proverbium natum illud
[ut dicatur] posse taurum tollere, qui vitulum sustulerit."
7 Igitur ne maiorem iniuriam in secreto frater acciperet,
26 consurrexi ad officium nuptiale. Iam Psyche puellae caput
involverat flammeo, iam embasicoetas praeferebat facem, iam
ebriae mulieres longum agmen plaudentes fecerant thalamumque
2 intexta exornaverunt veste, cum Quartilla [quoque]
iocantium libidine accensa et ipsa surrexit correptumque
3 Gitona in cubiculum traxit. Sine dubio non repugnaverat
puer, ac ne puella quidem tristis expaverat nuptiarum nomen.
4 Itaque cum inclusi iacerent, consedimus ante limen thalami
et in primis Quartilla per rimam improbe diductam
5 applicuerat oculum curiosum lusumque puerilem libidinosa
speculatur diligentia. Me quoque ad idem spectaculum lenta
manu traxit, et quia considerantium haeserant vultus,
quicquid a spectaculo vacabat, commovebat obiter labra et
me tamquam furtivis subinde osculis verberabat *
6 / Abiecti in lectis sine metu reliquam exegimus noctem * L

L (= lmrtp), O (= BRP)

25 5 *del. Fraenkel* 6 *om.* lr, *del. Buecheler* qui B: quae *cett.*

26 fecerunt L intexta *Auratus*: incesta 2 cum *Buecheler*: tum *del. Buecheler*

"Is she any younger than I was when I first took on a man? Juno strike me down if I can remember ever being a virgin! Even as a baby I messed with my playmates, and the older I grew the bigger the boys got – until today. I suppose this is where that saying comes from about being able to lift a bull after you've lifted a calf." So, to forestall any larger indignity that my dear Giton might incur out of view, I embraced a nuptial role.

26 In a wink Psyche was covering the girl's head in the red veil, Toddy was bearing forth the torch, tipsy women were making a cheering corridor, the bridal bower was being decked in tapestry; and Quartilla, inflamed by the lewd tableau, stood up and personally pulled Giton off to the bedroom. The boy did not hesitate, no doubt of it; and prospect of "marriage" didn't seem to faze the girl either. So the door was closed and down they lay, and there we sat outside the room. Quartilla was first in line to apply a curious eye to a naughtily crafted chink in the door, and in lustful concentration she watched their childish antics. Seductively she drew me into the view. Since this made our faces touch, she'd take time off to turn her lips to brush my cheeks over and over with stolen kisses *

We hurled ourselves onto the beds and passed what remained of the night without anxiety *

Pannychis (*Sat.* 25.1) is the first of a pair of very young girl-children (younger than a confirmed boy equivalent) threatened with or pressed into sexual service. She is an attendant/intern to Quartilla, priestess of Priapus, whose rank and duties are a shallow cover for a career as sex worker. Now, for the amusement of paying and approving clients, Quartilla's assistant Psyche proposes a full-fledged "wedding" of the little girl to Giton. Encolpius is doubly scandalized, taking Pannychis, at no more than seven, as far too young for such use. Quartilla begs to disagree, having been deflowered at that age, evidently without harm. Encolpius' discomfort was also with Giton as groom, Encolpius not believing Giton had the resolution to go through with it. What startled him particularly was that, hustled into this situation, the girl showed no dejection or fear, and Giton no hesitation; an irony that repeats elsewhere. The scene, mercifully, fades out.

7 / Venerat iam tertius dies [id est expectatio H
liberae cenae] sed tot vulneribus confossis fuga
8 magis placebat quam quies. Itaque cum maesti deliberaremus
quonam genere praesentem evitaremus procellam, unus
9 servus Agamemnonis interpellavit trepidantes et "Quid
vos?" inquit, "Nescitis, hodie apud quem fiat?
Trimalchio, lautissimus homo … horologium in
triclinio et bucinatorem habet subornatum, ut subinde
10 sciat quantum de vita perdiderit." Amicimur ergo
diligenter obliti omnium malorum, et Gitona
libentissime servile officium tuentem [usque hoc]
iubemus in balneum sequi …

27 Nos interim vestiti errare coepimus, immo iocari
magis et circulis ludentium accedere, cum subito
/ videmus senem calvum, tunica vestitum russea, inter HL

H, L (= lmrtp)
26 7 *del. Buecheler* 9 *lac. ind. Strelitz*
10 *del. Heraeus* balneum *Buecheler*: balneo
lac. post sequi *ind. Friedlaender*
27 morari *Nisbet* ludentium *Mueller* (-tum *Heinze*):
ludentes *Delz*: ludentem *libri, del. Buecheler*

5
Dinner With Trimalchio

The "day after tomorrow" had come, but after taking such a pounding we felt more like running away than relaxing. While we were gloomily pondering some way to escape the coming storm, one of Agamemnon's servants broke into our anxious reveries:

"What's the matter?" he asked. "Don't you know who the host is today? It's Trimalchio, and he's very chic – he keeps a clock in his dining room with a bugler at the ready to remind him constantly of where his life has gone." We forgot our troubles, dressed carefully, and bade Giton attend us to the baths acting as our valet, which he did most willingly …

27 Meanwhile, still clothed, we were wandering about cracking jokes and joining knots of guests, when all of a sudden our eyes were drawn to a bald old man clad in a red tunic,

---

A number of features mark this consecrated dinner episode, fully bracketed within the narrative, as we have it, and buffered before by four, and after by seven, distinct other scenarios, unspooling continuously from a common tape. The most obvious difference from them is its size relative to any other, occupying about fifty pages, or one-third, of the *Satyrica* total. The presence of greater length is a detail one could ignore, were it not for a second one: there has been a change of actors. Encolpius, Ascyltus, and Giton, the seemingly indispensable protagonists, are largely missing in action on stage, moved to the side in spectating roles, to make way for a different cast. To an extent, the manuscript tradition neatly mirrors these differences. The content prior to the dinner exists overwhelmingly in a blend of traditions L and O, and the latter, the coeval *Cena Trimalchionis*, for the most part, only in H. And then the significant differences start to pile up. In the early Middle Ages, around 800, these three traditions were merged into an archetype of Petronian material that had survived to that point. But then, for the reason probably of sexual content, LO became damaged in different ways, the first by accident and the second by expurgation; and H, the *Cena*, was left in peace, saved by the lack of pederastic romance. It offered instead, in unfamiliar Latin and by way of a break, an absorbing, funny, *Babette's Feast* of old gentlemen and their wives enjoying a splendid dinner, found in a distinct account made from a medieval copy in the early fifteenth century before it disappeared again for two more. It is posited that the anchoring role played by H within those three or four books of our archetype (out of possibly sixteen) ironically saved LO from extinction. The relative state of preservation, if not the quality, of these double traditions is plain to see. We have already experienced a plethora of gaps in the former. How does H compare? Here we are fortunate in two ways and less fortunate in a third. The first ten chapters of H are in L too, and the sixteenth-century gap hunters identified only a couple. After that, not a single starred gap occurs in H, which was lost, of course, and out of their reach, but one may safely say that the text of H was left tamper-free and ready to be enjoyed verbatim. (cont'd)

2 pueros capillatos ludentem pila. Nec tam pueri nos,
quamquam erat operae pretium, ad spectaculum duxerant
quam ipse pater familiae, qui soleatus pila prasina
exercebatur. Nec amplius eam repetebat quae terram
contigerat, sed follem plenum habebat servus
3 sufficiebatque ludentibus. Notavimus etiam res novas.
Nam duo spadones in diversa parte circuli stabant,
quorum alter matellam tenebat argenteam, alter
numerabat pilas, non quidem eas quae inter manus
[lusu] expellentium vibrabant, sed eas quae in terram
4 decidebant. Cum has ergo miraremur lautitias,
/ accurrit Menelaus et "Hic est" inquit, "apud quem H
cubitum ponetis, et quidem iam principium cenae
5 videtis." Etiamnum loquebatur Menelaus, cum
/ Trimalchio digitis concrepuit, ad quod signum HL
6 matellam spado ludenti subiecit. Exonerata ille
vesica aquam poposcit ad manus, digitos paululum
adspersos in capite pueri tersit ...

H, L (= lmrtp)

27 pila *del. Seager* 2 qui L: quia H 3 lusu H: luxu L: *del. Smith* expellentium *scribo:* expellentes *Smith*: expellente; *adiunctionem videas* 4 ergo om. L miramur H ponetis *lego*: ponitis; *sed non in triclinium convivae intrare coeperunt; v. ad* 33.2 permittitis: permittetis *Memm.* quidem *Buecheler*: quid 5 etiamnum *Scheffer*: et iam non digitos] digitis *Sullivan* (*cf. Cic. Off.* 3.75) supposuit L 6 *lac. ind. Buecheler*

engaged in a game of catch-ball with some long-haired boys. It was not so much the boys who caught our attention, though they were worth a look, as the gentleman himself, beslippered and taking his exercise with a green ball. If the ball dropped he didn't pick it up. A servant just gave the players another one from a well-stuffed bag. We noted some further twists: there were two eunuchs standing on opposite sides of the ring, one holding a silver chamber pot, the other taking the tally – not of the times the balls passed between the players from hand to hand, but of the times they fell to the ground. While we were admiring the spectacle, Menelaus hurried up. "This is the man," he said, "who is your dinner host, and you are now in fact witnessing the curtain raiser." Even as Menelaus spoke, Trimalchio snapped his fingers – the signal for the eunuch to position the chamber pot for him in mid-game. He relieved himself, called for water, briefly splashed his fingers, and wiped them dry on the hair of one of the boys …

(cont'd) That was in the "fortunate" column. Although the copying of H in 1423 was reasonably competent, it is marred by haste, "*culpa velocitatis,*" as Buecheler has it. There were many unfamiliar words that could not just be guessed at successfully; and they stayed as nonsense words in the text. In return for our trio, who are indeed present but in an almost furtive overhearing capacity (though invited to offer academic content), watched carefully by Agamemnon, we are introduced to about twelve freedmen (manumitted slaves), friends all ready to join in free discussion on a full range of topics of daily interest. There was some internal tourism: the sights and marvels of Trimalchio's home, his slaves and interactions with them, his observations and comments. The entry of the edible and drinkable menu and the presentation and discussion of it were an important part. And dominating all was the benediction of our generous host. A couple of ghost stories had to be told, followed by the arrival of Habinnas and Scintilla, intimate family friends. With everyone drinking steadily, interactions became louder and sometimes testier. Fortunata, Trimalchio's wife, wanted to dance. He had his Will brought in and read. As people became drunker, our young guest scholars began to feel trapped and stifled and a bath seemed like a good idea. A cock crew and Trimalchio grew nervous. A new work detail entered, among whom was a boy, quite nice-looking (*non inspeciosus*), whom Trimalchio kissed inappropriately. Fortunata was furious, said some bad words, and there was an angry, weepy exchange, which concluded with Trimalchio's invaluable autobiography, complete with details of Fortunata's support and of her own past. The intensely maudlin coda ended with the showing of the burial cloth, then music loud enough to bring in the fire brigade, and the trio slipped away, dodging their chaperone. Only one thing further to mention: the freedman banter. This famous account of their viva voce discussion, as reproduced by Petronius, one may say without fear of contradiction, is a bold, incomparable adventure in Latin, and "worth the visit." See below at *Sat.* 41.

28 Longum erat singula excipere. Itaque intravimus
balneum, et sudore calfacti momento temporis ad frigidum
2 eximus. Iam Trimalchio unguento perfusus tergebatur, non
3 linteis, sed palliis ex lana mollissima factis. Tres
interim iatraliptae in conspectu eius Falernum potebant,
/ et cum plurimum rixantes effunderent, Trimalchio hoc H
4 suum propin esse dicebat. / Hinc involutus coccina HL
gausapa lecticae impositus est praecedentibus phaleratis
cursoribus quattuor at chiramaxio, in quo delicias eius
vehebatur, puer vetulus, lippus, domino [Trimalchione]
5 deformior. Cum ergo auferretur, ad caput eius symphoniacus
cum minimis tibiis accessit et, tamquam in aurem aliquid
6 secreto diceret, toto itinere cantavit. Sequimur nos
admiratione iam saturi et cum Agamemnone ad ianuam
pervenimus, / in cuius poste libellus erat cum hac H
7 insciptione fixus: "Quisquis servus sine dominico iussu
8 foras exit, accipiet plagas centum." / In aditu autem HL
ipso stabat ostiarius prasinatus, cerasino succinctus
9 cingulo, atque in lance argentea pisum purgabat. Super
limen autem cavea pendebat aurea, in qua pica varia

H, L (= lmrtp)
28 calefacti L 3 mollissima lana L 3 bibebant L
del. Sullivan 5 auferetur (*sic*) H: afferetur L
propin esse *Heraeus*: propinasse 4 ferebantur L
symphoniacus cum minimis *Wehle*: cum minimis symphoniacus
(symphoniacis L) 6 iam admiratione L 8 autem *om. L* *lance om.* H

28 I shall spare the many other details. We entered the baths, and after warming up to a sweat in no time we exited to the cold room, where Trimalchio was now being oiled and rubbed down with shawls of the softest wool instead of the usual towels. Three masseurs were drinking Falernian wine in full view. As they squabbled over it, a lot was spilled, and Trimalchio quipped that they were toasting his health. Then, enveloped in a scarlet robe, he was deposited on a litter, in front of which were stationed four caparisoned runners and a go-cart carrying his favourite slave boy, a little, old-looking fellow with eye inflammation, uglier than his master. As he was being borne off, a musician stepped up and played into his ear along the route on tiny pipes, as if telling him a secret. We followed behind, lost in admiration, up to the door of the dining room, where we met Agamemnon. A notice had been pinned to its post, which read:

> ANY SLAVE LEAVING THE PREMISES WITHOUT PERMISSION FROM THE MASTER WILL RECEIVE ONE HUNDRED LASHES.

In the doorway stood a butler liveried in yellow with a cherry cummerbund, shelling peas into a silver bowl. Above the doorstep hung a golden birdcage containing a magpie, which greeted the guests as they went in.

29 intrantes salutabat. Ceterum ego dum omnia stupeo, paene
resupinatus crura mea fregi. Ad sinistram enim intrantibus
non longe ab ostiarii cella canis ingens, catena vinctus,
in pariete erat pictus superque quadrata littera scriptum,
2 "CAVE CANEM." Et collegae mei quidem riserunt, ego autem
collecto spiritu non destiti totm parietem persequi.
3 Erat enim venalicium <cum> titulis pictum, et ipse
Trimalchio capillatus caduceum tenebat Minervaque
4 ducente Romam intrabat. Hinc quemadmodum ratiocinari
didicisset deinque dispensator factus esset, omnia
diligenter curiosus pictor cum inscriptione reddiderat.
5 In deficiente vero iam porticu levatum mento in tribunal
6 excelsum Mercurius rapiebat. Praesto erat Fortuna <cum>
cornu abundanti [copiosa] et tres Parcae aurea pensa
7 torquentes. Notavi enim in porticu gregem cursorum cum
8 magistro se exercentem. Praeterea grande armarium in
angulo vidi, in cuius aedicula erant Lares argentei
positi Venerisque signum marmoreum et pyxis aurea non
pusilla, in qua barbam ipsius conditam esse dicebant ...
9 Interrogare ergo atriensem coepi, quas in medio

H, L (= lmrtp)

29 2 *num quid ante* et *deest?* 3 enim *scripsi pro* autem *moleste iteratum; adiunct.videas add. Burman* Romam] tema *vel* tenia L: moenia *Heinze* 4 dein L 5 mento] merito *Memmianus*: vento *Fuchs* 5 capiebat L 6 *add. Wehle,* abundanti *delens sed* copioso *retinens*: delevit *Goesius* 7 cursorium *Memmianus* 8 marmorium positum H *lac. ind. Buecheler* 9 ego L

29 While gaping at the sights, I almost fell over and broke a leg, for upon the wall on the left going in, just beyond the butler's lodge, was a picture of a very large dog attached to a chain, above which was inscribed, in block capitals, BEWARE OF THE DOG. My friends laughed as I regained my composure and fixed my attention on the wall frieze for its entire length. First, a slave market, complete with price tags; and there was Trimalchio as a long-haired boy, entering Rome carrying a wand, with Minerva escorting him; next to that Trimalchio learning his sums; next to that Trimalchio promoted to steward – all rendered by the painter in careful detail, including caption. In the final panel, as the colonnade ended, there was Trimalchio, with Mercury lifting him by the chin and bearing him high onto a dais. Fortuna was there with her Horn of Plenty; also the Three Fates, spinning their golden threads. And right inside the colonnade I noticed a team of runners doing stretches with their coach. Finally, off in the corner was a large sideboard, in whose niches stood household gods in silver, a statue of Venus in marble, and a large jewel box in which, I was told, lay Trimalchio's first beard …

I asked the majordomo the subjects of the paintings before us. "The *Iliad* and the *Odyssey*," he replied, "and the gladiatorial show staged by Laenas."

Curiously, the dinner with Trimalchio contains fifteen references to dogs, and only one exists in the whole *Satyrica* outside it, at *Sat.* 95. Why this should be, and what it means to those formerly servile dinner guests, one can only speculate. Dogs in the *Cena* are used in a quasi-jocular manner, as presences prone to cause disturbances in line with the CAVE CANEM theme. There are plenty of other gags and risible scenarios in the dinner as a whole, usually terrible and hardly worth recording let alone repeating; but here, large, fierce, hunting-type dogs are legion, on chains (four times) or unrestrained (twice) or in a picture (once), as a kind of running joke, provoking excitement and laughter at their lack of proper control which Trimalchio almost seems to invite. Beginning students of classics and archaeology, like myself, recognize the CAVE CANEM mosaic at Pompeii often as their first introduction to the art and the empathy we share with the classical world. The motif starts here, then repeats at *Sat.* 72 with a real chained dog that knocks Ascyltus into a pool, dragging Encolpius in too. And just prior, at *Sat.* 64, another large, live dog on a chain, Scylax, is goaded into nearly ripping the limbs off the overmatched Margarita, lap-dog of Trimalchio's mascot Croesus. Amusing? Possibly. And who forgets the one-word scolding, of Trimalchio by his wife in the drunken, waning moments of the banquet, for rashly overstepping decency with a pass at an attractive slave boy: "*Canis!*" (*Sat.* 74). Other relevant references are at *Sat.* 40 and *Sat.* 64.

picturas haberent. "Iliada et Odyssian," inquit,
30 / "ac Laenatis gladiatorium munus." Non licebat H
ulteriora etiam considerare ...
Nos / iam ad triclinium perveneramus, in cuius HL
parte prima procurator rationes accipiebat. Et quod
praecipue miratus sum, in postibus triclinii fasces
erant cum securibus fixi, quorum imam partem quasi
embolum navis aeneum finiebat, in quo erat scriptum:
2 "C. Pompeio Trimalchioni, seviro Augustali, Cinnamus
3 dispensator." Sub eodem titulo et lucerna bilychnis de
camera pendebant, <erant> et duae tabulae in utroque
poste defixae, quarum altera, si bene memini, hoc
4 habebat inscriptum: "III. et pridie kalendas Ianuarias
C. noster foras cenat," altera lunae cursum stellarumque
septem imagines pictas; et qui dies boni quique
5 incommodi essent, distinguente bulla notabantur. / His H
Repleti voluptatibus cum conaremur in triclinium
intrare, exclamavit unus ex pueris, qui supra hoc
6 officium erat positus: "Dextro pede." Sine dubio
paulisper trepidavimus, ne contra praeceptum
7 aliquis nostrum limen transiret. / Ceterum ut pariter HL

H, L (= lmrtp)
30 multa etiam *Scheffer*: multa iam *Anton*: multaciam H:
audacter sed veri simile ulteriora etiam *Mueller*
lac. ind. Buecheler veneramus L imam m^{m}: unam
3 etiam lucerna L *add. Buecheler*

30 There was no time for further study …

By now we were at the dining room. In the entranceway a steward was doing the accounts. I observed the ceremonial bundle of twigs, pegged to the two doorposts by the axes in them – a most intriguing touch. The lower ends were done up in bronze to represent a ship's prow, upon which was inscribed

PRESENTED TO C. POMPEIUS TRIMALCHIO, MEMBER OF THE AUGUSTAN BOARD, BY CINNAMUS THE BUTLER.

Double lanterns hung from the ceiling down below the inscription, to where there was a tablet attached to either post. One read (if memory serves) DECEMBER 30 AND 31: OUR GAIUS IS DINING OUT. The other had on it the moon's current phase, painted versions of the seven planets, and the good and bad days of the month marked off by different tacks. After having our fill of these wonders, and just as we were making to enter, "Right foot first," bawled the slave boy designated for this task. Not surprisingly we were unnerved for a moment by the prospect of crossing the threshold in

---

The reference, even revelation, on this page of the dinner as a feat of recall, taken with Encolpius' remarks in *Sat.* 56 that "there were hundreds of these things, most of which I have now forgotten," and *Sat.* 65, "the very memory of which revolts me, to tell you the truth," are of course modest attempts by Petronius to knit the narrative, and are not for a moment to be taken seriously or as successful from a literal or seriously literary perspective. We may concede the presence of the narrator in every scene, but there is far too much action, minute physical detail, and character-driven dialogue throughout the *Satyrica* to make an accurate reproduction a remotely feasible human feat of memory. Even an omniscient narrator would have had to take copious notes.

movimus dextros gressus servus nobis despoliatus
procubuit ad pedes ac rogare coepit, ut se poenae
8 eriperemus: nec magnum esse peccatum tuum, propter
quod periclitarentur; subducta enim sibi vestimenta
dispensatoris in balneo, quae vix fuissent decem
9 milia sestertiorum. Rettulimus ergo dextros pedes
dispensatoremque in oecario aureos numerantem deprecati
10 sumus, ut servo remitteret poenam. Superbus ille
sustulit vultum et, "Non tam iactura me movet" inquit,
11 "quam neglegentia nequissimi servi. Vestimenta mea
cubitoria perdidit, quae mihi natali meo cliens quidam
donaverat, Tyria sine dubio, sed iam semel lota. Quid
ergo est? Dono vobis eum."

31 Obligati tam grandi beneficio cum intrassemus
triclinium occurrit nobis ille idem servus pro quo
rogaveramus, et stupentibus spississima basia impegit
2 gratias agens humanitati nostrae. "Ad summam, statim
scietis," ait, "cui dederitis beneficium. Vinum
dominicum ministratoris gratia est."

H, L (= lmrtp)
30 7 ad] ante L 8 decem] X l *(i.q. milia); sine virgula Benedictinus* 9 oecario *Heraeus*: thecario *Giardina, quod alibi non invenio*: precario ut *om.* L 11 donaverat cliens quidam L, eum *omittens* **31** spississima basia stupentibus L

contravention of a rule. Just as we were putting our steps in synch, a stripped slave fell at our feet and begged us to get him off his punishment. The offence which he stood accused of, he said, was hardly serious. The steward's clothes, costing barely more than ten thousand sesterces, had been stolen from him at the baths. So we withdrew our feet to petition the steward in his lodge, where he was counting up gold pieces, to let the slave off. "It's not the loss of the clothes that bothers me," he said, tossing his head imperiously. "It's the carelessness of that no-good slave. He lost the dinner outfit which a client gave to me for my birthday – Tyrian cloth of course, and washed only once. Oh, well. He's yours."

31 We were much obliged for so great a favour. After we finally entered the dining room, the slave on whose behalf we had petitioned rushed up and to our astonishment kissed us profusely and thanked us for our compassion. "You will soon know the man you rescued," he concluded: "Master's wine is butler's benediction."

Encolpius' response to the personality and performance of Trimalchio and his associates is as mixed as the sallies of his host, and depend upon the context. Plenty of admiration (not all of it ironical) is shown for the physical characteristics of the dinner party, usually in the first half; but habituation, time, intoxication, and weariness with excess and novelty add an increasing sting of disapproval to the narrative commentary. Encolpius is less impressed, in particular, with Trimalchio's dozens of departures from behavioural and educated norms and customs (*Sat.* 59.3 *ut insolenter solent*), which could be seen as pointed eccentricities and impulsive moves designed first to impress his own freedman class by emulation of his betters, but then in reality as practical, simplifying adjustments to those standard behaviours, to which his success as an oligarchically rich businessman entitled him. It was this unselfconscious display of freedom to send up such protocols that gave pause and resentment in the clever but naturally conservative, conventional Encolpius, whether it was in altering the rules of a game of catch-ball, or the order of precedence for reclining at the dinner table (see next page).

3 Tandem ergo discubuimus pueris Alexandrinis aquam
in manus nivatam infundentibus aliisque insequentibus ad
pedes ac paronychia cum ingenti subtilitate tollentibus.
4 Ac ne in hoc quidem tam molesto tacebant officio, sed
5 obiter cantabant. Ego experiri volui an tota familia
6 cantaret, itaque potionem poposci. Paratissimus puer non
minus me acido cantico excepit, et quisquis aliquid
7 rogatus erat ut daret: pantomimi chorum, non patris
8 familiae triclinium crederes. Allata est tandem gustatio
valde lauta, nam iam omnes discubuerunt praeter ipsum
9 Trimalchionem, cui locus novo more primus servabatur.
Ceterum in promulsidari erat asellus Corinthius cum bisaccio
positus, qui habebat olivas in altera parte albas, in
10 altera nigras. Tegebat asellum duae lances, in quarum
marginibus nomen Trimalchionis inscriptum erat et argenti
pondus. Ponticuli etiam ferruminati sustinebant glires
11 melle ac papavere sparsos. Fuerunt et thumatula ferventia
supra craticulam argenteam posita, et infra craticulam
Syriaca pruno cum granis Punici mali.

H, L (= lmrtp)
31 6 ut daret: *verba fere* simul cantabat *post* u.d. *excidisse putavit Buecheler*: daret *del. Gaselee*, ut daret *Mueller in quarta*
8 tandem *Heinze*: tamen H: tum L ipsum L: unum H
11 thumatula] *vel* thymatula *def. Bodel, item ad* 49.10: tumatula: tomacula l^{m} p, *ex quo patavina* t. ferventia *hunc ordinem habet Tornaesius in* t^{m}: *post* argenteam HL

As we at last took our places, a detail of Alexandrian boys poured snow-cooled water over our hands and another took charge of our feet, removing the whitlows with the utmost delicacy. And instead of being reduced to silence by this unpleasant job, they sang throughout. Wanting to find out if the entire household sang, I ordered a drink, and another boy was no less quick to oblige with a tinny tune, as did every boy when meeting a request. It seemed more like a musical stage than a gentleman's dining room.

After a pause, while everyone took their places with the exception of Trimalchio, for whom rather unusually the place of honour had been kept in reserve, the hors-d'oeuvre was brought in – a very elaborate affair. To whet our appetites we were presented, upon a tray of Corinthian bronze, with panniers of olives on either side of a little donkey, carrying black olives in one and green olives in the other. Over it, the donkey had two platters, supported on welded metal struts. Etched on the platter borders was Trimalchio's name together with the weight in silver. One contained dormice dredged in honey and poppyseed, and the other sausages sizzling upon a silver griddle under which sat dark Syrian plums topped with pink pomegranate seeds.

32 In his eramus lautitiis, cum ipse Trimalchio ad
symphoniam allatus est, positusque inter cervicalia
2 minutissima expressit imprudentibus risum. Pallio enim
coccineo adrasum excluserat caput, circaque oneratas
veste cervices laticlaviam immiserat mappam fimbriis
3 hinc atque illinc pendentibus. Habebat enim in minimo
digito sinistrae manus anulum grandem subauratum,
extremo vero articulo digiti sequentis minorem, ut mihi
videbatur, totum aureum sed plane ferreis veluti
4 stellis ferruminatum. Et ne has tantum ostenderet
divitias, dextrum nudavit lacertum armilla aurea cultum
33 et eboreo circulo lamina splendente conexo. Ut deinde
pinna argentea dentes perfodit, "amici," inquit, "nondum
mihi suave erat in triclinium venire, sed ne diutius
absentivus morae vobis essem, omnem voluptatem mihi
2 negavi. Permittitis tamen finiri lusum." Sequebatur puer
cum tabula terebinthina et crystallinis tesseris,
notavique rem omnium delicatissimam. Pro calculis enim albis
3 ac nigris aureos argenteosque habebat denarios. Interim dum

---

H, L (= lmrtp)
32 minutissima L: munitissima H 2 excluserat H: incluserat L 4 conexo *Buecheler*: connexum **33** triclinium absens more vobis venire sed ne diutius absenti vos essem, voluptatem H: triclinium venire sed ne diutius absentius essem, omnem vol. L: *corr. Heinze, quem secutus Giardina, sed* absentius *pro* absens *desperans* 2 permittetis *Memmianus* albis *om.* H ac] aut L

32 As we fell to these delicacies, the orchestra struck up a fanfare, as Trimalchio was brought in, propped up by tiny pillows: a sight bringing titters from the unwary. For his head, clean-shaven, and just protruding out of a crimson cravat, was enveloped by a broad-purple-striped open-necked shirt with tassels dangling on either side. On the littlest digit of his left hand was a large gilt ring; and on the next finger, distal joint, a smaller one, apparently of solid gold, except for welded iron studs, to look like stars. As if this were not enough proof of wealth, he kept bare a right upper arm to display an armlet of gold and an ivory bangle, linked by a gleaming metal clasp.

33 Picking his teeth with a silver pin, "Friends," he announced, "it didn't feel right coming into the dining room just yet, but not wanting to hold you up any longer by my absence I sacrificed the good time I was having. You will let me finish my game, I hope." He was followed by a boy carrying a board of terebinth-wood with crystal pieces; and I noted a felicitous innovation: instead of the usual black and white chips were coins of silver and gold.

ille omnium textorum dicta inter lusum consumit,
gustantibus adhuc nobis repositorium allatum est cum
corbe, in quo gallina erat lignea patentibus in orbem
4 alis, quales esse solent quae incubant ova. Accessere
continuo duo servi et symphonia strepente scrutari
paleam coeperunt, erutaque subinde pavonina ova
5 divisere convivis. Convertit ad haec scaenam Trimalchio
vultum et, "Amici," ait, "pavonis ova gallinae iussi
supponi. Et mehercules timeo ne iam concepti sint;
6 temptemus tamen, si adhuc sorbilia sunt." Accipimus nos
cochlearia non minus selibras pendentia ovaque ex farina
7 figurata pertundimus. Ego quidem paene proieci
8 partem meam, nam videbatur mihi in pullum coisse. Deinde
ut audivi veterem convivam: "Hic nescio quid boni debet
esse," persecutus putamen manu pinguissimam ficedulam
inveni piperato vitello circumdatam.

34 Iam Trimalchio eadem omnia lusu intermisso
poposcerat, feceratque potestatem clara voce si quis
nostrum iterum vellet mulsum sumere, cum subito signum
symphonia datur et gustatoria pariter a choro cantante
2 rapiuntur. Ceterum inter tumultum cum forte paropsis
excidisset et puer iacentem sustulisset, animadvertit

H, L (= lmrtp)
33 3 textorum *obscurum sed bellum* dicta *om.* L
esse solent *desunt in* H incumbunt *Benedictinus*
8 mihi om. H circumdatam] piperatam *ex* piperato *ortum* L

Thus, with Trimalchio coming out with words of every stripe as the game progressed, and us still on the first course, the next dish was brought in. Upon it was a basket in which sat a wood-carved hen with wings spread out in the familiar incubating pose. Two slaves came up instantly, and upon a drum roll began to rummage in the straw beneath. Out came peahen's eggs, which were promptly divided among the guests. Trimalchio looked up at this tableau and said, "Friends, it was I who told them to put peahen's eggs under the hen; but I'm afraid they may have formed. Let's see if they are still soft." With teaspoons weighing at least half-a-pound we proceeded to tap on these eggs, made of a rich dough. I almost threw mine on the floor, as it looked as if it had hatched into a chick. But when I overheard a veteran guest say, "There should be something good here," I poked my finger into the outer layer, to find a wagtail figpecker dredged in a seasoned yolk.

34 Trimalchio now suspended his game and demanded to be served the same dishes, loudly offering a second glass of dessert wine to anyone wishing it. Suddenly, at a drum roll, the hors-d'oeuvre tray was snatched away by slaves singing in formation. In all the hubbub a dish got knocked over.

Trimalchio colaphisque obiurgari puerum ac proicere
3 rursus paropsidem iussit. Insectus est <supel>lecticarius
argentumque inter reliqua purgamenta scopis coepit
4 everrere. / Subinde intraverunt duo Aethiopes capillati H
cum pusillis utribus, quales solent esse <eis> qui harenam
in amphitheatro spargunt, vinumque dedere in manus: aquam
enim nemo porrexit.
5 / Laudatus propter elegantias dominus "Aequum," HL
inquit, "Mars amat. Itaque iussi suam cuique mensam
assignari. Obiter et putidissimi servi minorem nobis
aestum frequentia sua facient."
6 Statim allatae sunt amphorae vitreae diligenter
gypsatae, quarum in cervicibus pittacia erant affixa
cum hoc titulo: "Falernum Opimianum annorum centum."
7 Dum titulos perlegimus, complosit Trimalchio manus et
"eheu," inquit, "ergo diutius vivit / vinum quam H
homuncio. Quare tangomenas faciamus. / Vinum vita est. HL
Verum Opimianum praesto. Heri non tam bonum posui, et

H, L (= lmrtp)
34 2 obiugari H: obiurgari L 3 insecutusque L *add. Dousa* everrere *Goesius*: verrere 4 esse] habere *Braswell* *suppleo*: esse <eorum> qui *Mueller*: esse quis *vel* quibus 5 iussi *Burman*: iussit et H: ei L putidissimi *Heinze*: pudissimi H: pdissimi L sua frequentia L 7 eheu *Heinze*: heheu H: heu L vivit L vinum vita *Goesius*: vita vinum H

When Trimalchio noticed a boy moving to pick it up where it lay, he had him rebuked with a box on the ears and a command to throw it down again. A cleaner stepped forward and commenced sweeping up the silver together among the other rubbish. Immediately two long-haired Ethiopian slaves came in carrying small leather flasks, like those used for wetting the sand in the arena. From these they poured wine to rinse our hands. We never got water.

After compliments for the stylish touches, Trimalchio remarked, "Mars likes a fair fight, so everyone is given his own table. This will stop us from getting too hot from these smelly slaves as they go about their business."

Immediately some wine flagons were brought out. They had been carefully corked, and contained tags with the following information tied around their necks:

> FALERNIAN WINE OF THE OPIMIAN VINTAGE
> GUARANTEED ONE HUNDRED YEARS OLD

While we were reading this, Trimalchio clapped his hands and said with a groan, "See how much longer wine lives than us poor men! Drink down, then. Wine is life. It's genuine Opimian. Yesterday I had less good put out and the guests were much fancier."

8 multo honestiores cenabat." Potantibus ergo nobis et
accuratissime lautitias mirantibus larvam argenteam
attulit servus sic aptatam, ut articuli eius vertebraeque
9 luxatae in omnem partem flecterentur. Hanc cum super
mensam semel iterumque abiecisset et catenatio mobilis
aliquot figuras exprimeret, Trimalchio adiecit:
10 / "Eheu nos miseros quam totus homuncio nil est
Sic erimus cuncti, postquam nos auferet Orcus,
Ergo vivamus, dum licet esse bene."

35 Laudationem ferculum insecutum est plane non pro
expectatione magnum; novitas tamen omnium convertit
2 oculos. Rotundum enim repositorium duodecim habebat signa
in orbem disposita, super quae proprium convenientemque
3 materiae structor imposuerat cibum: super geminos
testiculos ac rienes, super cancrum coronam, super leonem
4 ficum Africanum, super virginem stericulum, super
libram stateram in cuius parte scriblita erat, in altera
placenta, / super scorpionem <scorpionem> [pisciculum] H
marinum, /super sagittarium oclopetam, super capricornum HL

H, L (= lmrtp)
34 8 nobis hic *Buecheler: ante* lautitias curatissime H
aptam L luxatae *Heinze*: laxatae H: locatae L
verterentur H 9 et] ut *Jahn* **35** est insecutum H; *cf.* 65.1
2 repositorium enim rotundum L materiae *susp. Jacobs*
super scorpionem <scorpionem> marinum *Sullivan et ego*

As we proceeded with our drinking in scrupulous awe at these fancy touches, a slave brought in a silver skeleton constructed so that its joints and bones could be twisted and turned in all directions. Trimalchio flopped it on the table-top a couple of times so its moving parts could assume various poses, and articulated the following:

> "Alas for us poor wretches, how all of man is nil!
> Thus everyone shall be when off we go to Hell.
> So let us live it up, now when we're feeding well!"

35 Following the applause was a dish that didn't meet our expectations for size, but its sheer novelty drew every gaze. It was a round platter with the twelve signs of the Zodiac etched upon it in a continuous circle. Upon each sign the chef had placed an appropriate or suitable piece of food. Thus upon Aries was a ram's head chickpea, upon Taurus a bit of beef stew, upon Gemini testicles and kidneys, upon Cancer a herbal wreath, upon Leo a fig from Africa, upon Virgo a barren sow's womb, upon Libra a scale with different pastries in each pan, upon Scorpio a sea-weever, upon Sagittarius an

locustam marinam, super aquarium anserem, super pisces
5 duos mullos. In medio autem caespes cum herbis excisis
6 circumferebat Aegyptius puer clibano argenteo panem ...
atque ipse etiam taeterrima voce de Laserpiciario mimo
7 canticum extorsit. Nos ut tristiores ad tam viles
accessimus cibos, "Suadeo," inquit Trimalchio, "cenemus;
36 hoc est ius cenae." Haec ut dixit, ad symphoniam
quattuor tripudiantes procurrerunt superioremque partem
2 repositorii abstulerunt. Quo facto videmus infra
[scilicet in altero ferculo] altilia et sumina leporemque
in medio pennis subornatum, ut Pegasus videretur.
3 Notavimus etiam circa angulos repositorii Marsyas
quattuor, ex quorum utriculis garum piperatum currebat
4 super pisces, qui quasi in euripo natabant. Damus omnes
plausum a familia inceptum et res electissimas ridentes
5 aggredimur. Non minus et Trimalchio eiusmodi methodio
6 laetus "Carpe," inquit. Processit statim scissor et ad
Symphoniam gesticulatus ita laceravit obsonium, ut

H, L (= lmrtp)
35 6 *lac. ind. Buecheler* extorquet L 7 ius] in H
36 2 *del. Pithoeus* 3 utriculis H *Pithoeus*: int culis L
qui quasi *Gaselee ex quique compendio ambiguo in* H: qui L
natabat H 4 coeptum L 6 ita gesticulatus L

oxpecker, upon Capricorn a lobster, upon Aquarius a goose, upon Pisces two mullet.

The space in the middle contained a piece of cut turf upon which sat a honeycomb. An Egyptian slave carried bread around in a silver bin ... as Trimalchio himself belted out a song from the musical *The Silphium Gatherer* in a quite execrable voice. As we rather gloomily addressed this very ordinary fare, Trimalchio said, "Come on, let's eat. Here's food for thought!"

36 At this point the orchestra clashed and four dancers leaped in and swept off the upper tray of the dish, to reveal beneath it capons and sow's udders arranged around a hare fitted with wings to look like Pegasus. We saw also, positioned at the four outer corners of the platter, four satyrs, from whose wineskins a peppered fish sauce trickled over fish that seemed to be swimming in a kind of channel. The household clapped and we all followed suit, laughing as we tucked into this gourmet fare. Trimalchio, equally thrilled by this *coup de théâtre*, then gave the order, "Carve'er!" Up stepped a carver and, in time to music, made such a mess of the birds that anyone

7 putares essedarium hydraule cantante pugnare. Ingerebat
nihilo minus Trimalchio lentissima voce: "Carpe, carpe."
Ego suspicatus ad aliquam urbanitatem totiens iteratam
vocem pertinere, non erubui eum qui supra me accumbebat
8 hoc ipsum interrogare. At ille, qui saepius eiusmodi
ludos spectaverat, "Vides illum," inquit "qui obsonium
carpit? Carpus vocatur. Ita quotiensque dicit 'Carpe,'
eodem verbo et vocat et imperat."

37 Non potui amplius quicquam gustare, sed conversus
ad eum, ut quam plura exciperem, longe accersere fabulas
coepi sciscitarique, quae esset mulier illa, quae huc
2 atque illuc discurreret. "Uxor," inquit Trimalchionis:
3 Fortunata appellatur, quae nummos medio metitur. Et modo
modo quid fuit? Ignoscet mihi genius tuus, noluisses
4 de manu illius panem accipere. Nunc, nec quid nec quare,
5 in caelum abiit et Trimalchionis topanta est. Ad summam,
6 mero meridie si dixit illi tenebras esse, credet.
/ Ipse nescit quid habeat, adeo saplutus est; sed haec H
lupatria providet ommia, et ubi non putes. Est sicca,
sobria, bonorum consiliorum – tantum aurum vides –, est

H, L (= lmrtp)
36 6 esse darium H *coniuncta a I.F. Gronovio*: darium L
7 Carpe *alterum om.* L ad *om.* H 8 inquit illum L
ita] itaque L, *haud male* **37** quam *om.* L arcessere L
praeter l sciscitari H illa mulier L 3 modo *alterum*
om. L eius L 6 credet] *deest* L *plerumque postea in Cena*

would have thought he was a charioteer fighting to the tune of a water organ – with Trimalchio pronouncing all the while in an insistent tone, "Carve'er, Carver!" I had an inkling that the frequent repetition bore on some joke or other and without hesitation quizzed my neighbour on this very point. A frequent witness of such scenes, he replied, "See the man who is carving the bird? Well, his name is Carver. So every time the master says "Carve'er!" in one word he is both summoning and commanding him!"

37 After eating my fill I turned to my neighbour to find out more – to seek all the detail on the woman who was bustling back and forth. "That's Trimalchio's wife," he replied. "Her name is Fortunata and she's worth a bushel or two. Not long ago she was nothing, didn't have a crumb to share with you, begging your pardon. And today, ours not to reason why, she's in heaven – Trimalchio's universe. In a nutshell, if she told him it gets dark at mid-day he'd believe her. He's got no idea how much he has – that's how rich he is – but this bitch, she keeps track of everything, even where you'd least expect it.

She's cool, calm and collected – see all the gold? – but, my, she's got a

---

Fortunata receives her introduction in confidence from a freedman neighbour of Encolpius at table, whose name is not supplied at this point. We would know him shortly as Hermeros, and at his time he has an important role to play: first crediting the opulence and independence of the household, then indicating another unnamed freedman at the end of the table who has made good (Diogenes), and finally taking the lead in a scolding of Ascyltus and Giton for affectatiousness and merriment at Trimalchio's rebus performance (*Sat.* 57). Trimalchio is still present, but Encolpius had picked the close-by Hermeros carefully, to be out of hearing range to others, for private, unmediated answers. Trimalchio, more in amusement than surprise, lets the row play out, until he eventually intervenes to end things, praising his colleague by name for showing his mettle. We note that the *scholastici* line up and differentiate into two groups: the supercilious Ascyltus and Giton, and the respectful Agamemnon and Encolpius.

tamen malae linguae, pica pulvinaris. Quem amat, amat;
8 quem non amat, non amat. Ipse Trimalchio fundos habet
quantum milvi volant, nummorum nummos. Argentum in
ostiarii illius cella plus iacet quam quisquam in
9 fortunis habet. Familia vero, babae, babae, non
mehercules puto decumam partem esse quae dominum suum
10 noverit. Ad summam, quemvis ex istis babaecalis in rutae
38 olium coniciet. Nec est quod putes illum quicquam emere.
Omnia domi nascuntur: lana, cedria, piper; lacte
2 gallinaceum si quaesieris, invenies. Ad summam, parum
illi bona lana nascebatur: arietes a Tarento emit et eos
3 culavit in gregem. Mel Atticum ut domi nasceretur, apes
ab Athenis iussit afferri; obiter et vernaculae quae sunt,
4 meliuculae a Graeculis fient. Ecce intra hos dies scripsit,
ut illi ex India semen boletorum mitteretur. Nam mulam
5 quidem nullam habet quae non ex onagro nata sit. Vides
tot culcitas: nulla non aut conchyliatum aut coccineum
6 tomentum habet. Tanta est animi beatitudo. Reliquos tamen
7 collibertos eius cave contemnas. Valde sucosi sunt. Vides
illum qui in imo imus recumbit: hodie sua octaginta

H

37 8 argenti *Giardina*, 38.15 *conferens Trimalchio supervacaneum Buecheler, del. Mueller: convenit tamen colliberto domini nomine crebro uti* quantum *Scheffer*: qua **38** cedria *Smith*: citrea *Jacobs*: credrae 2 ad summam *melius convenit ante lacte convenit Keibel* 5 culcitras 6 sucossi

wicked tongue on her: a couch magpie. She knows who she likes and who she doesn't like. As for Trimalchio, he's got estates that only a buzzard could cover, and piles of money. There's more silver lying around in the butler's lodge than your average fortune. As for slave holdings, my oh my! I shouldn't think ten per cent of them can recognize their master. In a nutshell, he'd knock any of these jokers here into a briar patch!

38 "And don't think he needs to buy anything. Everything's home grown – wool, cedar oil, pepper. If you asked for hen's milk you'd get it. Once when he didn't like the quality of his wool he imported rams from Tarentum to tup his ewes. And he wanted to produce genuine Attic honey on his estate so he ordered bees from Athens, ensuring at the same time that the native strain would be upgraded by the Greek stock.

"In fact only a couple of days ago he wrote asking for mushroom spores to be sent to him from India. And not one she-mule of his was not sired by a wild ass. See all these cushions? Not one doesn't have its stuffing dyed in purple or scarlet. That's how big he thinks. And don't underestimate his colleagues: they're really rolling in it. See the man lying at the end of the bottom couch? Today he's worth eight hundred thousand.

8 possidet. De nihilo crevit. Modo solebat collo ligna
portare. Sed quomodo dicunt - ego nihil scio sed audivi -
cum Incuboni pilleum rapuisset, [et] thesaurum invenit
9 Ego nemini invideo si quid deus dedit. Est tamen sub alapa
et non vult sibi male. Itaque proxime cenaculum hoc
10 titulo proscripsit: "C. Pompeius Diogenes ex kalendiis
11 Iuliis cenaculum locat: ipse enim domum emit." Quid ille
12 qui libertini loco iacet, quam bene se habuit. Non
impropero illi. Sestertium suum vidit decies, sed male
vacillavit. Non puto illum capillos liberos habere, nec
mehercules sua culpa; ipso enim homo non melior; sed
13 liberti scelerati, qui omnia ad se fecerunt. Scito autem,
sociorum olla male fervet, et ubi semel res inclinata
14 est, amici de medio. Et quam honestam negotiationem
15 exercuit, quod illum sic vides. Libitinarius fuit.
Solebat sic cenare quomodo rex: apros gausapatos, opera
pistoria, avis, ... cocos, pistores. Plus vini sub mensa

H

38 8 modo *hic Wehle: post* collo cum *vel* quom (Incuboni) *Buecheler*: quomodo H, *perperam iteratum del. Scheffer* 9 quid *Buecheler*: quod *Scheffer*: quo sub_alapa H: subalapo *Heinze; ad sensum cf. Cueva CP* 96, 68–76 10 cenaculum *Buecheler*: cum, *post quod lacunam susp. alii.* locat *patavinus:* loca 11 ille *patavinus*: illi libertino *Heinze* 12 ipso H^m: ipse 15 opera pistoria *del. Jacobs* avis *Scheffer*: vis, *post quod lacunam susp. Bucheler; locus nondum sanatus*

"He started with nothing. Not long ago he carried his wood around on his own neck. But you know what they say – I don't know for sure but I heard – he snatched the cap off a goblin's head and found treasure. I don't envy anyone their god-given luck. Still, he's under the hammer and putting on the best face. For instance he recently advertised his flat like this:

> C. POMPEIUS DIOGENES HAS A FLAT FOR RENT
> FROM THE FIRST OF JULY. HE'S BOUGHT A HOUSE.

As for the man in the freedman's place on the couch, he was riding high all right. I'm not blaming him, but he had a million and took a bad fall. I don't think he can call the hair on his head his own. By god it wasn't his fault – there's no better man around – but his freedman colleagues were crooks and made off with everything. It just shows you, a committee's pot boils badly, and when things start to go down your friends are out of there. And what a good job he had for seeing him on his way. He was an undertaker. He used to eat like a king – boars in the blanket, fancy baked goods, gourmet poultry … and he had his own cooks and bakers too. More wine flowed under this table

16 effundebatur, quam aliquis in cella habet. Phantasia,
non homo. Inclinatis quoque rebus suis, cum timeret ne
creditores illum conturbare existimarent, hoc titulo
auctionem proscripsit: "<C.> Iulius Proculus auctionem
faciet rerum supervacanearum."

39 Interpellavit tam dulces fabulas Trimalchio: nam
sublatus erat ferculum, hilaresque convivae vino
2 sermonibus publicatis operam coeperant dare. Is ergo
reclinatus in cubitum, "hoc vinum," inquit, "vos oportet
3 suave faciatis. Pisces natare oportet. Rogo, me putatis
illa cena esse contentum, quam in theca repositorii
videratis? 'Sic notus Ulixes?' Quid ergo est? Oportet
4 etiam inter cenandum philologiam nosse. Patrone meo ossa
bene quiescant, qui me hominem inter homines voluit esse.
Nam mihi nihil novi potest afferri, sicut ille ferculus
5 iam semel habuit praxim. Caelus hic, in quo duodecim dii
habitant, in totidem se figuras convertit, et modo fit
aries. Itaque quisque nascitur in illo signo, multa
pecora habet, multum lanae, caput praeterea durum,
frontem expudoratum, cornum acutum. Plurimi hoc signo
6 scholastici nascuntur et arietilli." Laudamus urbanitatem

H

38 15 aliquis *susp. Buecheler,* alius *suadens* 16 *supplevit* T. *vel* C. *Buecheler* auctionem *Scheffer*: caucionem interpellabit *vulgo correctum* 3 putabatis *Buecheler* *Verg. Aen.* 2.44 4 fericulusta mel *seiunctum a I.F. Gronovio*: ferculus iam semel *Heraeus diffidenter*

than most people have in their cellars. He wasn't a man, he was a dream. So when his fortunes slid and he didn't want his creditors to think he'd declare bankruptcy he advertised an auction like this:

> G. JULIUS PROCULUS IS HAVING AN AUCTION OF SURPLUS STOCK."

39 This course had by now been removed, and the guests, in high spirits, had begun to get interested in the wine and general conversation, when into such sweet reflections, reclining on an elbow, Trimalchio spoke: "I want you to do justice to the wine," he pronounced. "Fish have got to swim. Tell me, do you think I was content to serve for dinner only what you saw on the bottom layer of the dish? 'Thus know you Ulysses?' Well then? Dining is for acquiring knowledge too. It was my master – may he rest in peace – who wanted me to be a man among men. And you can't teach me a thing, as that dish has shown once and for all. The sky here, where the twelve gods live, turns into twelve figures, and it first becomes Aries. Anyone born under this sign has plenty of sheep and plenty of wool, and also a hard head, lots of cheek, and a sharp horn. Most students are born under this sign, also muttonheads." We applauded our astrologer's wit,

mathematici; itaque adiecit: "Deinde totus caelus
taurulus fit. Itaque tunc calcitrosi nascuntur et
7 bubulci et qui se ipsi pascunt. In geminis autem
nascuntur bigae at bovess et colei at qui utrosque
8 parietes linunt. In cancro ego natus sum. Ideo
multis pedibus sto, et in mari et in terra multa
possideo; nam cancer et hoc et illuc quadrat. Et
ideo iam dudum nihil supra illum posui, ne genesim
9 meam premerem. In leone cataphagae nascuntur et
10 imperiosi; in virgine mulieres et fugitivi et
11 quicumque aliud expendunt; in scorpione venenarii
et percussores; in sagittaro strabones, qui holera
12 spectant, lardum tollunt; in capricorno aerumnosi,
13 quibus prae mala sua cornua nascuntur; in aquario
copones et cucurbitae; in piscibus obsonatores et
rhetores. Sic orbis vertitur tamquam mola, et semper
aliquid mali facit, ut homines aut nascantur aut
14 pereant. Quod autem in medio caespitem videtis et
super caespitem favum, nihil sine ratione facio.
15 Terra mater est in medio quasi ovum corrotundata,
et omnia bona in se habet tamquam favus."

40 "Sophos!" universi clamamus et sublatis manibus

H

39 8 supra *ex compendio in* H: super *aliis visum non recte* 10 mulieres] mulierosi *I.F. Gronovius* expendunt *Burman:* expediunt 14 super] supra *scripsit Buecheler*

as he went on: "Next, the whole sky turns into Taurus, so then are born folks who kick up, ploughmen, and people who chew their own cud. In Gemini are born yoked pairs, and bulls, and big bollockses, and folks who whiten both walls. I was born under Cancer, so I stand on lots of feet and own plenty of land and sea, since a crab can cover both areas. Also I've never in a long while put anything on top of Cancer so as not to weigh my birth sign down. Under Leo are born greedy-gutses and bossy folks. Under Virgo are born ladies' men and runaways and people in shackles. Under Libra are born butchers and parfumiers and anyone who weighs stuff. Under Scorpio are born poisoners and muggers. Under Sagittarius are born the squinters, who look at vegetables but pick up bacon. Under Capricorn are born sad sacks, who grow horns from their troubles. Under Aquarius are born innkeepers and melon heads. Under Pisces are born caterers and rhetoricians. So round the world goes like a mill wheel, always bringing something bad with it as people get born or die. And as for the turf with the honeycomb on it that you see in the middle – everything is there for a reason – the earth is our mother in the middle, rounded off like an egg, and she has all the good things inside her, like a honeycomb."

40 "Bravo!" we shouted in unison, and raised our arms and swore

ad cameram iuramus Hipparchum Aratumque comparandos
illi [homines] non fuisse, donec advenerunt ministri ac
toralia praeposuerunt toris, in quibus retia erant
picta subsessores cum venalibus et totus venationis
2 apparatus. Necdum sciebamus <quo> mitteremus
suspiciones nostras, cum extra triclinium clamor
sublatus est ingens, et ecce canes Laconici etiam circa
3 mensam discurrere coeperunt. Secutum est hos repositorium,
in quo positus erat primae magnitudinis aper, et qidem
pilleatus, e cuius dentibus sportellae dependebant duae
palmulis textae, altera caryotis altera thebaicis
4 repleta. Circa autem [minores] porcelli ex coptoplacentis
facti, quasi uberibus imminerent, scrofam esse positam
5 significabant. Et hi quidem apophoreti fuerunt. Ceterum
ad scindendum aprum non ille Carpus accessit, qui altilia
laceraverat, sed barbatus ingens, fasciis cruralibus
alligatus et alicula subornatus polymita, strictoque
venatorio cultro latu apri vehementer percussit, ex
6 cuius plaga turdi evolaverunt. Parati aucupes cum
harundinibus fuerunt et eos circa triclinium volitantes
7 momento exceperunt. Inde cum suum cuique iussisset
referri Trimalchio, adiecit, "Etiam videte, quam porcus

H

40 comparatos *Rohde delevi*: homini *Heinze; adiunctionem videas* toralia praeposuerunt *Mentel*: tolaria proposuerunt toris *del. Fraenkel* 2 *add. Mentel* 4 delevi; *adiunctionem videas* imminentes *prop. Mentel* 7 etiam] iam *Jacobs*

Hipparchus and Aratus could never match him. At which point servants stepped up and laid cushions before the couches with representations on them of nets and beaters with spears and the whole baggage of hunting.

While we were still wondering what to make of this, a huge clamour arose outside the dining room and Laconian hounds were soon dashing about the very table. Behind them followed a platter upon which had been placed a wild boar, of monstrous size, wearing a cap, from whose tushes dangled little palmweave baskets filled with two different kinds of dates. About the boar were pastry piglets placed in the suckling position to signify a brood sow. These were party favours to take home.

Meanwhile there approached to carve the boar not the famous Carver who had made such a mess of the fowl but a bearded giant with legs bound in puttees and wearing a woven hunting jacket. He pulled out a hunting knife, gave the boar's flank a vigorous slash, and out of the aperture flew – thrushes! Reed-bearing fowlers were in position, and they soon caught the birds as they fluttered about the dining room. Trimalchio commanded that each guest be brought his own bird and then went on: "See that pig:

8 ille silvaticus lotam comederit glandem." Statim puer
ad sportellas accesserunt, quae pendebant e dentibus,
thebaicasque et caryotas ad numerum divisere cenantibus.

41 Interim ego, qui privatum habebam secessum, in multas
cogitationes diductus sum, quare aper pilleatus
2 intrasset. Postquam itaque omnes bacalusias consumpsi,
duravi interrogare illum interpretem meum quod me
3 torqueret. At ille: "Plane etiam hoc servus tuus
indicare potest; non enim aenigma est, sed res aperta.
4 Hic aper, cum heri summa cena eum vindicasset, a
convivis dimissus <est>; itaque hodie tamquam libertus
5 in convivium revertitur." Damnavi ego stuporem meum et
nihil amplius interrogavi, ne viderer numquam inter
honestos cenasse.

6 Dum haec loquimur, puer speciosus, vitibus hederisque
redimitus, modo Bromium, interdum Lyaeum Euhiumque
confessus, calathiscouvas circumtulit et poemata domini
7 sui acutissima voce traduxit. Ad quem sonum conversus
Trimalchio "Dionyse," inquit, "liber esto." Puer detraxit
8 pilleum apro capitique suo imposuit. Tum Trimalchio rursus
adiecit, "Non negabitis me, "inquit, "habere Liberum patrem."

H
40 7 lotam *Muncker*: totam **41** 2 bacalusias *non in prompto*
2 quod *Buecheler*: quid 3 hoc etiam *mavult Buecheler*
4 cena eum *Buecheler*: cenam *add. Heinze*
7–8 alii Liber ... liber *scribunt ioci causa*

what a fine dish of acorns our forest hog has eaten!" he said. In a trice slave boys approached the little baskets hanging from the boar's tushes and divided up the dates evenly among the guests.

41 All the while, I was taking a private moment to ponder, this way and that, why the boar had come in with a cap on. After testing every stupid reason I could think of, I steeled myself and put to my informant the problem that had been plaguing me. "Why," he replied, "even your slave knows the answer to that. No mystery in it. As plain as can be. This boar was going to be the main item at yesterday's dinner but the guests declined it. So today it comes back to the banquet with the cap of freedom." I cursed myself for my denseness and asked no more, in case I should seem never to have dined in respectable company.

As we were conversing, a good-looking boy wreathed in leaves of vine and ivy, recalling simultaneously Bacchus in his various aspects – Bromius, Lyaeus, Euhius – carried grapes around in a basket while reciting his master's poetry in a very shrill voice. Trimalchio turned to the sound and said, "Dionysus, be Liber!" The boy pulled the freedom cap off the boar and put it on himself. "No one can say," was Trimalchio's follow-up remark, "that I don't have my father Liber!" We applauded Trimalchio's pun and soundly kissed the boy as he passed before us.

A typical example of the ambience of boy-watching and appreciation, presumed and promoted.

laudavimus dictum [Trimalchionis] et circumeuntem puerum
sane perbasiamus.
9 Ab hoc ferculo Trimalchio ad lasanum surrexit.
Nos libertatem sine tyranno nacti coepimus invitare
10 <nos largius> convivarum sermones. Dama itaque primus
cum pataracina poposcisset, "Dies," inquit "nihil est.
Dum versas te, nox fit. Itaque nihil est melius quam de
11 cubiculo recta in triclinium ire. Et mundum frigus
habuimus. Vix me balneus calfecit. Tamen calda potio
12 vestiarius est. Staminatas duxi, et plane matus sum.
Vinus mihi in cerebrum abiit."
42 Excepit Seleucus fabulae partem et "Ego," inquit,
2 "non cotidie lavor; balniscus enim fullo est: aqua dentes
habet, et cor nostrum cotidie liquescit. Sed cum mulsi
pultarium obduxi, frigori laecasin dico. Nec sane lavari
3 potui; fui enim in funus. Homo bellus, tam bonus
Chrysanthus animam ebulliit. Modo modo me appellavit.
4 Videor mihi cum illo loqui. Heu, eheu. Utres inflati
ambulamus. Minoris quam muscae sumus. <Muscae> tamen
aliquam virtutem habent, nos non pluris sum quam bullae.

H
41 8 circumeuntem *Scheffer*: circumeuntes 9 *add. Courtney*
10 Dama *Heinze*: clamat pataracina *obscurum non desperandum*
42 2 balniscus *Scheffer*: baliscus cor] corpus *Jacobs*
laecasin *Burman*: laecasim 4 *om.* H, *add. Heinze*

This course finished, Trimalchio rose to go to the toilet, releasing us to discussion from the floor without his domineering presence. Dama was first. He called for a toast, then, "A day is nothing;" he said, "turn around and it's night. Might as well go straight from the dining room into the bedroom. And we've been having a real cold spell. Not even a bath gets me warm. But a hot drink is my overcoat. I've knocked back a few and I'm really pissed: wine gone straight to my head!"

42 Seleucus seconded the point: "I certainly don't bathe every day," he said. "Bathing tans your hide and water's got teeth in it. Every day we lose a bit of our insides. But give me a layer of grog and I'll tell the cold to go fuck itself! In fact I couldn't bathe today since I had to go to a funeral. It was Chrysanthus. That fine fellow has breathed up his last. Only the other day he called out to me and I can hear myself talking to him. Dear, oh dear, just walking bags of air we are! Less than flies we are! At least flies have

---

Too much of Trimalchio on the set raises design and production challenges for the author's staging of the *Cena*, and the host's presence during the freedmen's obviously planned linguistic contribution, as envisaged by the author, would simply not work. Petronius neatly solved both challenges by making Trimalchio disappear for a goodly spell on a bathroom visit, with means and reason clearly defined: *Trimalchio ad lasanum surrexit*, and *libertatem sine tyranno nacti (sumus)*. The intended benefit was immediate. In quick succession (they had to watch the time) there was simple **Dama**'s colourful, unelaborate advice to get pissed in cold weather; **Seleucus**, gloomy because of an attended funeral; quickly cut off by **Phileros** setting the record straight on the decedent, **Chrysanthus**: lived long and lucky, died rich, a lech to the last, not excluding boys and maybe the family dog; **Ganymedes** on crooked politicians paid off by bakers: town's going down like a calf's tail; **Echion**, the sports fan looking forward to a great show, with more coming up on the roster; finally the unspeaking **Diogenes,** remade a success. Agamemnon's silence throughout was to provoke Echion shortly (*Sat.* 46). A believer in education, he describes how he is raising his touchingly curated son, Primigenius. We should note that the guest scholastici were as silent during the freedman conversation, in the absence of Trimalchio, as they were in his presence – not "paying their way." Certainly Ascyltus and Giton had no interest, and not even Encolpius and Agamemnon were drawn in. Trimalchio's return broke the freedman flow for a while, until the outburst from **Hermeros** in *Sat.* 58 against Ascyltus, and Giton, concisely told he had a "muttonhead for a master" (Ascyltus). **Mammea**, **Norbanus, Phileros** the lawyer, Niceros, on it goes: absent freedmen colleagues mostly, some who had done well enough even to stand for office. We note, too, halfway and satiety sloshing in; *Sat.* 49: *nondum efflaverat omnia …* ; then *Sat.* 65, 67, 68, 69, 70, 72: growing resentment and distaste, a basis for Petronius to work out his last great authorial challenge: how to shut this thing down. But a few details remain: early life, courtship, and alliance of Trimalchio and Fortunata. In the Introduction the freedman dialogue is broached within the broad issue of Petronius translation.

5 Et quid si abstinax non fuisset! Quinque dies aquam in os
suum non coniecit, non micam panis. Tamen abiit ad plures.
Medici illum perdiderunt, immo magis malus fatus; medicus
6 enim nihil aliud est quam animi consolatio. Tamen bene
elatus est, vitali lecto, stragulis bonis. Planctus est
optime - manu misit aliquot - etiam si maligne illum
7 ploravit uxor. Quid si non illam optime accepisset! Sed
mulier quae mulier milvinum genus. Neminem nihil boni
facere oportet; aeque est enim ac si in puteum conicias.
Sed antiquus amor carcer est."

43 Molestus fuit, Philerosque proclamavit: "Vivorum
meminerimus. Ille habet, quod sibi debebatur: honeste
vixit, honeste obiit. Quid habet quod queratur? Ab asse
crevit et paratus fuit quadrantem de stercore mordicus
tollere. Itaque crevit quicquid tetigit tamquam favus.
2 Puto mehercules illum reliquisse solida centum, et omnia
3 in nummis habuit. De re tamen ego verum dicam, [qui]
linguam caninam comedi<t>: durae buccae fuit, linguosus,
4 discordia, non homo. Frater eius fortis fuit, amicus amico,

---

H

42 5 ad *Scheffer*: at 6 stragulis *patavina*: stagulis
planctus *patavina*; plautus manu misit aliquot *patavina*
7 carcer *ex* cancer *correctum in* H **43** Philerosque *Buecheler:*
phileros qui ab asse crevit *Scheffer*: abbas secrevit
tetigit *Delz; cf. 76.8*: crevit 3 *correxit Jacobs*

got some value, but we're nothing but bubbles of air. And you wouldn't believe how he fasted. For five whole days not a splash of water, not a crumb of bread, and he still joined the majority. The doctors killed him, or bad luck, if you like. A doctor's only for peace of mind. Still, he got a fine funeral with all the trimmings – bed, clothing. And the weeping and wailing was as good as can be – he'd freed some slaves – even if his wife was a bit stingy with her tears. And how well he treated her. There's a woman for you. Race of vultures. Never do one a favour – might as well throw it down a well. And an old flame's nothing but a jailhouse."

43 Seleucus had become a bore. "Let's remember people's lives," proclaimed Phileros. "He got what he was owed: lived straight, died straight. He's got nothing to complain about. He started with nothing and was quite ready to pick a penny from a dunghill with his teeth. So everything he got his hands on grew like a honeycomb. Migod, I think he left a hundred thousand clear, and all in cash. But let's be truthful about it if a little cynical: he talked tough and had a big mouth: a walking argument. Now his brother:

manu plena, uncta mensa. Et inter initia malam parram
pilavit, sed recorrexit costas illius prima vindemia:
vendidit enim vinum, quantum ipse voluit. Et quod illius
mentum sustulit, hereditatem accepit, ex qua plus
5 involavit quam illi relictum est. Et ille stips, dum
fratri suo irascitur, nescio cui terrae filio
patrimonium elegavit. Longe fugit, quisquis suos fugit.
6 Habuit autem oricularios servos, qui illum pessum
dederunt. / Numquam autem recte faciet, qui cito credit, HL
/ utique homo negotians. Tamen verum quod <suum> H
7 frunitus est, quam diu vixit. <Est> cui datum [est], non
cui destinatum. Plane fortunae filius, in manu illius
plumbum aurum fiebat. Facile est autem, ubi omnia
quadrata currunt. Et quot putas illum annos secum tulisse?
Septuaginta et supra. Sed corneolus fuit, aetatem bene
8 ferebat, niger tamquam corvus. Noveram hominem olim
oliorum, et adhuc salax erat. Non mehercules illum puto
in domo canem reliquisse. Immo etiam pullarius erat,
omnis minervae homo. Nec improbo; hoc solum enim secum tulit."

H, L (= lmrtp)
43 4 plena et uncta *ordinem in* H *invertebat Heinze post Reinesium* quantum] quanti *post Scheffer Buecheler* 5 fugit *patavina*: fuit oricularios *[de aure] Reinesius*: oracularios 6–7 *bis restitui semelque delevi; cf.* 75.3 sic peculium tuum fruniscaris 8 pullarius] puellarius H, *quod Burman vel mutatum esse in textu statuit*

brave, friend to a friend, generous, hospitable. Starting out he drew a bad hand, but first harvest caulked his ribs – he sold wine, all he could get. But the inheritance he got really kept his chin above water, and he stole more than his share. Then the fool picked a fight with his brother and made out a will to some son of a sea-cook. Run from your family and you run a long way. He took bad advice from his slaves and they ruined him. Trusting someone quickly means you'll never do the right thing, at least in business. Still, he enjoyed himself all his life, no question. It's what you get that matters, not what you're promised. He was fortune's friend: put lead into his hand and it'd turn into gold. But it's easy when all the horses come in for you. What age d'you think he made it to? – Seventy-plus. Looked good for his age: hard as horn, hair black as a crow; knew him from way back – horny to the last. God, I don't think he let the family dog alone. And little boys, too: fond of them; jack-of-all-trades. Not blaming, mind: the one thing he hung on to."

From the other side of the intellectual spectrum, we get from Phileros here a loose defence of the deceased Chrysanthus: "fond of little boys he was." Not openly critical, but containing the slightest of hesitations, a subtle self-consciousness in the *non improbo* none the less.

44 Haec Phileros dixit, illa Ganymedes: "narratis quod
nec ad caelum nec ad terram pertinet, cum interim nemo
2 curat, quid annona mordet. Non mehercules hodie buccam
3 panis invenire potui. Et quomodo siccitas perseverat.
Iam annum esuritio fuit. Aediles male eveniat, qui cum
pistoribus colludunt: 'Serva me, servabo te.' Itaque
populus minutus laborat; nam isti maiores maxillae semper
4 Saturnalia agunt. O si haberemus leones, quos ego hic
5 inveni cum primum ex Asia veni. Illud eerat vivere.
Si simila Siciliae inferior erat, et larvas sic istos
6 percolopabant, ut illis Iuppiter iratus esset. [Sed]
Memini Safinium: tunc habitabat ad arcum veterem, me
7 puero, piper, non homo. Is quacumque ibat, terram
adiurebat. Sed rectus, sed certus, amicus amico, cum quo
8 audacter posses in tenebris micare. In curia autem quomodo
singulos [vel] pilabat [tractabat], nec schemas loquebatur
9 sed derectum. Cum ageret porro in foro, sic illius vox
crescebat tamquam tuba. Nec sudavit umquam nec expuit,
10 puto eum nescio quid assi a dis habuisse. Et quam benignus

---

H

44 3 esuritio *Buecheler*: esurio 5 si simila Siciliae inferior erat *Simon*: similia sicilia interiores et H, *prope desperanda, sed retinet Whittick*: si milia si cilia *Heraeus* istas *Scheffer* 6 *del. Scheffer* 8 *del. Scheffer* derectum *Reiske*: dilectum 9 eum *Mentel*: enim assi a diis *Burman*: asi a dis

44 That came from Phileros, and it was now Ganymedes' turn: "That's all neither here nor there," he said, "and meanwhile nobody cares about the price of grain this year. My god, today I couldn't find a mouthful of bread. And the drought hangs on! For a year we've been going hungry. Curse those politicians: they're in bed with the bakers: it's look after me and I'll look after you. So the little guy suffers while the big shots take a holiday every day. If only we had those tigers today that I found here when I first arrived from Asia! That was the life. If the flour from Sicily was below standard they boxed those spooks' ears so hard like Jupiter was angry at them. Do you remember Safinius? He lived by the old archway when I was a boy. More of a chili pepper than a man. The ground he walked on almost caught fire. But he was straight and true, friend to a friend. You could easily play 'flash' with him in the dark. But in court he'd take on anybody and no fancy talk either: straight shooter. When he pleaded a case his voice would swell like a trumpet, and no sweating or hawking: he had a bit of coolness in him, god-given.

Two intriguing references to children's games, one at *Sat.* 44.7, much like "rock, paper, scissors" in North America, which in South Africa was known as "flashing" (Latin *micare*!); another at *Sat.* 64.12, *bucca, bucca,* generally taken to be the analogy or origin of a game we called *buk-buk,* as chanted in Afrikaans (*buk-buk, staan styf: hoeveel vingers op jou lyf*: Bucky, bucky, stand steady, how many fingers on your body?), are quite astounding, not only for the fact that boys (girls?) have been playing them all this time, but because they are known to us by a word of the same meaning in the first, and by a word of much the same sound in the second, and possibly also the same meaning. A complication arises with the closeness of pronunciation between *buk,* meaning bend (imperative) and *bok,* meaning a ram or buck. The correct text was debated back in the day. Despite the tempting connection in other Indo-European languages (viz. German *bucken,* bend over), the Latin word remains an unclaimed orphan; all *OLD* can muster is "a catchword of uncertain meaning used in a game," with Petronius given as the only source; and we have been led away by the connection with "cheek" (*bucca*). Afrikaans encourages us to search anew for a relation: Petronius ends the chant in the same number-guessing riddle: *Quot sunt hic?* And *bucca,* Old Norse for a goat, and *buc,* Old English for a male deer, are reflected in the variant *bok, bok* in the Afrikaans, i.e., goat, goat. *Bucca* has lurked in total obscurity in Latin, but for a children's game. The object of the game, banned periodically at school for roughness, was to form teams to leapfrog onto opponents' bent backs, the receiving side supported by a post for staying upright (and adding collision to the dangers). The "fingers" are players piling on; and a good game ended in a free-for-all double collapse. Ullman 1943, p. 38, tried comparative linguistics, but admitted to getting no further than *OLD*. It took T.J. Haarhoff, a South African classicist, to explain it (1944, p. 118), though the linguistics are not settled. See at *Sat.* 64 for the context.

resalutare, nomina omnium reddere, tamquam unus de nobis
11 Itaque illo tempore annona pro luto erat. Asse panem quem
emisses, non potuisses cum altero devorare. Nunc oculum
12 bublum vidi maiorem. Heu, heu, quotidie peius. Haec
13 colonia retroversus crescit tamquam coda vituli. Sed
quare non? Habemus aedilem trium cauniarum, qui sibi
mavult assem quam vitam nostram. Itaque domi gaudet,
plus in die nummorum accipit, quam alter patrimonium
14 habet. Iam scio unde acceperit denarios mille aureos.
Sed si nos coleos haberemus, non tantum sibi placeret.
15 Nunc populus est domi leones, foras vulpes. Quod ad me
attinet, iam pannos meos comedi, et si perseverat haec
16 annona, casulas meas vendam. Quid enim futurum est, si
nec dii nec homines huius coloniae miserentur? Ita meos
fruniscar, ut ego puto omnia illa a diibus fieri.
17 / Nemo enim caelum caelum putat, nemo ieunium servat, HL
nemo Iovem pili facit, sed omnes opertis oculis bona
18 sua computant. / Antea stolatae ibant nudis pedibus in H
clivum, passis capillis, mentibus puris, et Iovem aquam
exorabant. Itaque statim urceatim plovebat: aut tunc aut

H, L (= lmrtp)

44 13 sed quare non? *sic interpunxit Burman*: sed quare? Non *maluit Scheffer* non] *ante* trium *proposuit Buecheler*: nos *Mentel* habet *patavina*: haberet 16 huius *Scheffer*: eius diibus *Buecheler*: aedilibus fieri *Mentel*: fleri 17 pili H: pluris L

But how kindly he greeted people, calling all by their own name, just like one of us.

The result was that wheat was cheap as dirt in those days. The loaf you bought for a penny would feed at least two people. Now I've seen bigger buns. Dear, oh dear, things get worse every day. This town's going down like a calf's tail, and no wonder: we have a city manager who's worth about three figs, who puts profits for himself in front of our own lives.

"So he happily sits at home taking in more in a day than a decent inheritance. I personally know where he got a thousand gold pieces. If we had any balls he wouldn't be half so fond of himself, but today people are tigers in private and jackals in public. In my own case I've sold the rags off my back for food, and if the prices stay up I'll be selling my house. What's to become of us when neither gods nor men take pity on this town? So help me if I don't think the gods are behind it all.

"There's no place in people's thoughts for heaven, nobody fasts, and nobody gives a damn for Jupiter. When people close their eyes it's to count their money. Before, the women would have made their journey up the hill veiled and barefooted, hair loose, hearts pure, and pray to Jupiter for rain. And in no time the rain came down in buckets,

numquam. Et omnes redibant udi tamquam mures. Itaque dii
pedes lanatos habent, quia nos religiosi non sumus.
Agri iacent – ."

45 "Oro te," inquit Echion centonarius, "melius loquere.
2 'Modo sic, modo sic,' inquit rusticus: varium porcum
perdiderat. / Quod hodie non est, cras erit: sic vita HL
3 truditur. / Non mehercules patria melior dici potest, si H
homines haberet. Sed laborat hoc tempore, nec haec sola.
4 Non debemus delicati esse, ubique medius caelus est. Tu
5 si aliubi fueris, dices hic porcos coctos ambulare. Et
ecce habituri sumus munus excellente in triduo die festa;
familia non lanisticia, sed plurimi liberti. Et Titus
noster magnum animum habet et est caldicerebrius: aut hoc
aut illud, erit quid utique. Nam illi domesticus sum, non
6 est mixcix. Ferrum optimum daturus est, sine fuga,
carnarium in medio, ut amphitheatur videat. Et habet
unde: relictum est illi sestertium trecenties, decessit
illius pater. Male! Ut quadringenta impendat, non sentiat
7 patrimonium illius, et sempiterno nominabitur. Iam nannos
aliquot habet et mulierem essedariam et dispensatorem

H, L (= lmrtp)
44 18 redibant *Jacobs et Wehle*: ridebant udi *Triller*: ut dii
45 2 truditur: tiditur 3 sola *Reiske*: sua 4 aliubi *Scheffer*: alicubi in triduo *Heinze*: inter duo 5 quid *Muncker*: quod 6 male! *sic scripsit Mueller* 7 nannos *Buecheler post* nanulos *vel* nanios *vel* naniolos *Scheffer et Heinze*: Manios

like never before. And they'd all go home wet as sewer rats. So since we have no religion the gods keep their slippers on. The fields lie idle ..."

45 "Please, please," interjected Echion the rag merchant, "no more gloomy talk. 'First this way then that,' said the farmer giving chase to his spotted pig. If not today, then tomorrow: that's life for you. God, you couldn't name a better country if it had real men in it. But right now we're in trouble, and we're not the only ones. We should stop complaining. The sky's still in the same place. If you came from someplace else you'd say the pigs here walked around ready-cooked. Look, we've got a holiday coming up in three days, with a terrific show – not just exhibition gladiators but lots of freedmen. Our friend Titus is generous and impulsive. Whatever he puts on you can be sure it'll be something good. I know him well: does nothing by halves. Top-quality steel is what we'll have, with no running away. Mayhem out in the open where everybody can see it. He can afford it too. His father died (sorry about that) and left him thirty million. He could spend four hundred thousand without feeling it, and get our undying gratitude too. He's got some dwarves and a female charioteer, and also the steward of Glyco, caught giving Glyco's wife a good time. You'll see the spectators squaring off, cuckolds versus lover-boys.

Glyconis, qui deprehensus est, cum dominam suam
delectaretur. Videbis populi rixam inter zelotypos
8 et amasiunculos. Glyco autem, sestertiarius homo
dispensatorem ad bestias dedit. Hoc est se ipsum
traducere. Quid servus peccavit, qui coactus est facere?
Magis illa matella digna fuit quam taurus iactaret. Sed
9 qui asinum non potest, stratum caedit. Quid autem Glyco
putabat Hermogenis filicem umquam bonum exitum facturam?
Ille milvo volanti poterat unques resecare; colubra
restem non parit. Glyco, Glyco dedit suas; itaque
quamdiu vixerit, habebit stigmam, nec illam nisi Orcus
10 delebit. Sed sibi quisque peccat. Sed subolfacio quia
nobis epulum daturus est Mammea, binos denarios mihi et
meis. Quod si fecerit, eripiet Norbano totum favorem.
11 Scias oportet plenis velis hunc vinciturum. Et revera,
quid ille nobis boni fecit? Dedit gladiatores sestertiarios
tam decrepitos, quos si si sufflasses cecidissent; iam
meliores bestiarios vidi. Occidit de lucerna equites,
putares eos gallos gallinaceos; alter burdubasta, alter
loripes, tertiarius mortuus pro mortuo, qui habebat
12 nerva praecisa. Unus alicuius flaturae fuit, Thrax, qui
et ipse ad dictata pugnavit. Ad summam, omnes postea
secti sunt; adeo de magna turba 'Adhibite' acceperant,

H
45 10 eripiet *Scheffer*: eripiat *Buecheler*: erripiat
11 tam *scribo; cf.* 87.3, 110.7: iam decrepitos H
habebat *Buecheler* 12 adhibite *Buecheler*: adhebete

"As for Glyco, well, he's got no class. By throwing his steward to the animals he's just showing himself up. It's no crime of the servants. They do what they're told. It's that piss-pot of a woman who should have felt the horns instead. But if you can't beat the ass you beat the saddle. How did Glyco think a sprout from Hermogenes would turn into anything good? Hermogenes could've clipped the claws off a buzzard in full flight, and a snake doesn't give birth to a piece of cord. Well, Glyco certainly paid the price, and as long as he lives he'll carrying the mark which only death can erase. Still, everyone is entitled to their mistakes.

"Now I've got a whiff of the feast Mammea is set to be throwing for us. Two denarii all round. If he pulls it off he'll steal all Norbanus' votes. Norbanus of course should be winning in a breeze, but truth to tell what has he done for us that was any good? He put on some cheap gladiators, so clapped out that they'd have fallen over if you blew on them. I've seen animal fighters that were better. As for the mounted gladiators he killed off – they stepped right off a lamp stand, and you'd think they were a bunch of strutting roosters: one as thin as a mule crop, one with foot rot, and one hamstrung replacement from the knackers' yard. There was a 'Thracian' with a bit of puff, but he also fought by the numbers. The result was that at the end they got a good whipping, with a big crowd yelling 'Lay it on!' to accompany the total rout. 'But still,' Norbanus says, 'I gave you a show.' Well done for that, I say. But add it up: I'm giving you more than I'm getting. One hand washes the other.

13 plane fugae merae. 'Munus tamen,' inquit, 'tibi dedi.'
Et ego tibi plodo. Computa, et tibi plus do quam accepi.
46 Manus manum lavat. Videris mihi, Agamemnon, dicere:
'Quid iste argutat molestus?' Quia tu, qui potes loquere,
non loquis. Non es nostrae fasciae, et ideo pauperorum
verba derides. Scimus te prae litterss fatuum esse.
2 Quid ergo est? Aliqua die te persuadeam, ut ad villam
venias et videas casulas nostras? Inveniemus quod
manducemus, pullum, ova: belle erit, etiam si omnia
hoc anno tempestas disparpallavit: inveniemus ergo unde
3 saturi fiamus. Et iam tibi discipulus crescit cicaro meus.
Iam quattuor partis dicit; si vixerit, habebis ad latus
servulum. Nam quicquid illi vacat, caput de tabula non
tollit. Ingeniosus est et bono filo, etiam si in aves
4 morbosus est. Ego illi iam tres cardeles occidi, et dixi
quia mustella comedit. Invenit tamen alias nenias, et
5 libentissime pingit. Ceterum iam Graeculis calcem
impingit et Latinas coepit non male appetere, etiam
si magister eius sibi placens sit nec uno loco consistit,

H

46 loquere non loquis *Burman*: loqui non loquere *Scheffer*: loquere non loqui 2 disparpallavit *Cholodniak, ex* dispar pallavit *Anton*: depravavit *vel* dispar depravavit *Mueller*: despoliavit *Rose*: dispare pallavit 3 partis *Scheffer*: parti aves *Triller et Reiske*: naves 5 sit] fit *Mueller, praeeuntibus doctis multis; alii tamen coniunctivum; Petersmann* 220 *videas*

46 "Agamemnon, I can see you saying, 'What is that old bore banging on about?' It's because you know how to speak and keep your mouth shut. You're not cut from our cloth, so you laugh at a poor man's words. We know you're crazy about literature. What of it, then? Some day can I get you to come to our place to visit the house? We'll have enough to eat – chicken, eggs. It'll be nice even though this year a storm tore through everything. But we'll have enough to fill our bellies.

"And already my little lad is growing up to be a worthy pupil for you, already says his four times table. If he survives you'll have a faithful follower at your side. Even in his free time his head doesn't leave the slate.

"He's bright and there's good stuff in him, even if he's crazy about birds. I just killed his three finches – told him the ferret ate them. But he found other hobbies, and he loves to paint. Also, he's now got his Greek behind him and is taking well to his Latin, even if his teacher's too fond of himself and can't sit still for long – comes and goes.

sed venit, <it. Scit qui> dem litteras, sed non vult
6 laborare. Est et alter non quidem doctus, sed curiosus,
qui plus docet quam scit. Itaque feriatis diebus solet
7 domum venire, et quicquid dederis, contentus est. Emi ergo
nunc puero aliquot libra rubricata, quia volum illum ad
domusionem aliquid de iure gustare. Habet haec res panem.
Nam litteris satis inquinatus est. Quod si resilierit,
destinavi illum artificium doceri, aut tonstrinum aut
praeconem aut certe causidicum, quod illi auferre non
8 possit nisi Orcus. Ideo illi cotidie clamo: 'Primigeni,
crede mihi, quicquid discis, tibi discis. Vides Phileronem
causidicum: si non didicisset, hodie famem a labris non
abigeret. Modo modo collo suo circumferebat onera venalia,
nunc etiam adversus Norbanum se extendit. Litterae
thesaurum est, et artificium numquam moritur.'"

47 Eiusmodi fabulae vibrabant, cum Trimalchio intravit
et detersa fronte unguento manus lavit spatioque minimo
2 interposito, "Ignoscite mihi," inquit, "amici, multis iam
diebus venter mihi non respondit. Nec medici se inveniunt.
Profuit mihi tamen malicorium et taeda ex aceto. Spero

H
46 5 sed ... litteras *sic recupero; alii* sed venit <vult> dem litteras 7 artificium *Scheffer*: artificii doceri *malo, passivum cum acc.rei, v. L.& S. p.* 605: docere tonstrinum *Scheffer*: constreinum

Knows his books but doesn't want to work. There's another teacher, not so learned but hard working, teaches more than he knows. He even comes to our house on holidays and is content with whatever I pay him. And so I bought my son some legal books, since I want him to get a taste of the law for home needs. There's bread in it. Besides, he's been dipped in literature quite enough. If he pulls through, my plan is to teach him a trade, hairdressing or auctioneering, or of course lawyering. No one can take that away from him until he dies.

"So every day I cry, 'See now, Primigenius, everything you learn you learn for yourself. Look at Phileros the lawyer: if he wouldn't have studied, today he couldn't keep back starvation. Just the other day he was carrying stuff for sale on his own neck and now he's measuring himself against Norbanus. Education is a treasure, and a trade's for life.'"

47 Stories like these were flying about when Trimalchio returned. He wiped his brow, cleaned his hands with an aromatic crème, and after the briefest pause, "Forgive me, friends," he announced, "for many days now my gut has not been cooperating. The doctors are stumped. I've been getting some relief from an infusion of pomegranate rind and vinegar resin.

tamen, iam veterem pudorem sibi imponit. Alioquin circa
4 stomachum mihi sonat, putes taurum. Itaque si quis
vestrum volue sua re causa facere, non est quod illum
pudeatur. Nemo nostrum solide natus est. Ego nullum puto
tam magnum tormentum esse quam continere. Hoc solum
5 vetare ne Iovis potest. Rides, Fortunata, quae soles me
nocte desomnem facere? Nec tamen in triclinio ullum vetui
facere quod se iuvet, et medici vetant continere. Vel si
quid plus venit, omnia foras parata sunt: aqua, lasani et
6 cetera minutalia. Credite mihi, anathymiasis in cerebrum
it et in toto corpore fluctum facit. Multos scio sic
7 periise, dum nolunt sibi verum dicere." Gratias agimus
liberalitati indulgentiae eius, et subinde castigamus
8 crebris potiunculis risum. Nec adhuc sciebamus nos in
medio [lautitiarum], quod aiunt, clivo laborare. Nam
commundatis ad symphoniam mensis tres albi sues in
triclinium adducti sunt capistris et tintinnabulis culti,
quorum unum bimum nomenculator esse dicebat, alterum trimum,
9 tertium vero iam sexennem. Ego putabam petauristarios
intrasse et porcos, sicut in circulis mos est, portenta

H

47 3 veterem *Heinze*: ventrem imponit] imponet *probat Buecheler* 4 vetare *del. Kaibel non inepte* lasani *Buecheler:* lasanum *Scheffer*: lassant 6 anathy*miasis Gronovius*: anathimia is 7 libera liberalitati 8 *del. Fraenkel* quod *Heinze*: quo clivo *Heinze*: divo commundatis *Heinze*: cum mundatis sexennem *Wehle*: senem

I hope it rights itself soon. Meanwhile my stomach is rumbling like a bull. So if any one of you wants to do his business don't be shy. None of us was born solid and there's no greater torture, I say, than holding yourself in. This is the one thing that not even Jupiter can deny us. What are you laughing at, Fortunata? It's you who keeps me awake at night.

"All the same, I've never forbidden anybody in the dining room from seeking relief, and the doctors say you shouldn't hold it in. If there's more on the way, everything's ready outside – water, chamber pots, and all the other paraphernalia. Believe you me, gas travels to the brain and floods your whole body. I know many a person who has died from not facing up to the truth."

We thanked our host for his generous consideration and moved quickly to stifle our mirth with sipping aplenty. We did not know it then, but we were still only on mid-slope, you might say. When the tables were cleared, to the clash of music, into the dining room were led three white pigs dressed up in bridles and bells. The announcer proclaimed one to be called twosie, the second threesie, and the third sixie. I imagined that acrobats were coming and that the pigs would be performing tricks, as in your typical sideshows.

10 aliqua facturos; sed Trimalchio expectatione discussa
"Quem," inquit, "ex eis vultis in cenam statim fieri?
Gallum enim gallinaceum, penthiacum, et eiusmodi nenias
rustici faciunt: mei coci etiam vitulos aeno coctos solent
11 facere." Continuoque cocum vocari iussit, et non expectata
electione nostra, maximum natu iussit occidi, et clara voce:
12 "Ex quota decuria es?" Cum ille se ex quadragesima
respondisset, "Empticius an," inquit, "domi natus?" "Neutrum,"
inquit cocus, "sed testamento Pansae tibi relictus sum." "Vide
13 ergo," ait, "ut diligenter ponas; si non, te iubebo in decurionem
viatorum conici." Et cocum quidem <domini> potentiae admonitum
48 in culinam obsonium duxit. Trimalchio autem miti ad nos vultu
respexit et, "Vinum," inquit, "si non placet, mutabo; vos illud
2 oportet bonum faciatis. Deorum beneficio non emo, sed nunc
quicquid ad salivam facit, in suburbano nascitur meo, quod
ego adhuc non novi. Dicitur confine esse Tarraciniensibus et
3 Tarentinis. Nunc coniungere agellis Siciliam volo, ut cum
4 Africam libuerit ire, per meos fines navigem. Sed narra tu
mihi, Agamemnon, quam controversiam hodie declamasti?

H
47 10 aeno coctos *Mentel*: oenococtos *Orelli probabiliter*: eno cocto 11 iussit *alterum susp. Buecheler*: *cur non prius* 12 natus *Buecheler*: natus es, *sed es expunctum* 13 cocum quidem *Buecheler*: quidem cocum potentiae *Scheffer*: <domini> potentiae *faveo*: potentia H **48** 2 meo *Goesius*: eo

But Trimalchio up-ended the speculation. "Which of these pigs," he asked, "do you want turned into dinner right now? Fowl and hash and suchlike are clodhopper's fare. My cooks are used to doing veal boiled whole in the pot." Immediately he gave the order for a cook to be summoned and, not waiting for our selection, commanded the oldest pig to be butchered. "What detachment?" he asked the cook. "Fortieth," was the reply. "Purchased or house born?" asked Trimalchio. "Neither," said the cook. "I was left to you in Pansa's will." "Be sure you prepare the pig carefully or I'll have you tossed into the fetchers' detachment." Whereupon the dish led the cook, suitably admonished of his master's authority, off to the kitchen.

48 Whereupon, Trimalchio turned to us with a kindly expression. "If you don't like the wine," he said, "I'll change it. But give it all the attention it deserves. By the grace of god I never buy my wine. Everything you will taste today comes from an estate of mine which I haven't seen yet. I am told it's somewhere between Tarracina and Tarentum, touching both borders. My plan now is to have Sicily addded on, so that when I feel like a trip to Africa I never leave my own property. But, Agamemnon, why don't you

Ego etiam si causas non ago, in domusionem tamen litteras
didici. Et ne me putes studia fastiditum, II bybliothecas
habeo, unam Graecam, alteram Latinam. Dic ergo, si me amas,
5 peristasim declamationis tuae." Cum dixisset Agamemnon,
"Pauper et dives inimici erant," ait Trimalchio "quid est
pauper?" "Urbane," inquit Agamemnon, et nescioquam
6 controversiam exposuit. Statim Trimalchio "Hoc," inquit,
"si factum est, controversia non est; si factum non est,
7 nihil est." Haec aliaque cum effusissimis prosequeremur
laudationibus, "Rogo," inquit "Agamemnon mihi carissime,
numquid duodecim aerumnas Herculis tenes, aut de Ulixe fabuam
quemadmodum illi Cyclops pollicem poricino extorsit? Solebam
8 haec ego puer apud Homerum legere. Nam sibyllam quidem Cumis
ego oculis meis vidi in ampulla pendere, et cum illi pueri
dicerent, 'Sibylla, ti theleis?' respondebat illa: 'Apothanein
thelo.'"

49 Nondum efflaverat omnia, cum repositorium cum sue ingenti
2 mensam occupavit. Mirari nos celeritatem coepimus et iurare, ne
3 gallum quidem gallinaceum tam cito percoqui potuisse, tanto
quidem magis, quod longe maior nobis porcus videbatur esse
quam paulo ante aper fuerat. Deinde magis magisque Trimalchio

---

H

48 4 etiam *Wehle*: autem domusionem *Wehle*: divisione II *Buecheler post Mentel*: tres 7 illi Cyclops] ille Cyclopi *Giardina et Melloni* poricino *obscurum*: porcino *Buecheler*: forcipe *Studer*: *del. Fuchs* **49** 3 <et> tanto *suppl. Buecheler* apparuerat *Heinze*: aper fuerat

tell me about today's declamation? I don't plead cases in public but I've studied up for household needs. In case you think I don't care much for learning, I've got two libraries, one for Greek, one for Latin. So please give me your presentation in outline."

"There was a rich man and a poor man," began Agamemnon, "who were enemies." "What's a poor man?" interrupted Trimalchio. "How witty!" replied Agamemnon, as he launched into some debate or other. Trimalchio's response was instantaneous: "If this happened you can't call it a debate, and if it didn't happen you can't call it anything."

This and more we awarded lavish applause, until Trimalchio said, "Dear Agamemnon, do you know the Twelve Labours of Hercules, or the story of Ulysses getting his thumb screwed off by the Cyclops? When I was a boy I used to read this stuff in Homer. Yes, and with my own eyes I even saw the Sybil of Cumae suspended inside a glass jar; and when children would ask her, 'Sybile, que veux-tu?' she'd say, 'Je veux mourir.'"

49 Even as he was blathering, a dish with an enormous pig upon it took possession of the table. We were amazed at the speed of preparation and swore that not even a fowl could have been cooked in that time, not to mention an obviously much larger pig than the one that had just put in an appearance. Next, Trimalchio, peering at it closer and closer, said,

4 intuens eum, "Quid? Quid?" inquit, "Porcus hic non est
5 Exinteratur? Non mehercules est. Voca, voca cocum in
medio." Cum constitisset ad mensam tristis et diceret
se oblitum exinterare, "Quid? Oblitus?" Trimalchio
exclamat, "Putes illum piper et cuminum non coniecisse.
6 Despolia!" Non fit mora, despoliatur cocus atque inter
duos tortores maestus consistit. Deprecari tamen omnes
coeperunt et dicere, "Solet fieri: rogamus, mittas;
7 postea si fecerit, nemo nostrum pro illo rogabit." Ego
crudelissimae severitatis, non potui me tenere, sed
inclinatus ad aurem Agamemnonis, "Plane," inquam, "hic
debet servus esse nequissimus; aliquis oblivisceretur
porcum exinterare? Non mehercules illi ignoscerem, si
8 piscem praeterisset." At non Trimalchio, qui relaxato
in hilaritatem vultu, "ergo," inquit, "quia tam malae
9 memoriae es, palam nobis illum exintera." Recepta cocus
tunica cultrum arripuit porcique ventrem hinc atque
10 illinc timida manu secuit. Nec mora, ex plagis ponderis
inclinatione crescentibus thumatula cum botulis effusa sunt.

50 Plausum post hoc automatum familia dedit et "Gaio
feliciter," conclamavit. Nec non cocus potione honoratus

H

49 6 mittas *Heinze*: mittes 10 thumatula] *notam ad* 31.11 *videas* botulis *Scheffer*: botulius **50** honoratus *Scheffer*: oneratus

"What's this I see? Has this pig not been cleaned? No, I do declare! Bring in the cook!" So there stood the cook all sad-faced and admitting he'd forgotten to gut the pig. "Forgotten? Forgotten?" shrieked Trimalchio. "You'd think he was talking about the seasoning! Strip him!" Quick as a flash the cook was stripped and stood up between two torturers, a sorry man indeed. We all started pleading for him. "These things happen," we said. "Please let him off. If he does it again no one will say a word in his defence."

I, sternest of disciplinarians, couldn't restrain myself. Leaning over to Agamemnon's ear, I said, "This is obviously a very careless slave. How could anyone forget to gut a pig? I wouldn't let him off even if it was a fish." This was not for Trimalchio, though. "Well," he said, his face softening into a smile, "since your memory is so terrible you'd better gut it in front of us."

The cook retrieved his shirt, snatched up a knife, and with trembling hand cut into the pig's belly in several places. Out of the gashes gaping large from the weight of the contents there quickly spilled – sausages and blood puddings.

50 The household joined in cheering this jape: "Bravo, Gaius!"

est et[iam] argentea corona, poculumque in lance accipit
2 Corinthia. Quam cum Agamemnon propius consideraret, ait
Trimalchio: "Solus sum qui vera Corinthea habeam."
3 Expectabam, ut pro reliqua insolentia diceret sibi vasa
4 Corintho afferri, sed ille melius, "Et forsitan," inquit,
"quaeris, quare solus Corinthea vera possideam: quia
scilicet aerarius, a quo emo, Corinthos vocatur. Quid est
5 autem Corintheum, nisi quis Corinthum habet? Et ne me
putetis nesapium esse, valde bene scio, unde primum
Corinthea nata sint. Cum Ilium captum est, Hannibal, homo
vafer et magnus stelio, omnes statuas aeneas congessit et
6 eas incendit; factae sunt in unum aera miscellanea. Ita
ex hac massa fabri sustulerunt et fecerunt catilla et
paropsides <et> statuncula. Sic Corinthea nata sunt, ex
7 omnibus in unum, nec hoc nec illud. Ignoscetis mihi quod
dixero: ego malo mihi vitrea, certe non olunt. Quod si
non frangerentur, mallem mihi quam aurum; nunc autem
51 vilia sunt. Fuit tamen faber qui fecit phialem vitream

H

50 1 *del. Buecheler* 4 quaeritis *Wehle, sed ad Agamemnonem* vera Corinthea *maluit Buecheler* nisi quis Corinthum *susp. Mueller,* nisi quis a Corintho *praebens bene* habet *Buecheler:* habeat 5 et ne] set ne *potius Buecheler, bene* stelio *Heinze*: scelio 6 *add. Scheffer* 7 quod *Muncker*: quid certe non olunt (olent *Jahn*) *Buecheler*: certae (certi *alii*) nolunt *Orelli*: certe nolunt **51** *cf. Isid. Etym.* xvi.16., *Ioan. Sar. Policr. iv.5: nec plus memoriae Petronii confirmant*

The cook too was saluted with a toast and a silver wreath, and was given a goblet on a Corinthian tray. When Trimalchio noticed Agamemnon inspecting it closely he said, "I am the only person who has genuine Corinthian plate." I expected him to match his earlier boasts with the statement that he imported it from Corinth, but he went one better: "Perhaps you are wondering," he said, "how I can be the sole possessor of genuine Corinthian. It's of course because the metalsmith who I buy from is called Corinthus. So no one has Corinthian unless he has Corinthus. And don't take me for an ignoramus who doesn't know where the first Corinthian came from.

"When Troy was captured, that cunning snake Hannibal piled all the bronze statuary together and set it on fire, so all the different bronze pieces melted into one. From this lump of bronze craftsmen got their material to make bowls and dishes and statuettes. That's how Corinthian came about. All into one, and not a bit from here and a bit from there. If you'll forgive me for saying so I like glass better myself because it doesn't smell. If glass didn't break I think I'd prefer it to gold. But now it's cheap.

51 "Once there was a craftsman who made a goblet of unbreakable glass.

2 quae non frangebatur. Admissus ergo Caesarem est cum suo munere
... Deinde fecit reporrigere Caesarem et illam in pavimentum
3 proiecit. Caesar non pote valdius quam expavit. At ille sustulit
4 phialem de terra; collisa erat tamquam vasum aeneum; deinde
5 martiolem de sinu protulit et phialem otio belle correxit. Hoc
facto putabat se solium Iovis tenere, utique postquam ille
dixit: "Numquid alius scit hanc condituram vitreorum?"
6 Vide modo: postquam negavit, iussit illum Caesar decollari,
quia enim, si scitum esset, aurum pro luto haberemus. In
52 argento plane studiosus sum. Habeo scyphos urnales plus minus
... quemadmodum Cassandra occidit filios suos, et pueri mortui
2 iacent sic ut vivere putes. Habeo capidem quam reliquit patronus
<mihi> meus, ubi Daedalus Niobam in equum Troianum includit.
3 "Nam Hermerotis pugnas et Petraitis in poculis habeo, omnia
ponderosa; meum intellegere nulla pecunia vendo."

H
51 2 Caesarem *Scheffer*: <ad> *Caesarem Heinze*: Caesari *lac. ind. Fuchs* 5 solium *Heinze*: coleum ille *Heinze*: illi
52 *lac. ind. Heinze, in qua nota numeri tum alia pauca continebantur;* C *add. Wehle* sic ut vivere *Heinze*: sicuti vere 2 capidem quam *patavina*: capidem quas: capides M quas *Buecheler* patronus meus *patavina: suppl. Buecheler in adn.* patrono <meo> Mummius *item Buecheler*: patronorum <optimus> *Watt*: patronorum meus 3 pugnas et *Burman*: pugnasset

Admitted into the presence of Caesar with his gift, he had the emperor reach for it as he dropped it onto the floor. Caesar couldn't have been more shaken. The craftsman picked up the goblet, now dented like a bronze pot, took a small hammer from his pocket, and calmly fixed it fine with no trouble at all.

"This done, he thought he was over the moon, especially after Caesar asked him if anyone else knew this process for making glass. Wait! As soon as he said no, Caesar had his head cut off, because if the secret got out he thought it would make gold cheap as dirt.

52 "I'm a great connoisseur of silver. I've got lots of urn cups … Cassandra killing her sons, with the dead boys lying there looking like they're alive. I've got a bowl which my master left me with Daedalus on it shutting up Niobe in the Trojan Horse. I've got goblets with the fights of Hermeros and Petraites on them, all in solid silver. Yes, my education I'll never part with for all the money in the world."

4 Haec dum refert, puer calicem proiecit. Ad quem respiciens
Trimalchio, "Cito," inquit, "te ipsum caede, quia nugax es."
5 Statim puer demisso labro <ora>re. At ille, "Quid me rogas?
Tamquam ego tibi molestus sim. Suadeo, a te impetres, ne sis
6 nugax." Tandem ergo exoratus a nobis missionem dedit puero.
Ille dimissus circa mensam percucurrit <Trimalchionis, qui>
7 [et] "aquam foras, vinum intro," clamavit. Excipimus urbanitatem
iocantis, et ante omnes Agamemnon qui sciebat quibus meritis
8 revocaretur ad mensam. Ceterum laudatus Trimalchio hilarius
bibit et iam ebrio proximus, "Nemo," inquit, "vestrum rogat
Fortunatam meam ut saltet? Credite mihi, cordacem nemo
9 melius ducit." Atque ipse erectis supra frontem manibus
Syrum histrionem exhibebat concinente tota familia:
10 "Madeia, Perimadeia!" Et prodisset in medium, nisi Fortunata
aurem accessisset; [et] credo, dixerit non decere gravitatem
11 eius tam humiles ineptias. Nihil autem tam inaequale erat; nam

---

H
52 5 labro orare *Scheffer*: labrore: orare <coepit> *Strelitz*
6 *post alterum* nugax *lac. putabat Buecheler ob* ergo, *non admodum aptum post* percucurrit *lacunam alteram ind. Buecheler, non tamen mihi magna, si* aquam *non ad minctionem sed ad* aquam *e calice effusam refert; exigitur solum nomen* Trimalchionis, *quod cum* qui *supplevi, lacunam implens; adiunctionem videas*

As Trimalchio was speaking, a boy dropped a goblet. Trimalchio looked up at him. "Go get yourself a beating for being careless!" he said. At once the boy pouted and began to plead. "Why ask me?" was Trimalchio's riposte. "Am I your problem? Why don't you see that you're not careless?" And so again, after our entreaties, he pardoned the boy, who celebrated his release with a lap around the table …

"Water out, wine in!" Trimalchio proclaimed, and we welcomed our wag's witticism, Agamemnon to the fore. He knew the requirements of a repeat dinner invitation. After this praise, Trimalchio drank all the more exuberantly and was becoming quite drunk. "Will none of you," he said, "ask Fortunata here to dance? Believe me, no one does a better shimmy."

Whereupon he raised his hands over his head and did Syrus the mime, with his entire household singing along, "Have some Madeira, m'dear!" He would have leaped before us, had not Fortunata leaned into his ear and said something to the effect that such low tomfoolery ill became his station.

11 modo Fortunatam <verebatur> modo ad naturam suam revertebatur.
53 Et plane interpellavit saltationis libidinem actuarius,
2 qui tamquam urbis acta recitavit: "VII Kalendas Sextiles: in
praedio Cumano quod est Trimalchionis nacti sunt pueri XXX,
puellae XL; sublata in horreum ex area tritici millia modium
3 quingenta, boves domiti quingenti. Eodem die: Mithridates
servus in crucem actus, quia Gai nostri genio male dixerat.
4 Eodem die: in arcam relatum est quod collocari non potuit,
5 sestertium centies. Eodem die: incendium factum est in hortis
6 Pompeianis, ortum ex aedibus Nastae vilici." "Quid?" inquit
7 Trimalchio, "Quando mihi Pompeiani horti empti sunt?" "Anno
priore," inquit actuarius, "et ideo in rationem nondum
8 venerunt." Excanduit Trimalchio et "Quicumque," inquit,
"mihi fundi empti fuerint, nisi intra sextum mensem sciero,
9 in rationes meas inferri vetuo." Iam etiam edicta aedilium
recitabantur, et saltuariorum testamenta, quibus Trimalchio
10 cum elogio exheredebatur; iam nomina vilicorum et repudiata
a circ[um]itore liberta in balneatoris contubernio
deprehensa et atriensis Baias relegatus, iam reus factus
dispensator, et iudicium inter cubicularios actum.

H

52 11 verebatur add. *Heinze,* suam *post* naturam *ponens* modo fortunatam suam revertebatur modo ad naturam H; *sic scribo post Mueller, quod renuit Buecheler,* suam <verebatur> malens: modo Fortunatam <sequebatur>, modo . . . *Giardina et Melloni post Fuchs*[2] **53** 9 elogio *patavinus*: elegio 10 del. *Buecheler*

But it was an unequal struggle, as he alternately deferred to Fortuna and reverted to his own nature.

53 With a dry report, Trimalchio's accountant put a firm stop to the prospect of a lewd dance, reciting as if from the city Gazetteer:

> JULY 26. ON THE ESTATE OF TRIMALCHIO AT CUMAE. BORN: BOYS, 30, GIRLS, 40. TAKEN FROM THRESHING FLOOR TO GRANARY: WHEAT, 500,000 PECKS. OXEN BROKEN IN: 500. ALSO ON THIS DAY: SLAVE MITHRIDATES CRUCIFIED FOR TAKING IN VAIN THE NAME OF OUR GAIUS. ALSO ON THIS DAY: STORED IN THE SAFE WHEN IT COULD NOT BE INVESTED, 10,000,000 SESTERCES. ALSO ON THIS DAY: FIRE BROKE OUT IN POMPEIAN GARDENS, BEGUN AT HOME OF GROUNDSMAN NASTA.

"What's that?" said Trimalchio, "When did I buy my gardens at Pompeii?" "Last year," was the reply, "so it hadn't got into the books until now." Trimalchio became angry. "Any property bought in my name that I don't hear about within six months must not go into the accounts."

Then also were recited the edicts of the aediles, and gamekeepers' wills specifically disinheriting Trimalchio in codicils. Groundsmen's records were then read out, then that of a freedwoman divorced by a watchman after being caught in bed with a bath attendant, then a hall attendant banished to Baiae, then also a wine steward on a charge, then a decision rendered between bedroom stewards.

11 Petauristarii autem tandem venerunt, Baro
insulsissimus cum scalis constitit puerumque iussit per
gradus <ire> et in summa parte odaria saltare, circulos
deinde ardentes transilire et dentibus amphoram sustinere.
12 Mirabatur haec solus Trimalchio dicebatque ingratum
artificium esse. Ceterum duo esse in rebus humanis quae
libentissime spectaret, petauristarios et cornicines;
13 reliqua [animalia] acroamata tricas meras esse. "Nam et
comoedos," inquit, emeram, sed malui illos Atellanam
facere, et choraulem meum iussi Latine cantare.

54 Cum maxime haec dicente eo puer [Trimalchionis]
delapsus est. Conclamavit familia, nec minus convivae
non propter hominem tam putidum, cuius etiam cervices
fractae libenter vidissent, sed propter malum exitum
2 cenae, ne necesse haberent alienum mortuum plorare. Ipse
Trimalchio cum graviter ingemuisset superque bracchium
tamquam laesum incubuisset, concurrere medici, et inter
primos Fortunata crinibus passis cum scypho, miseramque

H
53 11 *addidi post Muncker* deinde circulos *maluit Buecheler* transilire *Heinze*: transire 12 cornicines *Heinze*: cornices *del.* Buecheler acroamata tricas *Scheffer*: cromataricas sed *Heinze*: et Atellanam *Scheffer*: Atellam **54** eo *Mueller*: Gaio *delevi; post* puer *lac. ind. Scheffer, non Wehle, qui* in bracchium huius *emendat; adiunct. videas* etiam] et *Buecheler*

At length trapezists entered the room. A simple-minded giant stood next to a ladder as he gave a boy the order to climb the rungs and at the top to dance a jig and then jump through a flaming hoop with an amphora in his teeth. Only Trimalchio was impressed by this. He said it was an underappreciated skill. In fact, he said, there were only two human activities he could watch anytime: trapeze acts and horn playing. As for the other "turns": stuff and nonsense. "For instance," he went on, "I once bought Greek comic actors, but I had them doing Roman farces, which I prefer, and I told my chorus leader to sing in Latin."

54 In the midst of this information the boy fell off the ladder. The servants shrieked, as did the guests – not out of their concern for an individual so foul that they would have been content to see his neck broken: it was for the bad end to the dinner and in case they had to mourn the death of a nobody.

Trimalchio himself gave a deep groan and cradled his arm, which seemed to be injured. Up ran doctors, with Fortunata to the fore, hair streaming, goblet in hand, proclaiming her sorry and unhappy estate, and the fallen

3 se atque infelicem proclamavit. Nam puer quidem qui H
ceciderat circumibat iam dudum pedes nostros et missionem
rogabat. Pessime mihi erat, ne his precibus [periculo]
aliquid catastropha quaereretur. Nec enim adhuc exciderat
4 cocus ille qui oblitus fuerat porcum exinterare. Itaque
totum circumspicere triclinium coepi ne per parietem
automatum aliquod exiret, utique postquam servus verberari
coepit, qui bracchium domini contusum alba potius quam
5 conchyliata involveerat lana. Nec longe aberravit suspicio
mea; in vicem enim poenae venit decretum Trimalchionis
quo puerum iussit liberum esse, ne quis posset dicere
tantum virum esse a servo vulneratum.
55 / Comprobamus nos factum / et quam in praecipiti res HLO/H
2 humanae essent / vario sermone garrimus./ "Ita," inquit HLO/H
Trimalchio, "non oportet hunc casum sine inscriptione
transire," statimque codicillos poposcit et non diu
cogitatione distorta haec recitavit:
3 / "Quod non expectes, ex transverso fit <ubique, HL
Nostra> et supra nos Fortuna negotia curat.
/ Quare da nobis vina Falerna, puer." H

H, L (= lmrtp), O (= BRP)
54 3 *delevi ut glossema*: per ridiculum *Keller bene*: periculo
5 poenae *Hadrianides*: cenae vulneratum *Scheffer*: laceratum,
livoratum *vidit proposita Buecheler*: liberatum 55 1 nos om. LO
varioque LO sermone garrimus *om.* B 2 distortus *Fuchs*
3 expectas L *add. Heinze* supra *Heinze*: super negotium L

boy too had long started on his rounds of our feet, begging for pardon. I had a most uneasy feeling these entreaties were the cue for another prank, since I hadn't yet forgotten the cook who'd neglected to gut the pig. And so I began to look about the entire dining room on the chance that some device should pop out of the wall, my efforts redoubling when a slave was administered a flogging for wrapping a white bandage round his master's bruised arm instead of purple. And nor were my suspicions far off. Instead of the boy's being punished, down from Trimalchio came a decree commanding him to be set free, so that no one could say that a man of such account had been hurt by a slave.

55 We commended this act, then chattered variously over the knife-edge proclivities of human affairs. "What has thus befallen," pronounced Trimalchio, "must not be allowed to go unrecorded." He immediately called for paper and after no long wrestle with reflection came out with the following:

"Accidents will happen, when you least expect 'em,
And luck it is who does our biz.
And so, my boy, bring round the Château Pomeroy."

4 Ab hoc epigrammate / coepit poetarum esse mentio HLO
diuque summa carminis penes Mopsum Thracem memorata
5 est, donec Trimalchio, "Rogo," inquit, "magister,
quid putas inter Ciceronem et Publilium interesse?
Ego alterum puto disertiorem fuisse, alterum
honestiorem. Quid enim his melius dici potest?

6 'Luxuriae rictu Martis marcent moenia.
Tuo palato clausus pavo pascitur
Plumato amictus aureo Babylonico,
Gallina tibi Numidica, tibi gallus spado;
Ciconia etiam, grata peregrina hospita
Pietaticultrix gracilipes crotalistria,
Avis exul hiemis, titulus tepidi temporis,
Nequitiae nidum in caccabo fecit tuae.
Quo margaritam caram tibi, bacam Indicam?
An ut matrona ornata phaleris pelagiis
Tollat pedes indomita in strato extraneo?
Zmaragdum ad quam rem viridem, pretiosum vitrum?
Quod Carchedonios optas ignes lapideos?

H, L (= lmrtp), O (= BRP)
55 4 et poetarum coepit LO morata *Heinze*: memorata
5 putes LO Publilium *restituit Buecheler*: Publium
fuisse *om.* B 6.2 pascitur *Scaliger*: nascitur
6.3 auro HO 6.6 pietatis cultrix HO 6.8 tuae *Fraenkel*:
tuo *Heinze*: meo 6.9 margaritam caram *Ribbeck*: margarita
cara tibi, bacam indicam *Heinze*: tibi baca indica O
6.10 an HO: aut L onerata L 6.12 ad aquam H

Out of this epigram the discussion turned to poets, and for some time it was Mopsus of Thrace who held sway, until Trimalchio asked, "Please, professor, in your opinion what is the main difference between Cicero and Publilius? I think Cicero was more eloquent but Publilius nobler. How could it be put better than the following:

'In the maw of luxury wilt the walls of Mars:
A peacock's pastured, your palate the prisoner's bars,
Gorgeous in plumage of golden Babylon.
There too the guinea hen, therewith your capon;
A stork even, the welcome foreign guest,
Slim legged rattlebeak, loyal builder of her nest,
Avian winter exile, symbol of summer hot –
O infamy! – right in your cooking pot.
Why prized by you the pearl, the jewel of Ind?
For wife, to trappings of the sea a-pinned,
To spread her legs in stranger's bed, untamed?
The emerald, green precious glass, what boon?
And Carthaginian rubies choosing, fire in stone?

Nisi ut scintillet probitas e carbunculis
Aequum est induere nuptam ventum textilem,
Palam prostare nudam in nebula linea?'

56 / "Quod autem," inquit, "putemus secundum litteras H
difficillimum esse artificium? Ego puto medicum et
2 nummularium: medicus qui scit quid homuncionem intra
3 praecordia sua habeant et quando febris veniat, etiam
si illos odi pessime, quod mihi iubent saepe anatinam
4 parari; nummularius, qui per argentum aes videt. Nam
mutae bestiae laboriosissimae boves et oves: boves,
quorum beneficio panem manducamus; oves, quod lana illae
5 nos gloriosa faciunt. Et facinus indignum aliquis
6 ovillam est et tunicam habet. Apes enim ego divinas
bestias puto, quae mel vomunt, etiam si dicuntur illud
a Iove afferre; / ideo autem pungunt, quia ubicumque HL
dulce est, ibi et acidum invenies."

7 / Iam etiam philosophos de negotio deiciebant, cum H
8 pittacia in scypho circumferri coeperunt; puerque super
hoc positus officium apophoreta recitavit: "argentum
sceleratum": allata est perna, supra quam acetabula erant
posita; "cervical": offla collaris allata est; "serisapia

H, L (= lmrtp), O (= BRP)
55 6.14 e B: est *ceteri* carbunculis *Buecheler*: -os *vel* -us
induere *Sambucus*: inducere linea *Sambucus*: lunae **56**
putemus *scribo*: putamus 3 anatinam *Jahn* 5 est et *Scheffer*:
esset ideo autem: apes ideo L

Can honour thence from baubles shine alone?
Right is it for bride the wind to wear?
Parade in stuff of mist, on view and bare?'

56 "So, then," Trimalchio said, "next to writing, what should we regard as the hardest profession? I think it's being a doctor or a teller. A doctor has to know what's going on in people's insides when their fever's coming on – though I hate 'em in the worst way for ordering concoctions of duck meat all the time. As for a teller, he's got to find the copper under the silver wash.

"Among the dumb animals the hardest workers are oxen and sheep. The oxen give us our bread to chew, and the sheep make us look grand with their wool. It's a crime they don't deserve, with people eating mutton and wearing leather. As for bees now, I think they're supernatural beasties since they spew up honey, though they're supposed to get it from Jupiter. That's why they sting, of course, because everywhere there is sweet, there also you will find the bitter."

He was still tossing philosophers out of their jobs as a goblet came round with tags on it, and a designated boy read out the takeaway gifts. "Hokey Silver" produced a hock of ham with a cruet sitting on it; and "Neck Pillow" produced a collar of meat.

et contumelia": xerophagiae e sale datae sunt et contus
9 cum malo; "porri et persica": flagellum et cultrum
accepit; "passeres et muscarium": uvam passam et mel
Atticum; "canale et pedale": lepus et solea est allata;
"cenatoria et forensia": offlam et tabulas accepit;
"muraena et littera": murem cum rana alligata fascemque
10 betae. Diu risimus: sexcenta huiusmodi fuerunt, quam iam
exciderunt memoriae meae.

57 Ceterum Ascyltus, intemperantis licentiae, cum
omnia sublatis manibus eluderet et usque ad lacrimas
rideret, unus ex conlibertis Trimalchionis excanduit -
2 is ipse qui supra discumbebat - et "Quid rides,"
inquit, "vervex? An tibi non placent lautitiae domini
mei? Tu enim beatior es et convivare melius soles. Ita
tutelam huius loci habeam propitiam, ut ego si secundum
illum discumberem, iam illi balatum clusissem. Bellum
3 pomum, qui rideatur alios; larifuga nescioquis, nocturnus,
qui non valet lotium suum. Ad summam, si circumminxero
illum, nesciet qua fugiat. Non mehercules soleo cito

H
56 8 xerophagiae *Reiske*: aecrophagie e sale *Burman*: saele contus *Burman*: centus 9 canale ... allata *hic ponit Fraenkel: ante* muraena canale et pedale *Buecheler*: canalem et pedalem muraena et littera *Buecheler*: murenam et litteram alligata *Buecheler*: alligatam 10 exciderunt *Hadrianides*: ceciderunt **57** 2 clusississem *Friedlaender:* 3 mehercules *Buecheler:* me herculem

"Continuing Education" and "Bad Apple" got a beanie and a rotten apple. "Leeks and Peaches" got a rusty pipe and a pair of breeches. "Sparrows and Flypaper" got a cup of grapejuice and some Attic honey. "Canine Podiatry" got a hare and an old boot. "Dinner Togs and Legal Togs" got a bib and a tablet. "Eel and Letters" got the letter "L" and some bees. There were hundreds of these things, most of which I have now forgotten, and we laughed for ages.

57 Meanwhile Ascyltus, with typical lack of restraint, was flapping his hands at everything in mock appreciation and laughing himself to tears. One of Trimalchio's freedman colleagues, on my immediate left, lost his temper. "What are you laughing at, muttonhead?" he said. "Don't you like my patron's games? Of course you're richer and used to dining better.

"So help me, guardian deity of this place permitting, if I were sitting on the same couch as him I'd soon stop his bleating! He's a fine fruit to laugh at others, some runaway fly-by-night not worth his own piss! In fact, if I pissed around him in a circle he wouldn't know how to get out. I don't usually come this fast to the boil,

4 fervere, sed in molle carne vermes nascuntur. Ridet.
Quid habet quod rideat? Numquid pater fetum emit lamna?
Eques Romanus es; et ego regis filius. 'quare ergo
servivisti?' Quia ipse me dedi in servitutem et malui
civis Romanus esse quam tributarius. Et nunc spero me
5 sic vivere, ut nemini iocus sim. Homo inter homines sum,
capiti aperto ambulo; assem aerarium nemini debeo;
constitutum habui numquam; nemo mihi in foro dixit,
6 'Redde quod debes.' Glebulas emi, lamellulas paravi;
viginti ventres pasco et canem; contubernalem meam
redemi, ne quis in <capillis> illius manus tergeret;
mille denarios pro capite solvi; sevir gratis factus sum;
7 spero, sic moriar, ut mortuus non erubescam. Tu autem tam
laboriosus es, ut post te non respicias? In alio peduclum
8 vides, in te ricinum non vides. Tibi soli redicl[e]i
videmur; ecce magister tuus, homo maior natus: placemus
9 illi. Tu lacticulosus, nec mu nec ma argutas, vasus
fictilis, immo lorus in aqua, lentior, non melior. Tu
beatior es: bis prande, bis cena. Ego fidem meam malo
quam thesauros. Ad summam, quisquam me bis poposcit?
Annis quadraginta servivi; nem tamen scit utrum servus
essem an liber. Et puer capillatus in hanc coloniam veni:

H

57 4 molli *patavina* 5 sum *Burman*: suos 6 *add. Burman; post* illius *Watt*: <capite> *Reinesius; cf.* 27.6
7 ricinum *Mentel*: ricium 9 lacticulosus *Scheffer*: laeticulosus 9 sciit *Scheffer, quod plerumque edd. malunt*

but it's in soft meat where the worms are born.

"He's laughing. What's he got to laugh about? Did his father pay cash for him?

You're a Roman knight? I'm the son of a king. 'So why did you become a slave?' I did it willingly, because I wanted to live my life the laughing-stock of nobody. I'm a man among men and walk with my head high. I owe nobody a brass penny and never got summonsed. No one ever had to tell me in court to 'Pay back what you owe!' I bought some land and raised some cash. I feed twenty bellies and a dog. I bought out my woman: didn't want somebody wiping his hand on her hair. I paid a thousand for my own freedom and became a councillor, without paying. When I die I'll have nothing to blush for, that's my ambition.

"As for you, are you too busy to look around? You spot a flea on someone else and don't see the louse on yourself. We seem funny only to you. Look at your professor, an older man. We're fine with him. You're still on your mother's milk, can't even say googoo, wet clay, yes, a strap in the water and not even as useful though limper. You're richer? Two lunches? Two dinners? I'll stake my reputation over any fortune. So did anybody have to ask me twice? For forty years I was a slave but nobody could tell if I was a slave or free. I first came to this town as a long-haired boy. The town hall had not

10 adhuc basilica non erat facta. Dedi tamen operam ut
domino satisfacerem, homini maiesto et dignitos[s]o,
cuius pluris erat unguis quam tu totus es. Et habebam
in domo qui mihi pedes opponerent hac illac; tamen –
11 genio illius gratias – enatavi. Haec sunt vera athla:
nam [in] ingenuum nasci tam facile est quam 'Accede
istoc.' Quid nunc stupes tamquam hircus in ervilia?"

58 Post hoc dictum Giton, qui ad pedes stabat, risum
iam diu compressum etiam indecenter effudit. Quod cum
animadvertisset adversarius Ascylti, flexit convicium
2 in puerum et, "Tu autem," inquit, "etiam tu rides, cepa
cirrata? Io Saturnalia: rogo, mensis December est? Quando
vicesimam numerasti? … quid faciat, crucis offla,
corvorum cibaria. Curabo, iam tibi Iovis iratus sit, et
3 isti qui tibi non imperat. Ita satur pane fiam, ut ego
istud conliberto meo dono; aliquin iam depresentiarum
reddidisssem. Bene nos habemus, at isti nugae - [qui tibi
non imperant]: plane qualis dominus, talis et servus.
4 Vix me teneo, nec sum caldicerebrius, <sed> cum coepi,

H
57 10 maiesto *Muncker*: mali ista: malista *George*
11 *del. Buecheler* **58** 2 tu rides *patavina*: turdes
io *Heinze*: o cirrata *Reinesius*: pirrata *lac. ind.*
Buecheler, in qua fere nescit *ponit* tibi *patavina*: ubi
3 conliberto *Scheffer*: cum liberto at *Burman;* aut
nugae *Buecheler*: geuge *del. Fraenkel* 4 nec *Jahn*: at
caldicerebrius *Jahn*: caldus cicer eius *suppl. Buecheler*

been built yet. But I made it my business to please my master, a man of class dignity and presence: more under his fingernail than in all of you. Yes, I had people in the house sticking out their feet now and then, but thanks to my master's backing I kept afloat. These are the real challenges: when you're freeborn it's as easy as a 'Get over here!' Why are you still gaping, like a goat in a beanfield?"

58 After that expression, Giton, from his station at my feet, let out the unseemly guffaw so long held in check. At this Ascyltus' opponent turned his wrath upon the boy. "You laughing too, onion curls?" he said. "Merry Saturnalia! What month is it, December? When did you pay your five per cent?

"He's got no idea, this gallows-bait, this crow's meat. I'll soon see you feeling the wrath of Jupiter, and him also who doesn't control you. If it means my bread, I'll let it go for my colleague's sake, otherwise I'd've paid you back double-quick. We're doing fine until these losers ... Well, like master like slave. I can barely hold it in and I'm not hot- tempered by nature. But get me going and I don't give a coin-toss for my mother!

matrem meam dupundii non facio. Recte, videbo te in
5 publicum, mus, immo terrae tuber: nec sursum ne deorsum
non cresco, nisi dominum tuum in rutae folium [non]
coniecero, nec tibi parsero, licet mehercules Iovem Olympium
clames. Curabo, longe tibi sit comula ista besalis et
6 dominus dupunduarius. Recte, venies sub dentem: aut ego non
me novi, aut non deridebis, licet barbam auream habeas.
7 Athena tibi irata sit, curabo, et <ei> qui te primus
'Deuro de,' fecit. Non didici geometrias, critica et
alias nenias, sed lapidarias litteras scio, partes
8 centum dico ad aes, ad pondus, ad nummum. Ad summam, si
quid vis, ego et tu sponsiunculam: exi, defero lamnam.
Iam scies patrem tuum mercedes perdidisse, quamvis et
rhetoricam scis. Ecce:
'Qui de nobis longe venio, late venio? Solve me.'
9 Dicam tibi: qui de nobis currit et de loco non movetur?
Qui de nobis crescit et minor fit? Curris, stupes
10 satagis, tamquam mus in matella. Ergo aut tace, aut

H

58 5 [non] coniecero *Heinze; cf.* 58.2: non coniecero *Giardina:* non conieci *Scheffer:* non coniecit parsero *Reinesius*: par ero 7 Athana *Heinze*: Sathana *add. Reinesius* critica *Reiske*: cretica alias nenias *lego*: *alii alia*: alogias menias lapidarias *patavina*: lipidarias 8 lamnam *Heinze*: lamna scis *Reiske*: scio qui de *Buecheler*: quidem 9 curris *susp. Buecheler, cui placet* muttis

"I'll be seeing you in court, good and proper, you mouse, you toadstool! I'll grow up nor down before I throw your master into the brambles, and I'll spare you neither, cry to high heaven though you might. Those cheap curls'll help you not a bit, I'll make sure of that, and nor will your no-good master. Feel my teeth, you will. As sure as I know myself you'll not make a fool of me, even if your beard turned gold.

"You'll feel Athena's wrath, I'll see to it, as will he who first told you to 'Step Forward.' I never learned theorems or theory and other mumbo-jumbo, but I know my capitals and can do my hundred in weights and measures and coin. So: let's you and me make a wager, if you like. Here's my money, where's yours? You'll soon find out your father lost his investment, though you may know your rhetoric. Okay,

> 'I go far, I go wide, what am I?'

Here's a clue: 'I run, I stay in place, you all have me, I get bigger, I get smaller, what am I?' Had enough? Dazed and confused, like a mouse in a chamber pot?

meliorem noli molestare, qui te natum non putat; nisi si
me iudicas anulos buxeos curare, quos amicae tuae
11 involasti. Occuponem propitium. Eamus in forum et pecunias
12 mutuemur: iam scies hoc ferrum fidem habere. Vah, bella
res est vulpis uda. Ita lucrum faciam et ita bene moriar
aut populus per exitum meum iuret, nisi te ubique toga
13 perversa fuero persecutus. Bella res et iste qui te haec
docet, mufrius, non magister. <Nos aliter> didicimus:
dicebat enim magister: 'Sunt vestra salva? Recta domum;
14 cave, cum circumspicias; cave maiorem maledicas.' At nunc
mera mapalia; nemo dupondii evadit. Ego, quod me sic
vides, propter artificium meum diis gratias ago."

59 Coeperat Ascyltos repondere convicio, sed
Trimalchio delectatus collibertati eloquentia, "Agite,"
inquit, "scordalias de medio. Suaviter sit potius. Et
tu, Hermeros, parce adulescentulo. Sanguen illi
2 fervet: tu melior esto. / Semper in hac re qui vincitur HL
vincit. / Et tu cum esses capo, cocococo, aeque cor non H
habebas. Simus ergo, quod melius est, ut primitus
3 hilares et Homeristas spectemus." Intravit factio statim
hastisque scuta concrepuit. Ipse Trimalchio in pulvino

H, L (lmrtp)
58 12 ut *Heinze*: aut: et *Giardina et Melloni* ubique toga *Buecheler*: toga ubique 13 *add. Heraeus* 14 at nunc mera *Heraeus*: aut numera **59** 2 aeque *Heinze*: atque habebas *Mentel*: habeas ut primitus *Watt:* a primitiis *Buecheler*: a primitis

Well, either shut up or don't bother a better man who doesn't even think you exist, unless of course you expect me to be impressed with the wooden rings you stole from your girlfriend! Let the God of Business decide. Let's go to the market and borrow some money. You'll soon see the credit in this iron one. Hah! Nothing worse than a soaked fox. As I hope to keep my profits and die rich so people can swear upon my grave, I'll hunt you down everywhere with my black cap on. Nothing worse also than the man who taught you these habits, a muttonhead not a master. We learned another lesson. Our teacher would say, 'Got your things? Straight home, then. Don't look around. Don't be cheeky to your elders.' But now it's a shamble-shack, and nobody winds up with a thing. As for me, the man you see owes all to his trade and thanks god for it."

59 Ascyltus was beginning to respond to this abuse when Trimalchio, delighted with the eloquence of his colleague, interposed. "Come on now, you two," he said, "enough of this wrangling. Let's be nice to each other instead. As for you, Hermeros, go easy on the lad. His blood runs hot. You set a better example. In such matters it's always the person who yields that wins. And when you were a young bantam it was cock-a-doodle-doo without half his sense. Let's go on having fun like before and watch the Homeric troupe." Immediately the company made their entry with a clash of spears against shields as Trimalchio settled down into a cushion.

consedit, et cum Homeristae Graecis versibus
colloquerentur, ut insolenter solent, ille canora voce
Latine legebat librum. Mox silentio facto, "Scitis,"
4 inquit, "quam fabulam agant? Diomedes et Ganymedes duo
fratres fuerunt. Horum soror erat Helena. Agamemnon
illam rapuit et Dianae cervam subiecit. Ita nunc Homeros
dicit quemadmodum inter se pugnent Troiani et Tarentini.
5 Vicit scilicet et Iphigeniam, filiam suam, Achilli dedit
uxorem. Ob eam rem Aiax insanit et statim argumentum
6 explicabit." Haec ut dixit Trimalchio, clamorem
Homeristae sustulerunt, interque familiam discurrentem
vitulus in lance du<ce>naria elixus allatus est, et
7 quidem galeatus. Secutus est Aiax strictque gladio,
tamquam insaniret, <vitulum> concidit, ac modo versa
modo supina gesticulatus mucrone frusta collegit
mirantibus [vitulum] partitus est.

60 Nec diu mirari licuit tam elegantes strophas;
Repente lacunaria sonare coeperunt totumque triclinium
2 intremuit. Consternatus ego exsurrexi et timui, ne per
tectum petauristatarius aliquis descenderet. Nec minus
reliqui convivae mirantes erexere vultus, expectantes
3 quid novi de caelo nuntiaretur. Ecce autem diductis

H

59 4 Tarentini *Scheffer*: Parentini 6 *add. Burman*
7 vitulum *de infra transtulit Mueller* supina *Scheffer*: spuma
frusta *patavina*: frustra **60** 3 diductis *Scheffer*: deductus

And when the Homeric actors began speaking their Greek verse, as is their inconvenient habit, Trimalchio, in a singsong voice, followed from a libretto in Latin. Presently, when silence fell, he spoke. "Do you know what story they're telling? Diomede and Ganymede were brothers who had a sister. That was Helen. Agamemnon abducted her and left a deer for Diana in her place. In this way, then, Homer is recounting how the Trojans and the Tarentines got to fighting. Agamemnon won, of course, and he gave his own daughter to be the bride of Achilles. This made Ajax go mad, and – it'll be all over soon, you'll see."

When Trimalchio had finished, the Homeric actors raised a cry, the servants dashed about, and in was brought a whole boiled veal on a two-hundred-pound silver tray, complete with helmet. There followed "Ajax," sword in hand, acting the madman, as he attacked the veal with forehand and backhand slashes, gathered up the meat on his swordpoint, and parcelled it out to the admiring company.

60 But we were given little time to admire these fancy turns. At once the ceiling panels groaned and the entire dining room shook. Alarmed, I jumped to my feet, in apprehension of some acrobat making his descent through the roof. The other guests matched my wonder as they turned expectant gazes upwards for some novel pronouncement from the skies.

lacunaribus subito circulus ingens, de cupa videlicet
grandi excussus, dimittitur, cuius per totum orbem
coronae aureae cum alabastris unguenti pendebant.
4 Dum haec apophoreta iubemur sumere, respiciens ad
mensam … : iam illic repositorium cum placentis
aliquot erat positum, quod medium Priapus a pistore
factus tenebat, gremioque satis amplo omnis generis
5 poma et uvas sustinebat more vulgato. Avidius ad pompam
manus porreximus, et repente nova ludorum commissio
6 hilaritatem [hic] refecit. Omnes enim placentae omniaque
poma etiam minima vexatione contacta coeperunt effundere
7 crocum, et usque ad os molestus umor accidere. Rati ergo
sacrum esse fer[i]culum tam religioso apparatu perfusum,
consurreximus altius et, "Augusto, patri patriae,
feliciter!" diximus. Quibusdam tamen etiam post hanc
venerationem poma rapientibus et ipsi mappas implevimus
ego praecipue, qui nullo satis amplo munere putabam me
onerare Gitonis sinum.

8 Inter haec tres pueri candidas succincti tunicas
intraverunt, quorum duo <tres> Lares bullatos super mensam

H

60 3 de … excussus *del. Fraenkel* 4 *lac. ind. Buecheler, qualis fere* rem novam notavi aliquot *patavina*: aliquod 5 commissio *Nisbet et Delz*: missio *Buecheler*: remissio *del. Friedlaender* 6 ad os *Buecheler*: ad os nobis *Delz* ferculum *Reinesius*: peniculum *Scheffer, cui favet Buecheler*: periculum 7 ipsi *Buecheler*: ipsas sinum *patavina*: unum 8 *addidi*

Lo and behold, the ceiling panels quickly parted, and down dropped a large hoop, seeming to have been salvaged from a good-sized wine barrel, from the entire gilt circumference of which dangled alabaster flasks of perfume.

As we were being invited to take them as leaving gifts, I looked over at the table, upon which a platter of gateaux had been set, with a pastry Priapus commanding the centre, dangling from his ample "lap" grapes and all kinds of other fruit, in the familiar pose. We greedily reached for the display, and in no time at all a new round of gags restored our fun, since every cake and piece of fruit, given the tiniest squeeze, ejaculated liquid saffron, and the nasty juice landed right in our faces. We assumed that a course so drenched in a commodity used in religion had some sacral significance and sat up to attention with a toast to "Augustus Father of the Country." But even after such a worshipful moment, some of the guests made a grab for the fruit, and we too filled our napkins, in my conviction that no prize was too valuable for stuffing Giton's pockets.

In the meantime three boys came in, white tunics hitched high. Two of them placed three household deities with medallions upon the table,

posuerunt, unus pateram vini circumferens, "Dii
propitii!" clamabat ... aiebat autem unum Cerdonem,
9 alterum Felicionem, tertium Lucrionem vocari. Nos etiam
veram imaginem ipsius Trimalchionis, cum iam omnes
basiarent, erubuimus praeterire.

61 Postquam ergo omnes bonam mentem bonamque valetudinem
sibi optarunt, Trimalchio ad Nicerotem respexit et,
2 "Solebas," <inquit>, "suavius esse in convictu; nescioquid
nunc taces nec muttis. Oro te, sic felicem me videas, narra
3 illud quod tibi usu venit." Niceros delectatus affabilitite
amici, "Omne me," inquit, "lucrum transeat, nisi iam dudum
4 gaudimonio dissilio, quod te talem video. Itaque hilaria
mera sint, etsi timeo istos scholasticos, ne me
[de]rideant. Viderint: narrabo tamen; quid enim mihi
aufert qui ridet? Satius est rideri quam derideri."
5 "Haec ubi dicta dedit," talem fabulam exorsus est:
6 "Cum adhuc servirem, habitabamus in vico angusto:
nunc Gavillae domus est. Ibi, quomodo dii volunt, amare
coepi uxorem Terentii coponis: noveratis Melissam
Tarentinam, pulcherrimum bacciballum. Sed ego non

H

60 8 *lac. susp. Buecheler* Lucrionem *Reinesius*: lucronem
9 veram] auream *Jahn*: ceream *Reinesius* **61** 2 *suppleo*
nunc *Scheffer*: nec muttis *Scheffer*: mutes 3 dissilio
patavina: dissileo 4 *del. Mentel* viderint *patavina:*
riserint *Scheffer*: viderit 5 haec ... dedit *Verg. Aen.* 2.790

as the third brought round a bowl of wine. "May the gods bless us!" he piped. Trimalchio said their names were Increase, Prosperity, and Profit. There was a lifelike statuette of Trimalchio too, and since everyone else kissed it we were too ashamed to pass.

61 When all had finished toasting their own health and faculties, Trimalchio looked over to Niceros. "You used to be better company at table," he said. "But now so quiet – nary a grunt! Go on, make me happy and tell us that adventure you had." Niceros was delighted at his friend's cordial approach. "All profit to the winds," said he, "if I could have held back my pleasure at seeing you in such fine fettle. So let's make our happiness complete, though I'm afraid of being laughed at by our intellectuals here. They'd better behave, since I'm going ahead with my story. Besides, I lose nothing if people laugh, so long as it's laughed with and not laughed at." Thus spake Niceros, as he commenced the following tale:

"When I was still in service, we used to live in Narrow Lane, in what is now Gavilla's house. There as the gods willed it I fell in love with the wife of Terence the innkeeper. You all knew Melissa from Tarentum. Pretty as a peach she was.

mehercules corporaliter <illam> [autem] aut propter res
8 venerarias curavi, sed magis quod benemoria fuit. Si quid
ab illa petii, numquam mihi negatum: fecit assem,
semissem habui, in illius sinum demandavi, nec umquam
9 fefellitus sum. Huius contubernalis ad villam supremum
diem obiit. Itaque per scutum per ocream egi aginavi,
quemadmodum ad illam pervenirem: <scitis> autem, in
62 angustiis amici apparent. Forte dominus Capuae exierat ad
2 scruta scita expedienda. Nactus ego occasionem persuadeo
hospitem nostrum ut mecum ad quintum miliarium veniat.
3 Erat autem miles, fortis tamquam Orcus. Apoculamus nos
4 circa gallicinia; luna lucebat tamquam meridie. Venimus
inter monimenta. Homo meus coepit ad stelas facere, sed
5 ego <pergo> cantabundus et stellas numero. Deinde ut
respexi ad comitem, ille exuit se et omnia vestimenta
secundum viam posuit. Mihi [in] anima in naso esse, stabam
6 tamquam mortuus. At ille circumminxit vestimentaque sua, et

---

H

61 7 illam *add. Buecheler* autem *om. patavina* venerarias] venerias *Scheffer* benemoria *Orelli*: bene moriar 8 Si … fefellitus sum *non omnino a codice vel lingua abhorrendum; versionem Anglicam videas* 9 *add. Buecheler* **62** Capuae] Capua *Anton:* Capuam *Scheffer* 3 apoculamus *Scheffer*: apoculanius 4 ad stelas *Reiske*: stellas pergo *add. Heraeus* cunctabundus *Delz* stellas] stelas *Buecheler* 5 viam *Scheffer*: iam mihi [in] anima *Muncker*: in animo

Mind you, it was not for her body or the sex that I cared for her, so much as for her sweet nature. If I asked her for anything she never said no. If she earned a penny I'd have a ha'penny. Put it in her pocket and she'd never cheat me out of it. When her old man passed away out on the estate I decided by hook or by crook to be at her side. You know, 'a friend in need.'

62 "It chanced that the master had gone to Capua to take care of some odds and sods. Jumping at the opportunity, I persuaded a house guest to come with me as far as the fifth milestone. He was a soldier too, strong as all get-out. Off we shagged at about cockcrow, with the moon still shining bright as day. When we got to the cemetery, my companion went to relieve himself against the stones as I wandered on, humming and counting the stars. After a moment, looking round for him, I saw he'd disrobed and placed all his clothes beside the road. My heart jumped into my mouth and I stood rooted like a corpse while he urinated around them – and suddenly he had turned into – a wolf!

subito lupus factus est. Nolite me iocare putare; ut
7 mentiar, nullius patrimonium tanti facio. Sed, quod
8 coeperam dicere, postquam lupus factus est, ululare coepit
et in silvas fugit. Ego primitus nesciebam ubi essem, deinde
9 accessi, ut vestimenta eius tollerem: illa autem lapidea
facta sunt. Qui mori timore nisi ego? Gladium tamen strinxi
et mataiotata umbras cecidi, donec ad villam amicae meae
10 pervenirem. In larvam intravi, paene animam ebullivi,
sudor mihi per bifurcum volabat, oculi mortui, vix unquam
11 refectus sum. Melissa mea mirari coepit, quod tam sero
ambularem et 'Si ante,' inquit, 'venisses, saltem nobis
adiutasses; lupus enim villam intravit et omnia pecora
<laniavit>. Tamquam lanius sanguinem illis misit. Nec tamen
derisit, etiam si fugit; servus enim noster lancea collum
12 eius traiecit.' Haec ut audivi, operire oculos amplius non
potui, sed luce clara hac nostri domum fugi tamquam copo
compilatus, et postquam veni in locum illum in quo lapidea
13 vestimenta erant facta, nihil inveni nisi sanguinem. Ut vero
domus veni, iacebat miles meus in lecto tamquam bovis, et
collum illius medicus curabat. Intellexi illum versipellem

H

62 9 mataiotata *percipio* ex mataiotatos *Kelly*: ma tan Hekatan *Heraeus*: matauitatau H *de onomatopoeia fortasse; adiunct.videas* 10 undabat *Nisbet* 11 coepit *del. Fraenkel* villam] ovilia *George lac. ind. Buecheler, Hofmann anacoluthon; sed sic suppleo, vel* necavit; *adiunct.vide* 12 clara hac nostri H *volo*

Don't think I'm joking. I wouldn't lie for any money. Well, as I was saying, he turned into a wolf, howled, and ran off into the forest. For a moment I hadn't a clue where I was. But then I came back to pick up his clothes. They'd turned into stone! I almost died of fright, like no one before. I managed to draw my sword, and, whacking all the time uselessly at the shadows, I arrived at my girlfriend's house, white as a ghost, near death, sweat in rivers down my thighs, eyes glazed over. I almost didn't pull through.

"Melissa was surprised at me being on the road so late: 'If you'd come earlier,' she said, 'at least you could have helped us. A wolf got into the compound and killed all the sheep – spilled their blood like a butcher. He didn't get the last laugh, though he got away. One of our servants ran his neck through with a spear.' On hearing this I could close my eyes no more.

"When it was broad daylight I high-tailed it back to the master Gaius' home like a pilfered publican. Arriving at the spot where the clothes had turned into stone, all I found was blood. When I finally got home my soldier friend was on his bed, stretched out like an ox, with a doctor tending to his neck. I knew then he was a werewolf, and – ever afterwards –

nec postea cum illo panem gustare potui, non si me
14 occidisses. Viderint qui de hoc aliter exopinassent:
ego si mentior, genios vestros iratos habeam."

63 Attonitis admiratione universis, "Salvo," inquit
Trimalchio, "tuo sermone si qua fides est, ut mihi pili
horruerunt, quia scio Niceronem nihil nugarum narrare;
2 immo certus est et minime linguosus. Nam et ipse vobis
3 rem horribilem narrabo: asinus in tegulis. Cum adhuc
capillatus essem, nam a puero vitam Chiam gessi,
ipsimi nostri delicatus decessit, mehercules margaritum
4 catamitus] et omnium nummorum. Cum ergo illum mater
misella plangeret et nostrum plures in tristimonio essemus,
subito strigae coeperunt: putares canem leporem persequi.
5 habebamus tunc hominem Cappadocem, longum, valde audaculum,
6 et qui valebat: poterat bovum iratum tollere. Hic audacter
stricto gladio extra ostium procucurrit, involuta sinistra
curiose, et mulierem tamquam hoc loco – salvum sit quod tango –

H

62 14 qui de hoc aliter *lego*: alii quid de hoc *Buecheler*: qui hoc de alibi **63** inquit Trimalchio *ordo meus*: inquit tuo sermone 3 ipsimi nostri *Scheffer*: ipim mostri 4 catamitus *Jacobs ex caccitus* H *memoriam non Petronii recuperat sed glossae in codice; ergo delevi* nummorum *ego; cf.* 69.8: numerum 4 nostrum plures *Heinze*: nos tum plures 5 valebat *susp. Giardina et Melloni* poterat *om. patavina* bovem *Reiske*: iovem

I couldn't break bread with him, not even if you'd have killed me. If people have another explanation for this, that's their lookout. But if I'm lying, sick your angry guardian spirits on me."

63 All were dumbfounded. "I believe your story," said Trimalchio. "And, honestly, it made my skin creep, since I know Niceros doesn't tell tall tales – always straight and to the point. Anyway, I've got a scary one too – really weird. When I still wore my hair long (and even as a boy I lived in the lap of luxury), one of the master's favourite boys died. God, he was a pearl beyond price! So as his heartbroken mother was mourning him, with a good many of us sharing in the sorrow, suddenly the witches started up. You'd think it was a hare with a dog on its tail.

"In those days we had a Cappadocian servant, tall, completely fearless, and strong enough to lift an angry bull. This fellow boldly drew his sword, dashed outside with left arm carefully wrapped, and ran one of the women through the middle: right about here – touch wood.

mediam traiecit. Audimus gemitum, et – plane non mentiar –
7 ipsas non vidimus. Baro autem noster introversus
se proiecit in lectum, et corpus totum lividum
habebat quasi flagellis caesus, quia scilicet illum
8 tetigerat mala manus. Nos cluso ostio redimus iterum ad
officium, sed dum mater amplexaret corpus filii sui,
tangit et videt manuciolum de stramentis factum. Non cor
habebat, non intestina, non quicquam: scilicet iam puerum
strigae involaverunt et supposuerant stramenticium
9 vavatonem. Rogo vos, oportet credatis, sunt mulieres
plussciae, sunt Nocturnae, et quod sursum est, deorsum
10 faciunt. Ceterum baro ille longus post hoc factum numquam
coloris sui fuit, immo post paucos dies phreneticus periit."

64 Miramur nos et pariter credimus, osculatique mensam
rogamus Nocturnas ut suis teneant, dum redimus a cena.
2 Et sane iam lucernae mihi plures videbantur ardere
totumque triclinium esse mutatum, cum Trimalchio, "Tibi
dico," inquit, "Plocame, nihil narras? Nihil nos
delectaris? Et solebas suavius esse, canturire belle
deverbia, adicere melica[m]. Heu, heu, abistis, dulces
3 caricae." "Iam," inquit ille, "quadrigae meae
decucurrerunt, ex quo podagricus factus sum. Alioquin cum

H

63 6 gemitum et] gemitum sed *Jacobs*: gemitum at *Scheffer*

64 2 suavius *Buecheler*: suavis belle deverbia adicere melicam] belle melicam, deverbia adicere *Goesius*

We didn't actually see the witches, I must admit, but we heard the groan.

"Our giant came back inside and threw himself down on his bed, his whole body black and blue as if he'd been thrashed with whips. He'd obviously been touched by the evil hand. We barred the door and returned to our duties, and the boy's mother embraced the dead boy's body, only to feel and see – a straw doll! It had no heart, no gut, no nothing. Obviously the witches had made off with the child and left a straw doll behind. You'd do well to believe this, I tell you. There are women out there with supernatural powers – witches, who make things topsy-turvy. As for the giant, after this incident he never got his colour back and in fact died a few days later, out of his mind."

64 Again we marvelled and all believed, kissing the table and beseeching the witches to keep their distance as we made our way home from dinner.

To be sure, now the lighted lamps seemed to be multiplying and the whole dining room transforming as Trimalchio spoke. "Hey, Plocamus, don't you have a story? No entertainment for us? You used to be better company, with your poetry chanting and singing accompaniment. 'Ah, sweet figs of yesteryear!'"

"It was the gout," Plocamus replied, "that put an end to my galloping. And anyway,

essem adulescentulus, cantando paene tisicus factus sum.
4 Quid saltare? Quid deverbia? Quid tonstrinum? Quando
5 parem habui nisi unum Apelletem?" Oppositaque ad os manu
nescio quid taetrum exsibilavit, quod postea Graecum esse
affirmabat.

Nec non Trimalchio ipse cum tubicines esset imitatus,
6 ad delicias suas respexit, quem Croesum apellabat. Puer
autem lippus, sordidissimus dentibus, catellam nigram
atque indecenter pinguem prasina involvebat fascia
panemque semesum ponebat supra torum [atque] ac nausea
7 recusantem saginabat. Quo admonitus officio Trimalchio
Scylacem iussit adduci, "praesidium domus familiaeque."
Nec mora, ingentis formae adductus est canis catena
vinctus, admonitusque ostiarii calce ut cubaret, ante
8 mensam se posuit. Tum Trimalchio iactans candidum panem,
9 "Nemo," inquit "in domo mea me plus amat." Indignatus
puer, quod Scylacem tam effuse laudaret, catellam in
terram deposuit hortatusque <est> ut ad rixam properaret.
Scylax, canino scilicet usus ingenio, taeterrimo latratu
triclinium implevit Margaritam Croesi paene laceravit.
10 Nec intra rixam tumultus constitit, sed candelabrum etiam
supra mensam eversum et omnia vasa crystallina comminuit

H

64 5 apposita *Heinze* 6 sordidissimis *Scheffer*: sordidissimus semesum *Burman*: semissem *del. Buecheler* ac *Buecheler*: hac 9 terra *patavina add. Buecheler, qui* scilicet canino *"praestat"*

as a young man I sang so much I nearly brought on consumption. Dancing? Recitation? Harmonies? No one could hold a candle to me, except maybe Apelles." He then stuck a hand against his mouth and lisped out something awful, which, after he had finished, he assured us was Greek.

This tempted Trimalchio into doing an imitation of trumpet playing – until he looked over to his pet boy, whom he called Croesus. This was a blear-eyed, rotten- toothed child who was wrapping an obscenely fat puppy in a green scarf and stuffing it to the point of bursting with the half-eaten bread he was laying on the couch. This attention gave Trimalchio a thought, and he commanded the presence of Scylax, "Guardian of the Home and Hearth." In no time at all, in was led on a chain a gigantic hound. After a kick from the porter for encouragement, it laid itself down before the table. Trimalchio flipped it some white bread. "In my whole house," he said, "nobody loves me more than him."

The boy took offence at this effusive praise of Scylax, so he deposited his puppy on the floor and goaded it into starting a fight. Scylax, no doubt responding to some normal canine instinct, filled the dining room with the most frightful barking and then almost tore Croesus' Margarita limb from limb. The hubbub did not stop there, for the very candelabrum upon the table tipped over, shattering all the glassware into little pieces and

11 et oleo ferventi aliquot convivas respersit. Trimalchio
ne videretur iactura motus, basiavit puerum ac iussit
12 supra dorsum ascendere suum. Non moratus ille usus <est>
equo manuque plana scapulas eius subinde verberavit,
interque risum proclamavit, "Bucca, bucca, quot sunt hic?"
13 Repressus ergo aliquamdiu Trimalchio camellam grandem
iussit misceri <et> potiones dividi omnibus servis, qui
ad pedes stabant, adiecta exceptione: "Si quis," inquit,
"noluerit accipere, capit illi perfunde. Interdiu severa
nunc hilaria."

65 Hanc humanitatem insecutae sunt matteae, quarum
etiam recordatio me, si qua est dicenti fides, offendit.
2 Singulae enim gallinae altiles [pro turdis] circumlatae
sunt et ova anserina pilleata, quae ut comessemus
ambitiosissime <a> nobis Trimalchio petiit, dicens
3 exossatas esse gallinas. Inter haec triclinii valvas
lictor percussit, amictusque veste alba cum ingenti
4 frequentia comissator intravit. Ego maiestate conterritus
praetorem putabam venisse. Itaque temptavi assurgere et
5 nudos pedes in terram deferre. Risit hanc trepidationem
Agamemnon et, "Contine te," inquit, "homo stultissime.
Habinnas sevir est idemque lapidarius, qui vide[re]tur
monimenta optime facere."

H

64 12 *add. Buecheler* plana *Scheffer*: plena 13 *add. Anton:* potionesque *Buecheler* **65** 2 *deleo add. Scheffer*

showering some of the guests with hot oil. Not wanting to appear upset at the breakage, Trimalchio kissed the boy and told him to climb onto his back. The boy quickly mounted his horsey and proceeded to whack Trimalchio on the shoulders over and over with the flat of his hand, amid laughter, crying, "Bucky, Bucky, how many fingers?" Momentarily subdued, Trimalchio ordered a large punch bowl to be mixed, with drinks to be apportioned to all the slaves standing on duty, but with the following caveat: "If anyone refuses to drink, stick his head in it. Daytime's for serious, night time's for fun!"

65 This generous gesture was followed by dainties, the very memory of which revolts me, to tell the truth. Instead of getting thrushes, we were handed round a fat capon each, and goose eggs wearing bonnets. Trimalchio was most insistent that we eat them, saying they were "boneless poultry."

As this took place, an escort struck upon the doors of the dining room and there entered a white-tunicked celebrant at the head of a substantial retinue. I panicked at the pomp, thinking a praetor was visiting, and struggled to rise and plant my bare feet upon the floor. Agamemnon laughed at my consternation. "Get a grip, you silly man!" he said. "It's Habinnas the city councillor, a stonemason reputed to make the finest tombstones."

6 Recreatus hoc sermone reposui cubitum, Habinnamque
7 intrantem cum admiratione ingenti spectabam. Ille autem
iam ebrius uxoris suae umeris imposuerat manus,
oneratusque aliquot coronis et unguento per frontem in
oculos fluente praetorio loco se posuit continuoque vinum
8 et caldum poposcit. Delectatus hac Trimalchio hilaritate
et ipse capaciorem poposcit scyphum quaesivit quomodo
9 acceptus esset. "Omnia," inquit, "habuimus praeter te;
10 oculi enim mei hic erant. Et mehercules bene fuit. Scissa
lautum novendiale servo suo misello faciebat, quem
mortuum manu miserat. Et puto, cum vicensimariis magnam
mantissam habet; quinquaginta enim millibus aetimant
11 mortuum. Sed tamen suaviter fuit, etiam si coacti sumus
66 dimidias potiones supra ossucula eius effundere." Tamen,
inquit Trimalchio, "quid habuistis in cena?" "Dicam,"
inquit, "si potuero; nam tam bene memoriae sum, ut
2 frequenter nomen meum obliviscar. Habuimus tamen in primo
porcum botulo coronato et circa sangunculum et gizeria
facta et certe betam et panem autopyrum de suo sibi,
quem ego malo quam candidum; et vires facit, et cum
3 mea re causa facio, non ploro. Sequens ferculum fuit
sc[i]rib[i]lita frigida et supra mel caldum infusum

H
65 8 Trimalchio hac *Buecheler in adn.* 10 lautum novendiale *Buecheler*: laucum novendialem **66** 2 butulo *Jac. Gronovius:* poculo sangunculum *Heraeus*: saucunculum certe] circa *prop. Buecheler; vide* 66.4 3 *corr. patavina*

Reassured by this explanation, I settled down again and watched the entrance of Habinnas with vast admiration. Of course he was intoxicated by now, and was resting his hands upon his wife's shoulders. Staggering beneath several wreaths, perfume running down his forehead and into his eyes, he plopped down into the place of honour and called immediately for wine and warm water. Trimalchio was delighted by this show of spirit and ordered a larger cup for himself as he asked Habinnas how he had been treated. "We had everything," he said, "except you. So my eyes were elsewhere. Still, we had a really good time. Scissa put on a nice ninth day funeral party for an unfortunate slave of hers whom she freed when he died. She'll be paying a pretty penny in manumission tax, I expect, since the deceased's fortune is valued at fifty thousand. But it all went well despite having to pour half our drink over his remains."

66 "But what did you have for dinner?" asked Trimalchio. "I'll tell you, if I can remember," replied Habinnas. "My memory's so great I often forget my own name. Anyway, for the first course we had pig in a wreath of sausage links, garnished with blood puddings and giblets, cooked to perfection, and beets, of course, and real wholemeal bread, which I prefer over white because it builds you up, and when I go to the bathroom no regrets. Second course was chilled honey tart doused with a warmed concoction of

excellente Hispanum. Itaque de sc[i]rib[i]lita quidem non
4 minimum edi, de melle me usque tetigi. Circa cicer et
lupinum, calvae arbitratu et mala singula. Ego tamen duo
sustuli et ecce in mappa alligata habeo; nam si aliquid
5 muneris meo vernulae non tulero, habebo convicium. Bene
me admonet domina mea. In prospecto habuimus ursinae
frust[r]um, de quo cum imprudens Scintilla gustasset, paene
6 intestina sua vomuit; ego contra plus libram comedi, nam
ipsum aprum sapiebat. Et si, inquam, ursus homuncionem
7 comest, quanto magis homuncio debet ursum comesse? In
summo habuimus caseum mollem ex sapa et cocleas singulas
et cordae frusta et hepatia in catillis et ova pilleata et
rapam et senape et catillum concacatum, pax Palamedes. Etiam
in alveo circumlata sunt oxycomina, unde quidem etiam
improbe ternos pugnos sustulerunt. Nam pernae missionem
67 dedimus. Sed narra mihi, Gai, rogo, Fortunata quare non
2 recumbit?" "Quomodo nosti," inquit, "illam," Trimalchio:
"nisi argentum composuerit, nisi reliquias pueris diviserit,
3 aquam in os suum non conieciet." "Atqui," respondit Habinnas,
"nisi illa discumbit, ego me apoculo." Et coeperat surgere,
nisi signo dato Fortunata quater amplius a tota familia esset
4 vocata. Venit ergo galbino succincta cingillo, ita ut infra

---

H

66 7 ex sapa *Buecheler*: et sapa concacatum *Burman*: concagatum palam aedes *Öberg* improbe *Mueller*: improbi *post Jac. Gronovio Buecheler in adn.*: improbiter nos pugno **67** apoculo *patavina;* 62.3

vintage Spanish wine. So I had plenty of the tart, and honey up to here. Dried chickpeas and lupins were out, with all the filberts we wanted and an apple for each guest. But I took two – and here they are wrapped in my napkin – since if I don't bring a gift back to my favourite boy I'll have a row on my hands, as my wife did well to remind me. We had bear steak laid out for us, which Scintilla carelessly tucked into, and then she almost threw up her guts. But I ate more than a pound. It tastes like boar. If bears eat people, I argue, all the more reason for people to eat bears. As the last course we had creamed cheese in wine sauce, one snail each, pieces of tripe, side dishes of liver, eggs in bonnets, and a godawful stew (sorry, Palamedes), with turnip and mustard greens in it. We even had cumin seed munchies, brought round in a basket, from which the greedy ones took several handfuls. We passed on the ham.

67 "But tell me, Gaius, if you please: why isn't Fortunata dining with us?" "Oh, you know her," Trimalchio replied. "Until she's put out the silverware and doled out the leftovers to the boys, she won't touch a drop of water." "Well," said Habinnas, "if she doesn't come and take her place I'm buggering off." And he'd have risen to his feet unless, at a signal, Fortunata was shouted for close to five times by the combined staff, and in she came, dress hitched tight by a yellow sash, with the effect of revealing

cerasina appareret tunica et periscelides tortae
5 phaecasiaeque inauratae. Tunc sudario manus tergens,
quod in collo habebat, applicat se illi toro, in quo
Scintilla Habinnae discumbebat uxor, osculatque
plaudentem, "Est te," inquit, "videre?" …
6 Eo deinde perventum est, ut Fortunata armillas suas
crassissimis detraheret lacertis Scintillaeque miranti
ostenderet. Ultimo etiam periscelides resolvit et
7 reticulum aureum, quem ex obrussa esse dicebat. Notavit
haec Trimalchio iussitque afferri omnia et "Videtis,"
inquit, "mulieris compedes: sic nos barcalae despoliamur.
Sex pondo et selibram debet habere. Et ipse nihilo minus
habeo decem pondo armillam ex millesimis Mercurii factam."
8 Ultimo etiam, ne mentiri videretur, stateram iussit
9 afferri et circumlatum approbari pondus. Nec melior
Scintilla, quae de cervice sua capsellam detraxit
aureolam, quam Felicionem appellabat. Inde duo crotalia
protulit et Fortunatae in vicem consideranda dedit et,
"Domini," inquit, "mei beneficio nemo habet meliora."
10 "Quid," inquit Habinnas, "excatarissasti me, ut tibi
emerem fabam vitream? Plane si filiam haberem, auriculas
illi praeciderem. Mulieres si non essent, omnia pro luto

H
67 5 *an* manus sudario? *vide* 67.13 faciem sudario *lac. ind. Buecheler* 6 ex obrussa *patavina*: ex sobriissa 7 mulieris *Mentel*: muliebres *Heinze*: mulieres 8 ultimo etiam *iteratum non concinne* circumlatum *Heinze*: circulatum H: *cur non* circumlatam

below it a cerise petticoat, twisted stockings, and gilt slippers. She wiped her hands on a cloth that she kept tucked into her neck, slid onto the couch containing Scintilla, Habinnas' wife, and kissed her welcoming friend. "Is it really you I see?" she said …

By now we had got to the point where Fortunata removed the bangles from her great fat arms to show them off for Scintilla's admiration. She finally even undid her stockings and gold hairnet, which she said was of pure spun gold. Trimalchio took stock of this and commanded all her jewellery to be brought. "Behold, the shackles of a woman!" he said: "That's where our money goes, poor slobs that we are. She must have three kilos of stuff here, not counting this ten-pound armlet of mine out of the point-zero-one per cent Mercury tax." To prove he wasn't lying, he then even had a scale brought in so that the weight could be passed around for verification.

Not to be outdone, Scintilla pulled off her necklace with its golden locket (which she referred to as Felicio), taking out of it a pair of ear-rings which she presented for Fortunata's personal inspection. "Thanks to the generosity of my husband," she said, "nobody's got better ones." "What!" exclaimed Habinnas. "Cleaned me out for a couple of glass beans? If I had a daughter I'd make sure to cut off her ear lobes! If women didn't exist,

haberemus; nunc hoc est caldum potare et frigidum meiere."
11 Interim mulieres sauciae inter se riserunt ebriaque
iunxerunt oscula, dum altera diligentiam matris familiae
12 iactat, altera delicias et indiligentiam viri. Dumque sic
cohaerent, Habinnas furtim consurrexit pedesque Fortunatae
13 correptos super lectum immisit. "Au, au," illa proclamavit,
aberrante tunica super genua. Composita ergo in gremio
Scintillae incensissimam rubore faciem sudario abscondit.

68 Interposito deinde spatio cum secundas mensas
Trimalchio iussisset afferri, sustulerunt servi omnes
mensas et alias attulerunt, scobemque croco et minio
tinctam sparserunt et, quod numquam ante videram, ex
2 lapide speculari pulverem tritum. Statim Trimalchio
"Poteram quidem," inquit, "hoc fer[i]culo esse contentus;
secundas habetis mensas. <Sed> si quid belli habes, affer."
3 Interim puer Alexandrinus, qui caldam ministrabat,
luscinias coepit imitari clamante Trimalchione subinde:
4 "Muta." Ecce alius ludus. Servus qui ad pedes Habinnae
sedebat, iussus, credo, a domino proclamavit subito
canora voce
"Interea medium Aeneas iam classe tenebat."

H
67 10 c. m. et f. p. H; *adiunct. videas* 11 ebriaque *Mueller*: ebrieque indulgentiam *patavina* 12 correptos *Scheffer*: correctos 13 incensissimam *Reinesius*: indecens imam
68 2 *corr. patavina add. Buecheler Verg. Aen.* 5.1

we'd get everything cheap as the dirt, but now, instead, all we do is drink in warm and piss out cold."

Meanwhile the two women were giggling tipsily together and sharing woozy hugs and kisses, with one touting herself as a diligent wife and the other a negligent husband with a toyboy habit. Thus collapsed in one another's arms, Habinnas stole up, grabbed Fortunata by the feet, and swung her over the back of the couch. "Oh! Oh!" she cried, as her shift rode up over her knees. Settling into Scintilla's lap, she buried her furious blushes behind a handkerchief.

68 There was a brief interval, after which Trimalchio commanded the service of the second setting. Slaves removed the entire first setting and replaced it with the new one, scattering sawdust tinted with saffron and red lead and mixed with powdered mica – a touch I hadn't seen before. Trimalchio promptly remarked, "I could have just settled for what you see, since there is your second setting, but we should have something nice to put on it, I suppose."

Meanwhile an Alexandrian boy, providing the warm water, gave an imitation of a nightingale's song, with Trimalchio shouting all the while, "Change it! Change it!" That was another gag. The slave sitting at the feet of Habinnas, at the prompting of his master, I suppose, suddenly declaimed in singsong tones:

"Meanwhile the main with fleet did Aeneas hold."

Both wives had reason to complain, as did Scintilla at *Sat.* 69. 1, and Fortunata at *Sat.* 74. 9 ff. Here scholars differ on who said what: my view of the order is first Scintilla, then Fortunata, who was perhaps known for strong views on the subject (see *Sat.* 74.9), and paid the penalty of humiliation.

5 Nullus sonus umquam acidior percussit aures meas; nam
praeter errantis barbariae aut adiectum aut deminutum
clamorem miscebat Atellanicos versus, ut tunc primum
6 me etiam Vergilius offenderet. Lassus tamen cum aliquando
desisset, adiecit Habinnas: "Et numquam didicit. Sed ego
7 ad circulatores eum mittendo erudibam. Itaque parem non
habet, sive muliones volet sive gingriatores imitari.
Desperatum valde ingeniosus est: idem sutor, idem cocus,
8 idem pistor, omnis musae mancipium. Duo tamen vitia habet,
quae si non haberet, esset omnium nummorum: recutitus est
et stertit. Nam quod strabonus est, non curo: sic Venus
spectat. Ideo nihil iacet, vix. oculo mortuo umquam. Illum
69 emi trecentis denariis." Interpellavit loquentem Scintilla
et, "Plane," inquit, "non omnia artificia servi nequam
2 narras. Agaga est; at curabo, stigmam habeat." Risit
Trimalchio et, "Agnosco," inquit, "Cappadocem: nihil sibi
defraudat. Et mehercules laudo illum; hoc enim nemo parentat.

H

68 5 adiectum *Scheffer*: abiectum deminutum *Scheffer*: diminutum offenderet *scribo*: offenderit 6 desisset *Scheffer*: dedisset numquam *Buecheler*: numquid erudibam *Buecheler*: erudiebam *Jahn*: audibant 7 gingriatores *Öberg*: circulatores desperatum *Buecheler*: desperatus 8 vitia *patavina*: vina iacet *scribo; adiunct. videas*: tacet emi trecentis *Scheffer*: emit retentis **69** 2 agnosco *scribo*: adcognosco defraudat *Hadrianides*: defraudit

No more grating sound ever struck upon my ears, since on top of noisily wandering up and down the keys in an atrocious foreign accent he threw in some Atellan verses – to the point that then for the first time even Vergil gave offence.

When at length the boy grew tired and stopped, Habinnas interjected: "And he got no formal training. I had him taught by just sending him round with the hawkers. The result is that no one can touch him when it comes to impersonating mule skinners and hawkers. He's so incredibly talented. He can sew, cook and bake – a jack of all trades. But he's got two faults, without which he'd be a 'Ten': he's circumcised and he snores. I don't count the squint, since Venus herself has a cast in her eye. But he never lies down and closes an eye. I bought him for three hundred denarii."

69 Scintilla interjected at this point: "Of course," she said, "you'll be leaving out all of this no-good slave's other tricks? He's a little pimp and I'll have him branded for it!" Trimalchio chuckled. "There's a Cappadocian for you," he said. "He doesn't sell himself short and by god I credit him for it. You can't wait for your funeral.

3 Tu autem, Scintilla, noli zelotypa esse. Crede mihi
vos novimus. Sic me salvum habeatis, ut ego sic solebam
ipsumam debattuere, ut etiam dominus suspicaretur:
et ideo me in vilicationem relegavit. Sed tace, lingua,
4 dabo panem." Tamquam laudatus esset nequissimus servus
lucernam de sinu fictilem protulit et amplius semihora
tubicines imitatus est succinente Habinna et inferius
5 labrum manu deprimente. Ultimo etiam in medium processit
et modo harundibus quassis choraulas imitatus est, modo
lacernatus cum flagellis mulionumm fata egit, donec vocatum
ad se Habinnas basiavit, potionemque illi porrexit, et,
"Tanto melior," inquit, "Massa, dono tibi caligas."

6 Nec ullus tot malorum finis fuisset, nisi epidipnis
allata, turdi siliginei uvis passis nucibus farsi.
7 Insecuta sunt Cydonia mala etiam spinis confixa, ut echinos
effingerent. Et haec quidem tolerabilia erant, si non
fer[i]culum longe monstrosius effecisset ut vel fame perire
8 mallemus. Nam cum positus esset, ut nos putabamus, anser
altilis circa pisces et omnium genera avium, "<Amici,>"
inquit Trimalchio, "quicquid videtis hic positum, de uno
9 corpore est factum." Ego, scilicet homo prudentissimus,

H

69 3 lingua *Scheffer*: linguam ammeam H 5 imitatus est *del. Fraenkel* 6 turdi siliginei *Heinze*: turdis iligine 7 mala etiam *transposui; cf.* 74.1 lucernamque etiam mero ut echinos effingerent *ego post Heinze*: ut echinos efficerent 8 genera avium: generum aves *maluit Buecheler in adn.* *add. Buecheler*

And you, Scintilla, don't be jealous. Believe me, we know you women. So help me if I didn't use to whack my mistress, to the point that even the master got suspicious. So he kicked me upstairs to country bailiff. But soft, my tongue: you shall have bread."

Acting as if he had been paid a compliment, the awful slave produced a clay lamp from his pocket and for a good half-hour did his trumpeter imitation, with Habinnas humming along as he pulled down his lower lip. Eventually the boy marched into the middle and first impersonated a flute soloist with a cracked flute, followed by the "Mule Skinner Blues," complete with cloak and whip, until finally Habinnas called him over for a kiss and handed him a drink. "Good boy, Massa," he said. "Some new boots for you."

There would have been no end to our ills had not the dessert arrived: pastry thrushes stuffed with nuts and raisins. This was followed by quinces pinned with toothpicks to make them look like sea urchins. Even all this would have been tolerable had not a dish far more appalling made us wish to die of hunger first. A dressed goose (as we supposed) was set down, ringed by fish and birds of all kinds. "Friends," said Trimalchio, "all you see on this dish has been made out of one ingredient." Of course I, being a very smart fellow, knew instantly what this was about.

statim intellexi quid esset, et respiciens Agamemnon,
"Mirabor," inquam, "nisi omnia ista de <cera> facta
sunt aut certe de luto. Vidi Roma Saturnalibus eiusmodi
70 cenarum imaginem fieri." Necdum finieram sermonem, cum
Trimalchio ait: "Ita crescam, patrimonio non corpore, ut
2 ista cocus meus de porco fecit. Non potest esse pretiosior
homo. Volueris, de vulva faciet piscem, de lardo palumbum,
de perna turturem, de collepio Gallinam. Et ideo ingenio
meo impositum est illi nomen bellissimum; nam Daedalus
3 vocatur. Et quia bonam mentem habet, attuli illi Roma
munus cultros Norico ferro." Quos statim iussit afferri
ut mucronem ad buccam probaremus.

4 Subito intraverunt duo servi, tamquam rixam ad
lacum fecissent; certe in collo adhuc amphoras habebant.
5 Cum ergo Trimalchio ius inter litigantes diceret, neuter
sententiam tulit decernentis, sed alterius amphoram fuste
6 percussit. Consternati nos [insolentia ebriorum] intentavimus
oculos in proeliantes notavimusque ostrea e gastris
7 labentia, quae collecta puer lance circumtulit. Has
lautitias aequavit ingeniosus cocus; in craticula enim

H
69 9 *suppl. Heinze* **70** vulva *Scheffer*: bulla 3 attuli *Heinze*: attulit miratus [est] *Kaibel* 4 collo *Heinze*: loco
6 ebriorum *non placet; an servorum, quod reiecit Buecheler in adn. perplexe; conatur* <velut> ebriorum *Fuchs damnavi*
gastris *Muncker*: castris

Looking over to Agamemnon, "I shouldn't wonder," I said, "if they're all made out of wax, or more likely clay. In Rome I've seen artificial food like this during the Saturnalia."

70 Barely had I finished before Trimalchio spoke up. "I'll stake my fortune, if not my waistline, on my cook's making all of this out of – pork. There's no one alive more valuable. Just ask, and he'll turn a fish out of a sow's womb, a rock pigeon out of lard, a turtle dove out of a ham, or a hen out of a pig's knuckle. So I had the fine idea of giving him the perfect name for him: Daedalus. And because he's got a good head on him I brought him a present from Rome of kitchen knives of Norican steel." Instantly he ordered them to be brought in for our inspection and led the admiration. He even suggested we test the blades for sharpness against our cheeks.

There suddenly entered a pair of slaves who looked as if they'd been quarrelling at the water trough. At all events they still had jars upon their necks. Trimalchio proceeded to pronounce the law on their rival positions, a ruling which neither party accepted, and they took to smashing the other's jar with sticks. It was an unsetttling scene, so we stared intently at the combatants, only to note oysters and scallops slithering out of their large jars – which a boy gathered up and sent around on a tray. Our ingenious cook proved equal to these marvels as, singing in an unpleasant, quavering voice, he produced snails on a silver platter.

argentea cochleas attulit et tremula taeterrima voce
cantavit.
8 Pudet referre quae secuntur: inaudito enim more
pueri capillati attulerunt unguentum in argentea pelve
pedesque recumbentium unxerunt, cum ante crura talosque
9 corollis vinxissent. Hinc ex eodem unguento in vinarium
atque lacernam aliquantum est infusum.
10 Iam coeperat Fortunata velle saltare, iam Scintilla
frequentius plaudebat quam loquebatur, cum Trimalchio,
"Permitto," inquit, "Philargyre [et Cario] etsi prasinianus
famosus, dic et Menophilae, contubernali tuae, discumbat."
11 Quid multa? Paene de lectis deicti sumus, adeo totum
12 triclinium triclinium familia occupaverat. Certe ego notavi
super me positum cocum, qui de porco anserem fecerat, muria
13 condimentis fetentem. Nec contentus fuit recumbere, sed
continuo Ephesum tragoedum coepit imitare et subinde
dominum suum sponsione provocare, "si prasinus proximis
circensibus primam palmam."
71 Diffusus hac contentione Trimalchio, "Amici," inquit, "et
servi homines sunt et aeque unum lactem biberunt, etiam
si illos malus fatus oppresserit. Tamen me salvo cito
aquam liberam gustabunt. Ad summam, omnes illos in testamento
2 manumitto. Philargyro etiam fundum lego et

H
70 8 inaudito *patavina*: inauditu 9 aliquantum est *Heinze*: liquatum est: liquatum est [infusum] *Salonius* 10 *del. Kaibel*
71 oppressit *Buecheler*

It shames me to recount the sequel. In an unheard-of ceremony, long-haired boys brought in a silver bowl of perfume and, first making sure to wreathe shins and ankles in garlands, daubed the feet of the reclining guests. Afterwards they replenished lamp and wine bowl with some perfume remaining.

At which juncture Fortunata felt like dancing, while Scintilla was doing more clapping than talking. "Philargyrus," interposed Trimalchio, "you have my permission to join us, though you're a notorious fan of the Greens. And this goes for your woman Menophila too." Say no more: we were almost turfed out of our couches, as the entire staff laid claim to the dining room. I can confirm seeing down on my left the cook who had made a goose out of a pig, reeking of pickles and sauce. Not content only to recline, he instantly broke into impersonating Ephesus the tragic actor, with interludes of challenging the master to bet against the Greens at the next races.

71 His feistiness put Trimalchio in a mellow mood. "Friends," he said, "slaves are also people, and have drunk of the same mother's milk. Just oppressed by an evil fate. Still, if I live so long they'll soon be tasting the water of freedom. In fact I've manumitted the lot of them in my will. I've left Philargyrus a property also, and his woman; and, to Cario, in addition

contubernalem suam, Carioni quoque insulam et vicesimam
3 et lectum stratum. Nam Fortunatam meam heredem
facio, et commendo illam omnibus amicis meis. Et haec
ideo omnia publico, ut familia mea iam nunc sic me amet
4 tamquam mortuum." Gratias agere omnes indulgentiae
coeperant domini, cum ille oblitus nugarum exemplar
testimenti iussit afferri et totum a primo ad ultimum
5 ingemescente familia recitavit. Respicatus deinde
Habinnam, "Quid dicis," inquit, "amice carissime?
6 Aedificas monimentum meum, quamadmodum te iussi? Valde
te rogo ut secundum pedes statuae meae catellam pingas
et coronas et unguenta et Petraitis omnes pugnas, ut mihi
contingat tuo beneficio post mortem vivere; praeterea ut
sint in fronte pedes centum, in agrum pedes ducenti.
7 Omnes genus enim poma volo sint circa cineres meos, et
vinearum largiter. Valde enim falsum est vivo quidem
domos cultas esse, non curari eas ubi diutius nobis
habitandum est. Et ideo ante omnia adici volo: 'Hoc
8 monimentum heredem non sequatur.' Ceterum erit mihi
curae ut testamento caveam ne mortuus iniuriam accipiam.
Praeponam enim unum ex libertis sepulcro meo custodiae
9 causa, ne in monumentum meum populus cacatum currat. Te
rogas ut naves etiam [monimenti mei] facis plenis velis

H

71 6 pingas] ponas *Buecheler*: fingas *Scheffer* 7 sequatur] sequitur *Buecheler* 9 *del. Mueller*: <in fronte> monumenti *Keller*: <in lateribus> monumenti *Buecheler in adn.*

an apartment block, his five per cent tax and his funeral costs. Fortunata's my principal trustee, and I commend her now to all my friends. I am announcing this now to let my staff show their love as if I had died."

All were proclaiming their thanks for their master's generosity when Trimalchio, dispensing with the preliminaries, commanded a copy of his Will to be provided. He then recited the whole thing from beginning to end, to the groans of his servants. Next he looked up at Habinnas. "What say you, dear friend?" he asked. "Will you build my tomb according to my instructions? I remind you especially to paint my puppy at the foot of my statue, with garlands and perfumes and all the fights of Petraites, so I can enjoy them when I die, courtesy of your kindness.

"I'd like a hundred feet of frontage and two hundred feet of depth into the field, since I want fruit trees of all kinds growing around my remains, with plenty of vines. It's really wrong to keep fine houses when we're alive and take no trouble on the ones we'll have to spend more time in. So I want the following put in the most prominent spot:

THIS TOMB NOT TO GO TO THE HEIR.

In addition, I shall be providing by codicil that the deceased suffers no disrespect. I shall have a guard at the entrance to the tomb, one of my freedmen, to make sure it doesn't turn into a public shit house. I want you to do ships too, going under full sail, and me sitting on a platform in my purple toga,

euntes, et me in tribunali sedentem praetextatum cum
anulis aureis quinque et nummos in publico de sacculo
effundantem: scis enim quod epulum dedi binos denarios.
10 Faciantur, si tibi videtur, et triclinia. Facias et totum
11 populum sibi suaviter facientem. Ad dexteram meam ponas
statuam Fortunatae meae columbam tenentem; et catellam
cingulo alligatum ducat; et cicaronem meum, et amphoras
copiosas gypsatas, ne effluant vinum. Et unam licet fractam
sculpas, et super eqam puerum plorantem. Horologium in
medio, ut quisquis horas inspiciet, velit, nolit, nomen
12 meum leget. Inscriptio quoque vide diligenter si haec
satis idoneas tibi videtur:

'C. POMPEIUS TRIMALCHIO MAECENATIANUS HIC REQUIESCIT. HUIC SEVIRATUS ABSENTI DECRETUS EST. CUM POSSET IN OMNIBUS DECURIIS ROMAE ESSE, TAMEN NOLUIT. PIUS, FORTIS, FIDELIS, EX PARVO CREVIT: SESTERTIUM RELIQUIT TRECENTIES, NEC UMQUAM PHILOSOPHUM AUDIVIT. VALE: ET TU.'"

72 Haec ut dixit Trimalchio, flere coepit ubertim.
Flebat et Fortunata, flebat et Habinnas, tota denique
familia, tamquam in funus rogata, lamentatione triclinium
2 implevit. Immo iam coeperam etiam ego plorare, cum
Trimalchio, "Ergo," inquit, "cum sciamus nos morituros
3 esse, quare non vivamus? Sic vos felices videam: coniciamus

---

H

71 10 faciantur *Goesius*: faciatur facias *Buecheler*: facies *def. Öberg* 11 ponas *patavina*: pones copiosas] copiose *George* unam] urnam *Jac. Gronov.* 12 pius *Reinesius*: plus

wearing five gold rings, pouring money into the public coffers from my own purse. You know that banquet I gave at two denarii a head. If you approve, I'd like you to do dining rooms, and the whole town having a good time. On the right of me put Fortunata's statue, with a dove in her hand and leading a puppy in its harness. Do my little tyke also, and wine jars with plenty of corking to stop the wine leaking. But you can carve one broken, with a weeping boy hugging it. Put a clock right in the centre, so that someone who wants to know the time has to read my name, like it or not. As for the inscription, give careful thought as to whether you find this suitable:

> HERE LIES GAIUS POMPEIUS TRIMALCHIO MAECENATIANUS HONORARY CITY COUNCILLOR HE COULD HAVE GONE TO ROME AND JOINED ANY COMMITTEE BUT DECLINED LOYAL BRAVE CONSTANT HE STARTED WITH NOTHING AND LEFT BEHIND THREE HUNDRED MILLION WITHOUT ONCE LISTENING TO A PHILOSOPHER FAREWELL GAIUS FAREWELL READER.

72 After he had finished, Trimalchio began to weep extravagantly. Fortunata wept. Habinnas wept. Before long every member of the staff filled the dining room with lamentation as if attending a funeral. In fact even I had begun to weep when Trimalchio broke in. "So," he said, "since we know we are going to die why don't we live a little?

nos in balneum, meo periculo: non paenitebit. Sic calet
tamquam furnus." "Vero, vero," inquit Habinnas: "de una die
4 duas facere, nihil malo." Nudisque consurrexit pedibus
et Trimalchionem gaudentem subsequi <coepit>.
5 Ego respiciens ad Ascylton, "Quid cogitas," inquam,
6 "ego enim si videro balneum statim expirabo." "Assentemur,"
ait ille, "et dum illi balneum petunt, nos in turba exeamus."
7 Cum haec placuissent, ducente per porticam Gitone ad ianuam
venimus, ubi canis catenarius tanto nos tumultu excepit,
ut Ascylto etiam in piscinam ceciderit. Nec non ego quoque
[ebrius] <et> qui etiam pictum timueram canem, dum natanti opem
8 fero, in eandem gurgitem tractus sum. Servavit nos tamen
atriensis, qui interventu suo et canem placavit et nos
9 trementes extraxit in siccum. Et Giton quidem iam dudum se
ratione acutissima redemerat a cane; quicquid enim a nobis
acceperat de cena, <cani> latranti sparserat, at ille
10 avocatus cibo furorem suppresserat. Ceterum cum algentes
udique petissemus ab atriense ut nos extra ianuam emitteret,
"Erras," inquit, "si putas te exire hac posse qua venisti.
Nemo umquam convivarum per eandem ianuam emissus est; alia
73 intrant, alia exeunt." Quid faciamus homines miserrimi et novi

---

H

72 4 plaudentem *Jacobs et Wehle add. Burman*: subsequitur *Gaselee* 7 *add. Mueller*: *sed potius* ebrius *deleam* 9 se ratione *Scheffer*: servatione *supplevi* at *Wehle egoque*: et 10 udique *Buecheler olim*: utique *Buecheler serius cum* H

I want to see you having fun, so let's go jump in the bath, my treat. You won't be sorry. It's hot as a furnace." "Yes, yes!" said Habinnas, "Nothing better than making two days out of one! He rose to his bare feet and quickly followed his cheering host.

I looked over to Ascyltus. "What's your opinion?" I asked. "Me, if I so much as clap eyes on a bath I'll expire on the spot." "Let's go along with it," said he, "and while they're heading for the bath we'll exit in the crush." This was agreed, so Giton led us across the portico to the door, where a chained dog greeted us with such a racket that Ascyltus actually fell into the pool. As for myself, who had started at the mere picture of a dog, I also got dragged into the deep while attempting a swimmer-rescue.

The hall porter saved our lives, intervening to both calm the dog and pull us shivering onto dry land. As for Giton, he had long since bought off the dog with a very sharp piece of thinking. All the food left over from the dinner, which we had given to him, he scattered in front of the barking dog, which, distracted by it, put its rage on hold. But, cold and dripping wet, when we asked the porter to let us out the door, "You are mistaken," he replied, "if you think you can leave the same way you came. No guest is ever sent off through the same door. There's one for coming, another for going."

generis labyrintho inclusi, quibus lavari iam iam coeperat
2 votum esse? Ultro ergo rogavimus ut nos ad balneum duceret,
proiectisque vestimentis, quae Giton in aditu siccare coepit,
balneum intravimus, angustum scilicet [et cisternae frigidariae
simile], in quo Trimalchio rectus stabat. Ac ne sic quidem
putidissimam eius iactationem licuit effugere; nam nihil
melius esse dicebat quam sine turba lavari, et eo ipso loco
3 aliquando pistrinum fuisse. Deinde ut lassatus consedit,
invitatus balnei sono diduxit usque ad cameram os ebrium
et coepit Menecratis cantica lacerare, sicut illi dicebant
4 qui linguam eius intellegebant. Certi convivae circa labrum
manibus nexis currebant et gingilipho ingenti [clamore]
exsonabant. Alii autem [aut] restrictis manibus anulos de
pavimento conabantur tollere, aut posito genu cervices post
5 terga flectere et pedum extremes pollices tangere. Nos, dum
illi sibi ludos faciunt, in solium, quod Trimalchioni
vaporabatur, descendimus.

H

73 2 angustum scilicet *per ironiam intellegas*: et ... simile *delenda fortasse*: *alii alia membra deleverunt* in quo *Buecheler*: in qua eius iactationem *Heinze*: ei actionem 4 certi *Öberg*: ceteri *delevi post Smith*: ingenti clamore *del. Salonius* aut *del. Buecheler* 5 illi *Buecheler in altera*: alii solium *Buecheler*: solo vaporabatur *Buecheler*: pervapatur: parabatur H^m: praeparabatur *aut* temperabatur *Heinze lac. ind. Buecheler*

73 What were we to do, poor devils trapped in a modern labyrinth, to whom now even a hot bath seemed a devout wish? So we voluntarily asked to be taken there, threw off our clothes – which Giton commenced to dry in the anteroom – and entered the hot baths, which were about as small as one would expect.

There stood Trimalchio, upright, and not yet in a condition to allow us to escape his filthy bragging. He liked nothing better, said he, than to have his bath without the crowd, and that in fact at this very site there had once been a granary. As he grew tired he sat down, and, tempted by the bathroom acoustics, opened his mouth, slackened by drink, to the rafters and proceeded to mangle some of the songs of Menecrates – or so said those who understood his speech.

Most of the guests held hands and ran around the rim of the pool giggling at the tops of their voices, while some tried to pick quoits off the floor with hands fastened behind them, or got down on their knees and tried to bend their necks behind them to touch their toes. So while the others were engaged in these games we slipped into the hot tub that was being cranked up for Trimalchio.

Ergo ebrietate discussa in aliud triclinium deducti
sumus, ubi Fortunata disposuerat lautitias [suas ita ut
supra] ... lucernas aeneolosque piscatores notavimus
et mensas totas argenteas calicesque circa fictiles
6 inauratos et vinum in conspectu sacco defluens. Tum
Trimalchio, "Amici," inquit, "hodie servus meus
barbatoriam fecit, homo praefiscini frugi et micarius.
Itaque tangomenas faciamus et usque in lucem cenemus."

74 Haec dicente eo gallus gallinaceus cantavit. Qua voce
confusus Trimalchio vinum sub mensa iussit effundi
2 lucernam etiam mero spargi. Immo anulum traiecit in
dexteram manum et, "Non sine causa," inquit, "hic bucinus
signum dedit; nam aut incendium oportet fiat, aut aliquis
3 in vicinia animam abiciet. Longe a nobis. Itaque quisquis
4 hunc indicem attulerit, corollarium accipiet." Dicto citius
[de vicinia] gallus allatus est, quem Trimalchio iussit ut
5 aeno coctus fieret. Laceratus igitur ab illo doctissimo coco
qui paulo ante de porco aves piscesque fecerat, in caccabum
est coniectus. Dumque Daedalus potionem ferventissimam
haurit, Fortunata mola buxea piper trivit.

H

73 5 suas *del. Buecheler del. Mueller cetera lac. ind. Mueller, quam Buecheler post* lucernas *locavit* 6 servus] Croesus *vel aliquod nomen Wehle* fecit: *de* facit *corr.* H **74** 4 *del. Mueller post* iussit occidi *aut* iugulari *excidisse putavit Buecheler* aeno coctus] oenococtus *Orioli*

After thus shaking off our wooziness, we were escorted into another dining room, where Fortunata had set out her own finery ... We took note of lamps with fishermen in bronze on them, tables of solid silver, porcelain goblets everywhere with gilt rims, and wine decanting from a cloth bag in full view. "Friends," said Trimalchio, "today a slave of mine is getting his first shave. He's a thrifty boy – touch wood – a real nit-picker. So down the hatch and let's dine till dawn!"

74 As he was speaking, a cock crew. Growing nervous at the sound, Trimalchio commanded wine to be poured under the table, and the lantern to be sprinkled with the unmixed kind. He even changed a ring from left to right hand. "Not without reason," he said, "did this bugler blow. There must be a fire somewhere or else somebody nearby is going to croak. Far be it from us! So anyone who brings in our informant will get a reward." No sooner were the words out than a cock was produced – which Trimalchio commanded to become coq-au-vin. So it was dismembered by that most skilled cook – who had so recently turned pork into birds and fishes – and tossed into a casserole pot. And while Daedalus basted the bird with the steaming juices, Fortunata ground in pepper from a boxwood mill.

6 Sumptis igitur matteis respiciens ad familiam Trimalchio,
"Quid vos," inquit, "adhuc non cenastis? Abite, ut alii
7 veniant ad officium." Subiit igitur alia classis, et illi
quidem exclamavere: "Vale, Gai!"; hi autem: "Ave, Gai!"
8 Hinc primum hilaritas nostra turbata est; nam cum puer
non inspeciosus inter novos intrasset ministros, invasit
9 eum Trimalchio et osculari diutius coepit. Itaque
Fortunata, ut ex aequo ius firmum approbaret, male dicere
Trimalchioni coepit et purgamentum dedecusque praedicare,
qui non contineret libidinem suam. Ultimo etiam adiecit
10 "Canis!" Trimalchio contra offensus [convicio] calicem
11 in faciem Fortunatae immisit. Illa tamquam oculum
perdidisset exclamavit manusque trementes ad faciem suam
12 Consternata est etiam Scintilla trepidantemque sinu
suo texit. Immo puer quoque officiosus urceolum frigidum
ad malam eius admoviit, super quem incumbens Fortunata
13 gemere ac flere coepit. Contra Trimalchio, "Quid enim?"
inquit, "Ambubaia non meminit se de machina? Illam sustuli,
hominem inter homines feci. At inflat se tamquam rana, et
14 in sinum suum non spuit, codex, non mulier. Sed hic qui

H

74 9 Trimalchioni *Buecheler post Anton*: Trimalchionem 10 *deleo* 12 malam *patavina*: malum 13 Ambubaia non meminit se de machina? *sic pungo*: ambubaia non me misit se de machillam: Ambubaiam non meminisse! *Nisbet*

As Trimalchio fell to these delicacies, he looked over at his staff. "Haven't you eaten yet?" he said. "Leave, so another shift can come on duty." And so another detachment arrived, with the former crying, "Goodbye Gaius!" and the latter, "Hello Gaius!" This resulted in the first serious disruption of the general hilarity, since a quite good-looking boy had come in among the new group and Trimalchio grabbed and set to kissing him for rather too long. Fortunata, asserting her manifest equality before the law, proceeded to curse him out and call him garbage and a disgrace for not controlling his own lust; and, in finishing, "You hound!"

Trimalchio in return took offence at this harangue and threw a cup in Fortunata's face. She shrieked as if she'd lost an eye, touching her face with trembling fingers. Scintilla got upset too and she enfolded her quivering friend in her lap. The boy in question, ever attentive, held a cold pitcher against Fortunata's cheek as she leaned on him weeping and groaning. "What have we here?" Trimalchio began. "Does this chorus girl not remember her cage? I rescued her and turned her into a human being, but she puffs herself up like a bullfrog and won't spit in her own lap. A blockhead, not a woman.

Trimalchio lets his guard down with a quite serious public indiscretion, caused by a night of drinking: launching himself at a moderately good-looking servant boy and kissing him to excess, then offering what one calls a "yeah, right" defence: the boy's thriftiness not his looks made him do it. He adds further mischief to his case by recalling his faithful attention to his master's sexual needs, not forgetting those of his mistress also (*Sat.* 75). Again, we suspect the author of having some fun.

in pergula natus est aedes non somniatur. Ita genium meum
15 propitium habeam, curabo domata sit Cassandra caligaria. Et ego
homo dipundiarius, sestertium centies accipere potui. Scis tu
me non mentiri. Agatho unguentarius here proxime seduxit me et,
'Suadeo,' inquit, 'non patiaris genus tuum interire.' At ego dum
16 bonatus ago et nolo videri levis, ipse mihi asciam in crus
17 impegi. Recte, curabo me unguibus quaeras. Et ut depraesenti-
arum intellegas quid tibi feceris: Habinna, nolo statuam eius
in monumento meo ponas, ne mortuus quidem lites habeam. Immo,
ut sciat me possum malum dare, nolo me mortuum basiet."

75 Post hoc fulmen Habinnas rogare coepit ut iam desinet irasci et
2 / "Nemo," inquit, "nostrum non peccat. Homines sum, non dei."/ HL
Idem et Scintilla flens dixit ac per genium eius Gaium H
3 appellando rogare coepit ut se frangeret. Non tenuit ultra
lacrimas Trimalchio et, "Rogo," inquit, "Habinna, sic peculium
tuum fruniscaris: si quid perperam feci, in faciem meam inspue.
4 Puerum basiavi frugalissimum, non propter formam, sed quia frugi
est: decem partes dicit, librum ab oculo legit; thraecium sibi
de diariis fecit, arcisellium de suo paravit et duas trullas.
5 Non est dignum quem in oculis feram? Sed Fortuna vetat. Ita
tibi videtur,fulcipedia? Suadeo bonum tuum concoquas, milva,

H, L (= lmrtp), O (= BRP)

74 14 sit *patavina*: si: sis *Orioli* 15 here *del. Nisbet*

75 1 inquit *om.* L non nostrum H 2 se frangeret *Heinze*: effrangeret 3 fruniscaris *patavina*: frunis canis

But if you're born in a hovel you don't dream of a mansion. As surely as I can count on my guardian angel I'll get this Cassandra in jackboots under control. I could have got a hundred million but I came cheap. You know the truth of that. Only the other day Agatho the parfumier took me aside and said, 'Look, don't let your line die out.' And I, playing Mister Nice Guy and not wanting to look flighty, stuck an axe in my own foot. I'll make a fine target for your fingernails! And just so you see what you've done to yourself – Habinnas! Don't put any statue of her on my grave. I don't want any grief when I'm dead. Also, so she knows how I can hurt, I don't want her to kiss me when I'm gone."

75 After this thunderbolt Habinnas tried to persuade Trimalchio to stop being angry. "Nobody's perfect," he said. "We're men, not gods." A weeping Scintilla added her voice. She called him "Gaius" and begged him upon his guardian spirit to relent. Trimalchio held back the tears no longer. "Habinnas," he said, "I appeal to you: by your nest egg which you hope to spend, if I did anything wrong spit in my face. I happened to kiss a very thrifty boy because he is thrifty and not because he is pretty. He can say his tens and read at sight. He's made himself a Thracian sword by saving up his pocket money. He's built a chair by himself, plus two ladles. Doesn't he deserve to be the apple of my eye? No way, says Fortunata. Isn't that right, Platform Heels? Go and mind your own business, you old buzzard.

et me non facias ringentem, amasiuncula, alioquin experieris
7 cerebrum meum. Nosti me: quod semel destinavi, clavo trabali
8 fixum est. Sed vivorum meminerimus. Vos rogo, amici, ut vobis
suaviter sit. Nam ego quoque tam fui quam vos estis, sed virtute
mea ad hoc perveni. Corcillum est quod homines facit, cetera
9 quisquilia omnia. 'Bene emo, bene vendo'; alius alia vobis
dicet. Felicitate dissilio. Tu autem, sterteia, etiamnum
10 ploras? Iam curabo fatum tuum plores. Sed, ut coeperam dicere,
ad hanc me fortunam frugalitas mea perduxit. Tam magnus ex
Asia veni quam hic candelabrus est. Ad summam, quotidie me
solebam ad illum metiri, et ut celerius rostrum barbatum
11 haberem, labra de lucerna ungebam. Tamen ad delicias [femina]
ipsimi [domini] annos quattuordecim fui. Nec turpe est quod
dominus iubet. Ego tamen et ipsimae [dominae] satis faciebam.
76 Scitis quid dicam: taceo, quia non sum de gloriosis. Ceterum,
quemadmodum di volunt, dominus in domino factus sum, et ecce
2 cepi ipsimi cerebellum. Quid multa? Coheredem me Caesari fecit,
3 et accepi patrimonium laticlavum. Nemini tamen nihil satis est.
concupivi negotiari. Ne multis vobis morerer, quinque naves
aedificavi, oneravi vinum - et tunc erat contra aurum - misi
4 Romam. Putares me hoc iussisse: omnes naves naufragerunt.

H

75 6 facias *Mentel*: facies 7 trabali *Scheffer*: tabulari
8 corcillum *Scheffer*: coricillum 10 summae *Mentel*: summa
metiri *Scheffer*: me uri 11 <ad> annos *Bodel* *del. Buecheler*
76 2 accepi *Scheffer*: accepit

Don't make me show my teeth, little love, or you'll be tasting my temper. You know me: once I'm set on something it's fixed with a spike.

"But let's get back to the real world. Friends, I want you to have fun. I was just like you are now and got to where I am on talent. Guts is what makes a man and you can forget all the rest. 'Buy at a good price, sell at a good price,' is what I say. Others'll tell you different, but it's me that's rolling in it. Still crying are you, sniffles? I'll give you something to cry about. But as I'd begun to say, saving up got me my pile. I arrived here from Asia about as big as this candlestick, and in fact I measured myself against it every day, smearing lamp oil on my mouth to put hair on my chin faster. All the same, for fourteen years I was my master's pet boy. No disgrace in following orders. I took care of the mistress too – you know what I mean and I won't say more since I'm not a blowhard.

76 "Anyway, as the gods willed it, I was put in charge of the house and became my master's brains. The rest? He made me co-heir with the Emperor and I got an inheritance fit for a senator. But nobody can ever have enough. I wanted to go into trading. I'll spare you the details. I had five ships built, onloaded a full cargo of wine (in those days worth its weight in gold), and sailed them off to Rome. You'd almost think I arranged it:

Factum, non fabula. Uno die Neptunus trecenties sestertium
5 devoravit. Putatis me defecisse? Non mehercules mi haec
iactura gusti fuit, tamquam nihil facti. Alteras feci maiores
et meliores et feliciores, ut nemo non me virum fortem
6 diceret. Sci<ti>s, magna navis magnam fortitudinem habet.
Oneravi rursus vinum, lardum, fabam, seplasium, mancipia.
7 Hoc loco Fortunata rem piam fecit; omne aurum suum, omnia
8 vestimenta vendidit et me centum aureos in manu posuit. Hoc
fuit peculii mei fermentum. Cito fit quod di volunt. Uno cursu
centies sestertium corrotundavi. Statim redemi fundos omnes,
qui patroni fuerant. Aedifico domum, venalicia coemo, iumenta;
9 quicquid tangebam, crescit tamquam favus, Postquam coepi plus
habere quam tota patria mea habet, manum de tabula: sustuli me
10 de negotiatione et coepi <per> libertos faenerare. Et sane
nolentem me negotium meum agere exhortavit mathematicus, qui
venerat forte in coloniam nostram, Graeculio, Serapa nomine,
11 consiliator deorum. Hic mihi dixit etiam quae oblitus eram; ab
acia et acu mi omnia exposuit; intestinas meas noverat; tantum
quod mihi non dixerat quid pridie cenaveram. Putasses illum
77 semper mecum habitasse. Rogo, Habinna – puto, interfuisti – :

H
76 6 *add. Buecheler* 8 fit *Scheffer*: fio iumenta<que> *in adn. Buecheler* 9 *add. Heinze* 10 nolentem *Scheffer*: nolente exhortavit H^{m}: exoravit 11 exposuit *Scheffer*: exposcit

they all went down. Fact not fable. On one day Neptune swallowed thirty million. Do you think I gave up? Not on your life. This loss just whetted my appetite as if nothing had happened. I built new ships, bigger, better, luckier. No one could say I wasn't brave. I put on wine again, plus lard, beans, unguents, slaves.

"Right then Fortunata did the decent thing and sold off all her gold and fine clothing and put a hundred gold pieces in my hand. This was the yeast to make my fortune rise. If the gods will it, it doesn't take long. I netted a million in one trip and immediately bought out the mortgages on all my patron's former properties. I built a manor house and bought slaves and stock.

"Everything I touched grew like honeycomb. When I was worth more than the town budget I threw in my hand. I went out of trading and into moneylending through freedman agents. I actually wanted to quit business altogether, but an astrologer talked me out of it, a Greek, name of Serapa, by chance just in town, the gods' confidante. He told me even things I'd long forgotten, and laid it all out with needle and thread. He knew my insides. Only thing he never told me was what I had for dinner yesterday. You'd think he'd been living with me forever.

'Tu dominam tuam de rebus illis fecisti. Tu parum felix in
2 amicos es. Nemo umquam tibi parem gratiam refert. Tu latifundia
possides. Tu viperam sub ala nutricas,' et, quod vobis non
dixerim, etiam nunc mihi restare vitae annos triginto et
menses quattuor et dies duos. Praeterea cito accipiam
3 hereditatem. Hoc mihi dicit fatus meus. Quod si contigerit
4 fundos Apuliae iungere, satis vivus pervenero. Interim dum
Mercurius vigilat, aedificavi hanc domum. Ut scitis, casa adhuc
erat; nunc templum est. Habet quattuor cenationes, cubicula
viginti, porticus marmoratos duos, susum cellationem, cubiculum
in quo ipse dormio, viperae huius sessorium, ostiarii cellam
5 perbonum; hospitium hospites <C> capit. Ad summam, Scaurus cum
huc venit, nusquam mavoluit hospitari, et habet ad mare paternum
hospitium. Et multa alia sunt, quae statim vobis ostendam.
6 Credite mihi, assem habeas, assem valeas; habes, haberis. Sic
amicus vester, qui fuit rana, nunc est rex. Interim, Stiche,
profer vitalia, in quibus volo me afferri. Profer et unguentum
et ex illa amphora gustum, ex qua iubeo lavari ossa mea."

H
77 de rebus illis: de machina *intellegas;* 74.13 amicis *Scheffer* quod] quid Scheffer 4 casa adhuc *scribo cum Corbett*: casa *tunc Watt*: casa *patavina*: cusuc marmoratos *Buecheler*: marmoratis *add. Heinze* 5 summam *Scheffer*: summa mavolt *Heinze*

77 "Say, Habinnas, you were there, I think: 'You got your wife out of *those certain circumstances*. You're not lucky in your friends. No one ever gives you the thanks you deserve. You possess estates. You suckle a viper at your bosom.' And here's a thing I've never told you. I've got thirty years, four months, and two days left to live. In addition, I'll be inheriting soon. It's all in my horoscope. If I can manage to link up my Apulian properties I'll die content.

"Meanwhile under the watchful eye of Mercury I built this house. As you know, I took a shack and turned it into a sanctuary: four dining rooms, twenty bedrooms, two marble colonnades, an upstairs guest suite, and a master bedroom – this viper's nest – a fine porter's lodge, and a roomy guest billet. In fact when Scaurus came visiting he'd stay nowhere else, and he's got relatives on the beach.

"There's lots besides that I'll be showing you soon. Take my word for it: have a penny, worth a penny. You are what you have. In this way your humble friend, once a frog, is now a prince. By the way, Stichus, bring out my burial dress, the perfume too, and a sample of wine from the jar I'm having to wash my bones."

78 Non est moratus Stichus, sed et stragulam albam et
praetextam in triclinium attulit … iussitque nos temptare
2 an bonis lanis essent confecta. Tum subridens, "Vide tu,"
inquit, "Stiche, ne ista mures tangant aut tineae; alioquin
te vivum comburam! Ego gloriosus volo efferri, ut totus mihi
3 populus bene imprecetur." Statim ampullam nardi aperuit
omnesque nos unxit et, "Spero," inquit, "futurum ut aeque me
4 iuvet tamquam vivum." Nam vinum quidem in vinarium iussit
infundi et "Putate vos," ait, "ad parentalia mea invitatos esse."
5 Ibat res ad summam nauseam cum Trimalchio ebrietate
turpissima gravis novum acroama, cornicines, in triclinium iussit
addici, fultusque cervicalibus multis extendit se supra torum
6 extremum et, "Fingite me," inquit, "mortuum esse. Dicite
aliquid belli." Consonuere cornic<in>es funebri strepitu.
Unus praecipue servus libitinarii illius, qui inter hos
honestissimus erat, tam valde intonuit, ut totam concitaret
7 viciniam. Itaque vigiles qui custodiebant vicinam regionem,
rati ardere Trimalchionis domum effregerunt ianuam et cum aqua
8 securibusque tumultuari suo iure coeperunt. Nos occasione
opportunissimam nacti Agamemnoni verba dedimus raptimque tam
plane quam ex incendio fugimus …

H

78 *lac. ind. Buecheler* 5 cornicines *patavina*: cornicipes 6 *add. patavina* libitinarii *Scheffer*: libertinarii qui … erat *del. Delz* 8 plane tamquam *Jahn* *lac. ind. Buecheler*

78 Quick as a wink, Stichus carried the white burial cloth and purple toga into the dining room, and Trimalchio invited us to feel the quality of the wool. Then, with the ghost of a smile, "Stichus," he said, "make sure these things are kept away from mice and moths, or I'll have you burned alive. I want to look splendid when I go, so the whole population can give me a good sendoff."

Straight away he opened a vial of nard, gave us all a daub, and, "I hope," said he, "I like this as much dead as I do alive." Then he even had wine poured into a mixing bowl. "Imagine," he said, "you've all been invited to my wake."

The thing was becoming utterly nauseating, with Trimalchio, disgustingly drunk, commanding horn players to be brought into the dining room for a novelty. Supported on plenty of pillows, he stretched himself flat along the full surface of the couch and said, "Pretend I'm dead. Say something nice." The horn players blew in unison the funeral blast. One of them, the servant of the undertaker (among the most respectable of the guests) blew so hard that he roused the entire neighbourhood.

Whereupon the firemen in charge of the district, thinking Trimalchio's house to be on fire, quickly smashed in the door and racketed about with their water and axe, a law unto themselves. We grabbed this heaven-sent opportunity to give Agamemnon the slip and ran off at full tilt as convincingly as if from a real fire …

79 / Neque fax ulla in praesidio erat, quae iter aperiret L
errantibus. Nec silentium noctis iam mediae promittebat
2 occurrentium lumen. Accedebat huc ebrietas et imprudentia
3 locorum etiam interdiu obscurorum. Itaque cum hora paene
tota per omnes scrupos gastrarumque eminentium fragmenta
traxissemus cruentos pedes, tandem expliciti acumine
4 Gitonis sumus. Prudens enim puer, cum luce etiam clara
timeret errorem, omnes pilas columnasque notaverat creta
quae lineamenta evicerunt spississimam noctem et notabili
5 candore ostenderunt [errantibus] viam. Quamvis non minus
sudoris habuimus etiam postquam ad stabulum pervenimus.
6 Anus enim ipsa inter deversitores diutius ingurgita ne ignem
quidem admotum sensisset. Et forsitan pernoctissemus in
limine, ni tabellarius [Trimalchionis] intervenisset <quasi>
7 ex vehiculo divus. Non diu ergo tumultuatus stabuli ianua
effregit et nos per eandem [terram] immisit *

8 Qualis nox fuit illa, di deaeque,
quam mollis torus. Haesimus calentes
Et transfudimus hinc et hinc labellis
Errantes animas. Valete, curae
Mortales. Ego sic perire coepi.

L (= lmrtp)
79 2 obscurorum *Burman*: obscura 3 scrupos *Scaliger*: scirpos 4 puer *Nisbet*: pridie *F. Daniel*: prudens creta, quae *F. Daniel*: certaque *deleo; adiunctionem videas* 6 *del. Delz* intervenisset *F. Daniel*, l[m]: invenisset *supplevi* ex vehiculo divus *lego post Watt* dives: x vehiculis divus 7 per eandem terram pt *deleo* tramisit *Watt*

6
Habits of The Heart, II

79 Without a torch to assist us in finding our way, and with little prospect of meeting any approaching light in the midnight silence, we just wandered about. Not helping was our drunken state and lack of familiarity with a neighbourhood that would be dingy even in broad daylight. So for nearly an hour we dragged our bloodied feet through all the loose cobblestones and projecting pottery chips until at last we were extricated by the sharp wits of Giton. The clever boy, afraid of getting lost even at high noon, had marked all the pillars and columns with chalk. The blazes shone forth through the thick darkness, and with their familiar whiteness guided the way. But arrival at our lodgings didn't put an end to the sweat. The old female caretaker, after a prolonged session of imbibing with her guests, wouldn't have felt a torch even if poked with one. We might have spent the rest of the night out on the step if a courier hadn't turned up as if by divine intervention. After a quick shout he smashed the inn's door and got us through it again *

Ye Gods and Goddesses, what a night it's been!
How soft the bed! With sweaty limbs we twined,
And kisses from the soul our lips conjoined!
Mortal cares avast! I've died and gone to heaven!

9 Sine causa gratulor mihi. Nam cum solutus mero
remisissem ebrias manus, Ascyltos, omnis iniuriae inventor
subduxit mihi nocte puerum et in lectum transtulit suum,
volutatusque liberius cum fratre non suo, sive non
sentiente [iniuriam] sive dissimulante, indormivit alienis
10 amplexibus oblitus iuris humani. Itaque ego ut experrectus
pertrectavi gaudio despoliatum torum …

Si qua est amantibus fides, ego dubitavi an utrumque
11 traicerem gladio somnumque morti iungerem. Tutius dein
secutus consilium Gitona quidem verberibus excitavi,
Asylton autem truci intuens vultu, "Quoniam," inquam
"fidem scelere violasti et communem amicitiam, res tuas
ocius tolle et alium locum quem polluas quaere."

12 Non repugnavit ille, sed postquam optima fide partiti
manubias sumus, "Age," inquit, "nunc puerum dividamus."
80 Iocari putabo discedentem. At ille gladium parricidali
manu strinxit et, "Non frueris," inquit, "hac praeda,
super quam solus incumbas. Partem meam necesse est vel
2 hoc gladio contemptus abscidam." Idem ego ex altera parte

L (= lmrtp)
79 8 mortales t[m]: mortalis ego sic] ego sum sic lt[v] *ex Cuiaciano*: ego sum r (ego sic r[c]) 9 remisissem *Jacobs*: *del. Mueller*: iniuriam suam l 10 *lac. ind. Jahn* 11 dein *Scaliger*: demum **80** incumbas *lego*: incumbis contemptus *Burman*: contentus abscindam lr[c]

My self-satisfaction proved groundless. Ascyltus, fount of all hurt, stole my boy away from me in the night, when I had relaxed my grip in drunken sleep, took him into his own bed, and after sporting all too freely with another's love who either felt nothing or pretended not to, in disregard for all human law, slept fast in the embrace of a stranger, leaving me to awake and feel a bed robbed of its joy.

Believe a lover if you can: I considered running them both through with my sword and making their sleep more permanent. But then I took a safer course, first rousing Giton with a pummelling and then fixing Ascyltus with my fiercest glare. "Since you have so wickedly betrayed your word and the friendship that we shared, hurry up and get your stuff together and go find another place to spread your filth!"

Ascyltus raised no objection. But when we had divided our spoils with scrupulous fairness, "All right," he declared, "now let's divide the boy too." A parting joke, I thought, but no:

80 With murd'rous hand he drew his sword. "You will not have the joy," he said, "of gloating over this prize in private. Since you are turning me out I'll need to take my cut of the sword too!" I matched his move, wrapping my arm in my cloak and striking a duelling pose.

feci et intorto circa bracchium pallio composui ad
3 proeliandum gradum. Inter hanc miserorum dementiam
infelicissimus puer tangebat utriusque genua cum fletu
petebatque suppliciter ne Thebanum par humilis taberna
spectaret neve sanguine mutuo pollueremus familiaritatis
4 clarissimae sacra. "Quod si utique," proclamabat,
"facinore opus, nudo ecce iugulum: convertite huc manus,
imprimite mucrones. Ego mori debeo, qui amicitiae
5 sacamentum delevi." Inhibuimus ferrum post has preces,
et prior Ascyltos, "Ego," inquit, "finem discordiae
imponam. Puer ipse quam vult sequatur, ut sit illi saltem
6 in eligendo fratre libertas." Ego <qui> vetustissimam
consuetudinem putabam in sanguinis pignus transisse,
nihil timui, immo condicionem praecipiti festinatione
rapui commisique iudici litem. Qui ne deliberavit quidem,
ut videretur cunctatus, verum statim ab extrema parte
7 verbi consurrexit <et> fratrem Ascylton elegit. Fulminatus
hac pronuntiatione sic ut eram [sine gladio] in lectulum
decidi, et attulissem mihi damnatus manus, si non inimici
8 victoriae invidissem. Egreditur <ergo> superbus cum praemio
Ascyltos et paulo ante carissimum sibi commilitonem
fortunaeque etiam similitudine parem in loco peregrino
destituit abiectum.

L (= lmrtp)
80 5 salva libertas rtp 6 *add. Pithou in altera*
add. Buecheler 7 *del. Fuchs* invidissem rpt: *inviderem* l
8 *supplevi*: *adiunctionem videas*

Amid our pathetic, crazy posturings, the unhappy boy, in tears, grasped our knees and begged and implored us not to let this humble inn witness a duel worthy of Thebes nor sully the sanctity of a famous relationship with each other's blood. "Besides," he cried, "if you must do the deed, I bare my throat: aim your blows here; thrust here with your sword-tips. It is I who deserve to die for destroying friendship's sacred bond."

These entreaties stopped the fight, and Ascyltus was the first to speak: "I'm willing to settle the dispute," he said. "Let the boy go with whomever he wants. At least he'll get to choose his lover." I supposed that our long-standing affair had crossed over into a pact written in blood, and was unafraid of the terms. Indeed I hurriedly embraced the condition of entrusting the dispute to our "judge." Giton took not even a moment to reflect in pretended hesitation, but immediately rose and picked as his lover – Ascyltus! Stunned by the verdict, I collapsed on the bed just like that, and would have followed this conviction with death by my own hand, had I not begrudged my foe that victory. So Ascyltus left proudly with his prize, forsaking, cast upon a foreign shore, his erstwhile dearest comrade-in-arms and sharer equally in vicissitude.

The curtain-fall on the Cena, coinciding with the end of "Book XV," as the manuscript H tells us, is a convenient time for Petronius to ring in changes, if his continuing peripatetic tale of Encolpius is to match the stupendous triumph of Trimalchio's banquet. At any rate, impeccable though Giton here is on the page, the motif of the conflicted romantic trio feels stale and stretched to its narratorial limit. Ascyltus, already reduced to a supercilious cipher in the Cena, had to go, and go he did, after a parting last fling with Giton to keep his role fresh enough to produce echoes in the memory, plus a return in hot pursuit of the boy. No matter: he was effectively banished from the big picture, made redundant by the author immediately with the one person who could, and would, refresh and brilliantly dominate the storyline right to the conclusion, apparently some few fractured "books" later: Eumolpus. Yes, the end of H has pushed the reader back to the L narrative tradition, which requires a pact, in return for the breadth and charm of its palette, to revisit the gaps and disjunctures so typical earlier in the tale. A good enough bargain, for the threatening soldier, the picture gallery, the teachings of Eumolpus, the Pergamene boy, the Sack of Troy, Eumolpus and Ascyltus at the baths, entrapment and escape plots at sea, the epic fight, the reconciliation, the widow of Ephesus, the storm and shipwreck, Croton, the charade, the Civil War, Circe, the geese darlings of Priapus, Philomela and chldren, a final failure with the boy, but then the twelfth-hour apparent "restoration," the Will. This must surely be the Encolpiad.

9 / Nomen amicitiae sic, quatenus expedit, haeret: LO
Calculus in tabula mobile ducit opus.
Dum fortuna manet, vultum servatis, amici;
Cum cecidit, turpi vertitis ora fuga.

/ Grex agit in scaena mimum: pater ille vocatur
Filius hic, nomen divitis ille tenet.
Mox ubi ridendas inclusit pagina partes
Vera redit facies, assimulata perit.

---

81 Nec diu tamen lacrimis indulsi, sed veritus <etiam> ne
Menelaus [etiam] antescholanus inter cetera mala solum me in
deversorio inveniret, collegi sarcinulas locumque secretum
2 et proximum litori maestus conduxi. Ibi triduo inclusus
redeunte in animum solitudine atque contemptu verberabam
aegrum planctibus pectus et / inter [tot] altissimos L
3 gemitus frequenter etiam proclamabam: "Ergo me non ruina terra
potuit haurire? Non iratum etiam innocentibus mare? Effugi
iudicium, harenae imposui, hospitem occidi, ut inter <tot>

L (= lmrtp), O (= BRP)
80 9 sic *Muncker*: amicitia est *libri* quate] *hic desinit* m dum *Jahn*: cum *carmen alterum alicunde ex alio loco translatum statuit Buecheler* assimulata *Dousa*: dissimulata **81–109** 9 *deficit* B; *lectiones tamen* B *sub "Autiss." in* p^{2v} *videmus* **81** *transposui; videas adiunctionem 2/3* tot *transponunt Jacobs et Buecheler* 3 effugi *Cuiacianus*

Thus friendship lasts so long as it will pay;
The dice on gaming board will have their fickle way.
My friends, I hold your gaze so long as Fortune smiles,
But when she frowns I know you're gone for miles!

****

The troupe's on stage to do the mime:
The father, son, and rich man have their time.
Not long beyond when comic script is done,
The face of truth returns, and fiction's gone.

****

81 All the same, I didn't weep for long. Still anxious not to compound my woes by having Menelaus the assistant teacher find me alone at the inn, I sadly gathered up my things and rented myself a quiet place by the sea. There I holed up for three days' worth of brooding upon my loneliness and humiliation. I racked my wounded soul with many a wail, and amid the profoundest groans proclaimed over and over, "And why couldn't I have been buried in that landslide? Or drowned in the sea, which takes it out even on the innocent? Did I evade the law, cheat the amphitheatre, kill my host,

audaciae nomina mendicus, exul, in deversorio Graecae urbis
4 desertus? Et quis hanc mihi solitudinem imposuit? Adulescens
omni libidine impurus et sua quoque confessione dignus exilio,
stupro liber, stupro ingenuus, cuius anni teneri ad tesseram
venierunt, quem tamquam puellam conduxit etiam qui virum
5 putavit. Quid ille alter? Qui [tamquam] die togae virilis
stolam sumpsit, qui ne vir esset a matre persuasus est, qui
opus muliebre in ergastulo fecit, qui postquam conturbavit
et libidinis suae solum vertit, reliquit veteris amicitiae
nomen et, pro pudor, tamquam mulier secutuleia unius noctis
6 tactu omnia vendidit. Iacent nunc amatores adligati noctibus
totis, et forsitan mutuis libidinibus attriti derident
solitudinem meam. Sed non impune. Nam aut vir ego liberque
non sum, aut noxio sanguine parentabo iniuriae meae."

82 Haec locutus gladio latus cingor, et ne infirmitas
militiam perderet, largioribus cibis excito vires. Mox in
publicum prosilio furentis more omnes circumeo porticus.
2 Sed dum attonito vultu efferatoque nihil aliud quam caedem
et sanguinem cogito frequentiusque manum ad capulum, quem
devoveram, refero, notavit me miles, sive ille planus fuit
3 sive nocturnus grassator, et "Quid tu," inquit, "commilito,

---

L (= lrtp)
81 3 *add. Jacobs* solitudinem
lt $^{m}p^{2}$ *ex Cuiaciano*: solicitudinem rtp^{1} *ex Benedictino*
5 *del. F. Daniel,* qui togae virilis die *maluit*: qui tamquam die
Scaliger: die qui tamquam 6 adligati *Buecheler*: obligati

only to languish in defiance of my bold record a penniless, friendless exile in some Greektown rooming house? And who made me an outcast? A young dude polluted by every vice and deserving of exile even by his own admission, not only free but freeborn, thus doubly degenerate – who sold his tender youth for a throw of the dice to someone thinking he was buying a man but got a pseudo girl instead.

"As for the other, on the day for celebrating his manhood he put on a dress – when his own mother convinced him he was no man – and worked a prison farm like a woman. And then his money ran out and he found new ground for his lust, abandoning the tie of a stable relationship and like a kept woman – for very shame! – selling out on the strength of a one-night stand! As I speak the lovers lie entwined the night long, and spent from mutual lusts are doubtless mocking my loneliness! But they will pay. If I'm the man, the free man, I think I am, I'll redress my wrong with their guilty blood!"

82 So saying I strapped sword to side, and not wanting to spoil my fighting trim by faintness built up my strength with extra amounts of food. Then I sprang outdoors and prowled the piazzas like a crazy man. But while with wild and deranged mien and many a slap upon freshly dedicated sword hilt I had only murder and mayhem on my mind, I had attracted the attention of a soldier with a night's conning and mugging ahead of him.

The remarkable paragraph at the end of *Sat.* 81, with Encolpius' over-the-top ruminations indicting Giton as a common out-and-out effeminate, with a history of servicing the lowest of the low at a prison farm – at the age of sixteen! – are so out of character with his subsequent sweet-boy personality, as we see it and Encolpius accepts it, that it makes me wonder whether it is all a deranged invention: not real but a love-addled fantasy, a grimy sexual hallucination. Do we not remember that Encolpius was so solicitous for his lover's tender well-being at Quartilla's party at *Sat.* 25 that he feared the boy was too bashful to cope with the simple defloration of a willing seven-year-old girl? I sense that reality regrounds Encolpius when Ascyltus steps into the picture to have Giton choose him and run away together.

ex qua legione es aut cuius centuria?" Cum constantissime et centurionem et legionem essem ementitus, "Age ergo," inquit ille, "in exercitu vestro phaecasiati milites ambulant?"
4 Cum deinde vultu atque ipsa trepidatione mendacium prodidissem, ponere iussit arma et malo cavere. Despoliatus ergo, immo praecisa ultione retro ad deversorium tendo paulatimque temeritate laxata coepi grassatoris audaciae gratias agere *

---

5 Non bibit inter aquas poma aut pendentia carpit
Tantalus infelix, quam sua vota premunt.
Divitis haec magni facies erit, omnia cenans
qui timet et sicco concoquit ore famem*

---

6 Non multum oportet consilio credere, quia suam habet fortuna rationem *

L (= lrtp)

82 3 phaecasiati *Turnebus*: phocasiati 4 ponere me *Buecheler* laxata *Muncker*: lassata *post* agere *lac. ind. Pithou* (p) 5 *hos versus non ad hunc locum attinere putat Buecheler post famem septem sententias ex Cena Trimalchionis aggeratas in fontibus* L *invenimus*: 43.6, 44.17, 45.2, 55.1, 55.2, 55.4, 56.6; *ad quas supplemus* 59.2 *et* 75.1

"Hey, soldier," he bawled, "what's your brigade? Who's your officer?" Unfazed, I provided some fictitious details of my posting. "Come, now!" was the response: "Do soldiers in your regiment walk around in their slippers?" My nervous demeanour quickly gave the game away, and he told me to check my weapon and watch myself. Thus robbed at once of sword and vengeance, I went back to my room, and as my temper slowly cooled I blessed that mugger's brazen action. *

****

Water everywhere he drinks not, plucks not sagging fruit,
Poor Tantalus, victim of his will.
This the tycoon's fate: to eat his loot
Timorous, dry mouthed, gorge but hunger still *

****

One shouldn't believe much in planning, since fate has its own way *

The chapters immediately after the *Cena*, *Sat.* 79–83 ff., including a febrile resurgence of the sexualized romance of Encolpius, Ascyltus, and Giton, then a visit to a picture-gallery, where inevitably Encolpius fixes upon objects of mythological art featuring the *raptus* of young boys by smitten divinities of both sexes, followed by the entry upon the scene of the arch-pederast Eumolpus, make up the critical mass to address in sum the type of sexual-desire-driven romance (i.e., lust) that dominates the *Satyrica*: paedophilia, defined by the *Oxford Dictionary and Thesaurus* (1993) as "sexual desire directed towards children." This is a subject that I, along with other Petronius scholar-teachers who are fond of all aspects of the author and his creations, would just as soon skirt; or else, in our age of rightly increasing non-problematized sexual curiosity and practice (among consenting adults), perhaps channel, without a high degree of accuracy, into categories of new cultural recognition, like bisexuality and gender-fluidity in nominal binary women and men. In the *Satyrica* this will largely affect the male principals, Encolpius, Giton, Ascyltus, and Eumolpus. We also have Lichas the sea-captain and the equestrian admirer of Ascyltus at the baths, to show universality, where the bisexual term works in practice but is still not authentic or culturally transferable. The end-zone line of consenting sex between teenage youth and outright child abuse is fiercely defended in law and custom in our era, as it can and must be. In the first century AD, though, a flourishing, uncompromising, predatory, abuse-prone servile environment ensured a steady supply, without opportunity for neutral judicial recourse. Standards of age-determined right and wrong for sexual interplay could be counted broadly and were perceived to function along lines of normal sexual development and balance. And even if recognized they could easily be flouted. Encolpius, the opinion maker of our narrative, is indeed at times a mouthpiece of sensitivity to underage sex, *en passant*, more in surprise than in censure, and he knows he is powerless to exert influence or intervene. Also, his own perspective does not boast a high degree of moral sufficiency.

83 In pinacothecam perveni vario genere tabularum
mirabilem. Nam et Zeuxidos manus vidi nondum vetustatis
iniuria victas, et Protogenis rudimenta cum ipsius naturae
2 veritate certantia non sine quodam horrore tractavi. Iam
vero Apellis quem [Graeci] monocnemon appellant, etiam
adoravi. Tanta enim subtilitate extremitates imaginum erant
ad similitudinem praecisae, ut crederes etiam animorum esse
3 picturam. Hinc aquila aquila ferebat caelo sublimis Idaeum,
illinc candidus Hylas repellebat improbam Naida. Damnabat
Apollo noxias manus lyramque resolutam modo nato flore
4 honorabat. Inter quos [etiam] pictorum amantium vultus
tamquam in solitudine exclamavi: "Ergo amor etiam deos
tangit. Iuppiter in caelo suo non invenit quod eligeret,
5 et peccaturus in terris nemini iniuriam fecit. Hylan Nympha
praedata amori sui, si venturum ad interdictum Herculem
credidisset. Apollo pueri umbram revocavit in florem, et
omnes fabulae quoquo <modo> habuerunt sine aemulo complexus.
6 At ego in societatem recepi hospitem Lycurgo crudeliorm."
7 Ecce autem, ego dum cum ventis litigo, intravit
pinacothecam senex canus, exercitati vultus et qui videretur
nescio quid magnum promittere, sed cultu non proinde speciosus,
ut facile apereret eum <ex> hac nota litteratorum esse, quos
8 odisse divites solent. Is ergo ad latus constitit meum *

L (= lrtp)
83 2 quem lrp: quam t *del. Jahn* monocnemon *corr. Scaliger*
4 *del. Mueller post Fraenkel, qui* pictorum *quoque* 5 Hylan
Scaliger: hilari quoquo <modo> *lego; adiunct. vide*: quoque modo
7 *add. Dousa* litteratorum *Dousa*: litteratum 8 *lac. ind.* t

7
The Wisdom of Eumolpus

83 I visited a picture gallery that contained a remarkable collection of paintings. For example, there I witnessed the hand of Zeuxis, unmarred by the ravages of time, and not without a certain dread I touched the sketches of Protagenes, in realism competing with Nature herself. But at the "Goddess on One Knee" of Apelles, or Monocnemon, as the Greeks call her, I worshipped in earnest. The outlines of the artist's figures had been executed with such subtlety and naturalness that you'd swear he'd captured their souls. In one a high-flying eagle was bearing the Boy of Ida off to heaven. In another a snowy- skinned Hylas was repulsing a shameless Naiad. And there was Apollo cursing his murd'rous hands as he adorned his unstrung lyre with a fresh posy. Beholding the faces of these lovers in paintings, I cried out as if in my isolation, "So love touches even the Gods! Jupiter, finding no one in heaven to call his own, came sinning down to earth, yet did no harm. And the Nymph who despoiled Hylas would have controlled her passion, had she realized Hercules would intervene. Apollo brought back the shade of his boy as a flower. All these stories show variously love with the field clear. It was only I who brought to my hearth a guest crueller than Lycurgus!"

Even as I was wrangling with the winds, there entered the gallery a white-haired gentleman with the wrinkles of experience and an air somehow of great things to come, though he was hardly dressed with similar distinction. One could tell at a glance he was from that tribe of scholars commonly spurned by the rich. Such a man stood at my side *

"Ego," inquit, "poeta sum et ut spero non humillimi
spiritus, si modo coronis aliquid credendum est, quae
9 etiam ad immeritos deferre gratia solet. 'Quare ergo,'
inquis, 'tam male vestitus es?' Propter hoc ipsum: amor
ingenii neminem unquam divitem fecit.
10 / Qui pelago credit, magno se faenore tollit; LO
Qui pugnas et castra petit, praecingitur auro;
Vilis adulator picto iacet ebrius ostro,
Et qui sollicitat nuptas, ad praemia peccat:
Sola pruinosis horret facundia pannis
Atque inopi lingua desertas invocat artes.

84 Non dubie ita est: si quis vitiorum omnium inimicus
rectum iter vitae coepit insistere, primum propter morum
differentiam odium habet; quis enim potest probare
2 diversa? Deinde qui solas extruere divitias curant,
nihil volunt inter homines melius credi quam quod ipsi
3 tenent. Insectantur itaque, quacumque ratione possunt,
litterarum amatores, ut videantur illi quoque infra
pecuniam positi" *
4 / "Nescio quo modo bonae mentis soror est paupertas" * L
5 / "Vellem tam innocens esset frugalitatis meae hostis
ut deliniri posset. Nunc veteranus est latro et ipsis
lenonibus doctior" *

L (= lrtp), O (= RP)
83 8 immeritos *Buecheler*: imperitos **84** insistere *Brassicanus*: inspicere 3 insectantur *Buecheler*: iactantur 5 lenonibus *Bongars* p^{2}: leonibus

"I," he began, "am a poet, and one of no mean inspiration, I hope, if laurels are anything to go by, when all it takes to win them is popularity with no skill involved. 'Why, then,' you ask, 'are you so badly dressed?' For this reason only: love of the creative intellect never made anyone rich.

Who trusts to the sea comes out far, far ahead;
Who seeks for the fray will have gold on his head.
Low toady lies tipsy on cloth of purple stain;
The pesterer of wives gets cash for his pain.
Alone shivers Eloquence, her rags with frost wrung,
As she summons a lost craft, no food on her tongue!

84 "And that's the truth. Anybody who's a sworn foe of all imperfection and tries to get on the right road in life is hated, firstly because he is different. It's hard to like your opposite. And secondly, the people whose only interest is in accumulating wealth, all they want is for other people to think that nothing beats their having it. So they attack the lovers of literature by whatever means, to ensure they stay lower on the moneyed scale *

Poverty is somehow the sister of the high mind *

I could only wish that my honesty's enemy were naïve enough to be won over. In fact he's a seasoned crook and smarter than a pimp *

85 "In Asiam cum a quaestore essem stipendio eductus,
hospitium Pergami accepi. Ubi cum libenter habitarem
non solum propter cultum aedicularum, sed etiam propter
hospitis formosissimum filium, excogitavi rationem, qua
2 non essem patri familiae suspectus [amator]. Quotiescumque enim
in conivivio de usu formosorum mentio facta est, tam
vehementer excandui, tam severa tristitia violari aures
meas obsceno sermone nolui, ut me mater praecipue tamquam
3 unum ex philosophis intueretur. Iam ego coeperam ephebum
in gymnasium deducere, ego studia eius ordinare, ego
docere ac praecipere, ne quis praedator corporis
admitteretur in domum *

4 Forte cum in triclinio iaceremus, quia dies sollemnis
ludum auctaverat pigritiamque recedendi imposuerat
hilaritas longior, fere circa mediam noctem intellexi
5 puerum vigilare. Itaque timidissimo murmure votum feci et,
'Domina,' inquam, 'Venus, si ego hunc puerum basiavero
ita ut ille non sentiat, cras illi par columbarum donabo.'
6 Audito voluptatis pretio puer stertere coepit. Itaque
aggressus simulantem aliquot basiolis invasi. Contentus
hoc principio bene mane surrexi electumque par columbarum

L (= lrtp)
85 *est nomen dicentis* Eumolpus (Eumolpius l) in $t^m p^m$
del. Fraenkel 4 auctaverat *Giardina*: attulerat *Buecheler*:
artaverat 6 puer stertere coepit] puer coepit stertere
Mueller: *cur non* stertere puer coepit; *cf.* 87.1 stertere patrem

85 [Eumolpus] "Sent out to Asia on the staff of the quaestor, I was put up at a private house in Pergamum. My billet was a most agreeable one: accommodations were lavish, and my host had a very good-looking son. So I devised a plan to disarm fatherly suspicion. If ever any mention came up in company of sex with handsome boys, I became so violently angry and so sternly reproving of the sullying of my ears with such revolting talk that the boy's mother in particular took me for one of those moral philosophers. I was soon accompanying the lad to the gym, supervising his reading, and providing all teaching and instruction, with the aim to keeping the house clear of any sexual predator *

"One time we were lolling about in the dining room, a holiday having extended our leisure, and a longish spell of merriment having made us reluctant to retire, when round about midnight I noticed that the boy was awake. So in the shyest of whispers I made a vow: 'Lady Venus,' I prayed, 'if I can get to kiss this boy without his feeling it, tomorrow I shall present him with a pair of doves.' Hearing the price I'd put on my pleasure, the boy began to snore. So I approached the little faker and landed a kiss or two. Satisfied with this beginning, next day I rose bright and early and brought the boy a fine pair of doves, as anticipated, and so fulfilled my vow.

This tale of the distant sexual affair overseas of the younger Eumolpus (see n. 11) with the youthful son of his host while on military billet is one of Petronius' best. As usual, enough information is supplied for the reader to inspect and judge the ethical framework of the encounter – which would pass muster in his era and not necessarily fall far short any more in ours. Mitigation enters immediately, from the erotic temptations of a foreign setting (*peregrina libido*), which not even the Widow of Ephesus could resist. The first clues are teasingly conventional, with *filius* (son) and then *formosorum* (good-looking young males), in the familiar setting of education and guardianship. But then, a line or two later, something of greater use: Eumolpus refers to his quarry as an *ephebe* (adolescent) no less than five times in rapid order, a term rare enough to occur only once elsewhere in Petronius, at *Sat.* 140.4, in the similar context of Philomela's son. I concede that *puer* appears five times also. Does the Greek locale exert some influence? Not as broad-ranging or restrictive as *puer* and slightly more technical, an *ephebe* would offer greater latitude in this sexual setting: a well-grown, independent youth, eighteen or nineteen, ready for military service; a couple of years older than Giton at sixteen, an age at which he may already have amassed an appallingly lurid sexual track record.

86 attuli expectanti ac me voto exsolvi. Proxima nocte cum
idem liceret, mutavi optionem et 'Si hunc,' inquam,
'tractavero improba manu et ille non senserit, gallos
2 gallinaceos pugnacissimos duos donabo patienti.' Ad hoc
votum ephebus ultro se admovit et, puto, vereri coepit ne
3 ego obdormissem. Indulsi ergo sollicito, totoque corpore
4 citra summam voluptatem me ingurgitavi. Deinde ut dies
venit, attuli gaudenti quicquid promiseram. Ut tertia nox
licentiam dedit, consurrexi <et> ad aurem male dormientis
'Dii,' inquam, 'immortales, si ego huic dormienti
abstulero coitum plenum et optabilem, pro hac felicitate
cras puero asturconem Macedonicum optimum donabo, cum hac
5 tamen exceptione, si ille non senserit.' Numquam altiore
somno ephebus obdormivit. Itaque primum implevi lactentibus
papillis manus, mox basio inhaesi, deinde in unum omnia
6 vota coniunxi. Mane sedere <puer> in cubiculo [coepit] atque
expectare consuetudinem meam. Scis quanto facilius sit
columbas gallos gallinaceos emere quam asturconem, et
praeter hoc etiam timebam ne tam grande munus suspectam
7 faceret humanitatem meam. Ergo aliquot horis spatiatus in
hospitium reverti nihilque aliud quam puerum basiavi. At

L (= lrtp)
86 patienti *susp. George* 4 <eandem> licentiam *subiecit Mueller* consurrexi] *post hoc lac. ind. Buecheler,* et *ante* dii *addens; hic Fraenkel* 6 *sic addidi;* <puer> sedere *Mueller expectat; suspectavit* coepit *Fraenkel, ego delevi*

86 "That evening, when the same opportunity arose, I changed my bid: 'If I can get to intimately caress this child without his feeling it,' I intoned, 'I shall give him a pair of fighting cocks for his compliance.' At this vow the lad snuggled up closer, afraid perhaps of my falling asleep. I soon put his mind at rest as I hungrily explored his entire body, stopping short of the final pleasure. When day arrived I made good on my promise to the happy fellow.

"The third evening offered the same licence, so I rose and whispered into the ear of my fitful sleeper. 'Gods Immortal,' I intoned, 'if I can get to steal from this sleeping boy full and blissful intercourse, in return for my ecstasy, tomorrow I shall present him with a fine Macedonian thoroughbred, but only on condition that he doesn't feel a thing.' Never did a lad fall into a deeper sleep. And so I filled my hands with his milk-white breasts, affixed my lips to his, and in one clinch had the answer to all my prayers.

"Morning found the boy sitting in his bedroom awaiting my visit. It's a good deal easier, as you know, to buy doves and cocks than a thoroughbred; and besides, I now had to fear that the sheer size of the gift would put my generosity under suspicion. So I went off for a walk of several hours, and upon returning had nothing more for the boy than a kiss.

Gift giving, of birds and animals to boy beloveds is conventional, but here it is given a clever comic twist not once but twice: first by the increments required to complete the seduction, each gift costlier than the previous. The passivity of the beloved during the process was also a byword, thus feigned sleep during a whispered request took care of that – until the price for compliance became too high and Eumolpus reneged. That passivity then changed and a satisfactory denouement was achieved, playing out in an unusual, unexpected way (second twist). At 87.6–10 (next page), the youth, having reached a stage of muscle growth to "take it" (*ephebus plenae maturitatis et annis ad patiendum gestientibus*), accepted and received three full doses of intercourse on two nights and was up for a fourth, when Eumolpus was forced through exhaustion to call it off. It is debated whether this Milesian-style tale was told to cheer Encolpius up. The text is lacunose at the start, and it is sited in the midst of discussion of poetry and art – but the type of art to inspire it – and there is evidence of its mood-altering effect on the hitherto glum Encolpius: *Sat.* 88 *erectus his sermonibus.*

ille circumspiciens ut cervicem meam iunxit amplexu,
'Rogo,' inquit 'domine, ubi est asturco?' *

87 Cum ob hanc offensam praeclusissem mihi aditum quam
feceram, iterum ad licentiam redii. Interpositis enim
paucis diebus cum similis nos casus in eandem fortunam
rettulisset, ut intellexi stertere patrem, rogare coepi
ephebum ut reverteretur in gratiam mecum [id est ut]
<et> pateretur satis fieri sibi, et cetera quae libido
2 distenta dictat. At ille plane iratus nihil aliud
dicebat nisi hoc: 'Aut dormi, aut ego iam dicam patri.'
3 Nihil est tam arduum quod non improbitas extorqueat.
Dum dicit, 'Patrem excitabo,' irrepsi tamen et male
4 repugnanti gaudium extorsi. At ille non indelectatus
nequitia mea, postquam diu questus est deceptum se et
derisum traductumque inter condiscipulos, quibus
5 iactasset censum meum, 'Videris tamen,' inquit, 'non
6 ero tui similis. Si quid vis, fac iterum.' Ego vero
deposito omni offensa cum puero in gratiam redii ususque
7 beneficio eius in somnum delapsus sum. Sed non fuit
contentus iteratione ephebus plenae maturitatis et annis
ad patiendum gestientibus. Itaque excitavit me sopitum
8 et, 'Numquid vis?' inquit. Et [non] plane iam <non> molestum

---

L (= lrtp)
86 7 amplexu *Scaliger*: amplexui **87** *del. olim Mueller*: id …
sibi *del. Haley*: *delevi supplevique* 4 censum *Daniel*: sensum
ususque *F. Daniel*: usque 8 *sic transpono*: [non] paene *Mueller*

At which he looked about, threw his arms around my neck and said, 'Please, sir, where's my thoroughbred?' *

87 "By this contravention I had cut off my usual access, but again I reverted to my wicked ways. After a few days' interval, similar circumstances brought us back to the same situation, so, after confirming that his father was snoring away, I asked the lad to be friends with me again and to let me make it up to him and all else that the swellings of passion demand. But I'd obviously angered him, so all he said was, 'Go to sleep or I'll tell my dad.'

"There is no goal too high to be beyond the reach of the wicked. Even as he was threatening to wake his father I crept in beside him and took my pleasure with little resistance. In fact my naughtiness did not displease: after long complaining about being let down, teased, and shown up in front of his classmates, to whom he had boasted of my wealth, he said, 'But you'll see, I won't be like you: you can do it again if you want.'

"The boy had clearly set aside all resentment and I had returned to favour, so I took him up on his kind offer and sank off to sleep. But the well-grown youth was not content with a single encore, and of an age keen to oblige. So he roused me from slumber and said, 'Do you want anything?' Well, certainly even now this was hardly an odious

erat munus. Utcumque igitur inter anhelitus sudoresque tritus
quod voluerat accepit, rursusque in somnum decidi gaudio
9 lassus. Interposita minus hora pungere me manu coepit et
10 dicere: 'Quare non facimus?' Tum ego totiens excitatus
plane vehementer excandui et reddidi illi voces suas:
'Aut dormi, aut ego iam dicam patri'" *

88 Erectus his sermonibus consulere prudentiorem coepi ...
aetates tabularum et quaedam argumenta mihi obscura
simulque causam desidiae praesentis excutere, cum
pulcherrimae artes perissent, inter quas pictura ne
2 minimum quidem sui vestigium reliquisset. Tum ille,
"Pecuniae," inquit, "cupiditas haec tropica instituit.
/ Priscis enim temporibus cum adhuc nuda virtus placeret, LO
vigebant artes ingenuae summum certamen inter homines
3 erat, ne quid profuturum saeculis diu lateret. Itaque
hercule herbarum omnium sucos Democritus expressit, et ne
lapidum virgultorum vis lateret, aetatem inter
4 experimenta consumpsit. Eudoxos [quidem] in cacumine
excelsissimi montis consenuit, ut astrorum caelique motus
deprehenderet. Et Chrysippus, ut ad inventionem sufficeret,

L (= lrtp), O (= RP)
87 10 dicam patri l, *qui ordo ad* 87.2 *convenit* **88** *lac. ind. Buecheler, fere et interrogare complens*: *modo cur non* aetates<que> ... excutere; *adiectionem vide* 3 hercule *Scaliger*: hercula O: *om.* L: torculo *Heinze*: falcula *Giardina* omnium herbarum L 4 *om.* L, *del. Buecheler* excellentissimi L

imposition. So somehow or other amid my panting and sweating the boy got his licking, and again I fell asleep spent with bliss. Less than an hour later I felt a poke from his finger. 'Let's do it!' he said. By then awoken once too often, I was understandably pretty furious and gave him his words back: 'Go to sleep or I'll tell your dad!'" *

88 This story cheered me up and I accepted counsel from a wiser head, extracting from him the dates of the paintings and some of the more obscure themes, along with the reasons for the current apathy that was producing the extinction of the loveliest of arts. For even painting had disappeared without a trace. "Greed for money," he continued, "has wrought these changes. In the good old days when simple achievement was its own reward, the liberal arts flourished and competition was keen among men to ensure that everything of benefit to posterity should not go undiscovered.

"Exactly this was the impulse behind Democritus' extractions of the sap from plants: in his desire to investigate the properties of every stick and stone, he threw his life away on experimentation. Eudoxus grew into old age on the summit of the highest mountain available just so he could observe the phases of the stars and sky. And Chrysippus, to sensitize his mind for inquiry, took hellebore three times to purge it.

5 ter helleboro animum detersit. Verum ut de plastas
convertar, Lysippum statuae unius lineamentis inhaerentem
inopia extinxit, et Myron, qui paene animas quidem
hominum ferarumque aere comprehendit, non invenit heredem.
6 At nos vino scortisque demersi ne paratas quidem artes
audemus cognoscere, sed accusatores antiquitatis vitia
7 tantum docemus et discimus. Ubi est dialectica? Ubi
astronomia? Ubi sapientia consultissima <vitae> via?
Quis umquam venit in templum et votum fecit, si ad
eloquentiam pervenisset? Quis, si philosophiae fontem
8 attigisset? Ac ne bonam quidem mentem aut bonam
valetudinem petunt, sed statim antequam limen [Capitolii]
tangant, alius donum promittit, si propinquum divitem
extulerit, alius, si thesaurum effoderit, alius si ad
9 trecenties sestertium salvus pervenerit. Ipse senatus,
recti bonique praeceptor, mille pondo auri Capitolio promittere
solet, et ne quis dubitet pecuniam concupiscere, Iovem quoque
10 peculio exornat. Noli ergo mirari, si pictura defecit, cum
omnibus diisque hominibusque formosior videatur massa auri quam
quicquid Apelles Phidiasque, Graeculi delirantes, fecerunt.

L (= lrtp), O (= RP)
88 5 revertar O comprehenderet L 7 *sic supplevi: cf.* 84.1 rectum iter vitae: inlustrissima via *Mueller nuper in adn.* quis <nostrum> *requirit Watt* attigisset O: invenisset L 8 *del. Fraenkel* 9 exornat *Sambucus*: exorat *libri*

"And then, to turn to the plastic arts, there is Lysippus' wasting to death while concentrating on the lines of a single statue. And Myron, all but trapping in bronze the souls of man and beast, could find no heir. Whereas we wallow in our wine and our women without venturing to discover the art that's all around us. We scorn the past and teach and learn only its vices. What's become of the art of debate? Astronomy? The pursuit of wisdom, life's wisest path? Who today enters a temple and says a prayer to achieve eloquence? Or to find the fountain of, say, Philosophy? It's not even 'a sound mind in a sound body' that they want.

"No sooner do they set foot on the temple door jamb than it's one chap vowing up a gift in return for seeing off a wealthy relative; another chap for digging up buried treasure, and a third chap for making thirty million – clear. Even the Senate, that repository of all that's good and right, routinely appropriates for the Capitol a half-ton of gold; and, in case someone fails to love money enough, gussies up Jupiter too with it. So don't be surprised if painting has gone extinct when to gods and men a lump of gold looks prettier than anything Apelles or Pheidias – those crazy Greeks – created.

89 Sed video te totum in illa tabula, quae Troiae halosin ostendit. Itaque conabor opus versibus pandere:

Iam decuma maestos inter ancipites metus
Phrygas obsidebat messis et vatis fides
Calchantis atro dubia pendebat metu,
Cum Delio profante [ferro] caesi vertices
Idae trahuntur scissaque in molem cadunt
Robora, minacem quae figurabunt equum.
Aperitur ingens antrum et obducti specus
Qui castra caperent. Huc decenni proelio
Irata virtus abditur, stipant graves
Danai recessus, in suo voto latent,
O patria, pulsas mille credidimus rates
Solumque bello liberum: hoc titulus fero
Incisus, hoc ad furta compositus Sinon
Firmabat et mens semper in damnum potens.
Iam turba portis libera ac bella carens
In vota properat. Fletibus manat genae
Mentisque pavidae gaudium lacrimas habete
Quas metus abegit. Namque Neptuno sacer

L (= lrtp), O (= RP)
89 totum te L 4 *del Scaliger, fortasse post F. Daniel*
6 figurabunt *Lachmann*: figurabant 10 Danai recessus *Scaliger, transponens* in suo voto *Scaliger*: et in voto 13 furta *Buecheler*: fata 14 mens *Pithoeus ex Autiss.*: mendacium
16 properat r: properant

89 "But I see you're absorbed in the painting depicting The Sack of Troy. Let's see if I can cover the topic in verse:

And now ten harvests to uncertain fear
The gloomy Trojans led, in seer
Calchas' words inferring only dread:
So at Apollo's urging forest tops they axe
On Ida; thus to fall, in stacks to roll,
These oaks, fashioning their charger tall.
A huge enclosure left, covered like a cave,
To hold an army, angry, brave,
Ten years in combat, weight of Greeks all pent
To crowd the nooks and lurk for their intent.
O land! We'd thought the thousand ships had gone,
And soil from war was freed: for one the best was hewn
A legend; Sinon, trickster well rehearsed,
Assured us, and our hopes, e'er potent to reverse.
Now when the crowd from gates released, at war no more
Hastes to prayer, cheeks with tears aflow,
But tears of joy from hearts atremble so,
Which fear ere now forbade. For Neptune's priest

Crinem solutus omne Laocoon replet
Clamore vulgus. Mox reducta cuspide
Uterum notavit, fata sed tardant manus,
Ictus resilit et dolis addit fidem.
Iterum tamen confirmat invalidam manum
Altaque bipenni latera pertemptat. Fremit
Captiva pubes intus, et dum murmurat,
Roborea moles spirat aliena metu.
Ibat iuventus capta, dum Troiam capit,
Bellumque totum fraude ducebat nova.
Ecce alia monstra: celsa qua Tenedos mare
Dorso replevit, tumida consurgunt freta
Undaque resultat scissa tranquillo mari,
Qualis silenti nocte remorum sonus
Longe refertur, cum premunt classes mare
Pulsum marmor abiete imposita gemit.
Respicimus: angues orbibus geminis ferunt
Ad saxa fluctus, tumida quorum pectora
Rates ut altae lateribus spumas agunt.
Dat cauda sonitum, liberae ponto iubae
Consentiunt luminibus …
fulmineum iubar

L (= lrtp), O (= RP)
89 21 tardant *Junius*: tradunt 22 ictusque *Autiss.*: l<a>etusque *ceteri* 38 ponto: *Puteolanus*: pontem 39 *versum excidisse statuit Lachmann*

Laocoon, his hair aflow, incites the host
To shouting. And then his lance he lards,
The paunch to nick. But Fate his hand retards,
And blow rebounds in credence to the trick.
Again, besides, he steels his shaking hand
With axe to strike the tow'ring flank and
Grunts within the captive youth, and while amutter,
Oaken monster snorts with alien flutter.
Goes forth the captive youth to capture Troy,
To fight a war entire by novel ploy.
Behold the portents further: where Ten'dos' spiny
Back doth fill the sea, a swell arises on the briny
Wave, and breaks, recoils upon tranquillity,
A sound like oarage in the silent night
Carried distant, then when fleets do smite
The main, and surface, fir a-plunging, groans in pain.
Up we look, and snakes are borne in double coil
By waves to rocks, their chests engorged, they roil
With hips the foam like lofty ships.
They clap their tails, their crests in harmony
With swell, their eyes …
a flashing beam

Incendit aequor sibilisque undae fremunt.
Stupuere mentes. Infulis stabant sacri
Phrygioque cultu gemina nati pignora
Lauconte. Quos repente tergoribus ligant
Angues corusci. Parvulas illi manus
Ad ora referunt, neuter auxilio sibi
Uterque fratri: transtulit pietas vices
Moraque ipsa miseros mutuo perdit metu.
Accumulet ecce liberum funus parens,
Infirmus auxiliator. Invadunt virum
Iam morte pasti membraque ad terram trahunt.
Iacet sacerdos inter aras victima
Terramque plangit. Sic profanatis sacris
Peritura Troia perdit primum deos.
Iam plena Phoebe candidum extulerat iubar,
Minora ducens astra radianti face
Cum inter sepultos Priamidas nocte et mero
Danai relaxant claustris et effundunt viros.
Temptant inn armis seduces, ceu vi solet
Nodo remissus Thessali quadrupes iugi
Cervicem et altas quatere ad excursum iubas.
Gladios retractant, commovent orbes manu

L (= lrtp), O (= RP)
89 40 fremunt *Haupt*: tremunt 43 Lauconte *Scaliger*: Lacoonti 49 infirmus *Poggio*: infirmis 58 ceu vi solet *Lachmann*: ceu ubi solet: ceu solet ubi r 59 nodo *Dousa*

To set the seas alight, the waves to hiss and scream.
Minds in stupefaction: priests in headbands rooted,
Along with twin son tokens of Laocoon, Phrygian-suited,
Then suddenly in coils the gleaming snakes do smother;
To mouths they raise their little hands, neither brother
For self but other, their love exchanging plans,
Poor boys for whom in very death their fear was mingled.
Lo the father now his children's bodies will collect,
So feeble to protect. The man they seize
Already death-sated: to earth they drag his knees.
So lies before his altar victim/priest,
The ground a-beating. With rites profaned
Troy quickly lost her gods, was doomed.
And now the moon cast up her pallid light,
The lesser stars a-guiding with her radiant sight:
Among the Trojans sunk in sleep and wine
The Greeks undo the bolt, pour forth men.
Their leaders test their weapons, as when
The steed of Thessaly from ropen yoke is sharply cut:
He nods his head and shakes his flowing mane, is out.
They draw their swords and set their shields on arm

Bellumque sumunt. Hic graves alius mero
Obtruncat et continuat in mortem ultimam
Somnos, ab aris alius accendit faces
Contra Troae invocat Troiae sacra."

90 / <Quidam> ex is, qui in porticibus spatiabantur, L
lapides in Eumolpum recitantem miserunt. At ille, qui
plausum ingenii sui noverat, operuit caput extraque templum
2 profugit. Timui ego ne me poetam vocare<n>t. Itaque
subsecutus fugientem ad litus perveni, et ut primum extra
3 teli coniectum licuit consistere, "Rogo," inquam, "quid
tibi vis cum isto morbo? Minus quam duabus horis mecum
moraris, et saepius poetice quam humane locutus es.
4 Itaque non miror, si te populus lapidibus persequitur.
Ego quoque sinum meum saxis onerabo, ut quotiescumque
coeperis a te exire, sanguinem tibi a capite mittam."
5 Movit ille vultum et, "O mi," inquit, "adulescens, non
hodie primum auspicatus sum. Immo quotiens theatrum, ut
recitarem aliquid, intravi, hac me adventicia excipere
6 frequentia solet. Ceterum ne [et] tecum quoque habeam
rixandum, toto die me ab hoc cibo abstinebo." "Immo,"
inquam ego, "si eiuras hodiernam bilem, una cenabimus" *
7 Mando aedicularum custodi cenulae officium *

L (= lrtp), O (= RP)
89 64 ab aris *Junius*: avaris 65 invocat *aliqui minores cum* lrp: invocant **90** *lac. ind.* rtp; *verbum tale* quidam *deest, quod suppleo* 2 me <quoque> *Fuchs sic supplet* t^m 4 persequitur l prosequitur rtp e capite *Memmianus* r 5 recitarem *Cuiacianus*: 6 *del. Buecheler* 6/7 *lacunae in libris indicantur*

To take up combat. And here there's one
Who maims the deep in wine, their slumbers he equates
To death's finality; another brands from altars lights,
Calls down on Trojans Trojans' sacred rites ..."

90 Some students strolling in the colonnade lobbed stones at Eumolpus in mid-song. Knowing only too well the acclaim in store for his talents, he shielded his head and fled the building. My fear was that they'd brand me a poet too, so I took after him as far as the shoreline where I could make my first stop beyond missile range. "Hey," I said, "what's your problem? Are you sick? You're in my company less than two hours and you've talked more often like a poet than a human being. I'm not surprised people see you off with stones! I'll be filling my own pockets with rocks too, so that any time you get beyond yourself I can let some blood out of your head!" He glanced at me. "My dear young fellow," he said, "I am no stranger to such auguries. Frankly every time I've gone to the hall to give a recitation I've had this reception from the audience. But I have no wish to quarrel with you as well, so I shall give up this diet for one full day." "All right, then," said I. "If you can swear off your daily rant we'll have dinner together" *

I put in an order with the housekeeper for a light supper *

The usual response from the young crowd to Eumolpus' more ambitious poetic sallies, it resembles the reaction at the school of rhetoric from an exiting throng of *scholastici iuvenes* to an extemporaneous declamation by the next speaker after Agamemnon (*Sat.* 6), with focus on critique of bad aphorisms and poor construction (*sententias ordinemque totius dictionis*). Encolpius was by nature a respectful student, and now again he had lost himself in the subjects at the picture gallery, particularly The Sack of Troy, before Eumolpus offers an extempore poetic rendering, followed, alas, by the stoning we witness. A Petronian running joke with a debatable purpose. For another barracking at the baths see below and at Note (16). For my money, The Sack of Troy and The Civil War are substantial efforts from the author. Without knowing the date of composition, we cannot gauge their triteness. See Introduction.

91 Video Gitona cum linteis strigilibus parieti
2 applicitum tristem confusumque. Scires non libenter
servire. Itaque ut experimentum oculorum caperem ...
Convertit ille solutum gaudio vultum et, "Miserere,"
inquit, "frater. Ubi arma non sunt, libere loquor. Eripe
me latroni cruento et qualibet saevitia paenitentiam
iudicis tui puni. Satis magnum erit misero solacium, tua
3 voluntate cecidisse." Supprimere ego querellam iubeo, ne
quis convicia deprehenderet, relicto Eumolpo – nam in
balneo carmen recitebat – per tenebrosum et sordidum
egressum extraho Gitona raptimque in hospitium meum
4 pervolo. Praeclusis deinde foribus invado pectus
amplexibus et perfusum os lacrimis vultu meo contero.
5 Diu vocem neuter invenit: nam puer etiam singultibus
6 crebris amabile pectus quassaverat. "O facinus," inquam,
"indignum, quod amo te quamvis relictus, et in hoc
pectore, cum vulnus ingens fuerit, cicatrix non est. Quid
7 dicis, peregrini amoris concessio? Dignus hac inuria fui?"

L (= lrtp)
91 2 scires <eum> *prop. Buecheler* *pauca excidisse statuit Buecheler* paenitentiam] sententiam *scripsit Scaliger, tum corr.* 3 ego <illum> *prop. Buecheler* convicia *scribo* (*vide* 10.5), *nisi* ne ... deprehenderet *irrepsit*: consilia

8
Habits of The Heart, III

91 I spotted a glum and upset-looking Giton leaning against a wall with towels and scrapers in his hands, obviously not enjoying his servant's role. As if to confirm this impression ... he turned a regard to me now, melting with joy: "Take pity, buddy," he began: "With no weapons in sight I'm free to speak. Rescue me from this bloodthirsty brigand and punish your repentant 'judge' however harshly you wish. It will be consolation enough for this poor miscreant to fall by your will."

I told him to forget our quarrel in case someone got wind of our insults. Leaving Eumolpus behind (he was spouting poetry in the bathhouse!), I dragged Giton through the dark and squalid exit and made off for my lodgings at top speed. There I barred the door, hugged him tightly around the chest and crushed my face against his tear-stained cheeks.

For a long time neither of us could find words, and the boy's sweet chest was heaving with sob after sob. "You don't deserve it for leaving me," I said, "but I love you, and my heart though deeply wounded bears no scar. And what did you mean by taking another lover? Did I deserve to be treated so badly?"

Postquam se <adhuc> amari sensit, supercilium altius sustulit. * "Nec amoris," <inquam,> "arbitrium ad alium detuli. Sed nihil iam queror, nihil iam memini, si bona fide sententiam emendas."
8 Haec cum inter gemitus lacrimasque fudissem, detersit ille pallio vultum et, "Quaeso," inquit, "Encolpi, fidem memoriae tuae appello: ego te reliqui an tu <me> prodidisti? Equidem fateor et prae me fero: cum duos armatos videram, ad fortiorem fugi." Exosculatus pectus sapientia plenum inieci cervicibus manus, et ut facile intellegeret redisse me in gratiam et optima fide reviviscentem amicitiam, <eum> toto corpore adstrinxi.

92 Et iam plena nox erat mulierque cenae mandata
2 curaverat, cum Eumolpus ostium pulsat. Interrogo ego:
"Quot estis?" obiterque per rimam foris speculari
dilgentissime coepi, num Ascyltos una venisset. Deinde ut
3 solum hospitem vidi, <Eumolpon> momento recepi. Ille ut se
in grabatum reiecit viditque Gitona in conspectu ministrantem,
movit caput et "Laudo," inquit "Ganymedem. Oportet
4 hodie bene sit." Non delectavit me tam curiosum principium
timuique ne in contubernium recepissem Ascylti parem.
5 Instat Eumolpus, et cum puer illi potionem dedisset, "malo

L (= lrtp)
91 7 *verbum tale exigitur; adiunctionem videas lac.* p^2, p^1 *cum t correcta* detuli *Buecheler*: tuli *aut* tulit inquam *fortasse opus est* sententiam *Buecheler*: paenitentiam 8 <eum> *add.* t; *supplevi* corpore *lego*: pectore *insulsum; adiunctionem videas* **92** 2 *suppleo; adiunctionem vide* 4 parem t^m: partem

When he sensed I loved him still, he raised his eyes.*

"I looked to you only to judge my love," I said. "But now no more complaints, no more grudges, if you'll promise faithfully to change your mind."*

When I'd poured this out amid sobs and tears he wiped my face with his cloak and said, "Please now, Encolpius, I appeal to the accuracy of your recollection: did I leave you or did you ditch me? This for my part I freely admit: when I saw two armed men I took refuge with the stronger." I kissed that breast so wise beyond its years and threw my arms round his neck. And to show him plainly how I'd reconciled and our friendship was truly revived I gave him the full-body press.

92 By now the night had fallen and the woman had produced our meal order just as Eumolpus was banging at the entrance. "How many are you?" I called out, peering cautiously through a crack in the door in case Ascyltus had come along. At the sight of one visitor I quickly let him in. He threw himself down on the cot and noted the presence of Giton, serving the meal. "I like your Ganymede," he said, motioning with his head: "Today should be a good one." I was not pleased at this studied overture, and worried that I'd taken in as colleague another Ascyltus. After the boy handed him a drink

---

Encolpius had good reason to be apprehensive. It has been only four chapters since his new friend Eumolpus showed his hand and burnished his brand with the expert account of the Pergamene Ephebe. That took place long ago, but Eumolpus' comparison now of Giton to a Ganymede signalled ominously that his sexual perspective fell along the same lines and had not changed. His courtship commenced in earnest at Sat. 94 and seemed effective enough to have Encolpius resigned yet somehow unconvinced at Sat. 100 of the supposed virtues of sharing.

te," inquit, "quam balneum totum," siccatoque avide
6 poculo negat sibi umquam acidius fuisse. "Nam et dum
lavor," ait, "paene vapulavi, quia conatus sum circa
solium sedentibus carmen recitare, et postquam de balneo
[tamquam de theatro] eiectus sum, circuire omnes angulos
7 coepi et clara voce Encolpion clamitare. Ex altera parte
iuvenis nudus, qui vestimenta perdiderat, non minore
8 [clamoris] indignatione Gitona flagitabat. Et me quidem
pueri tamquam insanum imitatione petulantissima deriserunt,
illum autem frequentia ingens circumvenit cum plausu et
9 admiratione timidissima. Habebat enim inguinem pondus tam
grande, ut ipsum hominem laciniam fascini crederes. O
iuvenem laboriosum! Puto illum pridie incipere, postero
10 die finire. Itaque statim invenit auxilium; nescio quis
enim, eques Romanus ut aiebat infamis, sua veste
errantem circumdedit ac domum abduxit, credo, ut tam
11 magna fortuna solus uteretur. At ego ne mea quidem
vestimenta ab officioso ... recepissem, nisi notorem
dedissem.Tanto magis expedit inguina quam ingenia
12 fricare." Haec Eumolpo dicente mutabam ego frequentissime
vultum, iniuriis scilicet inimici mei hilaris, commodis
13 tristis. Utcumque tamen, tamquam non agnoscerem fabulam,
tacui et cenae ordinem explicui *

L (= lrtp)
92 6 et postquam *Goldast*: at *aut* ut p *del. Buecheler* 7 *delevi; cf.* 100.4 10 aiebant *Dousa*: aiebat 11 *lac. ind. Buecheler,* custode *supplens;* capsarius *Scaliger* expedit *Dousa*: impedit

Eumolpus pressed on: "I'll have you over the whole bathful," he said, draining the cup greedily as he announced he'd never had a rougher time. "As I was taking my bath I ventured a poetry recital for the people sitting around the rim, and I was almost beaten black and blue! When I was thrown out of the pool I went round every nook and cranny shouting your name as loudly as I could. On the opposite side a naked youth who'd lost his clothes was yelling for 'Giton!' with equal vehemence. While I was mocked for a lunatic and mimicked in the meanest fashion by the boys present, he was surrounded by a large crowd of admirers, applauding in humblest obeisance. His parts, you see, were so large that you'd take his manhood for the man himself! What a youth for the job! I'd bet he starts yesterday and finishes tomorrow! So he found assistance pretty quickly – some scandalous Roman knight, they said, who intercepted him, covered him with his own clothes and led him off home to enjoy his good fortune in private, I imagine. In my case I wouldn't even have been able to get back my own clothes from that officious attendant without supplying a witness. Goes to show by how much more it profits to massage the groin than the brain." This account by Eumolpus I met with frequent changes of expression: happiness at the discomfiture of my enemy, sadness as his fortunes rose. But I stayed silent as if the story meant nothing to me, and got on with setting up the meal *

Starting with a typically poor reception at the bath house for Eumolpus' impromptu poetry recital, the account as told to Encolpius shifts to a youth (Ascyltus) not yet encountered by Eumolpus, yelling for one "Giton" and enveloped by cheering fans, in contrast to the physical and mental beating Eumolpus suffers. The author's constant drum-beat of disdain-signalling by the young at the fruits of Eumolpus' intellectual efforts – poetry and rhetoric – is difficult to parse without the proper context; and it may be never better put than by Eumolpus himself at Sat. 92.

93 "Vile est quod licet, et animus errore laetus iniurias diligit:

2 Ales Phasiacis petita Colchis
Atque Afrae volucres placent palato,
Quod non sunt faciles: at albus anser
Et pictis anas involuta pennis
Plebeium sapit. Ultimis ab oris
Attractus scarus atque arata Syrtis
Si quid naufragio dedit, probatur:
Mullus iam gravis est. Amica vincit
Uxorem. Rosa cinnamum veretur.
Quicquid quaeritur, optimum videtur."

3 "Hoc est," inquam, "quod promiseras, ne quem hodie
versum faceres? Per fidem, saltem nobis parce, qui te
numquam lapidavimus. Nam si aliquis ex is, qui in eodem
synoecio potant, nomen poetae olfecerit, totam concitabit
viciniam et nos omnes sub eodem casu obruet. Miserere
4 et aut pinacothecam aut balneum cogita." Sic me loquentem
obiurgavit Giton, mitissimus puer, et negavit recte facere,

L (= lrtp)
93 *ante hoc caput lac. ind. libri* 2 *miror si hoc carmen hic convenit* laetus *Gronovius*: lentus 2.2 Afrae *Puteanus*: aeriae 2.4 involuta *Busche*: renovata 2.6 Syrtis *Scaliger*: sitis 2.7 probamus *Memmianus* 2.10 quicquid ... videtur *cf.* 15.8 3 potant *Pithou*: poterit casu *audio*: causa; *adiunctionem videas*

93 "Propriety is expendable; our aspiration embraces deviance and revels in mischief.

The bird we hunt in Colchis, land of pheasant
And fowl of Guinea, to palates are pleasant
For not being an easy mark. But the snow white goose,
And the duck, in his many-coloured coat,
Taste ordinary. From farthest shores the wrasse
Is brought, and whatever the stranded boat
Can dredge from the Syrtes is nice.
The mullet's now a bore. A mistress beats
A wife; from cinnamon the rose retreats.
Most highly prized are the things that are scarce."

"Is this," I said, "how you keep your promise to lay off poetry for the day? For heaven's sake at least spare us, who never gave you a stoning. Any one out of the number of people drinking in this building would stir up the whole neighbourhood at the merest whiff of the word 'poet' and ensnare us in the same fate. Take pity on us and heed the lesson of the gallery and the bath house!" Giton, the soft-hearted boy, scolded me for such talk, saying I was wrong on two counts: for verbally abusing my elders, and for

quod seniori conviciarer simulque oblitus officii
mensam, quam humanitate posuissem, contumelia tollerem
multaque alia moderationis verecundiaeque verba, quae
formam eius egregie decebant *
94 / "O felicem," inquit "matrem tuam, quae te talem LO
peperit: macte virtute esto. Raram fecit mixturam
cum sapientia forma. Itaque ne putes te tot verba
2 perdidisse: amatorem invenisti. Ego laudes tuas
carminibus implebo. Ego paedagogus et custos etiam quo
non iusseris sequar. Nec iniuriam Encolpius accipit:
3 alium amat." Profuit etiam Eumolpo miles ille, qui mihi
abstulit gladium; alioquin quem animum adversus Ascylton
4 sumpseram, eum in Eumolpi sanguinem exercuissem. Nec
fefellit hoc Gitona. Itaque extra cellam processit
tamquam aquam peteret, iramque meam prudenti absentia,
5 extinxit. Paululum ergo intepescente saevitia, "Eumolpe,"
inquam, "iam malo vel carminibus loquaris quam eiusmodi
tibi vota proponas. Et ego iracundus sum et tu
6 libidinosus: vide quam non conveniat his moribus. Puta
igitur me furiosum esse, cede insaniae, id est foras exi." / L
7 Confusus hac denuntiatione Eumolpus non quaesiit iracundiae
causam, sed continuo limen egressus adduxit repente ostium
cellae meque nihil tale expextantem inclusit, exemitque raptim
clavem et ad Gitona investigandum cucurrit.

L (= lrtp), O (= RP)
93 4 *lac.ind. libri* **94** facit L 3 eum *om.* L 6 id est *del. Fraenkel*

forgetting my duty as host not to bring contention to the table I had so generously provided – and a profusion of other things of moderation and tact so perfectly in keeping with his beauty *

94 "Oh happy your mother must be," cried Eumolpus, "to have given birth to such a boy! Bless your kindness! Oh rare combination of beauty and brains! And don't think your words will go to waste: you have found a devotee and I shall fill my poems with your praises. As your guardian and your guide I shall follow you bidden and unbidden. And Encolpius won't mind since he loves another."

Good thing for Eumolpus that the soldier had relieved me of my sword: all the hostility pent up against Ascyltus I would have let with his blood. This was not lost on Giton. He left the room, ostensibly to get some water, and his tactful exit cooled my anger. When I'd got a grip on myself I spoke. "Eumolpus," I said, "I'd rather you recited your poetry than make such commitments. I have a hot temper and you are a lecher, which makes us completely incompatible. Just think of me as crazy, back off, and get out fast!" Eumolpus, though taken aback by my outburst, wasted little time seeking the reasons. Without a pause he stepped across the threshold, brought the door smartly shut, and locked me in, completely by surprise. Swiftly removing the key, he sped away to check up on Giton.

Such is the picture painted in recent chapters: of an impeccably mannered, considerate, soft-hearted Giton, so diametrically opposed to the Giton whom Encolpius charges with brutally sluttish behaviour at the height of his deprivation-anguish. Who is the real Giton? Of one thing we can be sure: there never was a more giftedly manipulative boy-lover than he.

8 Inclusus ego suspendio vitam finire constitui. Et
iam semicinctio <lecti> stantis ad parietem spondam
vinxeram cervicem nodo condebam, cum reseratis foribus
foribus intrat Eumolpus cumm Gitone meque a fatali iam
9 meta revocat ad lucem. Giton praecipue ex dolore in rabiem
efferatus tollit clamorem, me utraque manu impulsum
10 praecipitat super lectum <et>, "Erras," inquit, "Encolpi,
si putas contingere posse ut ante moriaris. Prior coepi;
11 in Ascylti hospitio gladium quaesivi. Ego si te non
invenissem, petiturus praecipitia fui. Et ut scis non
longe esse quaerentibus mortem, specta invicem quod me
12 spectare voluisti." Haec locutus mercennario Eumolpi
novaculum rapit et semel iterumque cervice percussa ante
13 pedes collabitur nostros. Exclamo ego attonitus,
secutusque labentem eodem ferramento ad mortem viam
14 quaero. Sed neque Giton ulla erat suspicione vulneris
laesus neque ego ullum sentiebam dolorem. Rudis enim
novacula <erat> et in hoc retusa, ut pueris discentibus
15 audaciam tonsoris dare [instruxerat thecam]. Ideo nec
mercennarius ad raptum ferramentum expaverat nec Eumolpus
interpellavit mimicam mortem.

L (= lrtp), O (= RP)

94 8 *add. Buecheler* revocat l: revocavit rtp 9 <dumque> me *Buecheler* *add. Fuchs* 11 petiturus lr: periturus per t, *ex quo* p 14 *supplevi; videas adiunctionem; cf.* ulla erat *supra* tonsoris *del. Fraenkel* *delevi; adiunctionem videas*

I was locked in, and resolved to take my life by hanging. I had buckled my belt round the bedframe stood on its end against the wall and was putting my neck into the loop when the door flew open and in walked Eumolpus with Giton, to bring me back from death to life. Giton notably was mad with grief and yelling as he shoved me with both hands above the bed and cried, "Encolpius, you are wrong if you think you can go to your death before me. I already tried to by the sword in Ascyltus" room.

"If I hadn't found you I'd have headed for a cliff. And just so you know that death is never far off for those who seek it, I want you to witness what you meant to me!"

With that he snatched a razor from Eumolpus' servant, slashed his throat across and back, and collapsed before our feet. I cried out in shock and, seeking death by the same blade, followed him to the ground. But of a wound Giton showed not the slightest sign, nor was I feeling any pain. It was a practice razor with a specially blunted blade to give apprentice barbers confidence – the reason why the servant had remained undismayed at its seizure and Eumolpus had let the mimic death run its course.

95 / Dum haec fabula inter amantes luditur, deversitor LO
cum partem cenae intervenit, contemplatus foedissimam
2 iacentium volutationem, "Rogo," inquit, "ebrii estis an
fugitivi an utrumque? Quis autem grabatum illum erexit
3 aut quid sibi vult tam furtiva molitio? Vos mehercules
ne mercedem cenae daretis fugere nocte in publicum
voluistis. Sed non impune. Iam enim faxo sciatis non
4 viduae hanc insulam esse sed M. Mannicii." Exclamat
Eumolpus, "Etiam minaris?" Simulque os hominis palma
5 excussima pulsat. Ille tot hospitum potionibus liber
urceolum fictilem in Eumolpi caput iaculatus est
solvitque clamantis frontem et de cella se proripuit.
6 Eumolpus contumeliae impatiens rapit ligneum candelabrum
sequitur abeuntem et creberrimis ictibus supercilium
7 suum vindicat. Fit concursus familiae hospitumque
ebriorum frequentia. Ego autem nactus occasionem
vindictae Eumolpum excludo, redditaque scordalo vice
sine aemulo scilicet et cella utor et nocte.
8 Interim coctores insulariique mulcant exclusum et
alius veru extis stridentibus plenum in oculos eius
intentat, alius furca de carnario rapta statum proeliantis
componit. Anus praecipue lippa, sordidissimo praecincta
linteo, soleis ligneis imparibus imposita, canem ingentis
magnitudinis catena trahit instigatque in Eumolpon. Sed

L (= lrtp), O (= RP)
95 ludit O 5 tot … liber *del. Fuchs* 7 Eumolpon *malit Mueller, clausulae gratia* sine aemulo scilicet *susp. Mueller*

95 As this romantic tale unspooled, the innkeeper entered the room with the rest of our supper, and with a look at the compromising tangle of bodies, "Hey!" he said: "Are you drunk? Runaways? Drunken runaways? And who stood up the bed? What do you mean by all this sneaky shuffling about? Aha! You were meaning to skip into the streets tonight to avoid paying for your dinner! You won't get away with it. I'll have you know that Marcus Mannicius owns this building, not some widow-woman!"

"Are you threatening us?" shouted Eumolpus, fetching him a resounding slap across the face. The innkeeper, disinhibited by all the drinks he'd had with his guests, flung a clay jug at Eumolpus' head, cutting his forehead in mid-shout, and then he bolted out of the room. Not one to take an insult lying down, Eumolpus grabbed a wooden candlestick, caught him on the way out, and reclaimed his pride with a thorough pummelling. Up rushed in a body the servants and a gaggle of drunken guests. I saw my chance to turn the tables and shut Eumolpus out, and in sweet revenge upon my rival put room and night to good use without him.

Meanwhile, the cooking staff and the tenants were punishing the stranded Eumolpus, one person jabbing him in the eyes with a spitful of sizzling tripe, another grabbing a barbecue fork from the grill and striking a gladiator's pose. An old woman took a leading part, tottering in on ill-matched wooden sandals, eyes weeping and filthy dress hitched up for action, and dragging on a chain an outsized dog, which she set upon Eumolpus.

ille candelabro se ab omni periculo vindicabat.
96 Videbamus nos omnia per foramen valvae, quod paulo ante
ansa osteoli rupta laxaverat, favebamque ego vapulanti.
2 Giton autem non oblitus misericordiae suae reserandum
3 ostiolum succurrendumque periclitanti censebat. Ego
durante adhuc iracundia non continui manum, sed caput
4 miserantis stricto acutoque articulo percussi. Et ille
quidem flens consedit in lecto. Ego autem alternos
opponebam foramini oculos iniuriaque Eumolpi / velut L
quodam cibo me replebam / advocationemque commendebam, LO
cum procurator insulae Bargates a cena excitatus a
duobus lecticariis in mediam rixam perfertur; nam erat
5 etiam pedibus aeger. Is ut rabiosa barbaraque voce in
ebrios fugitivosque diu peroravit, respiciens ad
6 Eumolpon, "O poetarum," inquit, "disertissime, tu eras?
Et non discedunt ocius nequissimi servi manusque
continent a rixa?" *
7 / "Contubernalis mea mihi fastum facit. Ita, si me
amas, maledic illam versibus, ut habeat pudorem." *
97 Dum Eumolpus cum Bargate in secreto loquitur, intrat
stabulum praeco cum servo publico aliaque sane <non> modica

L (= lrtp), O (= RP)
96 4 iniuria … commendebam *locus perturbatus*
inuriaque *"bonus codex" Scaligeri*: iniuriam *aut*
iniuriamque etiam *vix aptum; susp. Mueller post Wehle*
qui iam 6/7 *lac. ind. libri* **97** *add. Pithou*

He, however, rose to every challenge with the aid of his candlestick.

96 We were watching the whole thing through a hole in the door that had been formed shortly before by the handle breaking off, I cheering on his thrashing, Giton, true to his compassionate nature, saying we must open the door and aid our beleaguered colleague. But my resentment persisted and I couldn't stop myself giving the boy a rap on the head with the sharp end of my knuckles for his pains. Whereupon he burst into tears and sat down abruptly on the bed, while I applied one eye and then the other to the hole, gorging myself as if it were nourishment upon Eumolpus' discomfort and recommending mediation. At which point the building superintendent, Bargates by name, rousted from his dinner, was brought into mid-fray on a two-man litter (he had the gout). He began a long harangue in violent, uncouth tones against "drunks" and "runaways" but then saw Eumolpus. "Most eloquent of poets," he said, "that was you? Why aren't my shiftless slaves putting down their fists and leaving at the double?" *

"My woman is giving me grief, so I want you to put a hex on her with your poetry so she behaves" *

97 As Eumolpus and Bargates were having their tête-à-tête, a bailiff entered the inn, acccompanied by a policeman and a quite considerable

frequentia, facemque fumosam magis quam lucidam quassans
haec proclamavit:
2 PUER IN BALNEO PAULO ANTE ABERRAVIT, ANNORUM CIRCA
XVI, CRISPUS, MOLLIS, FORMOSUS, NOMINE GITON. SI QUIS
EUM REDDERE AUT COMMONSTRARE VOLUERIT, ACCIPIET
NUMMOS MILLE.
3 Nec longe a praecone Ascyltos stabat amictus discoloria
veste atque in lance argentea indicium et fidem praeferebat.
4 Imperavi Gitoni ut raptim grabatum subiret annecteretque
pedes et manus institis, quibus sponda culcitam ferebat,
ac sic ut olim Ulixes Polyphemi arieti adhaesisset, extentus
5 infra grabatum scrutantium eluderet manus. Non est moratus
Giton imperium momentoque temporis inseruit vinculo manus
6 et Ulixem astu simillimo vicit. Ego ne suspicioni relinquerem
locum, lectulum vestimentis implevi uniusque hominis vestigium
ad corporis mei mensuram figuravi.
7 Interim Ascyltos ut pererravit omnes cum viatore cellas,
venit ad meam, et hoc quidem pleniorem spem concepit quo
8 diligentius oppessulatas invenit fores. Publicus vero servus
insertans commissuris securem claustrorum [in]firmitatem
9 laxavit. Ego ad genua Ascylti procubui et per memoriam

L (= lrtp), O (= RP)
97 4 Polyphemi arieti *scripsi*: pro ariete: *lac. olim inter verba indicaverat Buecheler, tum fere* Cyclopis arieti *emendavit; adiunctionem videas* 5 imperium *displicet; susp. Mueller* 7 quo *Scaliger*: quod 8 commissuris *Pithou*: commissuras securem *Buecheler*: secure *aut* securas *del. Dousa*

entourage. Brandishing a torch that was emitting more smoke than illumination, he issued the following proclamation:

> 1000 SESTERCES REWARD FOR INFORMATION LEADING TO THE RECOVERY OR WHEREABOUTS OF A BOY, GONE MISSING AT THE BATHS, RECENTLY, AGED ABOUT SIXTEEN, HAIR CURLY, BOYISH, NICE-LOOKING, NAME OF "GITON"

Ascyltus in a particoloured tunic was standing almost beside the bailiff, holding up the notice and the bounty upon a silver tray. I instructed Giton to get under the bed quick as a flash and hook his hands and feet round the edges of the frame that supported the mattress, in the same way that Ulysses had attached himself once to the ram of Polyphemus, and thus stretched along the underside of the bed elude groping hands. Without hesitation Giton instantly slipped his hands into the straps and beat Ulysses at his own game. To disarm suspicion I stuffed the bed with clothes to form the contour of just one person of about my size.

Meanwhile Ascyltus, with a guard, had made the rounds of all the rooms and got to mine, and the rather better secured door before him caused his hopes to rise. The official, however, simply wedged his axe between the planking and raised the heavy bar. I threw myself at Ascyltus' knees, imploring him upon the memory of our friendship, and hard times shared,

---

True in its details or not, this poster has the classic description of Giton and boy-beloveds such as he. The trickiest word to translate would be *mollis*, soft, for which "girlish" suggests itself first. But ultimately it is a boy that is sought, and a "boyish" boy fills the bill.

amicitiae perque societatem miseriarum ut saltem ostenderet fratrem. Immo ut fidem haberent fictae preces, "Scio te," inquam "Ascylte, ad occidendum me venissse. Quo enim secures attulisti? Itaque satia iracundiam tuam: praebeo ecce cervicem, funde sanguinem, quam sub textu quaestionis petisti." Amolitur Ascyltos invidiam et se vero nihil aliud quam fugitivum suum dixit quaerere, nec mortem hominis concupisse [nec] supplicis, utique eius quem <etiam> post fatalem rixam habuisset
98 carissimum. At non servus publicus tam languide agit, sed
raptam cauponi harundinem subter lectum mittit, omniaque etiam
foramina parietum scrutatur. Subducebat Giton ab ictu corpus
et retento timidissime spiritu ipsos sciniphes ore tangebat ...
2 Eumolpus autem, quia effractum ostium cellae neminem
poterat excludere, irrumpit perturbatus et, "Mille," inquit
"nummos inveni"; iam enim persequar abeuntem praeconem et in
potestate tua esse Gitonem meritissima proditione monstrabo."
3 Genua ego perseverantis amplector, ne morientes vellet occidere,
et "Merito," inquam, "excandesceres, si posses perditum

L (= lrtp)
97 10 mortem hominis *ordo prop. Buecheler inter alia, argutias mirans del. Ernout add. Ernout* post] praeter *Conte*
98 retento *Mueller*: reducto *lac. ind.* tp, *in qua discedit Ascyltos* 2 tua l: sua rtp proditione *Pithou*: propositione
3 excandesceres *Pithou* perditum *Jacobs*: proditum

to at least produce my partner Giton. To add credence to my phony entreaties, "Ascyltus," said I, "I know you've come to kill me! Why else would you have brought axes? Well, satiate your rage. See, I bare my neck: spill the blood you sought on the pretext of a search!"

Ascyltus disclaimed revenge, saying he truly was after his runaway and nothing more, and had no desire to kill a man at his mercy, especially one of whom he was very fond still even after such a fateful quarrel.

98 The guard, however, had not relaxed. He snatched a cane rod from the innkeeper and prodded beneath the bed, even probing all the holes along the walls. Giton shrank out of range of the rod and did not dare to breathe, even as he brushed the bedbugs with his lips …

As for Eumolpus (the room's shattered door being in no condition to deny entry to anyone), he burst in excitedly. "The thousand sesterces are mine!" he cried. "I'll catch the bailiff before he leaves and turn you in! I'll tell him you've got Giton, as you richly deserve!" I grasped his knees to slow his effort to kill men already doomed. "You'd have every right," I said, "to be furious if you could show me the wretch, but he escaped into the crowd,

ostendere. Nunc inter turbam puer fugit, nec quo abierit
suspicari possum. Per fidem, Eumolpe, reduc puerum et vel
4 Ascylto redde." Dum haec ego iam credenti persuadeo, Giton
collectione spiritus plenus ter continuo ita sternutavit
5 ut grabatum concuteret. Ad quem motum Eumolpus conversus
salvere Gitona iubet. Remota etiam culcita videt Ulixem,
6 cui vel esuriens Cyclops potuisset parcere. Mox conversus
ad me, "Quid est," inquit, "latro? Ne deprehensus quidem
ausus es mihi verum dicere. Immo ni deus quidam humanarum
rerum arbiter pendenti puero excussisset indicium, elusus
circa popinas errarem" *
7 Giton longe blandior quam ego, primum araneis oleo
madentibus vulnus, quod in supercilio factum erat,
coartavit. Mox palliolo suo laceratam mutavit vestem,
amplexusque iam mitigatum osculis tamquam fomentis
8 aggressus est et, "In tua," inquit, "pater carissime,
in tua sumus custodia. Si Gitona tuum amas, incipe
9 velle servare. Utinam me solum inimicus ignis hauriret
vel hibernum invaderet mare. Ego enim omnium scelerum
materia, ego causa sum. Si perirem, conveniret inimicis" *
99 "Ego sic semper et ubique vixi, ut ultimam
quamque lucem tanquam non redituram consumerem" *

L (= lrtp)
98 3 reduc puerum lp[2]: redde puerum rtp[1] 4 ter lt[v]: *om.* rtp
5 motum] sonitum *Jahn* 6 conversus *del. Fraenkel*
6/9/ **99** 1 *lac. ind. libri* 9 vel *Buecheler*: ut

and where he's gone I can't imagine. I beg you, Eumolpus, bring the boy back and return him to Ascyltus if you like." Just as I was beginning to convince him, Giton sneezed three times in rapid succession with all the violence of his pent-up breath, so that the bed shook. "Bless you, Giton!" cried Eumolpus, turning towards the commotion. Removing the mattress, he beheld a Ulysses that even a ravening Cyclops could have pitied. Then he turned to me. "What's this, you kidnapper?" he said. "I caught you red-handed and still you try to lie to me. Yes, if some god refereeing human disputes hadn't wrung the evidence out of this dangling boy I'd now be traipsing round the tuck shops looking a proper fool" *

Giton, far more ingratiating than I, first stanched the gash on Eumolpus' brow with a gauze of cobwebs soaked in oil. Then he removed Eumolpus' tunic and replaced it with his own cloak, then embraced him, by now well soothed, then covered him with a poultice of kisses. "My dear, dear father," he cooed, "we are utterly in your power. If you love your Giton please try to help us. I wish wildfire'd consume me, me alone; I wish I'd drowned in the wintry sea. I'm the root and cause of all the trouble. If I died we'd be enemies no more" *

99 "I have always lived, no matter where I found myself, as if each day were my last and never to return" *

Profusis ego lacrimis rogo quaesoque ut mecum
2 quoque redeat in gratiam: neque enim in amantium esse
potestate furiosum aemulationem. Daturum tamen operam
ne aut dicam aut faciam amplius quo possit offendi.
Tantum omnem scabitudinem animo tamquam bonarum artium
3 magister delevet sine cicatrice. "Incultis," <inquam>,
"asperis regionibus diutius nives haerent, ast ubi
aratro domefacta tellus nitet, dum loqueris levis
pruina delabitur. Similiter in pectoribus ira considit:
feras quidem mentes obsidet, eruditas praelabitur."
4 "Ut scias," inquit Eumolpus, "verum esse quod dicis,
ecce etiam osculo iram finio. Itaque, quod bene eveniat,
expedite sarcinulas et vel sequimini me vel, si mavultis,
5 ducite." Adhuc loquebatur, cum crepuit ostium impulsum,
stetitque in limine barbis horrentibus nauta et,
"Moraris," inquit, "Eumolpe,tamquam prope diem ignores."
6 Haud mora, omnes consurgimus, et Eumolpus quidem
mercennarium suum iam olim dormientem exire cum sarcinis
iubet; ego cum Gitone quicquid erat in iter compono et
adoratis sideribus intro navigium *

L (= lrtp)
99 2 daturum me *vult Buecheler* delevet *Fraenkel*: deleret 3 *supplevi* in pectoribus *et* considit *supervacanea putavit Fraenkel* 5 miraris rt prope diem *Richard; cf.* 99.6 adoratis sideribus: propudium: properandum t^{m}: propitium (ventum) *coniecit Mueller* 6 iter *Buecheler*: artum *Conte*: alter *lac. ind. libri*

I shed plenteous tears and begged and besought Eumolpus to reconcile with me also: insane jealousy was a thing beyond a lover's control; nonetheless pains would be taken in the future not to speak or act in a manner that could bring offence. I prayed that he scrubbed the scales of animus, as a good teacher should, and leave no scar. "In wild and rugged climes," I said, "snow lasts; but where the soil lies tidy and tamed by the plough, light frost will melt away even as one speaks. Likewise in the human heart anger takes up residence. It haunts the brutish mind, but from the educated one it flows upon its way." "To show the truth of what you say," said Eumolpus, "with this kiss my anger I do end. To ensure our success I propose that you two pack up your bags and follow me. Or, if you prefer, I'll follow you." As he was speaking there came a loud knock at the door, and on the threshold stood a sailor, complete with shaggy beard. "Eumolpus, you are late!" he barked. "Don't you know it's almost day?" With no further delay we all got to our feet and Eumolpus instructed his servant, who had been fast asleep for some time, to take out his baggage. I, along with Giton, got things ready for travelling, and, offering up a prayer to the stars, boarded ship *

Eumolpus may have had his fill of the never-ending drama over Giton, and seems to decide on a clean break and a new locale, arranging for his new friends the long sea voyage through the Strait of Messina to Croton. The ship's captain he chose to take them there, one Lichas of Tarentum, and his pleasure-loving associate, Tryphaena, had unfortunately met the young men before in typically compromising circumstances, triggering a major collision of unknown previous events catching up fortuitously with the present. For assorted grifts, the youths were on the run from that very pair, who quickly had discovered their presence, and they needed to escape the very real danger of fatal retribution. Brought up to speed, Eumolpus directed operations from there, producing a long farce of concealment and attempted evasions, then an epic battle, then a truce and reconciliation, then a Milesian Tale, and finally a storm and shipwreck. It is one of Petronius' more carefully wrought episodes, quite long, with a text not too disturbed and brimming with the best word-play in Petronius, as the friends and antagonists stake out positions on either side. At first seeming long-winded, it is worth the effort, resolving into a well-crafted, interesting, and fit prelude to the poem on The Civil War, the outrageous scam in Croton, Encolpius' encounter with the glorious Circe, the ornery geese, Philomela, and the Will with the cannibal codicil.

100 "Molestum est quod puer hospiti placet. Quid
autem? Non commune est quod natura optimum fecit? Sol
omnibus lucet. Luna innumerabilibus comitata sideribus
etiam feras ducit ad pabulum. Quid aquis dici formosius
potest? In publico tamen manant. Solus ergo amor furtum
potius quam praemium erit? Immo vero nolo habere bona nisi
quibus populus inviderit. Unus, sed senex, non erit gravis;
etiam cum voluerit aliquid sumere, opus anhelitu prodet."
2 Haec ut infra fiduciam posui fraudavi animum dissidentem,
coepi somnum tunicula capite mentiri.

3 Sed repente quasi destruente fortuna constantiam meam
eiusmodi vox super constratum puppis congemuit: "Ergo me
4 derisit?" En haec quidem virilis et aegre auribus meis
familiaris animum palpitentem percussit. Ceterum eadem
indignatione mulier lacerata ulterius excanduit et, "Si
quis deus manibus meis," inquit, "Gitona imponeret, quam
5 bene exulem exciperem." Uterque nostrum tam inexpectato
ictus sono amiserat sanguinem. Ego praecipue quasi somnio
quodam turbulento circumactus diu vocem collegi
tremebundus manibus Eumolpi iam in soporem labentis
laciniam duxi et, "Per fidem," inquam, pater, cuius haec

L (= lrtp)
prodet t: perdet haec l: hoc 3 ingemuit *mavult Mueller*
4 en haec *scripsi; cf. Cic. Att.* 5.1.3 en haec ego patior
cotidie: et haec *Buecheler*: at haec; *neutraque apta*: aegre
scripsi: plane *Buecheler*: paene exciperem t^m: exciperet
5 circumactus *Cuper*: circumamictus *libri, sed supra* ictus
vide tremebundis l: tremulisque tp

9
Adventure at Sea

100 "It's a nuisance our host has taken a shine to the boy, but there it is. Isn't the best that nature has to offer common property? The sun brings light to all. The moon and the countless stars that shine with her lead even the wildest beasts to their food. What could be thought prettier than a flowing stream though it runs in our midst? Shall love then be the only thing we must steal and not claim? Yes; in fact I don't even want nice things unless people envy me them. One man, and an old one at that, will present no danger. And should he wish to get up to something, his heavy breathing will give him away!" Reflecting thus, with little conviction and with heart not sharing in the delusion, I pulled my tunic over my head and feigned sleep.

Suddenly, as if fortune meant to tear down all the resolution I had mustered, a voice rumbled over the stern deck: "Made a fool of me, did he?" – indeed a masculine voice and sounding somewhat familiar, which set my heart to pounding; and rising above it a feminine blast, filled with an equal indignation: "If some god," she said, "would let me get my hands on that exile Giton a fine welcome I'd give him!" These words, out of the blue, struck us both a physical blow and drained the blood away. I in particular felt as if I were being smothered in a long and violent nightmare. With trembling fingers I tugged at the end of Eumolpus' cloak (he'd just drifted off) and found my voice:

At about midpoint in the narrative is an episode that deserves to be everyone's favourite: its seagoing locale is absorbing and exciting; it is humorous, full of action, and reasonably long and compact; there is a new and unexpected love triangle; its characters are linked to the past, and there is a new feminine perspective. Moderating it all is a clear view of the influence of the era's obsession: rhetoric. (cont'd)

6 navis est, aut quos vehat dicere potes? Inquietatus ille
moleste tulit et, "Hoc erat," inquit, "quod placuerat tibi, ut
subter constratum [navis] occuparemus secretissimum locum
7 ne nos patereris requiescere? Quid porro ad rem pertinet, si
dixero Licham Tarentinum esse dominum huiusce navigii, qui
101 Tryphaenam exulem Tarentum ferat?" Intremui post fulmen
attonitus, iugulo detecto, "Aliquando," inquam, "totum me,
Fortuna, vicisti." Nam Giton super pectus meum positum
2 diu animam egit. Deinde ut effusus sudor utriusque spiritum
revocavit. Comprehendi <ego> Eumolpi genua et, "Miserere,"
inquam, "morientium, et pro consortio studiorum commoda manum:
mors venit, quae nisi per te <non> licet, potest esse pro
3 munere." Inundatus hac Eumolpus invidia iurat per deos deasque
se neque scire quid acciderit nec ullum dolum malum consilio
adhibuisse, sed mente simplicissima et vera fide in navigium
4 comites induxisse, quo ipse iam pridem fuerit usurus. "Quae
autem hic insidiae sunt," inquit, "aut quis nobiscum Hannibal
navigat? Lichas Tarentinus, homo verecundissimus et non tantum

---

L (= lrtp)
100 6 hoc … placuerat lt[v]rp[2] *ex Cuaciano*: hoc inquit placuerat rtp[1] *ex Benedictino* subter *Mueller*: super super constratum *del. Fraenkel,* navis *quoque Mueller in prima: cur non* navis *solum* 7 exulem *susp. Mueller*: uxorem t[m]
101 2 *supplevi; cf.* 97.9 ego ad genua Ascylti procubui et t[m]: id est *add. Scaliger* 4 nobicum tp[2]: nobis lrp[1]

"Pop!" I yelled, "For god's sake tell me whose ship this is and who's aboard!" Eumolpus didn't take kindly to being roused: "So this was your plan, was it," he said, "to occupy the most isolated spot available below deck to stop us from sleeping? What of it if I told you that Lichas is ship's master and he's taking Tryphaena on a trip abroad to Tarentum?"

101 After this thunderbolt I began to shake violently. "Fortune," I cried as I bared my throat, "at last your victory is complete!"As for Giton, he'd long since collapsed in a swoon over my chest. Presently our floods of sweat revived us and I grabbed onto Eumolpus' knees. "Show pity for the dying," I wailed, "and lend a hand to your comrades-in-letters! Death is upon us and may be a boon, unless you intervene!" Eumolpus was nonplussed by this paranoia and swore by all the company of heaven that he'd had no knowledge of prior events and had had no intention of playing any dirty trick. All he'd done, he said, was to invite in complete innocence and good faith some friends on a cruise he'd booked long ago. "But what's this trap you've fallen into?" he asked. "Who's this Hannibal sailing with us? – Why, Lichas of Tarentum, the most unassuming of men,

---

(cont'd) The episode contains only the latest and most extended of the debates and declamatory sallies that have penetrated the lives of the *Satyrica*'s characters. It began famously at the school of rhetoric and became a touchstone; it continued, more famously, with the talk at Trimalchio's dinner. And now, here's this long vignette aboard ship, with a density of practical examples to back it up. Encolpius, Giton, and Eumolpus, trapped and under sail, are at the mercy of personal enemies they have wronged and who wish to do them in. They must escape, but how? At a council of action, Giton starts with a proposal worthy of the Bertie Wooster Prize: have the helmsman change course for the shore for a claimed sick man aboard. No, says Eumolpus: won't work because ships don't change course, Lichas would visit the sick-bay, and they'd be seen. Now from Encolpius: slide down the rope to the tender and cut adrift. No, says Eumolpus, for the same reason, plus the need to kill the guard in the tender. Now Eumolpus: get in skin sacks and pose as baggage. Impracticable, says Encolpius, with a plan this time to pose as Ethiopian slaves. Unrealistic, says a chaffing Giton, with a second, ironic coda: jump overboard and leave it all to fate. Eumolpus refines the disguise plan with persuasive touches: full shaving and fake brands. They are spotted provoking this maritime ill omen and turned in. Eumolpus, as counsel, offers his usual flim-flam, causing the exasperated Lichas, captain and judge, to say at *Sat.* 107.7: *"Noli causam confundere, sed impone singulis modum!"* "You're confusing the issue with too many details" – which does so well for a tongue-in-cheek Petronian sphragis.

huius navigii dominus quod regit, sed fundorum etiam aliquot
et familiae negotiantis, onus deferendum ad mercatum conducit.
5 Hic est Cyclops ille et archipirata, cui vecturum debemus;
et praeter hunc Tryphaena, omnium feminarum formosissima,
6 quae voluptatis causa huc atque illuc vectatur." "Hi sunt,"
inquit Giton, "quos fugimus," simulque raptim causas odiorum
7 et instans periculum trepidanti Eumolpo exponit. Confusus
ille et consilii egens iubet quemque suam sententiam promere
et, "Fingite," inquit, "nos antrum Cyclopis intrasse.
Quaerendum est aliquod effugium, nisi naufragium imponimus
8 et omni nos periculo liberamus." "Immo," inquit Giton,
"persuade gubernatori ut in alterum portum navem deducat,
non sine praemio scilicet, et affirma ei impatientem maris
fratrem tuum in ultimis esse. Poteris hanc simulationem et
vultus confusione et lacrimis obumbrare, ut misericordia
9 permotus gubernator indulgeat tibi." Negavit hoc Eumolpus
fieri posse, "Quia magna," inquit, "navigia portubus se
curvatis insinuant, nec tam cito fratrem defecisse veri
10 simile erit. Accedit his quod forsitan Lichas officii causa

---

L (= lrtp)
101 4 quod regit *susp. Mueller* 5 hic est [Cyclops] ille [et] *Fraenkel* 7 imponimus *lego*: optamus *Mueller*: ponimus omni modo *Buecheler* et lacrimis et vultus confusione rtp gubernator *susp. Nisbet* 9 portubus ... curvatis *Verg. Aen.* 3.533

who in addition to being both captain and owner of this ship has several estates and a family business contracting for the shipping of cargo to market. This is the Polyphemus, the Bluebeard, to whom we owe our voyage. And then there's Tryphaena, a gorgeous woman who sails up and down the coast for the pleasure in it."

"They're the ones," gasped Giton, "we're running away from!" And he gave a rapid account to an anxious Eumolpus of why they hated us and of what danger we were in. Alarmed and at a loss for what to do, he asked each of us to come up with a suggestion. "Imagine," he said, "we've walked into the Cyclops' cave. We've got to find a way out short of causing a shipwreck and ending all our troubles."

"All right," said Giton, "let's persuade the helmsman to change course for another port – bribe him, naturally – saying your brother's seasick and on his last gasp. You'll be able to bolster the fiction with tears and worried looks, and make the helmsman sympathetic enough to do what you want."

Eumolpus said it wouldn't work. "Big ships need to find sheltered bays, and it'll hardly be credible that my brother got ill so quickly. Aside from that,

visere languentem desiderabit. Vides quam valde
nobis expediat ultro dominum ad fugientes accersere.
11 Sed finge navem ab ingenti posse cursu deflecti et Licham
non utique circumiturum aegrorum cubilia: quomodo possumus
egredi nave, ut non conspiciamur a cunctis? Opertis
capitibus an nudis? Opertis, et quis non dare manum
languentibus volet? Nudis, et quid erit aliud quam se
102 ipsos proscribere?" "Quin potius," inquam ego, "ad
temeritatem confugimus et per funem lapsi descendimus in
scapham praecisoque vinculo reliqua fortunae committimus?
2 Non ego Eumolpon in hoc periculum arcesso. Quid enim
attinet innocentem alieno periculo imponere? Contentus
3 sum, si nos descendentes adiuverit casus." "Non imprudens,"
inquit, "consilium," Eumolpos, "si aditum haberet. Quis
enim non euntes notabit? Utique gubernator, qui pervigil
4 nocte siderum quoque motus custodit. Et utcumque imponi
nil dormienti posset, si per aliam partem navis fuga
quaereretur: nunc per puppim, per ipsa gubernacula
delabendum est, a quorum regione funis descendit qui
5 scaphae custodiam tenet. Praeterea illud miror, Encolpi,
tibi non succurrisse, unam nautam stationis perpetuae
interdiu noctuque iacere in scapha, nec posse inde

L (= lrtp)
101 10 accersere *Buecheler*: accedere 11 aegrorum lp^2: aegrotorum rtp^1 **102** 2 casus *non damnandum; cf.* 15.6 4 nil ex nihil *Buecheler*: vel <nil> *Mueller*: velut *Conte*: vel: *del. Zinn* custodiam lt^{m}p^2: gubernacula rtp^1

maybe Lichas in his official capacity will want to pay a visit to the patient. A big help to our cause that would be, setting master on runaways voluntarily! But suppose we *can* get a ship on a major voyage diverted and Lichas somehow doesn't do the rounds of the sick bay, how can we disembark without being seen by the entire crew? Heads covered or free? Covered, and everybody would be wanting to lend the sick people a hand. Free, and we'd be advertising ourselves."

102 "Instead of this," said I, "why don't we resort to daring – slide down the rope into the tender, cut ourselves adrift, and leave the rest to fate? I'm not calling upon Eumolpus to attempt so dangerous a manoeuvre, since it's hardly appropriate to impose upon the innocent someone else's risk. But I'd be content to try our chances as we went over."

"Not a bad plan," said Eumolpus, "if it could get off the ground. But everybody will see us leaving. The helmsman will, at any rate, on his all-night watch to monitor the stars' positions. Though his eyes never close, it would be possible in theory to elude him if escape were being attempted from some other part of the ship, but one has to slide down from the rear deck and past the actual rudder, since that's where the rope descends.

"Anyway, Encolpius, I'm surprised it never occurred to you that there's a sailor stationed on permanent duty in the tender day and night. You won't

custodem nisi aut caede expelli aut praecipitari viribus.
6 Quod an fieri possit interrogate audaciam vestram. Nam
quod ad meum quidem comitatum attinet, nullum recuso
7 periculum quod salutis spem ostendit. Nam sine causa
[quidem] spiritum tamquam rem vacuam impendere ne vos
8 quidem existimo velle. Videte numquid hoc placeat: ego
vos in duas iam pelles coniciam vinctosque loris inter
vestimenta pro sarcinis habebo, apertis scilicet
aliquatenus labris, quibus et spiritum recipere possitis
9 et cibum. Conclamabo deinde nocte servos poenam graviorem
timentes praecipitasse se in mare. Deinde cum ventum
fuerit in portum, sine ulla suspicione pro sarcinis vos
10 efferam." "Ita vero," inquam ego, "tamquam solidos
alligaturus, quibus non soleat venter iniuriam facere?
An tamquam eos qui sternutare non soleamus nec stertere?
11 An quia hoc genus furti semel [mea] feliciter cessit? Sed
finge una die vinctos posse durare: quid eergo si diutius
aut tranquillitas nos tenuerit aut adversa tempestas?
12 Quid facturis sumus? Vestes quoque diutius vinctas ruga
consumit, et chartae alligatae mutant figuram. Iuvenes adhuc
laboris expertes statuarum ritu patiemur pannos et vincla?" *

L (= lrtp)
102 5 custodem *del. Fraenkel et Fuchs* 7 *del. Buecheler*
8 pro sarcinis *susp. Fraenkel et Fuchs* 11 mea lp: mihi rt:
del. Scaliger 12 *lacunam indicant libri*

be slipping his guard short of killing or bodily heaving him overboard. Ask yourselves whether you have the nerve to go through with it. As far as my participation goes, I refuse no challenge that offers hope of success. But I don't think you should be risking your necks quite so casually.

"Tell me if you like this idea at all: I'll put you each in one of these animal-skin sacks, wrap you up with leather straps, and treat you as my baggage along with my clothes – naturally leaving open here and there some of the top edging so you can get air and food.

"Then I'll raise the alarm that during the night both my slaves jumped into the sea to avoid worse ill treatment. Finally when we arrive in port I'll have you taken off as baggage without attracting the least suspicion."

"Oh, I see," said I: "You'll be trussing us up as if our guts were solid and unlikely to offend. Or as if we're the sort of people never to snuffle or sneeze. Or because this kind of trick worked on one occasion. Supposing we can last being tied up for a full day, what if becalming or rough weather keeps us in longer? What would happen to us? Clothes tied in a bundle too long are ruined by wrinkling, and bound paper changes shape. And young men not used to wear and tear? Would we survive being handled like statues, complete with the rags and the ropes?" *

13 "Adhuc," <inquam> "aliquod iter salutis quaerendum est.
Inspicite quod ego inveni. Eumolpus tamquam litterarum
studiosus utique atramentum habet. Hoc ergo remedio mutemus
colores a capillis usque ad ungues. Ita tamquam servi
Aethiopes et praesto tibi erimus sine tormentorum iniuria
14 hilares et permutato colore imponimus inimicis." "Quidni?"
inquit Giton, "Etiam circumcide nos, ut Iudaei videamur, et
pertunde aures, ut imitemur Arabes, et increta facies, ut suos
Gallia cives putet: tamquam [hic] solus color figuram possit
pervertere et non multa una oporteat sentiant [et non] nationi
15 <ut> mendacium constet. Puta infectam medicamine faciem
diutius durare posse; finge nec aquae asperginem imposituram
aliquam corpori maculam nec vestem atramento adhaesuram, quod
frequenter etiam non accersito ferrumine infigitur: age,
numquid et labra possumus tumore taeterrimo implere? Numquid
et crines calamistro convertere? Numquid et frontes
cicatricibus scindere? Numquid et crura in orbem pandere?
Numquid et talos ad terram deducere? Numquid <et> barbam

L (= lrtp)
102 14 quidni l: quid tu rtp: quidni tu t^{v} etiam l: et rtp oporteat *Heinze*: oportet ut *Buecheler et Crusius*: et *deleo post Buecheler*: omni *Crusius* ratione p^{2}: natione $lrtp^{1}$ [et non] nationi <ut> *scripsi; adiunctionem videas* 15 quod … infigitur *delet Pickard, ambitiose nimium* pandare *Stowasser* *add. Memmianus* r

"We still don't have a means of escape," I said. "How's this for an idea: Eumolpus as a man of letters surely has some ink. So let's use it to dye our skin from head to toe. That way, disguised as Ethiopian slaves, we can stay close to you, glad of not having to torture ourselves, and we can fool our enemies with the colour change."

"Oh yes!" said Giton. "And circumcise us also, so we pass for Jews. And put holes in our earlobes, so we look like Arabians. And chalk our faces, so the Gauls take us for one of them. To change our appearance we need more than a new colour.

"There's plenty else to fit into the national image for the deception to hold up. Just supposing the ink on our faces can last long enough, just supposing sea water doesn't cause spotting on our skin and our clothes don't get stuck to the ink, which happens often enough (no glue needed), how do we get our lips to puff up in those ghastly swellings? Do we have curling tongs to crimp our hair? Can we cut scars into our foreheads? Can we make ourselves bandy-legged and walk on our heels? Can we shape our beard-growth

peregrina ratione figurare? Color arte compositus inquinat
16 corpus, non mutat. Audite quod timenti succurrerit:
praeligemus vestibus capita et nos in profundum mergamus."

103 "Nec istud dii hominesque patiantur," Eumolpus exclamat,
"ut vos tam turpi exitu vitam finiatis. Immo potius facite
quod iubeo. Mercennarius meus, ut ex novacula comperistis,
tonsor est: hic continuo radat utriusque non solum capita
2 sed etiam supercilia. Sequar ego frontes notans inscriptione
sollerti, ut videamini stigmate esse puniti. Ita eaedem
litterae et suspicionem delinabunt suspicionem et vultus
umbra supplicii tegent."

3 Non est dilata fallacia, sed ad latus navigii furtim
processimus capitaque cum superciliis denudanda tonsori
4 praebuimus. Implevit Eumolpus frontes utriusque ingentibus
litteris et notum fugitivorum epigramma per totam faciem
5 liberali manu duxit. Unus forte ex vectoribus, qui acclinatus
lateri navis exonerabit stomachum nausea gravem, notavit
sibi ad lunam intempestivo inhaerentem ministerio, execratusque
omen, quod imitaretur naufragorum ultimum votum, in cubile
6 reiectus est. Nos dissimulata nauseantis devotione ad ordinem
tristitiae redimus, silentioque <lecto> compositi reliquas
noctis horas male soporati consumpsimus*

L (= lrtp)
102 15 peregrina ratione t^{m}: peregrinatione 16 timenti] amenti *Buecheler*: menti *Fraenkel* **103** 6 nos *Dousa*: non compositi *aliquis in Burman*: <lecto> compositi *ego*: lecto compositus vix prima silentia noctis carpebam *Frg*. 48.1: composito *lac. libri*

in the foreign style? Artificial colouring stains the body without changing it. Here's my desperation plan: let's tie our clothes round our heads and jump into the sea."

103 "Gods and man forbid!" exclaimed Eumolpus. "Putting an end to your lives so ignominiously! I'd much rather you did the following: As you could tell from his razor, my servant is a barber. Let him shave your heads right now, and eyebrows too, and I'll proceed to mark your foreheads with a realistic inscription to make it look like you've been branded as a punishment. The lettering will serve both to deflect the suspicion of the curious and to cast your faces in punishment's shadow!"

Without further ado we set this ruse in motion, and went stealthily to the ship's side for proffering of heads and eyebrows to the barber's cropping. Eumolpus then filled up our foreheads with large lettering and covered our entire faces most fulsomely with the familiar symbols for a runaway slave.

It chanced that one of the passengers, being seasick, was relieving his stomach of its contents over the side railing of the ship. Having seen in the moonlight the barber bent to his untimely task, he cursed the bad omen in this staging of the castaway's last desperate vow, and rushed back to his bunk. Pretending not to hear the sick man's imprecations, we resumed our sorry order of business, went to bed in silence, and slept badly through the hours of night remaining *

104 "Videbatur mihi secundum quietem Priapum dicere
'Encolpion, quem quaeris, scito a me in navem tuam esse
2 perductum.'" Exhorruit Tryphaena et, "Putes," inquit, "una
nos dormiisse; nam et mihi simulacrum Neptuni, quod
Bais <in> tetrastylo notaveram, videbatur dicere: 'in nave
3 Lichae Gitona invenies.'" "Hinc scies," inquit Eumolpus,
"Epicurum hominem esse divinum, qui eiusmodi ludibria
facetissima ratione condemnat" …
4 Ceterum Lichas ut somnium Tryphaenae expiavit, "Quis,"
inquit, "prohibet navigium scrutari, ne videamur divinae
mentis opera damnare?" …
5 Is qui nocte miserorum furtum deprehenderat, Hesus
nomine, subito proclamat, "Ergo illi [qui] sunt, qui nocte
ad lunam radebantur pessimo medius fidius exemplo? Audio
enim non licere cuiquam mortalium in nave neque ungues
neque capillis deponere nisi cum pelago ventus irascitur."
105 Excanduit Lichas hoc sermone turbatus et "Itane," inquit
"capillos aliquis in nave praecidit, et hoc nocte intempesta?

L (= lrtp)
104 videbatur mihi <inquit Lichas> desideratur quem t^{m}: quod: p: quid lt 2 Bais <in> tetrastylo *Buecheler*: Baistor asylo 3 contemnat *Heinze*: condemnat *lac. ind. Buecheler* 4 expiaret *Nisbet*: expavit *Delz* quis] quid *Burman* operam *Buecheler* *lac. ind. Buecheler* 5 Hesus nomine: laesus omine t^{m} *del. Segebade*

104 "I dreamed," said Lichas, "that Priapus spoke to me: 'The man you're looking for, Encolpius: I've had him brought onto your ship.'" Tryphaena shuddered. "You'd think we'd been in bed together," she said. "I had a dream of the statue of Neptune that I'd seen in the four-columned temple at Baiae, telling me that I'd find Giton on Lichas' ship." "Which goes to show," said Eumolpus, "that Epicurus was a genius when he dismissed such tricks of the mind with rational explanations" …

Meanwhile Lichas, after an incantation to avert the omen of Tryphaena's dream, said, "Who's to stop us from searching the ship, to make sure we don't run the risk of rejecting out of hand divine guidance?" …

The man who had witnessed our desperate nocturnal ruse, whose name was Hesus, suddenly exclaimed, "Aren't those the ones who were being shaved in the night by moonlight? By Heaven, what a dreadful precedent! I've heard that no living soul may cut his nails or hair on board ship except in time of a hard blow."

105 This information deeply troubled Lichas and he erupted in fury. "What's this?" he exclaimed. "Did someone cut his hair on my ship and on this night of a storm?

Attrahite ocius nocentes in medium, ut sciam quorum
2 capitibus debeat navigium lustrari." "Ego," inquit
Eumolpus, "hoc iussi. Nec in eodem futurus navigio
auspicium mihi feci, sed quia [nocentes] horridos
longosque habebant capillos, ne viderer de nave carcerem
nave facere, iussi squalorem damnatis auferri; simul ut
notae quoque litterarum non obumbratae comarum praesidio
3 totae ad oculos legentium acciderent. Inter cetera apud
communem amicam consumpserant pecuniam meam, a qua illos
proxima nocte extraxi mero unguentisque perfusos.
Ad summam, adhuc patrimonii mei reliquias olent" ...
4 Itaque ut tutela navis expiaretur, placuit
quadragenas utrique plagas imponi. Nulla ergo fit mora:
aggrediuntur nos furentes nautae cum funibus, temptantque
5 vilissimo sanguine tutelam placare. Et ego quidem tres
plagas Spartana nobilitate concoxi. Ceterum Giton semel
ictus tam valde exclamavit, ut Tryphaenae aures notissima
6 voce repleret. Non solum vero <ea> turbata est, sed
ancillae etiam omnes familiari sono inductae ad vapulantem
7 decurrunt. Iam Giton mirabili forma exarmaverat nautas
coeperatque etiam sine voce saevientes rogare, cum
ancillae pariter proclamant: "Giton est, Giton: inhibite

L (= lrtp)

105 2 *del. Fraenkel* obumbratae *Buecheler*: adumbratae accidērent *Heinze*: accederent *lac. ind.* t 4 utrique *Buecheler*: utrisque 6 vero *Fuchs*: ergo *add. Novak* etiam lt[v]: quoque rtp

Bring forth at once the guilty parties, so that I may know whose heads must roll to purify the ship!" "It was I," said Eumolpus, "who gave the order, and I certainly had no intention of bringing bad luck upon my own voyage. These prisoners' hair was long and scruffy, so I ordered them to be cleaned up so as not to let it seem like I was turning this ship into a dungeon; and also to make sure that their branding marks would not be concealed obligingly by their hair, and be on view for reading in their entirety. Moreover, they made light with my money on a girlfriend they shared, from whom I'd had to drag them away a night later soused in wine and scent. In fact they still reek of the dregs of my inheritance!" ...

Thus to appease the patron guardian of the ship, a sentence of forty lashes each was imposed. In a flash, angry members of the crew tied us up and set to placating their deity with our less than precious blood. I managed to absorb three lashes with a Spartan courage, though at his first blow Giton yelled loud enough to fill the ears of Tryphaena with his unmistakable voice. Nor was she alone in her distress, for all the maids too were prompted by the familiar sound to rush toward his torturer. Meanwhile Giton had disarmed the sailors with his amazing beauty and was meeting his cruel attackers with a plea in no need of words, as the maids cried out in unison, "It's Giton!

crudelissimas manus; Giton est, domina, succurre."
8 Deflectit aures Tryphaena iam sua sponte credentes
9 raptimque ad puerum devolat. Lichas, qui me optime
noverat, tamquam et ipse vocem audisset, accurrit et
nec manus nec faciem meam consideravit, sed continuo
ad inguina mea luminibus deflexis movit officiosam
10 manum et "Salve," inquit, "Encolpi." Miretur nunc
aliquis Ulixis nutricem post vicesimum annum cicatricem
invenisse originis indicem, cum homo prudentissimus
confusis omnibus corporis indiciorumque lineamentis
11 ad unicum argumentum tam docte pervenerit. Tryphaena
lacrimas effudit decepta supplicio – vera enim stigmata
credebat captivorum frontibus impressa – sciscitarique
submissius coepit, quod ergastulum intercepisset errantes,
aut cuius tam crudeles manus in hoc supplicium durassent.
Meruisse quidem contumeliam aliquam fugitivos, quibus in
odium bona sua venissent …

L (= lrtp)
105 8 deflectit] adrigit *Giardina* 9 luminibus deflexis *susp. Fraenkel qui cum aliis doctis manum interpolatoris in hoc capite et sqq. passim vidit: verba potius velut supervacanea loco non limato tribuas* 11 *lac. ind. Buecheler*

Giton! Stop your brutal lashes! It's Giton, my lady! Help him!" Tryphaena's ears needed no convincing, and she sped to the boy at top speed.

Lichas knew me perfectly, and might as well have recognized my voice. Up he ran, and, not pausing to inspect face or hands, with a quick downward glance at my groin and a practised feel, "Hello, Encolpius," he announced. Who can wonder today at the nurse of Ulysses recognizing that telltale scar after twenty years, when this man, after all the lines of body and outward markings had been erased, could with such perspicacity and cleverness light upon the one true confirmation of the runaway's identity?

A contrite Tryphaena, weeping copiously and quite taken in into thinking the brands upon our foreheads were real prisoner punishments, began inquiring as to what convict farm it was that had put an end to our wanderings and whose hands were cruel enough to carry out such a punishment, though runaways surely deserved some reproach for biting the hand that fed them …

Here is a fine, sexualized parody (Petronius/Encolpius over-egging it) of the recognition scene in Homer *Od.* 19.393–446, where Odysseus, years ago having been gashed above the knee by a tush in a boar hunt, had a prominent scar from the long flesh wound, by which his nurse Eurycleia was about to identify him, prematurely, to his wife Penelope. In a flash, to silence her, the quick-thinking chap grabbed Eurycleia by the throat with his right hand. Tryphaena's speculation about a convict farm does not, from this evidence, make it any more real than the brandings themselves.

106 Concitatus iracundia prosiluit Lichas et, "o te," inquit,
"feminam simplicem, tamquam vulnera ferro praeparata litteras
biberint! Utinam quidem hac se inscriptione frontis
maculassent: haberemus extremum solacium. Nunc mimicis
artibus petiti sumus et adumbrata inscriptione derisi!"
2 Volebat Tryphaena misereri, quia non totum voluptatem
perdiderat, sed Lichas memor adhuc uxoris corruptae
iniuriarumque, quas in Herculis porticu acceperat,
3 turbato vehementius vultu proclamat: "Deos immortales
rerum humanarum agere curam, puto, intellexisti, O
Tryphaena. Nam imprudentes noxios in nostrum induxere navigium,
et quid fecissent admonuerunt pari somniorum consensu. Ita vide
ut possit illis ignosci, quos ad poenam ipse deus deduxit.
Quod ad me attinet, non sum crudelis, sed vereor ne quod
4 remisero patiar." Tam superstitiosa oratione Tryphaena mutata
negat se interpellare supplicium, immo accedere etiam
iustissimae ultioni. Nec se minus grandi vexatam iniuria quam
Licham, cuius pudoris dignitas in contione proscripta sit *
107 "Me, ut puto, hominem non ignotum, elegerunt ad hoc
officium legatum petieruntque ut se reconciliarem aliquando
2 amicissimis. Nisi forte putate iuvenes casu in plagas
incidisse, cum omnis vector nihil prius quaerat quam cuius

L (= lrtp)
106 mimicis *Pithou*: inimicis *aut inimici* 2 iniuriarumque *vetus Pithoei Memm.* rp[2]: contumeliarumque ltp[1] 3 itaque *Fraenkel* possit *Tolosanus, id est Cuiacianus, secundum Pithou*: prosit 4 pudoris *del. Fraenkel*: pudor et *Buecheler* *lac. ind. libri* **107** legatum lt cum Tolosano: *om.* rp

106 Containing his anger no longer, Lichas leapt up. "You simple-minded woman!" he cried. "Scars done with a knife don't smudge! I only wish the brands were real. We'd be getting final consolation. But we've been made the victims of a charade. Fooled by a bogus inscription." Tryphaena was on the side of compassion, since she had not totally forgotten her pleasure, but the seduction of his wife and the insult to him in the colonnade of Hercules were still fresh in Lichas' mind, and he scowled all the fiercer. "Tryphaena," he said, "I think you have grasped how the immortal gods look after the affairs of men, now that they have lured these guilty malefactors unawares to our ship and advised us of their action in a set of matching dreams. We are therefore at risk of pardoning those whom God himself has delivered up for punishment. As far as I am concerned, I'm not a cruel man, but I'm afraid of suffering the consequences of leniency." This piece of superstitious rhetoric changed Tryphaena's mind. She was not against the carrying out of punishment, she said, and in fact supported what she saw as their just deserts, for the insult to her personally had been no less than his when her honour had been brought into public disrepute *

107 "As a man of some reputation, I suppose," said Eumolpus, "these young men have chosen me to effect the appointed task of seeking reconciliation between those who were once the best of friends – unless of course you believe they have walked into this trap completely by chance, though every passenger's first concern is into whose hands he is entrusting himself.

3 se diligentiae credat. Flectite ergo mentes satisfactione
lenitas, et patimini liberos homines ire sine iniuria quo
4 destinant. Saevi quoque implacabiles domini crudelitatem
suam impediunt, si quando paenitentia fugitivos reduxit,
5 et dediticiis hostibus parcimus. Quid ultra petitis aut
quid vultis? In conspectu vestro supplices iacent iuvenes,
ingenui honesti, et quod utroque potentius est,
6 familiaritate vobis aliquando coniuncti. Si mehercules
intervertissent pecuniam vestram, si fidem proditione
laesissent, satiari tamen potuissetis hac poena quam
videtis. Servitia ecce in frontibus cernitis et vultus
ingenuos voluntaria poenarum lege proscriptos."
7 Interpellavit deprecationem <supplicis> Lichas et, "Noli"
8 inquit, "causam confundere, sed impone singulis modum. Ac
primum omnium, si ultro venerunt, cur nudavere crinibus
capita? Vultum enim qui permutat, fraudem parat, non
9 satisfactionem. Deinde, si gratiam te legato moliebantur,
quid ita omnia fecisti, ut quos tuebaris absconderes? Ex
quo apparet casu incidisse noxios in plagas et te artem
quaesisse, qua nostrae animadversionis impetum eluderes.
10 Nam quod invidiam facis nobis ingenuos honestosque
clamando, vide ne deteriorem facias confidentia causam.
Quid debent laesi facere, ubi rei ad poenam confugiunt?

L (= lrtp)
107 3 destinarunt *Buecheler*   6 quam videtis *del. Fraenkel*
7 supplicis lt^{v}p^{2}, *id est Cuiacianus*: *om.* lrtp^{1} *del. Mueller*:
supplicii *Buecheler*   9 te *Buecheler*: a

So, unbend your minds in recognition of their efforts to make amends, and allow them as free men to go where they will without harm. Even the harshest, most unforgiving masters restrain their savagery when repentance brings the runaway back, and we spare the foe who has surrendered. What more do you seek or want from them? There lie before you young men in humble supplication, freeborn youths of honour, and more important still, your former associates. If – by Heaven! – they defrauded you of your money, if they betrayed your trust, now at least you could be content with the punishment you see. Observe on their foreheads the marks of servitude, their mien of freedom compromised by the voluntary acceptance of their sentence!"

"You're confusing the issue," said Lichas, "with too many details. First of all, if they came to me voluntarily, why did they get their heads shaved? One disguises oneself with the intention to commit fraud, not to make amends. Secondly, if they were trying to ingratiate me using you as their spokesman why did you do everything possible to keep your clients from view? From this it's clear we have guilty people stumbling by accident into my power, and that you've been employing your talents to evade the impact of our retribution. Your effort to shame us with glib appeals to their free and noble status will, I warn you, only weaken your case. What are grievants supposed to do in the event that their malefactors run straight into their own punishment?

11 At enim amici fuerunt nostri: eo maiora meruerunt
supplicia; nam qui ignotos laudit, latro appellatur, qui
12 amicos paulo minus quam parricida." Resolvit Eumolpus tam
iniquam declamationem et, "Intellego," inquit, "nihil magis
obesse iuvenibus miseris quam quod nocte deposuerunt
capillos: hoc argumento incidisse in navem videntur, non
13 venisse. Quod velim tam candide ad aures vestras perveniat
quam simpliciter gestum est. Voluerunt enim antequam
conscenderent exonerare capita molesto et supervacuo
pondere, sed celerior ventus distulit curationis
14 propositum. Nec tamen putaverunt ad rem pertinere, ubi
inciperent quod placuerat ut fieret, quia nec omen nec
15 legem navigantium noverant." "Quid," inquit Lichas,
"attinuit supplices radere? Nisi forte miserabiliores
calvi solent esse? Quamquam quid attinet veritatem per
interpretem quaerere? Quid dicis tu, latro? Quae [sola]
salamandria supercilia tua exussit? Cui deo crinem
devovisti? Pharmace, responde!"

108 Obstupueram ego supplicii metu pavidus, nec quid in re manifestissima dicerem inveniebam. Turbatus et deformis

---

L (= lrtp)
107 11 nostri lt[v]p[2v], *id est Cuiacianus*: mei tp[1] 12 hoc … venisse *susp. olim Mueller* 13 aures vestras lpt: vestras aures lp[2]: vestras aures rtp[1] *ex Benedictino* 15 del. *Pithou* exussit *Dousa*: excussit **108** *locus admodum corruptus vel lacunosus; utique sic punctum post* inveniebam *locandum constat*

"So they were our friends. In that case they deserve more severe punishment. The man who harms strangers we call a bandit; the man who harms friends, little short of parricide!"

Eumolpus rebutted this unfair riposte: "I note," he said, "that these unfortunate youths' worst mistake was to cut their hair at night, since that seems to prove they boarded your ship by accident and not by design. Let me reach your ears with a frank account of how innocently this came about. They wanted to unburden their heads of some uncomfortable excess weight before they went on board, but the wind freshened and forced a postponement of the planned grooming. And besides, they thought it quite immaterial where they should start doing what they'd previously decided to do, in all ignorance of the customs and superstitions of the sea." "And what," demanded Lichas, "was the purpose of shaving these petitioners' heads? To attract more sympathy by being bald, perhaps? In any case there's no point in trying to get the truth out of their counsel. What do you have to say, you brigand? Did a dragon burn off your eyebrows? Did you dedicate your locks to some god? Answer me, you witch!"

108 Trembling with dread of punishment, I was dumbstruck, and could find no words to explain what clearly needed no explaining. In my confused

... praeter spoliati capitis dedecus superciliorum etiam
aequalis cum fronte calvities, ut nihil nec facere deceret
2 nec dicere. Ut vero spongia uda facies plorantis detersa est
et liquefactum per totum os atramentum omnia [scilicet lineamenta]
3 fuliginea nube confudit, in odium se ira convertit ... Negat
Eumolpus passurum se, ut quisquam ingenuos contra fas legemque
contaminet, interpellatque saevientium minas non solum voce sed
4 etiam manibus. Aderat interpellanti mercennarius comes et unus
alterque infirmissimus vector, solacia magis litis quam virium
5 auxilia. Nec quicquam pro me deprecabar, sed intentans in oculos
Tryphaenae manus usurum me viribus meis clara libera voce clamavi,
ni abstineret a Gitone iniuriam mulier damnata et in toto navigio
6 sola verberanda. Accenditur audacia mea iratior Lichas,
indignaturque quod ego relicta mea causa tantum pro alio clamo.
7 Nec minus Tryphaena contumelia saevit accensa totiusque navigii
8 turbam diducit in partes. Hinc mercennarius tonsoria ferramenta
sua nobis et ipse armatus distribuit, illinc Tryphaenae familia
nudas expedit manus, ac ne ancillarum quidem clamor aciem
destituit, uno tantum gubernatore relicturum se navis ministerium
denuntiante, si non desinat rabies libidine perditorum collecta.
9 Nihilo minus tamen perseverat dimicantium furor, illis pro ultione,

---

L (= lrtp)

108 *lac. ind. Ehlers* 2 scilicet *del. Fuchs*: scilicet lineamenta *del. Gaselee* 2 *lac. ind Fraenkel* 8 tonsoria *emendo*: tonsor: *del. Burman, secl. Mueller in omnibus edd., sed cf. Mart.* 14.36 ferramenta tonsoria; mercennarius *substantivum est*

and ugly state, with the disgrace of having a head cropped and eyebrows as hairless as my forehead, it seemed only proper to say and do nothing. When the tears were wiped from my cheeks with a damp sponge, which made the ink run all over my face, covering everything in a sooty smear, Lichas' anger turned to revulsion … but Eumolpus, saying he would never allow anybody wrongfully and illegally to cause harm to freeborn men, confronted those brutal threats both verbally and physically, assisted in his efforts by his servant, with the odd weakling passenger lending moral support if not combat strength.

I too sought no quarter for myself, waving my fists in Tryphaena's eyes and shouting loudly and defiantly that I would not hold back unless that accursed woman, the only person on the whole ship who needed thrashing, refrained from hurting Giton.

My feisty showing only goaded Lichas to further anger, and the abandonment of my own cause in powerful vocal support of another offended him mightily. Tryphaena, incensed at my taunt, was no less beside herself, which prompted the taking of sides by the entire sailing party. On one side Eumolpus' servant passed out his hardware (arming himself first); on the other Tryphaena's retinue put up their naked fists, with the very servant girls shrieking on the battle line, and the lone voice of the helmsman threatening to abandon control of the ship unless this lust-fuelled lunacy among degenerates ceased. All the same, the furious fighting continued, the other side fighting for their revenge, we for our very lives.

nobis pro vita pugnantibus. Multi ergo utrimque sine
morte labuntur, plures cruenti vulneribus referunt veluti
10 ex proelio pedem, nec tamen cuiusquam ira laxatur. Tunc
fortissimus Giton ad virilia sua admovit novaculam
infestam, minatus se abscissurum tot miseriarum causam,
inhibuitque Tryphaena tam grande facinus non dissimulata
11 missione. Saepius ego cultrum tonsorium super iugulum
meum posui, non magis me occisurus quam Giton quod
minabatur facturus. Audacius tamen ille tragoediam
implebat, quia sciebat se illam habere novaculam, qua
12 iam sibi cervicem praeciderat. / Stante ergo utraque LO
acie, cum appareret futurum non tralaticium bellum,
aegre expugnavit gubernator, ut caduceatoris more
13 Tryphaena indutias faceret. Data ergo acceptaque ex more
patrio fide protendit ramum oleae a tutela navigii
raptum, atque in colloquium venire ausa,

14 "Quis furor," exclamat, "pacem convertit in arma?
Quid nostrae meruere manus? Non Troius heros
Hac in classe vehit decepti pignus Atridae,
Nec Medea furens fraterno sanguine pugnat.

L (= lrtp), O (= RP)
108 9 sine morte *del. Delz et Nisbet* veluti ex proelio *del. Fraenkel* 10 infestam *Pithou*: insertam *aut infertam* 12 tralaticium *Autiss., id est ex portione* B *deperdita*: stlatarium *aut* statarium L: *om.* R 13 ex patrio more *aut* patrio more L praetendit *Buecheler* 14 heros O: hostis L

Thus many fell on both sides (though none died), and still more retreated bloody from their wounds, just as in a real war, with no one's ardour cooling. Then Giton in an act of heroism took deadly razor to his manhood and threatened to slice away the root of all our ills: Tryphaena forestalled a crime so great, in heartfelt act of mercy. Many a time I too bared my neck to the barber's knife, with no more intent to kill myself than Giton had to carry out his threat, though he played his tragic part with greater assurance for knowing he had in his hand the same practice razor he'd used to "slash" his throat. As the combat lines stood firm and it was clear this would be no ordinary war, the helmsman with difficulty prevailed upon Tryphaena to offer a truce, like a herald. Then, after tokens were given and received in the traditional manner, she extended the olive branch that she'd snatched from the ship's figurehead and moved to start a parley:

> "What madness," (cried she) "changes peace into war?
> Was this our hands' deserts? No man of Troy
> In this ship bears off the troth of duped Atreides,
> No Colchian woman fights, inflamed by brother's blood.

As usual, the bone of contention becomes Giton, and for him as "Helen" a kind of Trojan War is fought on deck, with the interests of Encolpius pitted against the interests of Tryphaena, who, the evidence suggests, had had a fling with Giton, and maybe also Encolpius, which she would like to restart. See preparations at *Sat.* 110. This parallels an evident Encolpius-Lichas liaison earlier, now also on the point of rekindling. Amid it Petronius makes sure to keep the mood light and comic (he is no Apuleius: no one dies); and the armistice and then truce, complete with a signed text of the contractual details, are achieved pretty much on the strength of Giton's faked threat to slice off his private parts. Parody turns into farce.

Sed contemptus amor vires habet. Ei mihi, fata
Hos inter fluctus quis raptis evocat armis?
Cui non est mors una satis? Ne vincite pontum
Gurgitibus feris alios immittite fluctus."

109 Haec ut turbato clamore mulier effudit, haesit
paulisper acies, revocataeque ad pacem manus intermisere
bellum. Utitur paenitentiae occasione dux Eumolpus et
castigato ante vehementissime Licha tabulas foederis
2 signat, quis haec formula erat: "Ex tui animi sententia,
ut tu, Tryphaena, neque iniuriam tibi factam a Gitone
quereris, neque si quid ante hunc diem factum est
obiecis vindicabisve aut ullo alio genere persequendum
curabis; ut tu nihil imperabis puero repugnanti, non
amplexum, non osculum, non coitum venere constrictum,
nisi pro qua re praesentes numeraveris denarios centum.
3 Item, Licha, ex tui animi sententia, ut tu Encolpion nec
verbo contumelioso insequeris nec vultu, neque quaeres
ubi nocte dormiat, aut si quaesieris pro singulis iniuriis
4 numerabis praesentes denarios ducenos." In haec verba
foederibus compositis arma deponimus, / et ne residua in L
animis etiam post iusiurandum ira remaneret, praeterita
5 aboleri osculis placet. Exhortantibus universis odia
detumescunt, epulaeque ad certamen prolatae conciliant

L (= lrtp), O (= RP)
108 ei *Buecheler*: et immittite L: imponite O
109 2 quereris *Scaliger*: queraris 3 insequaris L si quaesieris *del. Mueller* ducenos *Autiss*: ducentos *cett.*

Love that's scorned will have the power. Alas for me: who
Amid these waves seizes arms, brings on the fates?
Who with one death has not enough? Surpass not the sea,
Unleash not fresh floods upon the savage deep!"

109 This came out in a hysterical wail, producing a momentary halt to the clash, as our hands stopped warring and returned to peace. Our leader Eumolpus, profiting from this opportune relenting, signed the peace treaty (after a blistering condemnation of Lichas), whose text read as follows: "You, Tryphaena, being of sound mind, undertake neither to complain of any wrong done to you by Giton, nor, if such wrong were done before this day, to prosecute for it, nor seek compensation for it, nor enter upon any other form of redress for it; and not to force your unwanted attentions upon the boy, neither to hug him, nor to kiss him, nor to engage in the sexual act with him. On pain of which for each offence you shall be fined two hundred denarii on the spot. And you, Lichas, being of sound mind, undertake not to reproach Encolpius abusively in either word or look, nor to ask where he spent the night. On pain of which for each offence you shall be fined two hundred denarii on the spot."

With the treaty framed in such terms, we laid down our arms, and, as a precaution against any anger in our souls lingering beyond the oath, agreed, with a kiss, to forget the past. To universal encouragement our resentments cooled, and the feast postponed by the conflict sealed our compact in good cheer.

6 hilaritate concordiam. / Exsonat ergo cantibus totum LO
navigium, et quia repentina tranquillitas intermiserat cursum, alius exultantes quaerebat fiscina pisces, alius hamis blandientibus convellebat praedam repugnantem.

7 Ecce etiam per antemnem pelagiae consederant volucres, quas structis harundinibus peritus artifex tetigit; illae viscatis illigatae viminibus deferebantur ad manus. Tollebat plumas aura volitantes, pinnasque per maria inanis spuma torquebat.

8 Iam Lichas redire mecum in gratiam coeperat, iam Tryphaena Gitona extrema parte potionis spargebat, cum Eumolpus et ipse vino solutus dicta voluit in calvos stigmosos iaculari, donec consumpta frigidissima urbanitate rediit ad carmina sua coepitque capillorum elegidarion dicere:

9 "Quod solum formae decus est, cecidere capilli
Vernantes comas tristis hiemps.
Nunc umbra nudata sua iam tempora maerent,
Area attritis ridet adusta pilis.
O fallax natura deum: quae prima dedisti
Aetati nostri gaudia, prima rapis" *

L (= lmrtp), O (RP)

109 5 concordiam *Buecheler*: concilium: hilaritatem [concilium] *Jacobs* 6 ergo om. L exultans O 7 structis *Butrica*: textis peritus artifex *an in tautologia interpolatio latitat?* 8 capillorum: in capillos suos Thol.lt[v], id est *Cuiacianus* 9 ridet *Birt*: ardet *post* rapis *lac. ind.* rtp[1]

The whole ship rocked with singing; and, in the sudden calm which had stopped our progress, one man tried to spear the flying fish with a trident, while another with tempting hooks to pull out the wriggling prey. And wondrously, along the sailyard, birds of the open sea had perched. A man skilled in his craft reached up to them with extended cane rods smeared in birdline, and the creatures, stuck fast, were lowered down to waiting hands. A breeze wafted up their down in billows, and their feathers eddied in the waters atop the airy foam.

By now Lichas was making up to me, and Tryphaena too was sprinkling Giton with the dregs from her cup, as Eumolpus, mellow also from the wine, took to hurling jibes at bald or branded men. Eventually, his stock of oafish wit running out, he resorted to poetry with an elegiac on hair:

"The one, true glory of my looks, my hair, has gone:
The locks of springtime driven out by winter gloom.
Now at last my brows lament their loss of shade
And scorched pate a clean threshing floor has made.
Cheating hearts of gods! The foremost joys you gave
Our lives, of these you do us first deprive!" *

10 "Infelix, modo crinibus nitebas 1
Phoebo pulchrior et sorore Phoebi. 3
At nunc levior aere vel rotunda 5
Horti tubere, quod creavit unda 2
Ridentis fugis et times puellas. 4
Ut mortem citius venire credas, 6
Scito iam capitis petisse partem." 7

110 Plura volebat proferre, credo, et ineptiora
praeteritis, cum ancilla Tryphaenae Giton in partem navis
inferiorem ducit corymboque dominae pueri adornat caput.
2 Immo supercilia etiam profert de pyxide sciteque iacturae
3 lineamenta secuta totam illi formam suam reddidit. Agnovit
Tryphaena verum Gitona, lacrimis turbata tunc primum bona
4 fide puero basium dedit. / Ego etiam si repositum in L
pristinum decorem puerum gaudebam, abscondebam tamen
frequentius vultum intellegebamque me non tralaticia
deformitate esse insignitum, quem alloquio dignum ne
5 Lichas quidem crederet. Sed huic tristitiae eadem illa
succurrit ancilla, sevocatumque me non minus decoro
exornavit capillamento; immo commendatior vultus enituit,
quia flavum corymbion erat *

L (= lrtp), O (B *post* nitebas *redintegrans*, RP)
109 10 *hunc ordinem versuum restituit Turnebus per coniecturam; numeri in margine ordinem fere librorum ostendunt* unda] imber *Jahn*: umor *Busche* **110** 5 sevocatumque *Goldast*: evocatumque flavum t^{m}: flaucorum *lac. ind. libri*

"Unhappy man, your locks did shine
More beauteous than sibling moon and sun;
But now, shining more than brass or round
Garden bulb, rain nourished in the ground,
You fear and flee the giggling girls around.
To let you know you'll soon be dead,
Look: already you've lost half your head!"

110 There was more of this available, I expect, and no less foolish, but Tryphaena's maid was now leading off Giton into a lower part of the ship and adorning the boy's head with a curly hairpiece belonging to her mistress. She even produced a pair of false eyebrows from a jewel box, and, expertly tracing the line of the missing ones, restored him to his full beauty. Tryphaena recognized her one and only Giton, and, amid her tears, for the first time kissed the boy with confidence.

I, rejoicing though I was in the return of the boy's original appeal, nevertheless hid my face often, conscious of having been marred by a deformity so considerable that not even Lichas would accept me as worthy of conversation. But the same maid as before relieved my despondency by taking me aside too and embellishing me with a no less flattering set of hair. In fact my looks were improved by the choice of a blond wig *

6 / Ceterum Eumolpos, et periclitantium advocatus et LO
praesentis concordiae auctor, ne sileret sine fabulis
hilaritas, multa in muliebrem levitatem coepit iactare: quam
7 facile adamant, quam cito etiam filiorum obliviscerentur,
nullam esse tam pudicam quae non peregrina libidine usque
8 ad furorem averteretur. Nec se tragoedias veteres curare
aut nomina saeculis nota, sed rem sua memoria factam, quam
expositurum se esse, si vellemus audire. Conversis igitur
omnium in se vultibus auribusque sic orsus est:

111 "Matrona quaedam Ephesi tam notae erat
pudicitiae, ut vicinarum quoque gentium feminas ad
2 spectaculum sui evocaret. Haec ergo cum virum extulisset,
non contentus vulgari more funus passis prosequi crinibus
aut nudatum pectus in conspectu frequentiae plangere, in
conditorium etiam prosecuta est defunctum, positumque in
hypogaeo Graeco more corpus custodire ac flere totis
3 noctibus diebus coepit. Sic afflictantem se ac mortem
inedia persequentem non parentes potuerunt abducere, non
propinqui; magistrati ultimo repulsi abierunt,

L (= lrtp), O (= BRP), Ioan.
110 7 esse feminam tam: feminam esse tam l **111** *et* **112** *fabula praeterea in Policratico Ioannis Saresberiensis ex nescioquo codice vel codicibus est transcipta* **111** 2 passis BPrtp: *sparsis* Rlr^{m} Ioan prosecuta] secuta *mavult Buecheler* defunctum *del. Reeve, sed decet Eumolpum largior sermo* Graeco more *in susp. venit Fraenkel*

Meanwhile Eumolpus, champion of defendants and sponsor of the present harmony, not one to let the hilarity abate without benefit of his anecdotes, launched a string of jibes at the fickleness of women: how easily they fall in love, how quickly they forget their own children, and how no woman was ever chaste enough to avoid going crazy with lust away from home. He was not referring to the tragedies of ancient legend, he said, nor to the figures recorded by history, but to an actual incident that he personally could recollect which he would relate to us if we cared to hear it. And so we all turned our faces and ears toward him as he began:

111 "There was a married woman in Ephesus with such a reputation for virtue that the women even of other cities in the region were drawn to come to gaze at her. And so it was that when she buried her husband she was not content in the ordinary way merely to follow behind his coffin with her hair loosened and beating upon her breast, bared to the mourners' view: she even followed his corpse into the crypt; and when the body was laid in its vault underground, Greek-style, she set to guarding it and weeping over it ceaselessly night and day.

"Not even her parents, nor her closest friends, could stop her from punishing herself in this way and seeking death by starvation. Finally the city magistrates were rebuffed and went away,

complorataque singularis exempli femina ab omnibus
4 quintum iam diem sine alimento trahebat. Assidebat
aegre fidissima ancilla, simulque et lacrimae commodabat
lugenti et quotiensque defecerat positum in monumento
5 lumen renovebat. Una igitur in tota civitate fabula erat,
solum illud affulsisse verum pudicitiae amorisque
exemplum omnis ordinis homines confitebantur, cum
interim impeerator provinciae latrones iussit crucibus
affigi secundum illam casulam, in qua recens cadaver
6 matrona deflebat. Proxima ergo nocte cum miles, qui
cruces asservabat ne quis ad sepulturam corpus
detraheret, notasset sibi [et] lumen inter monumenta
clarius fulgens et gemitum lugentis audisset, vitio
gentis humanae concupiit scire quis aut quid faceret.
7 Descendit igitur in conditorium, visaque pulcherrima
muliere primo quasi quodam monstro infernisque
8 imaginibus turbatus substitit. Deinde ut et corpus
iacentis conspexit et lacrimas consideravit faciemque
unguibus sectam, ratus scilicet id quod erat, desiderium
extincti non posse feminam pati, attulit in monumentum

L (= lrtp), O (= BRP), Ioan.

111 3 complorata ab omnibus ltr^{c} Ioan. 4 commodabat *Rittershusius*: commendabat quotienscumque R Ioan.: quotiensque B: quotie(n)s LP 5 cum *del. Jahn* asservabat L: servabat O Ioan. ad sepulturam *suspicor* corpus O Ioan: corpora L *del. Buecheler* 8 iacentis *mihi omnino non placet* contulit l Memmianus rp^{2}, *ex Cuiaciano fortasse*

as this model of wifely devotion, to universal sorrow, passed her fifth day without food. Her loyal maid sat beside her ailing mistress, lending her tears to the woman in mourning and refilling the lamp in the tomb as it would go out. Thus in the entire city there was only one topic of conversation, as men of all classes held her up as a truly unique and shining example of chastity and love.

"Meanwhile some robbers were crucified by order of the provincial governor right next to the sepulchre inside which the woman was mourning her recently departed spouse.

"During the subsequent night, the soldier posted at the crosses to see that no body was taken down for burial saw a light burning brightly amid the gravestones and heard sobs of mourning, and his curiosity, that very human weakness, impelled him to find out who or what was behind it.

"He went down into the crypt, whereupon, seeing a beautiful woman, he initially stood rooted, as if having a visitation by some supernatural spectre from the world below. But then he observed the corpse laid out, and he noticed her tears and her nail-scratched face, and came to the correct conclusion, I suppose: a woman unable to bear separation from her dead husband.

cenulam suam coepitque hortari lugentem ne perseveraret
in dolore supervacuo ac nihil profituro gemitu pectus
diduceret: omium esse eundem exitum [sed] et idem
domicilium, et cetera quibus exulceratae mentes ad
9 sanitatem revocantur. At illa ignota consolatione
percussa laceravit vehementius pectus ruptosque crines
10 super corpus iacentis imposuit. Non recessit tamen, sed
eadem exhortatione temptavit dare mulierculae cibum,
donec ancilla vini [certum ab eo] odore corrupta primum
ipsa porrexit ad humanitatem invitantis victam manum,
deinde refecta potione et cibo expugnare dominae
11 pertinaciam coepit et, 'Quid proderit,' inquit, 'hoc
tibi, si soluta inedia fueris, si te vivam sepelieris,
si antequam fata poscant, indemnatum spiritum effuderis?
12 "Id cinerem aut manes credis sentire sepultos?"
Vis tu reviviscere? Vis discusso muliebri errore, quam
diu licuerit lucis commodis frui? Ipsum te iacentis corpus

L (= lrtp), O (= BRP), Ioan.

111 8 esse exitum RP: exitum esse L: exitum *om.* B Ioan. *om.* A, *del. Orelli* 9 ignoti *coni. Buecheler*: ingrata *Rohde* corpus *Nodot*: pectus 10 *om.* L: certum *aut* certo *aut* certe O: certum habeo Ioan. 11 tibi] illi *Morgan* 12 *Verg. Aen.* 4.14 sentire L, Ioan. *ex Verg.* <Quid? Nonne> vis tu reviviscere? *Fuchs; cf. Sen. Epp.* 47 vis tu

"So he brought his supper into the tomb and began an effort to encourage the mourner to set aside her needless grieving and the marring of her breasts in useless lamentation. We all have to die and go to the same place, he said, together with those other things intended to mend a broken heart. But she took no consolation, and in her affliction she scratched at her breast the more fiercely and tore out her hair and laid it on top of the extended corpse.

"The soldier did not leave, however. Using the same line of encouragement, he sought to give food to the younger woman, until the maid, soon enticed by the aroma of the wine, first herself reached out a hand in defeat to take his compassionate offer, and then, restored by the food and drink, began to work upon her mistress's resolve. 'What will you achieve,' she asked, 'by starving yourself to death, burying yourself alive, yielding up your innocent breath before the Fates decree?

"'Think you that they care, these ashes, these departed souls?

"'Isn't it time to return to life? Isn't it time to set aside female delusions and enjoy the good things of life for the time that you can? The very body stretched out before you ought to counsel you to do just that.'

13 admonere debet ut vivas.'Nemo invitus audit, cum cogitur aut cibum sumere aut vivere. Itaque mulier aiquot dierum abstinentia sicca passa est frangi pertinaciam suam, nec minus avide replevit se cibo quam
112 ancilla quae prior victa est. Ceterum scitis quid plerumque soleat temptare humanam satietatem. Quibus blanditiis impetraverat ut matrona vellet vivere, isdem
2 etiam pudicitiam eius aggressus est. Nec deformis aut infacundus castae videbatur, conciliante gratiam ancilla subinde dicente:

'Placitone etiam pugnabis amori?
[Nec venit in mentem, quorum consederis in arvis?]'

Quid diutius moror? Ne hanc quidem partem corporis mulier
3 ab[sti]nuit, victorque miles utrumque persuasit. Iacuerunt ergo una non tantum illa nocte qua nuptias fecerunt, sed postero etiam ac tertio die, praeclusis videlicet

---

L (= lrtp), O (= BRP), Ioan.
111 12 admonere *vel* ammonere O Ioan.: commonere *aut* commovere L 13 nemo … vivere *om.* L: *ex* O *in* ltp aut … aut *del. Fraenkel*
112 quid L: quod O plerumque soleat temptare O: temptare plerumque soleat L: plerumque temptare soleat Ioan. vellet vivere BP: vivere vellet LR Ioan. 2 *Verg. Aen.* 4.38–9; *om.* Memm., *expunxit* r^c: deerat in L, *del. Buecheler* ne … abstinuit *aliquid corruptum;* partem corporis mulier O Ioan.: mulier corporis partem L: corporis *del. Iacobs bene*
3 *id est* abnuit *melior* videlicet] scilicet lr^c

"An invitation to eat and enjoy life never falls on deaf ears, and the woman too, parched from her fast of many days, allowed her resolve to be broken and ate her fill no less eagerly than the maid who had yielded before her.

112 "Well, you know of the temptations that attend satiety among us humans. The same seductive arguments that persuaded the woman to go on living were now turned upon her chastity. The virtuous lady found the soldier neither unattractive nor unpersuasive, in the face of the maid's persistent invoking of precedent to make the match:

"'Will you even reject a lover who pleases you?'

No need to elaborate: the woman ended her fast in that part of her body too, and the soldier won his battle upon both fronts. And so in each other's arms they lay, not only the night of their nuptials but the next one and the one after that, making sure of course to close the door of the crypt first,

---

Verg. *Aen.* 4.38–9. Cf. p.188 n. 27 for the second Vergil Dido parody.

conditorii foribus, ut quisquis ex notis ignotisque ad
monumentum venisset, putaret expirase super corpus
4 viri pudicissimam uxorem. Ceterum delectatus miles et
forma mulieris et secreto, quicquid boni per facultates
poterat coemabat et prima statim nocte in monumentum
5 ferebat. Itaque unius cruciarii parentes ut viderunt
laxatam custodiam, detraxere nocte pendentes supremoque
6 mandaverunt officio. At miles circumscriptus dum desidet,
ut postero die vidit unam sine cadavere crucem, veritus
supplicium, mulieri quid accidisset exponit; nec se
expectaturum iudicis sententiam, sed gladio ius dicturum
ignaviae suae. Commodaret modo illa perituro locum et
fatale conditorium <commune> familiari ac viro faceret.
7 Mulier non minus misericors quam pudica, 'Nec istud,' inquit,
'dii sinant, ut eodem tempore duorum mihi carissimorum
hominum duo funera spectem. Malo mortuum impendere quam
8 vivum occidere.' Secundum hanc orationem iubet ex arca corpus
mariti sui tolli atque illi quae vacabat cruci affigi. Usus
est miles ingenio prudentissimae feminae, posteroque die
populus miratus est qua ratione mortuus isset in crucem."

L (= lrtp), O (= BRP), Ioan.
112 3 quisquis L: quisque O Ioan. putaret *Buecheler*: putasset 5 cruciarii unius L detraxere O: detraxerunt L, Ioan. 6 desidet L Ioan.: residet O quid L Ioan.: quod O illa *om.* O Ioan. add. Buecheler: unum temptabat Mueller 7 inquit *om.* O Ioan. hominum duo *om.* L 8 ex arca post iubet Ost Ioan, *vel post* tolli L (lrp)

so that anyone visiting the tomb, friend or stranger, should think that this wife of unexampled virtue had expired upon her husband's corpse.

"As for the soldier, captivated by the lady's beauty and the secrecy, he would acquire whatever delicacies his means allowed and at first nightfall bring them back to the tomb. And so the parents of one of the crucified, upon seeing that guard had been relaxed, during the night took the body down from the cross and paid it the last rites.

"The soldier had been caught napping. Next day, when he saw that a cross was minus a body, he was afraid he'd be executed and told the woman what had happened. And he wouldn't be waiting around for the verdict of the court, he said: he'd carry out the sentence for his slackness with his own sword. But would she, he asked, grant the doomed man a place in the tomb and have that dire crypt share her husband and her man?

"The woman's heart was as soft as her morals were pure: 'God forbid,' she said, 'that I should behold the corpses of the two men I held dearest side by side! I'd sooner string up the one already dead than strike down the one still living!' So saying, she instructed the soldier to lift her husband's body from his coffin and affix it to the vacant cross. The soldier followed this resourceful woman's clever plan, and next day it was the people's turn to wonder how a corpse had got itself crucified."

113 Risu excepere fabulam nautae, [et] erubescente
non mediocriter Tryphaena vultumque suum super cervicem
2 Gitonis amabiliter ponente. At non Lichas risit, sed
iratum commovens caput, "Si iustus," inquit, "imperator
fuisset, debuit patris familiae corpus in monumentum
referre, mulierem affigere cruci."
3 Non dubie venerat in animum Hedyle expilatumque
4 libidinosa migratione navigium. Sed nec foederis verba
permittebant meminisse, nec hilaritas, quae occupaverat
5 mentes, dabat iracundiae locum. Ceterum Tryphaena in
gremio Gitonis posita modo implebat osculis pectus,
6 interdum concinnabat spoliatum crinibus vultum. / Ego L
maestus et impatiens foederis novi non cibum, non
potionem capiebam, se obliquis trucibusque oculis utrumque
7 spectabam. Omnia me oscula vulnerabant, omnes blanditiae,
quascumque mulier libidinosa fingebat. Nec tamen adhuc
sciebam utrum magis puer irascerer, quam amicam mihi
auferret, an amicae, quod puerum corrumperet: utraque
inimicissima oculis meis et captivitate praeterita
8 tristiora. Accedebat huc quod neque Tryphaena me
alloquebatur tamquam familiarem et aliquando gratum sibi
amatorem, nec Giton me aut tralaticia propinatione dignum
iudicabat aut, quod minimum est, sermone communi vocabat,
credo, veritus ne inter initia coeuntis gratiae recentem

L (= lrtp), O (= BRP)

113 et *om.* L 3 Hedyle *Buecheler* ex hedile, *cf.* 106. 2
8 vocabat *delebat quidam apud Hadrianidem*

113 This story was greeted with laughter from the sailors, and Tryphaena blushed furiously and rested her face affectionately upon Giton's neck. But Lichas did not laugh. Angrily shaking his head, "A good governor," he said, "would have taken the husband's body back to the tomb and put the woman on the cross."

He no doubt was reminded of Hedyle and how she'd cleaned out his ship and run off with another man. But the terms of the treaty forbade such reflections and the good cheer that had taken hold offered little room for resentment. And Tryphaena for her part had curled up in Giton's lap and was alternately kissing his chest and fussing with his hairless appearance. I found the new arrangements hard to stomach, and sulked and took no food and drink and glowered obliquely at the pair of them, as every kiss and every endearment that this oversexed woman contrived wounded me personally.

Yet I still could not make up my mind whether I was angrier at the boy for taking my girl, or at the girl for seducing my boy. In my eyes both things were despicable and even more depressing than my recent captive state. Making it worse was that Tryphaena would not speak to me as friend and former lover, and Giton did not think me worthy of toasting routinely nor (and this takes very little) include me in the general conversation, perhaps out of fear that in our reconciliation's infancy he might reopen the fresh scar.

9 cicatricem rescinderet. Inundavere pectus lacrimae
dolore partus, gemitusque suspirio tectus animam paene
submovit *

10 In partem voluptatis temptabat admitti, nec domini
supercilium induebat, sed amici quaerebat obequium *

11 "Si quid ingenui sanguinis habes, non pluris illam
facies quam scortum. Si vir fueris, non ibis ad spintriam" *

12 Me nihil magis pudebat quam ne Eumolpus sensisset,
quicquid illud fuerat, et homo dicacissimus carminibus
vindicaret …

13 Iurat Eumolpus verbis conceptissimis …

114 Dum haec taliaque iactamus, inhorruit mare nubesque
undique adductae obruere tenebris diem. Discurrunt nautae
2 ad officia trepidantes velaque tempestati subducunt. Sed nec
certus fluctus ventus impulerat, nec quo destinaret cursum
3 gubernator sciebat. <Nam> Sicilia[m] modo ventus flabat,
saepissime tamen Italici litoris aquilo possessor
convertebat huc illuc obnoxiam ratem, et quod omnibus

L (= lrtp)

113 9 partae *Mueller*: paratae 11 illam] illum *Courtney de Tryphaena puto, non Gitone* scortum *Putschius*: sportum Memm. r: sportam ltp: spurcam t: spintriam t[m] (*si hoc,* illum *legendum*)

114 2 certus *Jungermann*: certos 3 *suppleo deleo* flabat *scribo*: dabat tamen *emendo*: in oram t: *om.* lrp ratem *Goldast*; partem; *colloquium in adiunctione videas*

Tears born of humiliation streamed down my chest and the sobs I had concealed with sighs threatened to choke me *

Lichas made an effort to be included in the fun, shedding his master's reserve and trying for the easy acquiescence of a friend *

"If you have a drop of decent blood in your veins you'd see her as no more than a whore. If you're a real man you won't consort with such a low creature!" *

Nothing shamed me more than having Eumolpus discover how things had been and take it out on me with poetry in his own verbose way *

Eumolpus swore the most carefully worded oath *

114 As these words and suchlike flew back and forth between us, the sea grew rough and general overcast formed, making night out of day. The sailors rushed about in panic to their posts and furled the sails before the storm. Yet the wind drove upon the waves inconsistently and the helmsman was at a loss for where to set his course, because at one moment it blew from Sicily, followed in the next by the prevailing Northerly, offshore of the Italian littoral, which spun the hapless ship hither and yon.

There is a singular lack of clarity to these sentences, which our L tradition, not necessarily correctly, places after the story of the Widow of Ephesus, which did little indeed to reconcile the genders. There is hostility and name calling in the air, driven by sexual jealousy. A mood swing accompanied by lacunae suggests dislocation, but one tries first to make sense of the text we have. Encolpius is now unpaired and seething. His erstwhile lovers, Tryphaena and Giton, have warmed to each other and are fair targets. Lichas is a gooseberry, with overtures to Encolpius rejected, thus a good candidate for speaker, cajoling Encolpius and referring to Tryphaena as the whore, perhaps from her latest behaviour, if not as his travelling companion, *voluptatis causa*. A second possibility is offered by Courtney's 1970 emending of "her" to "him," i.e., having Lichas trying to detach Encolpius from Giton. Thus either Tryphaena or Giton qualifies as the "whore" a real man would avoid, depending on the gender of the demonstrative pronoun. What Encolpius feared from a poetic reveal would more likely be the dark back-story of Giton than his own earlier tryst with Tryphaena. This is only one possibility; others give roles to a woman speaker and the same pronoun dubiety.

procellis periculosius erat, tam spissae repente tenebrae
lucem suppresserant, ut ne proram quidem totam gubernator
4 videret. Itaque hercules postquam <tempestas> manifesta
5 convaluit, Lichas trepidans ad me supinas porrigit manus
et "Tu," inquit, "Encolpi, succurre periclitantibus,
id est vestem illam divinam sistrumque redde navigio.
Per fidem, miserere, quemadmodum quidem soles."
6 Et illum quidem vociferantem in mare ventus excussit,
repetitumque infesto gurgite procella circumegit atque
7 hausit. Tryphaenam autem prope iam <exanimatam>
fidelissimi rapuerunt servi, scaphaeque impositam cum
8 maxima sarcinarum parte subduxere certissimae morti. <At ego
Gitoni> applicitus cum clamore flevi et "Hoc," inquam,
"a diis meruimus, ut nos sola morte coniungerent. Sed non
9 crudelis fortuna concedit. Ecce iam ratem fluctus evertet,
ecce iam amplexus amantium iratum dividet mare. Igitur, si
vere Encolpion dilexisti, da oscula, dum licet, ultimum hoc
10 gaudium fatis properantibus rape." Haec ut ego dixi, Giton
vestem deposuit, meaque tunica contectus exeruit ad osculum
caput. Et ne sic cohaerentes malignior fluctus distraheret,

L (= lrtp)
114 4 hercules *mirum; obtrectat Mueller post* postquam *excidit aliquid, fere ut supplevi;* 5 id est *del. Fraenkel* 7 *add. Buecheler* subduxere *Buecheler*: abduxere 8 *lacunam signat* p: *potius addidit Gonsalius,* at *insero* 9 da *Jungermann*: ad 10 distraheret t^{m}: detraheret

And, more dangerous than any squall, so heavy a gloom had suddenly descended that it blotted out the daylight to the point that he could not even see the front outline of the prow. For sure, the storm was raging at its height, and Lichas, panic-stricken, stretched forth his hands to me in supplication: "Encolpius, help us in our peril and restore to the ship its sacred tunic and rattle! For God's sake show us the mercy so typical of you!"

Even as he cried out, the wind wrenched him overboard into the sea and the current caught him in a dangerous eddy, whirled him round, and swallowed him up. Tryphaena, however, was grabbed, barely conscious, by her ever-loyal slaves, put upon the life raft with the greater part of her belongings and thus rescued from a certain death *

I, clutching Giton to myself, wept and yelled: "The gods have seen it fitting to unite us at the last in death, but cruel fate says no! See now how the waves are capsizing the ship and the sea's wrath sunders the lovers' embrace! So if you truly loved your Encolpius, kiss me while you can and snatch a final joy from onrushing fate!"

When he heard this, Giton threw off his shirt and burrowed into my tunic, popping out his head for a kiss. And in case some particularly envious wave should try to part us while thus entwined,

11 utrumque zona circumvenienti praecinxit et "Si nihil
aliud, certe diutius," inquit, "iuncta mors nos feret,
vel si voluerit <mare> misericors ad idem litus expellere,
aut praeteriens aliquis tralaticia humanitate lapidabit,
aut quod ultimum est iratis etiam fluctibus, imprudens
12 harena componet." Patior ego vinculum extremum, et veluti
lecto funebri aptatus expecto mortem iam non molestam.
13 Peragit interim tempestas mandata fatorum et omnesque
reliquias navis expugnat. Non arbor erat relicta, non
gubernacula, non funis aut remus, sed quasi rudis atque
infecta materies ibat cum fluctibus *

14 Procurrere piscatores parvulis expediti navigiis ad
praedam rapiendam. Deinde ut aliquos viderunt qui suas
opes defenderent, mutaverunt crudelitatem in auxilium *

115 Audimus murmur insolitum et sub diaeta magistri quasi
2 cupientis exire beluae gemitum. Persecuti igitur sonum
invenimus Eumolpus sedentem membranae ingenti versus
3 ingerentem. Mirati ergo quod illi vacaret in vicinia
mortis poema facere, extrahimus clamantem iubemusque bonam
4 habere mentem. At ille interpellatus excanduit et "Sinite
me," inquit, "sententiam explere: laborat carmen in fine."
5 Inicio ego phrenetico manum iubeoque Giton accedere et

L (= lrtp)
114 11 mors] mare *Faber add. Mueller* 13 *et* 14 *lac. ind. libri*: 14 *omnino praeterea omittit* r 14 crudelitatem] cupiditatem *mavult Jacobs* **115** 3 extrahimus l: extraximus rtp reclamantem *Fraenkel*

he tied a belt around the both and, "At the least," he said, "death shall bear us off together for a good long while, and perhaps the sea will take pity and decide to cast our bodies onto the same shore, to be covered with stones by some beachcomber in an act of common decency, or buried randomly by the sand in the last rites of the roughest seas."

I accepted that final restraint and, as if arrayed for my coffin, I awaited my demise with equanimity. Meanwhile the storm ran the course of fate's bidding and assailed every last remnant of the ship. Not a mast was left, not the steerage, not a sheet or an oar. She was reduced to a rough, unworked lump of wood carried by the swell *

Fishermen in small, manoeuvrable craft hurried up to see what they could salvage, but upon seeing people still ready to protect their possessions dropped their callous design in favour of rendering assistance *

115 We heard a strange muffled noise emanating from beneath the captain's quarters, like the grunt of a seal trying to get out. So we followed the sound and discovered Eumolpus, seated, spilling out verses onto a large piece of parchment! We were amazed at his finding the time to do this in the face of death, dragged him off protesting, and told him to be sensible. He was furious at this intrusion. "Let me complete my thought," he said. "I'm having trouble with the poem's ending." He was clearly delirious, so I

in terram trahere poetam mugientem *
6 Hoc opere tandem elaborato casam piscatoriam
subimus maerentes, cibisque naufragio corruptis utcumque
7 curati tristissimam exegimus noctem. Postero die cum
poneremus consilium cui regioni crederemus, repente
video corpus humanum circumactum levi vertice ad litus
8 deferri. Substiti ergo tristis coepique umentibus oculis
9 maris fidem increpare et, "Hunc forsitan," proclamo, "in
aliqua parte terrarum secura expectat uxor, forsitan
ignarus tempestatis filius aut pater; utique reliquit
10 aliquem, cui proficiscens osculum dedit. Haec sunt
consilia mortalium, haec vota [magnarum cogitationum]. En
11 homo quemadmodum natat." Adhuc tamquam ignotum deflebam,
cum inviolatum os fluctus convertit in terram, agnovique
terribilem paulo ante et implacabilem Licham pedibus meis
12 paene subiectum. Non tenui igitur diutius lacrimas, immo
percussi semel iterumque manibus pectus et, "Ubi nunc est,"
13 inquam, "iracundia tua, ubi impotentia tua? Nempe piscibus
beluisque expositus es, et qui paulo ante iactabas vires
imperii tui, de tam magna nave ne tabulam quidem naufragus

L (= lrtp)

115 5 poetam l^{m}, *id est Scaliger*: porcam rtp: portam l *lac. ind. libri* 7 poneremus] promeremus *Mueller* 8 umentibus Tornaesius: viventibus maris malam fidem *quaerit Buecheler* increpare *scripsi; adiunctionem videas*: inspicere 9 pater *Buecheler*: patrem 10 *del. Fraenkel* 12 manibus l: manu rtp

gripped him and shouted to Giton to come and help me pull a bellowing bard to dry land *

After taking quite some time to complete this task, in a sorry state we approached a fisherman's shack. Our food had been spoiled by immersion but we made do somehow and passed the wretchedest of nights. Next morning, while we were discussing where to risk proceeding, I suddenly saw the body of a human being coming to shore in a gentle eddy. I rose sadly to my feet and with brimming eyes began to take the sea to task for its fickleness:

"Perhaps this man," I exclaimed, "has a wife, calmly waiting for him somewhere, perhaps a son or father, with no knowledge of the storm: someone, for sure, to whom he entrusted a kiss upon departing. Such are the plans and the ambitions of mortals, but now the man merely floats!" I was still shedding tears for a stranger, I thought, when a wave turned him face up and unscathed landwards and I saw it was Lichas, redoubtable and unbending only a moment earlier, now a virtual prisoner beneath my feet.

I could hold back the floodgates no longer and even pounded my fists repeatedly upon my chest. "Where now," I cried, "your anger and your fury? Why, you have been laid out for the fishes and the beasts of the sea; and you who just now could boast of a business empire have not a plank to cling to from all that mighty ship!

14 habes. Ite nunc mortales, et magnis cogitationibus
pectora implete. Ite cauti, et opes fraudibus
15 captas per mille annos disponite. Nempe hic proxima
luce patrimonii sui rationes inspexit, nempe diem
etiam, quo venturus esset in patriam, animo suo
16 fixit. Dii deaeque, quam longe a destinatione sua
iacet. Sed non sola mortalibus maria hanc fidem
praestant. Illum bellantem arma decipiunt, illum diis
vota reddentem, penatium suorum ruina sepelit. Ille
vehiculo lapsus properantem spiritum excussit, cibus
avidum strangulavit, abstinentem frugalitas. Si bene
17 calculum ponas, ubique naufragium est. At enim
fluctibus obruto non contingit sepultura. Tamquam
intersit, periturum corpus quae ratio consumat, ignis
18 an fluctus an mora. Quicquid feceris, omnia haec
eodem ventura sint. Ferae tamen corpus lacerabunt.
Tamquam melius ignis accipiat; immo hanc poenam
19 gravissimam credimus, ubi servis irascimur. Quae
ergo dementia est, omnia facere, ne qui de nobis
relinquat sepultura?" *
20 Et Licham quidem rogus inimicis collatus manibus
adolebat. Eumolpus autem dum epigramma mortuo facit,
oculos ad arcessendo sensus longius mittit *

L (= lrtp)
115 15 fixit *Oevering*: fingit 19 de *Jacobs*: e
19 *et* 20 *lac. ind. libri* 20 mittit] nictat *Giardina*

"Go forth, then, mortals: fill your heads with grandiose schemes! Go forth in shrewdness: disburse your ill-gotten gains for the next thousand years! Why, only yesterday this man was doing the accounts on his fortune and making a mental note of the exact day to return to his country. Ye gods and goddesses! How distant from his destination he now lies!

"But it is not only the seas that betray the trust of mortals. One man is let down by his equipment in mid-duel; another is buried when his house collapses, even as he does worship to the gods; another falls from his carriage and quickly yields his spirit up. A glutton chokes on his food and a light eater starves. Make your best move and still everywhere's a shipwreck!

"'But people lost at sea,' you say, 'get no burial.' As if the way you will die makes any difference, be it by fire or drowning or old age. Whatever you manage, all comes to the same thing. 'The wild beasts will tear his body to pieces.' Is fire any better? In fact we reserve it for slaves as the worst punishment when they displease us. What sort of madness is it therefore to do our best to see that there's nothing left of us to bury?" *

Thus the pyre that would consume Lichas now was raised by the hands of his enemies, and Eumolpus took on a faraway look to garner inspiration for an epitaph to the dead *

116 Hoc peracto libenter officio destinatum carpimus
iter ac momento temporis in montem sudantes conscendimus,
ex quo haud procul impositum arce sublimi oppidum
2 cernimus. Nec quod esset sciebamus errantes, donec a
vilico quodam Crotona esse cognovimus, urbem antiquissimam
3 et aliquando Italiae primam. Cum deinde diligentius
exploraremus qui homines inhabitarent nobile solum quodve
genus negotionis praecipue probarent post attritis
4 bellis frequentibus opes, "O mi," inquit, "hospites, si
negotiatores estis, mutate propositum aliudque vitae
5 praesidium quaerite. Sin autem urbanioris notae homines
6 sustinetis semper mentiri, recta ad lucrum curritis. In
hac enim urbe non litterarum studia celebrantur, non
eloquentia locum habet, non frugalitas sanctique mores
laudibus ad fructum perveniunt, sed quoscumque homines in
hac urbe videritis, scitote in duas partes esse divisos.
7 Nam aut captantur aut captant. In hac urbe nemo liberos
tollit, quia quisquis suos heredes habet, non ad cenas,
non ad spectacula admittitur, sed omnibus prohibetur
8 commodis, inter ignominosos latitat. Qui vero nec uxores
umquam duxerunt nec proximas necessitudines habent, ad
summos honores perveniunt, id est soli militares, soli
9 fortissimi atque etiam innocentes habentur.

L (= lrtp)
116 quod *Buecheler*: quid 6 laudibus *del. George* in hac urbe *repetita del. Buecheler* 7 cenas *Bongars*: scenas *Buecheler* 8 id … militares *del. Fraenkel, sed ante Kraffert*

10
Entering Croton: a Plan and a Poem

116 We readily performed this duty, embarked in our chosen direction, and almost immediately found ourselves having to sweat up a hill, from whose summit we saw in the near distance a town built upon a steep rise. We were lost, of course, and had no idea of its name until an estate manager told us it was Croton, the ancient city that was once the foremost in Italy. We then made a careful inquiry into what manner of men now inhabited that hallowed sod and what sort of business they favoured most, now that their resources had been depleted by almost constant warfare. "Strangers," the man said, "if you are entrepreneurs it's time to change your plans and find a different way to make a living. But if you happen to be men who can live by their wits and don't mind lying all the time, keep straight on for profit! Because in this city literary pursuits get no credit, eloquence has no place, and self-restraint and moral behaviour get no respect. Keep in mind that all the people you will encounter fall into one of two categories: they are either legacy hunters or their quarry. Nobody raises children here because people who have heirs get no invitations to dinners or shows, are excluded from all perquisites, and live in pathetic obscurity. On the other hand, men who have never married and have no close ties attain the top ranks. They are like a military caste, the sole claimants to courageousness and freedom from reproach.

9 Adibitis," inquit, "oppidum tamquam in pestilentia campos,
in quibus nihil aliud est nisi cadavera quae lacerantur
aut corvi qui lacerant" *

117 Prudentior Eumolpus convertit ad novitatem rei mentem
genusque divisionis sibi non displicere confessus est.
2 Iocari ego senem poetica levitate credebam, cum ille,
"Utinam quidem sufficeret largior scaena, id est vestis
humanior, instrumentum lautius quod praeberet mendacio
fidem: non mehercules rapinam istam differrem, sed continuo
3 vos ad magnas opes ducerem. Atquin promitto" ...
... quicquid exigeret, dummodo placeret vestis
rapinae comes, et quicquid Lycurgi villa grassantibus
praebuisset. Nam nummos in praesentem usum deum maitrem
pro fide reddituram ...

4 "Quid ergo," inquit Eumolpus, "cessamus mimum
componere? Facite ergo me dominum, si negotiatio placet."
5 Nemo ausus est artem damnare nihil auferentem. Itaque ut
duraret inter omnes tutum mendacium, in verba Eumolpi
sacramentum iuravimus: uri, vinciri, verberari ferroque

L (= lrtp)

116 9 adibitis *Scaliger*: audebitis *aut* videbitis *lac. ind. libri* **117** divisionis *scribo*: divinationis ltp: divitionis r; *adiunctionem videas* 2 post quidem dixit *insero* (inquit *Buecheler*) id est *del. Fraenkel* instrumentum lt^{m}: vestimentum rtp lautius *Gulielmus*: latius rapinam *Buecheler*: poenam 3 *lac. ind. Schmid* *lac. ind. Buecheler* 4 mimum *Pithou*: in unum 5 sacramentum *ut ex* 6 *del. Fraenkel*

"You will be entering a town," he said, "like the countryside in plague, where nothing exists besides corpses being picked and crows a-picking." *

117 Eumolpus was quicker than we to apply his brain to the novelty of the situation, and allowed that this kind of division was not displeasing. I thought the old boy was joking – using poetic licence – but he was not: "I wish," he continued, "we were equipped with a more generous set of props – nicer clothes, for example, and fancier trappings, to add credibility to a tall tale: by God, I'd soon be in at the trough and make rich men of you in no time at all! All the same, I promise" …

… whatever he required, as long as the cloak, my comrade in crime, would do, together with the proceeds from our knocking over Lycurgus' house. As for day-to-day expenses, surely the tutelage of the mother of the gods would provide the cash …

"Well, then," said Eumolpus, "let's get on with the performance! If you like the script make me the director." We had nothing to lose from this scheme, and nobody ventured to object. So in order for our secret to remain safe, we all swore a mutual oath after Eumolpus "to undergo fire, chains, lash and sword" – and all else that he enjoined; and just like real gladiators in solemnest ritual we commended ourselves body and soul to our 'master.'

necari, et quicquid aliud Eumolpus iussisset. Tamquam
legitimi gladiatores domino corpora animasque
6 religiosissime addicimus. Post peractum sacramentum
serviliter ficti dominum consalutamus, elatumque ab
Eumolpo filium pariter condiscimus, iuvenem ingentis
eloquentiae et spei, ideoque de civitate sua miserrimum
senem exisse, ne aut clientes sodalesque filii sui aut
7 sepulcrum quotidie causam lacrimarum cerneret. Accessisse
huic tristitiae proximum naufragium, quo amplius vicies
sestertium amiserit; nec illum iactura moveri, sed
destitutum ministerio non agnoscere dignitatem suam.
8 Praeterea habere in Africa trecenties sestertium fundis
nominibus depositum; nam familiam quidem tam magnam
per agros Numidiae esse sparsam, ut possit vel Carthaginem
9 capere. Secundum hanc formulam imperamus Eumolpo ut
plurimum tussiat, ut sit <modo astrictioris> modo
solutioris stomachi cibosque omnes palam damnet; loquatur
aurum et argentum fundosque mendaces et perpetuam terrarum
10 sterilitatem; sedeat praeterea quotidie ad rationes
tabulaeque testamenti omnibus <mensibus> renovet. Et ne
quid scaenae deesset, quotienscumque aliquem nostrum vocare
temptasset, alium pro alio vocaret, ut facile appareret
dominum etiam eorum meminisse qui praesentes non essent.

L (= lrtp)
117 6 ficti *delebat Fraenkel, def. Mueller* condiscimus *Gulielmus*: condicimus 9 *add. Wehle* sterilatatem rp: fertilitatem t: felicitatem l 10 *add. Buecheler*

After the swearing, we posing slaves hailed our master and agreed upon the story that Eumolpus had just lost his son, a young man of enormous persuasiveness and promise, and that this poor old man had left his city rather than be brought to tears every day by seeing his son's friends, associates, and grave.

Adding to his woes (we would say) was a recent shipwreck in which he had lost more than two millions – though it was not so much the loss of the money that affected him as the lack of recognition of his status without the servants. In any case (we would say) in Africa he had another thirty million tied up in land and loans, and enough retainers scattered about the Numidian countryside to capture Carthage if he wanted.

In line with this scenario we told Eumolpus to cough a lot and to openly swear off all food for his "alternating bouts of diarrhoea and constipation." He was to talk of his gold and his silver, of his disappointing farms, of how his land had gone permanently barren.

Also, he should be sitting down to his "Accounts" every day, and changing the clauses in his "Will" every month. For good measure, every time he tried to address one of us he was to get the name wrong – to suggest a master that obviously could only remember the slaves who were no longer with him.

11 His ita ordinatis, "quod bene feliciterque eveniret"
precati deos viam ingredimur. Sed neque Giton sub insolito
fasce durabat, et mercennarius Corax, detractator ministerii,
posita frequentius sarcina male dicebat properantibus
affirmabatue se aut proiecturum sarcinas aut cum onere
12 fugiturum. "Quid? Vos," inquit, "iumentum me putatis esse aut
lapidariam navem? Hominis operas locavi, non caballi. Nec minus
liber sum quam vos, etiam si pauperem pater me reliquit." Nec
contentus maledictis tollebat subinde altius pedem et strepitu
13 obsceno simul atque odore viam implebat. Ridebat contumaciam
Giton et singulos crepitus eius pari clamore prosequebatur …
118 / "Multos," inquit Eumolpus, "o iuvenes, carmen LO
decepit. Nam ut quisque versum pedibus instruxit sensumque
teneriore verborum ambitu intexuit, putavit se continuo in
2 Heliconem venisse. Sic forensibus ministeriis exercitati
frequenter ad carminis tranquillitatem tamquam ad portum
feliciorem refugerunt, credentes facilius poema extrui posse
3 quam controversiam sententiolis vibrantibus pictam. Ceterum

---

L (= lrtp), O (= BRP)
117 12 *sic interpunxi* 13 crepitus *Iunius*: strepitus *lac. ind.* L **118** inquit Eumolpus *om.* L teneriore B: teneriorem *ceteri* 2 feliciorem EI: faciliorem: *del. olim Buecheler*

With this down pat, we offered up a prayer to the gods for the success of the enterprise and set out on our way. But Giton soon faltered from his unaccustomed load, and Eumolpus' man Corax, a natural slacker, put down his pack all the time and cursed us out for going too fast. He was all for leaving it behind or making off with the contents. "Hey! You think I'm a beast of burden?" he said. "Or a granite barge? I hired on for a man's work, not a mule's! I'm just as free as you, though my father left me a poor man!"

And not content to curse, every so often he'd cock his leg and blanket the highway in disgusting noise and odour. Giton laughed at his insolence and matched him fart for fart at equal pitch *

118 "My young friends," began Eumolpus, "poetry has deluded many. Somebody writes a line in metre and weaves a new metaphor into the sense and he thinks he's gone straight to Mount Helicon.

"So when people are stressed by their legal representations they often take refuge in the tranquil and supposedly safer harbour of poetry, in the belief that it's easier than a brief adorned with dazzling tags. However, it is not a nobler spirit that seeks mere stylistic soundness,

neque generosior spiritus sanitatem amat, neque concipere aut
edere partum mens potest nisi ingenti flumine litterarum
4 inundata. Refugiendum est ab omni veborum, ut ita dicam,
vilitate et sumendae voces a plebe semotae, ut fiat 'odi
5 profanum vulgus et arceo.' Praeterea curandum est ne
sententiae emineant extra corpus orationis expressae, sed
intexto versibus colore niteant. Homerus testis et lyrici
Romanusque Vergilius et Horatii curiosa felicitas. Ceteri
enim aut non viderunt viam qua iretur ad carmen, aut visam
6 timuerunt calcare. Ecce belli civilis ingens opus quisquis
attigerit nisi plenus litteris, sub onere labetur. Non enim
res gestae versibus comprehendendae sunt, quod longe melius
historici faciunt, sed per ambages deorumque ministeria et
fabulosum sententiarum tormentum praecipitandus est liber
spiritus, ut potius furentis animi vaticinatio appareat quam
religiosae orationis sub testibus fides: tamquam, si placet,
hic impetus, etiam si nondum recepit ultimam manum:"

L (lrtp), O (BRP)
118 3 sanitatem] vanitatem p, E *teste Buecheleri dubio* concipere *Puteolanus*: conspicere L: conspici O inundanter O 4 refugiendum *Buecheler*: effugiendum semotae *Pius*: submotae *aut* summotae 5 rationis O versibus RP sed <ut> *aut* sed <velut> *Boschius et Buecheler* visam *Faber*: versum 6 sententiarum *susp. Courtney* tormentum] *varie emendatur, nusquam apte*, e.g. fermentum *Pellegrino, def. Conte*

and the mind cannot imagine and create poetry unless flooded with the mighty spate of literature. One must stay away from all words that I would call cheap, and must select phrasing distinct from the common coin, in line with Horace's 'I hate the uninitiated rabble and fend it off.' Furthermore, one should take pains to see that any aphorisms do not emerge from the substance of the delivery: they should shimmer like the colours of thread woven into a garment. Homer and the lyric poets attest to this, along with Roman Vergil, and Horace with his painstaking felicity. As for the rest, they never saw the road that leads to poetry, or if they saw it were afraid to set foot on it. Take the huge theme of the Civil War: anyone trying it would collapse under its weight unless he were brimming with literature. It is not a matter of needing to cover the events of history in poetry. Leave that to the historians, who do it much better. No: the spirit must be free – to roam through the puzzles and interventions of the gods and the twists and turns of oracular utterance – to create the effect of the poet's mind prophesying in a frenzied trance, and not of the testimony in a statement sworn before witnesses, some effort such as the following, perhaps, though it has not yet received the finishing touch *

Eumolpus' poem on The Civil War – commencing in the next chapter – if examined as it deserves, has less in common with Lucan's *Pharsalia* than one might have expected. Although long in the present context, at just under three hundred lines, with the setting for this study in poetic declamation not doing it credit, it is less than half the length of Lucan's first of ten books. So there is the scale. And Eumolpus is more interested in moral mythmaking and effects of language than history, or politics, or causation, or the personalities of the grand combatants. Borrowings from the *Aeneid* of Vergil suggest it is more to his taste than the *Pharsalia*, but Petronius' brief does not seem to be to follow others into criticism of Lucan himself for swelling up the poetry or falling short of Vergil. Eumolpus' version, granted, is shown as a "pearls-before-swine" compositional misjudgment, not really a decent imitation of anything, with a style and verve particular to the poet and man, Eumolpus himself. Is he, however, a butt of Petronian mockery? Such is the suspicion of Ernout, who believes he has collapsed *Pharsalia* Book 1 into what he calls, in the arresting phrase, "un merveilleux de pacotille," an amazement of gimcrack. That said, the elaboration itself bespeaks, on the part of Petronius, no mean compositional and linguistic effort, as anyone faced with the task of rendering the poem poetically will agree, and its adages and tropes do not deserve wholesale to be set aside or ironized (citation from A. Ernout 1950[3], p. 135).

119 "Orbem iam totum victor Romanus habebat,
qua mare, qua terrae, qua sidus currit utrumque.
Nec satiatus erat. Gravidis freta pulsa carinis
iam peragebantur: si quis sinus abditus ultra,
si qua foret tellus, fulvum quae mitteret aurum,
hostis erat, fatisque in tristia bella paratis
quaerebantur opes. Non vulgo nota placebant
gaudia, non usu plebeio trita voluptas.
Aes Ephyreiacum laudabat miles; in ima
quaesitus tellure nitor certaverat ostro.
Hinc Numidae accurant, illinc nova vellera Seres,
atque Arabum populus sua despoliaverat arva.
Ecce aliae clades et laesae vulnera pacis.
Quaeritur in silvis Tauri fera, et ultimus Hammon
Afrorum excutitur, ne desit belua dente
ad mortes pretiosa; fremens premit advena classes
tigris et aerata gradiens vectatur in aula,
ut bibat humanum populo plaudente cruorem.
Heu, pudet effari perituraque prodere fata:
Persarum ritu male pubescentibus annis

L (= lrtp), O (= BRP)
119 5 quae fulvum O 9 aes Ephyreiacum *Heinze, formam ignotam probans*: aespyre cum B *melius* ima *Gifanius*: unda 11 accurant *Colladonius*: accusant L: accusatius O 14 Tauri *Busche*: auro 16 fremens *Bouhier*: fames 17 aerata *Busche*: aurata 19 fata] facta *Burman*

119 "By now the Roman victor held the world in sway,
All land the sun and moon traverse, and all the sea,
But was not sated. Now remotest waters felt the oar
Of pregnant ship. If any hidden shore
Or bay had tawny gold to offer,
It was the foe, in search to fill the coffer
Backed by awful war, Fate-sanctioned. No common joy
Sufficed, the people felt their normal pleasure cloy.
The soldier wanted only bronze from Corinth, shine
To vie with purple, found in deepest mine
Such as Numidia provides, China virgin silk
And people of Arabia their own fields did milk.
Behold the other scars and scourges of a peace of pain:
Tauric forests searched for bears, Ammon
Outpost of Africa, combed for lion,
Tooth prized for killing. Exotic tiger tries the fleet,
In bronzen crate transported, padding feet,
To drink the blood of humans, before a clapping seat.
Alas! I blush to utter grim prophetic words,
How boys, in Persian custom, scarcely in their beards,

surripuere viros exsectaque viscera ferro
in venerem fregere, atque ut fuga nobilis aevi
circumscripta mora properantem differat annos …
Quaerit se natura nec invenit. Omnibus ergo
scorta placent placent fractique enervi corpore gressus
et laxi crines et tot nova nomina vistis
quaeque virum quaerunt. Ecce Afris eruta terris
citrea mensa greges servorum ostrumque renidens
ponitur ac maculis imitatur vilius aurum,
quae sensum trahat. Hoc sterile ac male nobile lignum
turba sepulta mero circum venit, omniaque orbis
praemia correptis miles vagus esurit armis.
Ingeniosa gula est. Siculo scarus aequore mersus
ad mensam vivus perducitur, atque Lucrinis
eruta litoribus vendunt conchylia cenas
ut renovent per damna famem. Iam Phasidos unda
orbata est avibus, mutoque in litore tantum
solae desertis adspirant frondibus aurae.
Nec minor in campo furor est, emptiqu Quirites
ad praedam strepitumque lucri suffragia vertunt.
Venalis populus, venalis curia patrum,
est favor in pretio. Senibus quoque libera virtus

L (= lrtp), O (= BRP)

119 22 aevi *Puteolanus*: aevo 23 *lac. ind. Buecheler*
28 citrea *Puteolanus*: aurea 29 vilius *Gronovius*: vilibus
30–2 *interpolata susp. Shackleton Bailey* 33 ingeniosa
gula est = *Mart.* 13.62.2 38 solae]surdae *Nisbet*

Are robbed of manhood, by knife their vitals cut
For sexual service, refuge of the nobler time to cheat
By holding back the onrush of the years, while
Nature seeks to find her course, to no avail.
All love their male-whoring, their tripping and prancing,
Their long hair, their great variety of clothing,
And what else tempts a man. See how the citron table,
Ripped from soil of Africa, mirrors slaves and purple:
There it sits evoking flecks of gold, but dearer,
To draw the senses: the wood, now barren and viler,
A mob surrounds, awash in drink, and footloose military
Armed, aggressive, salivates at the world's delicacy.
Greed is resourceful: the wrasse, off Sicily far under,
Comes live to table, and Lucrine oyster,
Scraped from shore, sells the dinner,
To whet the taste buds and be gone. The Phasian lagoon
Is stripped of fowl, and on the silent shore alone
The lonely breezes sigh amid the empty green.
No less a frenzy inhabits the hustings: Roman men
Sell their votes to bring in stuff and jingling gain.
The people for sale, for sale the Upper House:
Popularity for purchase: even in our elders the loss

exciderat, sparsisque opibus conversa potestas
ipsaque maiestas auro corrupta iacebat.
Pellitur a populo victus Cato; tristior ille est,
qui vicit, fasces pudet rapuisse Catoni.
[Namque hoc dedecoris populo morumque ruina]
non homo pulsus erat sed in uno uno victa potestas
Romanumque decus. Quare tam perdita Roma
ipsa sui merces eerat et sine vindice praeda.
Praeterea gemino deprensam gurgite plebem
faenoris ingluvies ususque exederat aeris.
Nulla est certa domus, nullum sine pignore corpus,
sed veluti tabes tacitis concepta medullis
intra membra furens curis latrantibus errat.
Arma placent miseris, detritaque commoda luxu
vulneribusque reparantur. Inops audacia tuta est.
Hoc mersam caeno Romam somnoque iacentem
quae poterant artes sana ratione movere,
ni furor et bellum ferroque excita libido?

120 Tres tulerat Fortuna duces, quos obruit omnes
armorum strue diversa feralis Enyo.
Crassum Parthus habet, Libyco iacet aequore Magnus,
Iulius ingratam perfudit sanguine Romam,

L (= lrtp), O (= BRP)
119 47 *del. Broukhusius* dedecori L 49 tam] iam *Tornaesius, probat Shackleton Bailey* 51 plebem *Burman*: praedam 52 ingluvies *Palmer*: illuvies 58 mersam *Scaliger*: mersant 60 excita *Junius*: excisa

Of freedom meant the loss of virtue. Cash was dangled.
It changed the balance, and all that power's for gold.
Cato's beaten, sent packing by the people, but victor
Is the glummer, ashamed of stealing Cato's lictor.
'Twas not a man that lost, but in him the losing
Of Roman pride, and hence the shame of Rome for being
The pawner of itself, with none redeeming.
The people too were caught in a double rut,
And wallowed in greedy usury and debt.
No house was theirs, no body unindentured:
The wasting disease to their silent marrow ventured,
Went about their limbs in a frenzy of barking misery.
They take to war, sad fools: bounty lost to luxury
They recoup with injury. If poor we're free to risk.
With Rome so fast asleep, so mired in muck,
What skills of sanity and reason could shift her? –
The fields we left to frenzy, bloodlust and disaster.
Three leaders Fortune raised, all of whom was Enyo
The bestial by dint of arms though variously to strow.
Crassus lies in Parthia, the Great on Libyan shore,
And Rome, ungrateful Rome, is soaked in Julian gore;

et quasi non posset tellus tot ferre sepulcra
divisit cineres. Hos gloria reddit honores.
Est locus exciso penitus demersus hiatu
Parthenopen inter magnae Dicarchidos arva,
Cocyti perfusus aqua; nam spiritus, extra
qui furit effusus, funesto spargitur aestu.
Non haec autumno tellus viret aut alit herbas
caespite laetus ager, non verno persona cantu
mollia discordi strepitu virgulta loquuntur,
sed chaos et nigro squalentia pumice saxa
gaudent ferali circum tumulata cupressu.
Has inter sedes Ditis pater extulit ora
bustorum flammis et cana sparsa favilla,
ac tali volucrem Fortunam voce lacessit:
'Rerum humanarum divinarumque potestas,
Fors, cui nulla placet nimium secura potestas,
quae nova semper amas et mox possessa relinquis,
ecquid Romano sentis te pondere victam,
nec posse ulterius perituram extollere molem?
Ipsa suas vires odit Romana iuvantus
et quas struxit opes, male sustinet. Aspice late
luxuriam spoliorum et censum in damna furentem.
Aedificant auro sedesque ad sidera mittunt,

L (= lrtp), O (= BRP)
120 65 tellus tot] tot tellus P, ex quo ltp, *Buecheler, "perperam," Mueller* 69 Cocyti *Sambucus*: Cocytia 70 expulsus *Nisbet* 79 potestas *susp. Mueller recte,* magistra *intuens*

And Earth, as if unable all the many graves to bear,
Has set apart the ashes. Such reward will glory share.
There is a spot, deep-sunken and a gaping wound
Between Parthenope and Puteoli of the hallowed ground,
Awash in water of Cocytus; and indeed the breath
Which wildly swirls abroad is wet with drops of death.
Not green in Fall is it, nor lush the field
In grasses, nor tender stalks in sounding song do yield
Their vernal chatter, disharmonious noise:
Chaos rules: filthy boulders, pumice-black, rise
Their tumuli rejoicing round in cypress of the dead.
Amid the realm did father Hades raise his head,
Sooty from flames of pyres and white from ashes,
And winged Fortune now in this address he lashes:
'O power behind all things both human and divine,
Fortune, never pleased by too secure a reign,
Always loving change and quick your field to leave,
By weight of Rome defeated, is it you perceive?
No more to raise her higher now she is to die?
For Roman youth itself does her own strength decry,
And opulence she built she carries ill. Afar behold
The riches of our booty and mad destruction of our gold:
In gold they build, erecting mansions to the skies.

expelluntur aquae saxis, mare nascitur arvis
et permutata rerum statione rebellant.
En etiam mea regna petunt. Perfossa dehiscit
molibus insanis tellus, iam montibus haustis
antra gemunt, et dum vanos lapis invenit usus,
inferni manes caelum sperare fatentur.
Quare age, Fors, muta pacatum in proelia vultum
Romanosque cie ac nostris da funera regnis.
Iam pridem nullo perfundimus ora cruore,
nec mea Tisiphone sitientes perluit artus,
ex quo Sullanum bibit ensis et horrida tellus
extulit in lucem nutritas sanguine fruges.'

121 Haec ubi dicta dedit, dextrae coniungere dextram
conatus rupta tellurem solvit hiatu.
Tunc Fortuna levi defudit pectore voces:
'O genitor, cui Cocyti penetralia parent,
si modo vera mihi fas est impune profari,
vota tibi cedent; nec enim minor ira rebellat
pectore in hoc leviorque exurit flamma medullas.
Omnia, quae tribui Romanis arcibus, odi
muneribus meis irascor. Destruet istas
idem, qui posuit, moles deus. Et mihi cordi
quippe cremare viros et sanguine pascere luxum.

L (l= lrtp), O (= BRP)
120 92 vanos *florilegium*: vanus O: varios L usum O 93 fatentur] iubentur l^{m}rt^{m}p e *nescioquo codice* 103 Cocyti cui BR 110 armare *Gronovius*

The tide's expelled by rocks as seas in fields arise:
Man changes things, on settled order making war,
And now my kingdom even seeks: gapes the earthen floor
For mad foundations, as now the mountains they strip,
Grottoes groaning; and while the stone gets empty grip
The souls below admit to longing for the skies.
So, Fortune, come recast on war your peaceful eyes,
Stir up the Romans and deal death to our domains!
Too long our visages were free from blood stains!
Nor has Tisiphone her thirsty limbs appeased
Since Sulla's sword drank deep and the land, confused,
Brought her blood-fed crops to light!'
121 And when he'd said these words, in striving right
To right hand join he rent the earth apart.
In these words answered Fortune, from her fickle heart:
'O father whom the bowels of Hell obey,
If it is right for me in freedom truth to say,
Your prayers will soon oblige; an equal anger torches
In my breast, no lesser flame my marrow scorches.
There's naught I gave to Rome I don't resent,
Of all the gifts I gave (and God destroy!) I do repent,
The same who built that mass. And now what I desire
Is sate with blood their excess; send men to the fire!

Cerno equidem gemina iam stratos morte Philippos
Thessaliaeque rogos et funera gentis Hiberae 112
et Libycae: cerno tua, Nile, gementia claustra 114
Actiacosque sinus et Apollinis arma timentes. 115
Iam fragor armorum trepidantes personat aures. 113
Pande,age, terrarum sitientia regna tuarum 116
atque animas accerse novas. Vix navita Porthmeus
sufficiet simulacra virum traducere cumba;
classe opus est. Tuque ingenti satiare ruina,
pallida Tisiphone, concisaque vulnera mande:
ad Stygios manes laceratus ducitur orbis.'

122 Vixdum finierat, cum fulgure rupta corusco
intremuit nubes elisosque abscidit ignes.
Subsedit pater umbrarum, gremioque reducto
telluris pavitans fraternos palluit ictus.
Continuo clades hominum venturaque damna
auspiciis patuere deum. Namque ore cruento
deformis Titan vultum caligine texit:
civiles scies iam tum spectare putares.
Parte aliena plenos extinxit Cynthia vultus
et lucem sceleri subduxit. Rupta tonabant

L (= lrtp), O (= BRP)
121 113 *sic post* 115 *collocat Suringar; alii alio transponunt; damnabat Mueller* 117 navita *susp. Mueller* Porthmeus O: certe L 125 palluit R, *Puteolanus*: polluit 127 Titan *Vat.lat.1671*: titubans 129 spectare *Crusius et Suringar*: spirare

I see Philippi's fields in double carnage strewn,
I see the pyres of Thessaly, corpses lying in Spain 112
And Libya. And, Nile, I see your barriers wallow 114
And bay of Actium dreading too the arrows of Apollo. 115
Already din of arms my eager ears does hold. 113
Come, array the realms of your thirsting world 116
And bring on the fresh souls. Will Charon the sailor
Avail to ferry all those souls of men in his painter?
He'd need a fleet. And you be sated on vast carnage,
Still-pale Tisiphone: devour your severed damage.
The world in tatters is led off to the Stygian shades!'

122 Barely had she finished when, by lightning rays
Rent, a cloud thundered, disgorging shattered flame.
The father of the shades recoiled, and pale in alarm
At his brother's might withdrew the earth's embrace.
And straight the ruin to come, a plague on human race,
Arrived in divine portent: with gory mouth the sun
Grew hideous and clothed her face in gloom,
As if already seeing, you would think, a Civil War.
And in another part did Cynthia her fullness withdraw
And from the crime withheld her light. Cliffs a-falling

verticibus lapsis montis iuga, nec vaga passim
flumina per notas ibant morienta ripas.
Armorum strepitu caelum furit et tuba Martem
sideribus tremefacta ciet, iamque Aetna voratur
ignibus insolitis et in aethera fulmina mittit.
Ecce inter tumulos atque ossa carentia bustis
umbrarum facies diro stridore minantur.
Fax stellis comitata novis incendia ducit,
sanguineosque recens descendit Iuppiter imbre.
Haec ostenta brevi solvit deus. Exuit omnes
quippe moras Caesar, vindictaeque actus amore
Gallica proiecit, civilia sustulit arma.
Alpibus aeriis, ubi Graio numine pulsae
descendunt rupes et se patiuntur adire,
est locus Herculeis aris sacer. Hunc nive dura
claudit hiemps canoque ad sidera vertice tollit:
caelum illinc cecidisse putes. Non solis adulti
mansuescit radiis, non verni temporis aura
sed glacie concreta rigent hiemis pruinis:
totum ferre potest umeris minitantibus orbem.
Haec ubi calcavit Caesar iuga milite laeto

L (= lrtp), O (= BRP)
122 132 lapsis *codd. aliquot saec. XV*: lassis
137 carentia BR: arentia *cett.* 138 minantur *Goldast*: minatur 144 numine *Burman*: nomine 148 tetigisse *cogitavit Mueller* adulti *Scaliger*: adusti 150 rigent *Lipsius*: riget BR: rigens *cett.*

Roared as mountaintops collapsed; rivers once a-wandering
Far and wide knew not their courses and soon did die.
And Mars (the din of warfare roiling in the sky)
Was summoned in the stars by quaking trumpet. Etna by
Unwonted fire consumed sends her towers of flame ahigh.
And there amid the mounds and bones robbed of a fire
The images of shades hissed their warnings dire.
Heaven's brand trailed her fire in new stars' company,
And Jupiter showered the blood of men killed recently.
Such were the portents quickly sent by God. All demur
Did Caesar end, and impelled by need to settle a score
Threw off the Gallic and assumed the Civil War.
In airy Alps, where, by a Greek god worn,
The crags descend and let the people enter,
There is a site of sacred altars to Hercules. In winter
Seals in harsh snow and lofts to stars a white crown:
Thence you'd think the sky had fallen. Of risen sun
No trace of ray melts it, nor a springtime blast:
All is stiff with solid ice and wintry hoar-frost,
And on its looming shoulders the world entire can rest.
When Caesar reached these ridges with his happy host

optavit locum, summo de vertice montis
Hesperiae campos iste prospexit et ambas
intentans cum voce manus ad sidea diit:
'Iuppiter omnipotens, et tu Saturnia tellus,
armis laeta meis olimque onerata triumphis,
testor, ad has acies invitum accersere Martem,
invitas me ferre manus. Sed vulnere cogor,
pulsus ab urbe mea, dum Rhenum sanguine tingo,
dum Gallos iterum Capitolia nostra petentes
Alpibus excludo, vincendo certior exul.
Sanguine Germano sexagintaque triumphis
esse nocens coepi. Quamquam quos gloria terret,
aut qui sunt qui bella vetant? Mercedibus emptae
ac viles operae, quorum est Roma noverca.
At reor, haud impune, nec hanc sine vindice dextram
vinciet ignavus. Victores ite furentes,
ite mei comites, et causam dicite ferro.
Namque omnes unum crimen vocat, omnibus una
impendet clades. Reddenda est gratia vobis,
non solus vici. Quare, quia poena tropaeis
imminet et sordes meruit victoria nostra,

L (= lrtp), O (= BRP)

122 153 optavitque *Sambucus*: oravitque 157 ornata *Bouhier*: oneranda *vel* ornanda *Burman* 160 tingo *Monacensis 23713*: vinco 163 tropaeis *Nisbet* 165 vetent *Moessler et Buecheler*: vident 167 at P: ut 168 furentes A: ferentes 170 notat *Schrader*

And had picked this spot, and from the topmost path
Surveyed afar the plains of Italy, outstretching both
His hands addressed the heavens thus:
'Jupiter omnipotent and thou too, Saturn's house,
By my exploits enriched, already triumph-grown,
Unwillingly do I, I swear, commit the battle line,
And raise these hands unwillingly, compelled by pain,
As driven from my city I stained in blood the Rhine
As Gaul a second time our Capitol did seek,
From Alps excluding, and by winning did exile provoke.
I found I had upon my hands the blood of Germans and
Too many triumphs. But who are they who fear renown?
Who forbidding war? Baggage bought with cash,
To whom my city has a stepmother been, so much trash.
But not for naught, I'll warrant: this hand the sloth
Ties not revengeless. Go, you victors, in wrath!
On, my comrades, with your steel you make your case,
For one crime cites us all and one brings all disgrace.
I must thank you for your contribution;
With you I won. But over our pride hangs retribution,
And our victory earns us nothing more than muck.

iudice Fortuna cadat alea. Sumite bellum
et temptate manus. Certe mea causa peracta est:
inter tot fortes armatus nescio vinci.'
Haec ubi personuit, de caelo Delphicus ales
omina laeta dedit pepulitque meatibus auras.
Nec non horrendi nemoris de parte sinistra
insolitae voces flamma sonuere sequenti.
Ipse nitor Phoebe vulgato laetior orbe
crevit et aurato praecinxit fulgure vultus.

123 Fortior ominibus movit Mavortia signa
Caesar et insolitos gressu prior occupat ausus.
Prima quidem glacies et cana vincta pruina
non pugnavit humus mitique horrore quievit.
Sed postquam turmae nimbos fregere ligatos
et pavidus quadrupes undarum vincula rupit,
incaluere nives. Mox flumina montibus altis
undabant modo nata, sed haec quoque – iussa putares –
stabant, et vincta fluctus stupuere ruina,
et paulo ante lues iam concidenda iacebat.
Tum vero male fida prius vestigia lusit
decepitque pedes; pariter turmaeque virique
armaque congesta strue deplorata iacebant.
Ecce etiam rigido concussae flamine nubes

L (= lrtp), O (= BRP)

122 178 omina A *et edd. priores nonnulli*: omnia

184 insolitos *Monacensis 23713*: insolito

ausus *Puteolanus*: haustus 191 ruina *Reiske*: pruina

The die must now be cast at Fortune's feet. So the luck
And skill of war we try. My case is surely won;
How can I know defeat in arms amid such valiant men?'
After these echoing words, the Delphic bird on high
Gave a happy omen as he swooped amid the sky.
And also, on the left side of that creepy clearing
Issued strange voices, with a flame appearing.
The sunlit brightness grew, brighter than ere now,
And surrounded his countenance in a golden glow.
123 The braver for the omens Caesar moved his colours
Martial, boldly striking first the foe all unawares.
At first the ice and earth in grip of whiten hoar
Did not resist, and lay in quiet fear;
But after cavalry broke the brittle sheet
And nervous horse unloosed the waters with his feet
The ice would turn to slush, and soon on high the first
Of rivers coursed, but then to freeze as if rehearsed,
And the currents in the grip of death were rooted,
And what ran recently in slime to the axe was suited.
Then the ground, before in doubt, now mocked a footing
And betrayed their steps; as one, men and the riding
And their mounds of arms, went down in awful heap.
And lo, the clouds, a-battered by an icy sweep,

exonerabantur, nec rupti turbine venti
derant aut tumida confractum grandine caelum.
Ipsae iam nubes ruptae super arma cadebant
et concreta gelu ponti velut unda ruebat.
Victa erat ingenti tellus nive victaque caeli
sidera, victa suis haerentia flumina ripis;
nondum Caesar erat, sed magnam nixus in hastam
horrida securis frangebat gressibus arva
qualis Caucasea decurrens arduus arce
Amphitryoniades, aut torvo Iuppiter ore,
cum se verticibus magni demisit Olympi
et periturorum disiecit tela Gigantum.
Dum Caesar tumidas iratus deprimit arces
interea voluceer motis conterrita pinnis
Fama volat summique petit iuga celsa Palati
atque hoc Romanos tonitru ferit omnia fingens:
iam classes fluitare mari totasque per Alpes
fervere Germano pefsusas sanguine turmas.
Arma, cruor, caedes, incendia totaque bella
ante oculos volitant. Ergo pulsata tumultu
pectora perque duas scinduntur territa causas.
Huic fuga per terras, illi magis unda probatur

L (= lrtp), O (= BRP)

123 200 unda *Puteolanus*: umbra 205 arce] axe r *ex Memmiano fortasse, quod item viderat Pithou* 208 disiecit *Gulielmus*: deiecit 210 volucris L 212 Romanos *Bouhier*: Romano fingens *Watt*

Discharged their load, and whirl of broken wind
Came up, and sky with swollen hail was stunned.
The very cloudburst fell about the soldiers' weapons,
And solid ice, wave-sized, rushed from the heavens.
Earth was overwhelmed by snow in huge amounts, and sky
Was, too; beaten were the rivers, left on banks to dry.
But not yet Caesar: leaning on his mighty spear
Those rugged fields he quartered with his step secure,
Like lofty Hercules when down the ramp of Caucasus
He sped, or Jupiter, when with countenance so fierce
He from the summits of great Olympus descended,
Dispersing Giants' weapons and their lives soon ended.
While Caesar, wrathful, pressed the swollen height
Birdlike rumour soared, pinions beating in her fright,
And made for the high ridges of lofty Palatine
In full invention striking Romans with her refrain:
The fleets were now asea, through Alps all up and down
The horsemen sweated, bathed in blood of German.
Arms and gore and slaughter, fire and total war,
Sped before the eyes and caused the breast to sear
From tumult, split in fright between two plans:
One preferred to flee by water, one along the lands,

et patria pontus iam tutior; est magis arma
qui temptare velit fatisque iubentibus uti. 220
Ac velut ex alto cum magnus inhorruit auster 233
et pulsas evertit aquas, non arma ministris,
non regimen prodest, ligat alter pondeera pinus, 235
alter tuta sinus tranqilla litora quaerit: …
hic dat vela fugae Fortunaeque omnia credit. 237
[Quantum quisque timet, tantum fugit ocior ipse.] 221
Hos inter motus populus, miserabile visu,
quo mens icta iubet, deserta ducitur urbe.
Gaudet Roma fuga, debellati Quirites
rumoris sonitu maerentia tecta relinquunt. 225
Ille manu pavida natos tenet, ille penates
occultat gremio deploratumque relinquit
limen et absentem votis interficit hostem.
Sunt qui coniugibus maerentia pectora iungant
grandaevos patres … 230a
onerisque ignara iuentus 230b
id pro quo metuit, tantum trahit. Omnia secum
hic vehit imprudens praedamque in proeliis ducit. 232
Quid tam parva queror? Gemino cum consule Magnus, 238
ille tremor Ponti saevique repertor Haedaspis

L (= lrtp), O (= BRP)
123 219 patria lB: patria est *cett.* 221 *ad* 237 *ex ordine casos sic transposuit Ehlers; alii aliter, ut ait Buecheler, moliti sunt* 236 sinus *Bursian*: sinu *lac. ind. Ehlers* 221 *del. Moessler* 230 *lac. ind. Mueller*

Though sea was safer than their country; the rest
Preferred to fight, in fealty to the fates' behest. 220
Just as when a southern squall erupts far out at sea 233
To drive and bowl the waves along, and crew will try
In vain to secure cargo and course, one the pine-load 235
Lashing, another seeking safer bay and beach-head;
One more lets out the sail to flee, trusting to Fate. 237
Amid all this confusion, and what a wretched sight, 222
Whereto a broken spirit led them people went in flight
From city: Rome rejoiced in it, burghers smit
By Rumour's echo their grieving homes abandoned. 225
One would hold his sons with trembling hand,
Another hid in lap his images, and weeping crossed
The threshold, as absent foe to death he cursed.
And then were those who hugged their wives in grief,
And aged fathers ... 230
The young men, unused to loading,
Took only what they feared to lose, the foolish taking
Everything with him, booty to the conflict bringing. 232
Why with such minutiae a fuss? With two consuls Magnus, 238
The bane of Pontus, of the wild Hydaspes first seer,

et piratarum scopulus, modo quem ter ovantem
Iuppiter horruerat, quem fracto gurgite Pontus,
et veneratus erat submissa Bosphoros unda
pro pudor, imperii deserto nomine fugit,
ut Fortuna levis Magni quoque terga videret.

124 Ergo tanta lues divum quoque numina vicit,
consensitque fugae caeli timor. Ecce per orbem
mitis turba deum terras exosa furentes
deserit atque hominum damnatum avertitur agmen.
Pax prima ante alias niveos pulsata lacertos
abscondit galea victum caput atque relicto
orbe fugax Ditis petit impacabile regnum.
Huic comes it submissa Fides et crine soluto
Iustitia ac maerens lacera Concordia palla.
At contra, sedes Erebi qua rupta dehiscit,
emergit late Ditis chorus, horrida Erinys
et Bellona minax facibusque armata Megaera
Letumque Insidiaeque et lurida Mortis imago.
Quas inter Furor, abruptis ceu liber habenis
sanguineam late tollit caput oraque mille
vulneribus confossa cruenta casside velat;
haeret detritus laevae Mavortius umbo
innumerabilibus telis gravis, atque flagranti

L (= lrtp), O (= BRP)
123 241 in gurgite rt^{m}pBR 245 vicit *Jacobs*: vidit
250 galea] palla *Schrader*

And the pirates' reef, whom only now did Jupiter fear
Thrice-triumphing, whom the Black Sea had venerated,
Depths destroyed, to whom Bosphoran wave prostrated,
Yes, he: for shame, he fled, gave up his claim,
Gave another scalp to fickle Fortune, Magnus' name!

124 And so the awful pestilence racked the very gods,
For heaven's panic approved the flight: in all lands
Those gods, a milder crew, left an earth gone mad
In loathing and turned away from men, the ruined team.
Peace was first goddess, turning her snow-white back
And hiding in her helmet a beaten hand. From the track
Of world she fled and made straight to the realm of Dis
Implacable. With her went a cringing Faith, and Justice
With her hair awry, and Concordia with torn gown.
In contrast rent the seat of Erebus open: from down
Emerged the chorus-line of Dis – grim Erinys
And terrifying Bellona and Megaera armed with torches
And ghastly face of Death, Ambush, and Ruin.
Among them Madness as if unleashed by broken rein
Raised his sweeping, bloodstained crown, and that mask
Of a thousand gashes he crammed within his gory casque;
The shield of Mars he bore upon his left arm,
By countless arrows scarred and battered, and from

stipite dextra minax terris incendia portat.
  Sentit terra deos mutataque sidera pondus
quaesivere suum; namque omnia regia caeli
in partes diducta ruit. Primumque Dione
Caesaris arma sui ducit, comes additur illi
Pallas et ingentem quatiens Mavortiius hastam.
Magnum cum Phoebo soror et Cyllenia proles
excipit ac totis similis Tirynthius actis.
  Intremuere tubae ac scisso Discordia crine
extulit ad superos Stygium caput. Huius in ore
concretus sanguis, contusaque lumina flebant,
stabant aerati scabra rubigine dentes,
tabo lingua fluens, obsessa draconibus ora,
atque inter torto laceratam pectore vestem
sanguineam tremula quatiebat lampada dextra.
Haec ut Cocyti tenebras et Tartara liquit,
alta petit gradiens iuga nobilis Appennini,
unde omnes terras atque omnia litora posset
aspicere ac toto fluitantes orbe catervas,
atque has erumpit furibundo pectore voces:
'Sumite nunc, gentes, accensis mentibus arma,
sumite et in medias immittite lampadas urbes.
Vincetur, quicumque latet; non femina cesset,
non puer aut aevo iam desolata senectus;

L (= lrtp), O (= BRP)
124 267 arma *Passerat*: acta 269 Magnum *Gevaerts*: magnaque 270 totis] tantis *Nisbet* 273 fletu *Buecheler* 274 irati O 277 sanguinea tremulam *Sambucus*

His dire right hand a brand to set the world ablaze.
Earth felt the gods; the stars without their poise
Reformed – every region of the sky in haste
To join the one side or the other. Dione first
Arose to bear her Caesar's colours. Pallas next
To her arrived, and Mars (a mighty spear he flexed).
But Magnus got Diana, Apollo and Cyllene's son,
And also Hercules of similar renown.
Trumpets trilled, and Discord, hair all rent,
Showed off to gods her Stygian head: mouth besprent
With solid blood, eyes black-and-blue and weeping,
Tongue aflow with pus, face alive with snakes.
The torments of her chest had torn her gown to flakes,
And in her trembling hand she shook a bloody lamp.
Now when she left Cocytus' gloom and Tartarean camp,
Off she marched to Appennine's high and famous reaches
To gain a view from thence of all the lands and beaches,
And to see the regiments a-moving through the world.
These words from that madly-heaving chest she hurled:
'Arise now, set your hearts aflame, ye lands:
Carry arms, and put amid the cities brands.
Those who try to hide will die: let try no woman,
Nor child, nor man at last by age undone;

ipsa tremat tellus lacerataque tecta rebellent.
Tu legem, Marcelle, tene. Tu concute plebem,
Curio. Tu fortem ne supprime, Lentule, Martem.
Quid porro tu, dive, tuis cunctaris in armis,
non frangis portas, non muris oppida solvis
thesaurosque rapis? Nescis tu, Magne, tueri
Romanas arces? Epidamni moenia quaere
Thessalicosque sinus humano sanguine tingue.'
Factum est in terris, quicquid Discordia iussit."

2 Cum haec Eumolpus ingenti volubilitate verborum
effudisset, tandem Crotona intravimus. Ubi quidem parvo
deversorio refecti, postero die amplioris fortunae domum
quaerentes incidimus in turbam heredipetarum sciscitantium
3 quod genus hominis aut unde veniremus. Ex praescripto ergo
consilii communis exaggerata verborum volubilitate, unde aut
qui essemus, haud dubie credentibus indicavimus. / Qui statim L
opes suas summo cum certamine in Eumolpum congesserunt ...

L (= lrtp), O (= BRP)
124 293 arces *Passerat*: acies moenia *Puteolanus*: nomina
Haec duo capita, **124**.2 *ad* **125**, *remissiora sunt quam quae nomine Petroniano sint digna* 3 *lac. ind. Buecheler*

The very earth must rock and broken houses never yield.
Arouse the people, Curio; Marcellus, law uphold;
And Lentulus, seek not brave Mars to stifle outright.
And as for you, god-born, what is this delay to fight?
No walls of towns to open, or their gates to smash,
Or treasure loot? And Magnus, Rome's hills to watch?
To walls of Epidamnus I counsel that you hie,
And with the blood of humans Saronic gulf to dye.'
On earth was done exactly as the goddess bade."

This all spilled forth from Eumolpus in a great gush of words, as we finally passed into Croton. There, after spending the night at a rather small lodging, on the following morning, as we looked for premises more in keeping with our station, we fell in with a crowd of legacy hunters, who wanted to know who we were and where we came from. And so we launched into our tall story along the pre-arranged lines and gave the details they sought, obviously having them convinced, as in no time at all they were vying with each other to shower Eumolpus with their resources …

4 Certatim omnes heredipetae muneribus gratiam
Eumolpi sollicitant *

125 Dum haec magno tempore Crotone aguntur … et
Eumolpus felicitate plenus prioris fortunae esset
oblitus [statim] adeo ut [suis] iactaret neminem
gratiae suae ibi posse resistere impuneque suos, si
quid deliquissent [in ea urbe] beneficio amicorum
2 laturos. Ceterum ego, etsi quotidie magis magisque
superfluentibus bonis saginatum corpus impleveram
putabamque a custodia mei removisse vultum Fortunam,
tamen saepius tam consuetudinem meam cogitabam quam
3 causam et, "Quid," aiebam, "si callidus captator
exploratorem in Africam miserit mendaciumque
deprehenderit nostrum? Quid, si etiam mercennarius
praesenti felicitate lassus indicium ad amicos
detulerit totumque fallaciam invidiosa proditione
4 detexerit? Nempe rursus fugiendum erit et tandem
expugnata paupertas nova mendacitate revocanda. Dii
deaeque, quam male est extra legem viventibus:
quicquid meruerunt, semper expectant" *

L (= lrtp)
124 4 ad **125** 4 *locus plenus iterationibus vel rebus insitivis vel supervacaneis, quas enodandas mihi non pretium operae esse statui.* **125** magno tempore *def. ablativum Petersmann, non insitionem quod suspicor lac. ind. Buecheler*

All the legacy hunters emulously courted his favour with gifts *

125 This continued in Croton for a considerable period of time, and Eumolpus, full of his good fortune and entirely forgetting his earlier days, began to boast that nobody in the town could avoid being under obligation to him and that we his colleagues could do anything and get away with it through the influence of his new friends. As for me, despite stuffing myself day after day with the good things of life, that only seemed to keep increasing, and beginning to think Fortune had taken her eyes off me, I returned over and over to my situation and its basis. "Suppose," I harped, "one of the legacy hunters is shrewd enough to send an investigator to Africa and catches us in a lie? Suppose that hireling, even, gets bored with his estate, spills the beans to his cronies, and in an act of spiteful betrayal gives the whole game away? Why, we'll have to take to our heels again and the poverty we'd kept at bay for so long will return to haunt us with a new round of beggary. The worst thing about living outside the law, God knows, is that you're always expecting exactly what you deserve!" *

It is Croton's women who dominate the last tableaux of our *Satyrica*, and what an enjoyable study they make: Circe, Chrysis, Proselenos, Oenothea, Philomela, even the see-saw girl; mistress or maid, priestess or shuffling retainer, venal matron-mother or brave young daughter: the perception of Petronius has seen to it that all, free or servile, rich or humble, young and beautiful or old and frail, dealt a bad hand by life or a good, try to play it as best they can, with style and self-respect. They all encounter Encolpius, this feckless, male-privileged, self-absorbed youth, in their chance ways, and the result is fascination and humour. Admittedly, Encolpius had the disadvantage of the condition of his condition. Also, for all his youth, good looks, and ego, he was dressed as a member of the servile class, i.e., appeared to be a slave. Even modern professional psychologists, hearing his backstory, would enjoy the articulate efforts of Encolpius and his intended beloved to attach a cause to the bedevilling mystery of his sexual failure. Now, for the first time, in our novel at least, he is very sexually attracted to a lovely, poised, "real woman." The tryst is organized in style by Chrysis, the sexy maid go-between; the encounter takes place under the most seductive of circumstances – and is an abject flop. The aftermath, and its failed aftermath, and the failed aftermath after that, must be left for personal reader fun. He came to our attention as having had two or three heterosexual escapades , unconfirmed, with grown women, maybe adulterous: Hedyle, Doris, and possibly Tryphaena, though her passion was for Giton. On-site relations with Ascyltus, Giton, and even Lichas make him, in modern parlance, a fit for a bisexual young man with definite paedophiliacal leanings. In the present novel there is little successful sex for him on offer, of any kind: a get-together with Ascyltus for old times' sake is unsatisfactory; emotional cuddles with Giton, also somehow below par. Now came the test of Circe, a resurgence of interest from an eager Chrysis, and resolution to his impotence, not quite confirmed at story's end.

126 "Quia nosti venerem tuam, superbiam tractas vendistique
2 amplexus, non commodas. Quo enim spectant flexae pectine
comae, quo facies medicamine attrita et oculorum quoque
mollis petulantia, quo incessus arte compositus et ne
vestigia quidem pedum extra mensuram errantia, nisi quod
3 formam prostituis ut vendas? Vides me: nec auguria novi
nec mathematicorum caelum curare soleo, ex vultibus tamen
hominum mores colligo, et cum spatiantem vidi, quid
4 cogitet scio. Sive ergo nobis vendis quod peto, mercator
paratus est, sive, quod humanius est, commodas, effice ut
beneficium debeamus. Nam quod servum te te et humilem
fateris, accendis desiderium aestantis. Quaedam enim
feminae sordibus calent, nec libidinem concitant, nisi
6 aut servos viderint aut statores altius cinctos. Harena
aliquas accendit aut perfusus pulvere mulio aut histrio
7 scaenae ostentatione traductus. Ex hac nota domina est
mea: usque ab orchestra quattuordecim transilit et in
extrema plebe quaerit quod quod deligat."
8 Itaque oratione blandissima plenus, "Rogo," inquam,
"numquid illa, quae me amat, tu es?" Multum risit ancilla
post tam rigidum schema et, "Nolo," inquit, "tibi tam
valde placeas. Ego adhuc servo numquam succubui, nec hoc

L (= lrtp)
126 tractas *scripsi*: iactas *Nisbet*: captas commodas *Lipsius*: commodos arte *Dousa*: tute 3 cogitet *Burman*: cogites 4 nobis *del. Fraenkel* 4 debeamus *Anton*: debeam 6 mulio l "Pith." t[m]: multo *cett.*

11
Circe and Polyaenus

126 "You know you're a charmer so you put on airs, and instead of lending your hugs you sell them. Why else the curled hair, buffed complexion, languid bedroom eyes, studied walk, not a foot out of place – unless you want to play the prostitute and sell your body? Look at me: I'm not a fortune teller or astrologer, but I can read people's character from the expression on their faces, and when I see a man's walk I know what's on his mind. So if you're selling us what I'm looking for, you have a buyer; but if you're generous enough to give it away you'll put us in your debt. Your look of a slave and of low status only increases the heat of passion, since some ladies like to get down and dirty and aren't aroused unless they're watching slaves or messengers showing their legs. The arena turns some women on, or perhaps a dust-choked mule skinner, or an actor making a fool of himself on a public stage. My mistress is one of these: from the front of the theatre she'll hop back fourteen rows and pick something she fancies from the lowest of the low."

I was buoyed by her flattering proposition. "Tell me," I asked, "is the one in love with me not you, perhaps?" The maid had herself a good laugh at such an unlikely notion. "I wouldn't give you the satisfaction," she said. "I've not gone to bed yet with a slave.

10 dii sinant, ut amplexus meos in crucem mittam. Viderint
matronae, quae flagellorum vestigia osculantur: ego
etiam si ancilla sum, numquam nisi in equestribus
11 sedeo." Mirari equidem tam discordem libidinem coepi
atque inter monstra numerare, quod ancilla haberet
matronae superbiam et matron ancilae haberet.
12 / Procedentibus deinde longius iocis rogavi ancillam LO
ut in platanona perduceret dominam. Placuit puellae consilium.
Itaque collegit altius tunicam flexitque se in daphnona,
13 qui ambulationi haerebat. Nec diu morata dominam producit et
latebris laterique meo applicat. Mulierem omnibus simulacris
14 emendatiorem. Nulla vox est quae formam eius possit
15 comprehendere, nam quicquid dixero, minus erit. Crines ingenio
suo flexi per totos se umeros effuderant, frons minima et quae
radices capillorum retro flexerat, supercilia usque ad malarum
scripturam currentia et rursus confinio luminum paene permixta,
16 oculi clariores stellis extra lunam fulgentibus, nares paululum
17 inflexae et osculum quale Praxiteles habere Dianam credidit.
Iam mentum, iam cervix, iam manus, iam pedum candor intra auri
18 gracile vinculum positus: Parium marmor extinxerat. Itaque tunc
primum Dorida vetus amator contempsi *

L (= lrtp), O (= BRP)
126 12 iocis *om.* O ancillam *om.* L produceret L
cohaerebat *mavult Mueller*: adhaerebat *Nisbet* 13 dominam
del. Fraenkel applicat meo L 15 scripturam *molestum
quibusdam*: stricturam *Gessner*: curvaturam *Fraenkel*
16 Dianam] Dionam *Meyer*: Dionen *Jahn*

And I hope to God I never have to put my arms around a cross. I'll leave kissing the whip marks to the ladies. Though I'm just a maid, it's only the knights who'll give me a ride!" I was struck by such dissonance of sexual tastes, and thought it odd that a maid should have the hauteur of a mistress and a mistress the earthiness of a maid.

Continuing our banter, I asked the maid to bring her mistress to a stand of plane- trees, and she agreed. Gathering in her dress, she turned off into the laurel grove adjoining the promenade.

Before long, she led her mistress out of the shadows and over to my side, a woman more flawless than any statue. No description could do justice to her beauty, and anything I said would be inadequate. Her hair was combed back from a tiny forehead, to reveal the roots, and then to cascade in natural curls the length of her shoulders; her eyebrows traced themselves to her cheekbones and on the inside almost met above the bridge of her nose; her eyes were brighter than the stars on a moonless night; her nostrils curved inward a fraction, and her mouth was as Praxiteles imagined Diana's. Her chin, her neck, her hands, her white feet enclosed within their dainty golden straps: she put Parian marble in the shade. For the first time I cared nothing for my old flame Doris *

Quid factum est, quod tu proiectis, Iuppiter, armis
inter caelicolas fabula muta iaces?
Nunc erat a torva submittere cornua fronte,
nunc pluma canos dissimulare tuos.
Nunc vera est Danae. Tempta modo tangere corpus:
iam tua flammifer membra calore fluent *

127 Delectata illa risit tam blandum, ut videretur mihi
plenum os extra nubem luna proferre. Mox digitis
gubernantibus vocem. "Si non fastiditis," inquit, "feminam
ornatam et hoc primum anno virum expertam, concilio tibi,
2 o iuvenis, sororem. Habes quidem [et] fratrem, neque enim
me piguit inquirere, sed quid prohibet et sororem
adoptare? Eodem gradu venio. Tu tantum dignare et meum
3 osculum, cum libuerit, agnoscere." "Immo," inquam ego,
"per formam tuam te rogo ne fastidias hominem peregrinam
inter cultores admittere. Invenies religiosus, si te
adorari permiseris. Ac ne me iudices ad hoc templum
[Amoris] gratis accedere, dono tibi fratrem meum."

L (= lrtp), O (= BRP)
126 18.2 iaces *Fraenkel*: taces **127** mihi extra nubem luna caput proferre L feminam] mulierem lt^{m} *auctore Scaligero, non codice* 2 *om.* delta, *del. Fraenkel* agnoscere *Pithoeus*: agnosce 3 *om.* LR, *del. Fraenkel*

What has become of you, O Jupiter, to cast aside
Your arms and loll among the gods, tongue still?
Now were the time to sprout horns from bestial head,
Or your snowy hair beneath down to conceal.
Here's a genuine Danae. Touch her if you can
And your limbs will melt in the flames of your passion *

127 She gave a delighted chuckle, so fetchingly that it seemed as if the moon had come out in full glory from behind a cloud. Then, tracing out her words with her fingers, she spoke. "If you don't despise a woman of standing, and one who's known a man for less than a year, I offer you a sister, young man. You already have a little brother (for I was bold enough to inquire), but what's to stop you from adopting a little sister too? I come on the same terms. Merely agree to accept my kisses whenever it shall please."

"Oh, yes!" said I, "I beg you by your beauty not to be loath to include a stranger among your acolytes. Let me worship and you'll have a devotee. And do not deem that I come to your temple at no cost: to you I sacrifice my little brother."

4 "Quid? Tu," inquit illa, "donas mihi eum sine quo non
potes vivere, ex cuius osculo pendes, quem si tu amas
5 quemadmodum ego te volo?" Haec ipsa cum diceret, tanta
gratia conciliabat vocem [loquentis], tam dulcis sonus
pertemptatum mulcebat aera, ut putares inter auras canere
Sirenum concordiam. Itaque miranti [et] toto [mihi] caelo
clarius nescioquid relucente libuit deae nomen quaerere.
6 "Ita," inquit, "non dixit tibi ancilla mea me Circen
vocari? Non sum quidem Solis progenies, nec mea mater,
dum placet, labentis mundi cursum detinuit; habebo tamen
quod caelo imputem, si non fata coniunxerint. Immo iam
7 nescio quid tacitis cogitationibus deus agit. Nec sine
causa Polyaenon Circe amat: semper inter haec nomina
magna fax surgit. Sume ergo amplexum, si placet. Neque
est quod curiosum aliquem extimescas: longe ab hoc loco
8 frater est." Dixit haec Circe, implicitumque me bracchiis
mollioribus pluma deduxit in terram vario gramine indutam.

9 Idaeo qualis fudit de vertice flores
terra parens, cum se concesso iunxit amori
Iuppiter et toto concepit pectore flamma:

L (= lrtp), O (= BRP)
127 4 quid tu *Pithoeus*: quid ni; quid tu *distinguunt quidam, sed cf.* 24.2 5 loquentis *redundat; adiunctionem videas* miranti … relucente *perturbata* et *del. Anton* miranti mihi … relucente *perturbata*: miranti mihi toto caelo *Rose*: mihi *delendum credo* 6 Circen me L habeo L 7 semper O: sed L 9 qualis *Hadrianides* concesso *Sambucus*: confesso

"What's this?" she replied. "You'd give up the one thing you can't live without, upon whose kisses you dote, whom you love in the very same way I want to love you?" As she said this she imbued her voice with such charm and sweet sounds to caress the enraptured air that one thought of the Siren chorus singing through the breezes.

As I marvelled and the sky seemed to take on a new brightness, I decided to ask the goddess her name. "Oh," she said, "did my maid not tell you I'm called Circe? Not that daughter of the Sun, of course, and no mother of mine could stop at will the motion of the turning world.

"Still, if the fates bring us together I shall see the hand of heaven in it. Yes, already a god is quietly working some purpose out. It's no accident that Circe should be in love with Polyaenus, since between those two names a strong spark will always flow! So come into my embrace, if you like, and don't be scared of a Peeping Tom. Your little brother's far away." With these words Circe enfolded me in her arms as soft as down and drew me towards the grass-bedecked earth.

Just as Mother Earth spread upon the crest
Of Ida posies, for Jupiter to join with his lawful love
And light the fire within his breast:

emicuere rosae violaeque et molle cyperon,
albaque de viridi riserunt lilia prato:
talis humus Venerem molles clamavit in herbas,
candidiorque dies secreto favit amori.

In hoc gramine compositi mille osculis lusimus quaerentes voluptatem robustam *

128 / "Quid est?" inquit, "numquid te osculum meum L
offendit? Numquid spiritus ienunio marcens? Numquid
alarum neglegens sudor? <Aut> si haec non sunt, numquid
2 Gitona times?" Perfusus ego rubore manifesto etiam si
quid habueram virium perdidi, totoque corpore velut
luxato, "Quaeso," inquam, "regina, noli suggillare
miserias. Veneficio contactus sum *
3 "Dic, Chrysis, sed verum: numquid indecens sum?
Numquid incompta? Numquid ab aliquo naturali vitio formam
meam excaeco? Noli decipere dominam tuam. Nescioquid
4 peccavimus." Rapuit deinde tacenti speculum, et postquam
omnes vultus temptavit, quales solent inter <se> amantes
risus effingere, excussit vexatam solo vestem raptimque
5 aedem Veneris intravit. Ego contra damnatus et quasi visu

L (= lrtp), O (= BRP)

127 9 clamavit] cumulavit *Courtney* **128** marcens *Buecheler*: aut *suppl. Buecheler* sudor] odor *Nisbet* 2 luxato *Jungermann*: laxato 4 quales solent *scripsi*: quos solet *addidi* fingere *Cuper*: frangere; *adiunct. videas*

Roses flashed, and violets too, and rushes smooth,
And white lilies smiling up from the green mead:
Such a bed cried out for love amid the soft sward,
As the day brightened in blessing upon our secret tryst.

Lying beside each other in the grass we kissed a thousand times, on the road to sturdy pleasures *

128 "What's the matter?" she cried. "Do my kisses offend? Is my breath stale from lack of food? Have I neglected my underarm perspiration? If none of the above, perhaps you are afraid of Giton?" I flushed an obvious scarlet and promptly lost whatever strength I'd had, my whole body going limp. "Please, highness," I begged, "don't compound my woes. I've been hexed!" *

"Tell me, Chrysis, and truthfully now: Am I ugly? Am I slovenly? Am I blind to some natural flaw in my beauty? Don't lie to your mistress. It's our fault, isn't it?" Chrysis wasn't speaking so Circe snatched a mirror from her and, after trying the gamut of faces that lovers pull to make each other smile, she shook out her dress, which had been mussed from contact with the ground, and rushed off into the shrine of Venus. Sentence passed, I felt as if I'd been given a fright from some apparition, and I began to ask myself searching questions as to whether I'd been cheated forever of real pleasure.

in horrorem perductus interrogare animum meum coepi an vera voluptate fraudatus essem.

6 / Nocte soporifera veluti cum somnia ludunt LO
errantes oculos effossaque protulit aurum
in lucem tellus: versat manus improba furtum
[thesaurosque rapit; sudor quoque perluit]
et mentem timor altus habet, ne forte gravatum
excutiat gremium secreti conscius auri:
mox ubi fugerunt elusam gaudia mentem
veraque forma redit, animus quod perdidit optat
atque in praeterita se totus imagine versat *

7 / "Itaque hoc nomine tibi gratias ago, quod me L
Socratica fide diligis. Non tam intactus Alcibiades in praeceptoris sui lectulo iacuit" *

129 "Crede mihi, frater, non intellego me virum esse. non sentio. Funerata est illa pars corporis, qua quondam Achilles eram" *

2 Veritus puer, ne in secreto deprehensus daret sermonibus locum, proripuit se et in partem interiorem aedium fugit *

L (= lrtp), O (= BRP)
128 6 *versum esse spurium conflatumque ex* 124.292 *et* 120.97 *confidit Buecheler* 7 lectulo rtp: lecto l
129 interiorem aedium l: aedium interiorem rtp

As in the night when sleepy dreams deceive the flighty
Eyes; the earth is turned and to the light the gold
Is brought. A greedy hand the loot does hold,
And panic grips the mind, in case perchance a party
Shall relieve our pockets of their secret coinage:
But soon, when joy retreats from our deluded mind
And shape of truth returns, the soul desires the find
It lost and travels backward to reclaim the image *

"Well, you have my thanks on one account: for loving me with a devotion truly Socratic. Not Alcibiades, lying in his teacher's bed, got away so unscathed!" *

129 "Believe me, dear boy, my sense of being a man is gone, along with the feeling. The part of me that once made me an Achilles lies dead and buried!" *

The boy, afraid lest he be caught meeting me in secret and set tongues wagging, wrenched himself free and fled into the inner recesses of the building *

Chapter 129 starts with another of those references to the need for extreme discretion to avoid a tell-tale disclosure of Encolpius and Giton's relationship, followed by denunciation, even in faraway Croton.

3 / Cubiculum autem meum Chrysis intravit LO
codicillosque mihi dominae suae reddidit, in quibus haec
4 erant scripta: "Circe Polyaeno salutem. Si libidinosus
essem, quererer decepta: nunc etiam languori tuo gratias
5 ago. In umbra voluptatis diutius lusi. Quid tamen agas,
quaero, et an tuis pedibus perveneris domum. Negant enim
medici sine nervis homines ambulare posse. Narrabo tibi,
6 adulescens, paralysin cave. Numquam ego aegrum tam magno
7 periculo vidi: medius [fidius] iam peristi. Quod si idem
frigus genua manusque temptaverit tuas, licet ad
8 tubicines mittas. Quid ergo est? Etiam si gravem iniuriam
accepi, homini tamen misero non invideo medicinam. Si vis
sanus esse, Gitonem relega. Recipies, inquam, nervos tuos,
9 si triduo sine fratre dormieris. Nam quod ad me attinet,
non timeo ne quis inveniatur cui minus placeam. Nec
speculum mihi nec famam mentitur. Vale, si potes."
10 Ut intellexit Chrysis perligisse me totum convicium,
"solent," inquit, "haec fieri, et praecipue in hac
civitate, in qua mulierss etiam lunam deducunt *
11 Itaque huius quoque rei cura agetur. Rescribe modo
blandius dominae animumque eius candida humanitate
restitue. Verum enim fatendum est: ex qua hora iniuriam
12 accepit, apud se non est." Libenter quidem parui

L (= lrtp), O (= BRP)
129 4 Circe Polyaeno salutem BR: *om. cett.* 6 ego BR: *om. ceteri, qui* L *penderent del. Thomas* 8 relega *Delz:* roga
11 ita r eius BR: *om. ceteri*

Whereupon Chrysis came into my room and handed me a letter from her mistress, which read as follows:

Dear Polyaenus,

Were I an oversexed woman I should complain of being disappointed, but I'm actually grateful for your limp performance. I've been dallying too long in the mere penumbra of pleasure. By the way, how are you? Did you make it home on your own two feet, I wonder, since doctors assure us we need our muscles for walking? Young man, a word of warning: be careful you don't seize up. I've never seen a sick person at greater risk. By Heaven, you're dead already in your mid-section, and if the same chill moves down to your knees or up to your hands, you might as well send for the trumpeters. So what's to do? I've been dealt a grave affront, but I certainly don't begrudge treatment to a man in such a plight. If you want to get better, send away Giton. You'll get your strength back, you'll see, if you don't sleep with your boyfriend for three nights. As far as I'm concerned, I'm not scared of being being unable to find someone else to please, since my mirror doesn't lie, and nor does my reputation.

Get well – if you can,
Circe.

After Chrysis saw I'd read the whole charge through, she spoke: "Things happen," she said, "especially in this town, where women bring down the moon … For this we'll find a cure also. Write a nice reply and restore her spirits by human frankness. But, I warn you, ever since she received this slight she's not been herself."

One wonders if the letter exchange may be a perverted reminiscence of Ovid's poetic *Heroides*, a cycle of imaginary love letters of legendary men and women as part of the medium of erotic elegy. Just before Ovid is the pioneering example in *Prop.* iv.iii from "Arethusa," a concealed real woman to her soldier husband: a dramatic monologue in the form of an epistle. See Luck 1959. The genre died with Ovid.

130 ancillae verbaque codicillis talia imposui: "Polyaenos
Circae salutem. Fateor me, domina, saepe peccasse; nam
et homo sum et adhuc iuvenis. Numquam tamen ante hunc
2 diem usque ad mortem deliqui. Habes confitentem reum:
quicquid iusseris, merui. Proditionem feci, hominem
occidi, templum violavi: in haec facinora quaere
3 supplicium. Sive occidere placet, <cum> ferro meo venio,
sive verberibus contenta es, curro nudus ad dominam.
4 Illud unum memento, non me sed instrumenta peccasse.
Paratus miles arma non habui. Quis hoc turbaverit nescio.
5 Forsitan animus antecessit corporis moram, forsitan dum
omnia concupisco, voluptatem tempore consumpsi. Non
6 invenio quod feci. Paralysin tamen cavere iubes: tamquam
etiam maior fieri possit quae abstulit mihi per quod [etiam]
te habere potui. Summa tamen excusationis meae haec est:
placebo tibi, si me culpam emendare permiseris" *
7 / Dimissa cum eiusmodi pollicitatione Chryside L
curavi diligentius noxissimam corpus, balneoque
praeterito modica unctione usus, mox cibis validioribus
pastus, id est bulbis cochlearumque sine iure cervicibus,
8 hausi parcius merum. Hinc ante somnum levissima ambulatione

---

L (= lrtp), O (= BRP)
130 hanc L 3 *add. Buecheler* 6 tamquam etiam *Buecheler:* tamquam iam *libri* *om* L *secl. Buecheler* 8 levissima lp: lenissima rt

I readily followed the maid's advice and put pen to paper as follows:

130 Dear Circe,

My lady, I confess to having made many mistakes, since I'm only human and young still. But before this day I'd never committed a capital offence. You have me dead to rights and I'd deserve any penalty you seek. I have committed treason, murder, temple desecration. For these crimes punish me. If the sentence is execution, I offer my own sword. If you find a whipping sufficient, to my mistress I offer my back. But take one thing into account: it was not I but my instruments that failed. The soldier was ready but he'd lost his sword. I have no idea who broke my line. Perhaps my mind ran ahead and my body didn't catch up. Perhaps while I was reaching for the skies my desire just spent itself. I have no idea what I did. You warn me to beware of paralysis. But how could its effects be worse than removing the actual means of having you? This is my plea in a nutshell: give me the chance to make it up to you and I promise to please.

Polyaenus. *

After dismissing Chrysis with such an undertaking, I gave some careful attention to my body: I skipped a hot bath but applied a moderate amount of crème. Then I took in food that gives strength – onions and snail necks, well drained – and I went easy on the wine. Next, before turning in, I went for a short walk to settle the digestion, and then to bed, without Giton.

Opinion differs over whether here Encolpius is opening a window to his past career by confessing to real crimes – of treason, murder, and temple robbery, such as got him a trip to the arena – or whether he is speaking only in a high-flown metaphor, equating the insults, disappointments, and deceptions inflicted upon Circe for his sexual failure – which he pretends to regard as a capital offence – with such crimes, just as grave and somehow analogous. I favour the latter, since it is more in the character of a not very courageous fantasist. Besides, those prior acts of criminality do seem like capital offences. Did he just lie? Now too he wants nothing more than to enjoy obscurity with his Giton, or maybe Circe.

compositus sine Gitone cubiculum intravi. [Tanta erat
placandi cura, ut timerem ne latus meum frater convelleret.]
131 Postero die, cum sine offensa corporis animique consurrexissem,
in eundem platanona descendi, etiamsi locum inauspicatum
timebam, coepique inter arbores ducem itineris expectare
2 Chrysidem. Nec diu spatiatus consideram, ubi hesterno die
3 fueram, cum illa intervenit comitem aniculam trahens. Atque
ut me consalutavit, "Quid est," inquit, "fastose, ecquid
bonam mentem habere coepisti?" …

4 Illa de sinu licium protulit varii coloris filis
intortum cervicemque vinxit meam. Mox turbatum sputo
pulverem medio sustulit digito frontemque repugnantis
signavit …

5 Hoc peracto carmine ter me iussit expuere terque
lapillos conicere in sinum, quos ipsa praecantatos
purpura involverat, admotisque manibus temptare coepit
6 inguinum vires. Dicto citius nervi paruerant imperio
7 manusque aniculae ingenti motu repleverunt. At illa
gaudio exultans, "Vides," inquit, "Chrysis mea, quod
aliis leporem excitavi?" *

L (= lrtp)
130 8 tanta … convelleret *adventicia damnanda; adiunct. videas* **131** 3 *lac. ind. Buecheler* 4 *lac. ind. Boschius*

[My desire to appease Circe had made me afraid that my little brother might wear me out.]

131 Next day I arose unsullied in body and soul and went down to the grove of plane- trees again, not without some trepidation at the unlucky setting, and began to wait among the trees for Chrysis to lead the way. I strolled about a little and then sat down at yesterday's site. At which point she appeared, pulling along a little old woman. After a cordial salute, "Well then, my finicky friend," she said, "have you started to come to your senses?" …

The old woman pulled from her pocket a necklace of threads braided in different colours and attached it round my neck. Next, with her middle finger she scooped up a wad of dirt which she mixed with spittle and smeared repulsively on my forehead …

After reciting this spell, the woman told me to spit three times and to flip the pebbles, pre-charmed and wrapped in a purple rag, onto my lap. Then she moved her hands forward to test the hardness of my erection. Sooner than words could say the sinews had followed her direction and they filled the old woman's hands with massive life. She was jubilant. "Chrysis, my dear," she said, "look at the hare I've started for other dogs to chase!" *

Like G.K. Chesterton's self-hating donkey, "the Devil's walking parody of all four-footed things," the old woman Proselenos "had [her] hour"; in fact a respectable eight chapters (*Sat.* 131–8), compared to Chrysis with fourteen (*Sat.* 126–39), Circe with nine (*Sat.* 126–34), and Oenothea with five (*Sat.* 134–8). More than a bawd, she was the under-retainer of Chrysis, delegated to deal with her specialty, the physical aspects of inciting Encolpius' arousal hence curing his impotence, in which she succeeded with quantities of spit, dirt, pebbles, and stimulation. But the effect was brief, and she was tossed out with her mistress Chrysis, though not beaten, perhaps because of her advanced years. I see some perceptively wrought pathos in her plight of physical decline and ugly, tottering, impoverished old age, which she is fully aware of and bitterly laments (*Sat.* 133–4). Under these conditions, her recourse, along with legions of other poor old women, was the bottle. For dogs flushing and chasing hares, see at *Sat.* 63.4.

8 / Nobilis aestivas platanus diffuderat umbras LO
et bacis redimita Daphne tremulaeque cupressus
et circum tonsae trepidanti vertice pinus.
Has inter ludebat aquis errantibus amnis
spumeus et querulo vexabat rore lapillos.
Dignus amore locus; testis silvestris aedon
atque urbana Procne, quae circum gramina fusae
et molles violas cantu sua furta colebant …

9 Premebat illa resoluta marmoreis cervicibus aureum
10 torum myrtoque florenti quietum <aera> verberabat. Itaque
ut me vidit, paulullum erubuit, hesternae scilicet iniuriae
memor; deinde ut remotis omnibus secundum invitantem
consedi, ramum super oculos meos posuit, et quasi pariete
interiecto audacior facta, "Quid est," inquit, "paralytice?
11 Ecquid hodie totus venisti?" "Rogas," inquam ego, "potius
quam temptas? Totoque corpore in amplexum eius immissus
non praecantatis usque ad satietatem osculis fruor." *

L (= lrtp), O (= BRP)
131 8 *versum* et bacis … *post illum* et circum *transp.* L errantibus O: trepidantibus L vexabat] versabat *Scaliger in Appendice Vergiliana* silvestris aedon *Scaliger ibidem:* silvester aedon *Pius*: isdon *vel* iasdon O: hirundo L furta *Buecheler:* rura *codd. praeter* r: iura

A noble plane its summer shade has spread,
And trembling cypresses, and Daphne berry-clad;
Round us stir the tonsured pines, tops a-sway.
Amid them too a foam-flecked stream at play,
Its waters winding, pebbles with a dewy murmur teasing.
Place designed for love! Country nightingale witnessing,
And swallow of the city. Round the grass they flit,
Above the violets tender, in song to celebrate our tryst.

There she lay, with her marble neck draped languidly along a golden couch, fanning the still air with a sprig of myrtle in bloom. Upon seeing me she flushed lightly, remembering yesterday's fiasco, no doubt.

She dismissed her attendants and invited me to sit beside her. Covering my eyes with the sprig and emboldened by this kind of screen thrown up between us, "What's up, my paralytic friend?" she said. "Do you come today a whole man?" "Instead of asking," I replied, "why don't you just try me?" And I flung myself bodily into her arms and took my fill freely of the most arousing kisses *

132 / Ipsa corporis pulchritudine me ad se vocante L
trahebat ad venerem. Iam pluribus osculis collisa labra
crepitabant, iam implicitae manus omne genus amoris
invenerant, iam alligata mutuo ambitu corpora animarum
quoque mixturam fecerant *
2 Manifestis matrona contumeliis lacerata tandem ad
ultionem decurrit vocatque cubicularios et me iubet
3 catomizari. Nec contenta mulier tam gravi iniuria mea
convocat omnes quasillarias familiae sordidissimam
4 partem ac me conspui iubet. Oppono ego manus oculis meis,
nullis precibus effusis, quia sciebam quid meruissem,
5 verberibus sputisque extra ianuam eiectus sum. Eicitur
et Proselenus, Chrysis vapulat, totaque familia tristis
inter se mussat quaeritque quis dominae hilaritatem
confuderit *
6 Itaque pensatis vicibus animosior verborum notas
arte contexi, ne aut Eumolpus contumelia mea hilarior
7 fieret aut tristior Giton. / Quod solum igitur salvo LO
pudore poteram, languorem simulavi,

L (= lrtp), O (= BRP)
132 *versus sequentes quinque ex alia parte huc translatos esse, statuit Buecheler* trahebar *Burman* 2 lacerata *tempto*: *cf.* 100.4: exacerbata *Buecheler*: vexata *Nisbet*: efferata *Mueller*: verborum *Conte*: verberata; *adiunctionem videas* catomizari *Salmasius*: catorogare 5 quid *mavult Buecheler* *lac. ind. Pithou* 7 poterat L simulare coepi L

132 With the sheer beauty of her body inviting me on, she drew me down to make love to her. We crushed our lips together in countless noisy kisses, our busy hands devised every kind of caress, our bodies were so tightly locked that our very souls commingled *

The lady was shattered at these palpable insults and stooped at last to revenge. She called to her stewards and instructed that I be soundly thrashed. Not stopping at this humiliation, she got out all her spinning girls and other household slaves of the lowest tier and told them to spit upon me. I shielded my eyes with my hands without a word of entreaty, since I knew it was all richly deserved. I was then tossed outside covered in lash marks and spittle. The old woman, Proselenos, followed, Chrysis got a beating, and the whole household was set to muttering disconsolately and wondering who was responsible for destroying their mistress' usual cheerfulness …

And so I took stock of my situation, and in a slightly better mood decided to conceal my whip marks with some care, to prevent Eumolpus deriving further amusement or Giton sorrow at my discomfiture. Then I did the only thing I could to ensure my privacy: I feigned an attack of illness. Burying myself in my bedclothes, I turned the full fire of my fury

conditusque lectulo totum ignem furoris in eam <rem> converti, quae mihi omnium malorum causa fuerat:

8 Ter corripui terribilem manu bipennem,
ter languidior coliculi repente thyrso
ferrum timui, quod trepido male dabat usum.
Nec iam poteram, quod modo conficere libebat;
namque illa metu frigidior rigente bruma
confugerat in viscera mille operta rugis.
Ita non potui supplicio caput aperire,
sed furciferae mortifero timore lusus
ad verba, magis quae poterant nocere, fugi.

9 Erectus igitur in cubitum hac fere oratione contumacem
vexavi: "Quid dicis," inquam, "omnium hominum deorumque
pudor? Nam ne nominare quidem te inter res serias fas est.
10 Hoc de te merui, ut me in caelo positum ad inferos traheres?
/ Ut traduceres annos primo florentes vigore senectaeque L
11 ultimae mihi lassitudinem imponeres? Rogo te, mihi
apodixin <non> defunctoriam redde." Haec ut iratus effudi,

/ illa solo fixos oculos aversa tenebat, LO
nec magis inceptoque vultum sermone movetur
quam lentae salices lassove papavere collo.

L (= lrtp), O (= BRP)
132 7 *supplevi;* aut *cf.* 132.12 partem; *adiunctionem videas*
8 terribili L 11 *add. Mueller,* nec *add. Buecheler versus carminis = Verg. Aen.* 6.469 *sq. cum* 9.436 *et Ecl.* 5.16

on that "object" which had been the root of all my troubles:

Thrice I grabbed the awful axe in fist,
And thrice, stalk-soft, the blade it promptly missed,
That gave cruel purpose to my trembling hand:
I could not do what recently I'd planned.
The thing, as cold as ice in wintertime for dread
In myriad wrinkles deep within my guts had fled.
I had no head for executioner to take,
But, cheated by the rascal's deathly quake,
Some words I used with more capacity to shake.

So I rose on one elbow and berated it for its stubbornness, approximately thus: "What do you have to say for yourself," I said, "you thing of universal disgrace to gods and humankind? See, I dare not even say your name in exalted company! What have I done to deserve your dragging me from a place in heaven right down to hell? Betraying my years in the first flush of their vigour by substituting the feebleness of extreme old age? Speak up, and you'd better make it good!" At my angry tirade,

"It turned away and eyes upon the ground did hold,
Nor more, me ranting, did its gaze unfold
Than bending willows or poppies on their drooping pole."

Of these three verses, the first two are verbatim from Verg. *Aen.* 469–70 with pronoun gender change (feminine to neuter subject); and the third a blend of half-lines from Verg. *Ecl.* 5.16 and *Aen.* 9.436. Considering the addressees (Dido v. Mentula) , the famous bathos is palpable. Cf. p. 149 n. 20 for the earlier Vergil Dido parody.

12 Nec minus ego tam foeda obiurgatione finita
paenitentiam agere sermonis mei coepi secreto rubore
perfundi, quod oblitus verecundiae meae cum ea parte
corporis verba contulerim, quam ne ad cognitionem quidem
13 admittere severioris notae homines solerent. Mox
perfricata diutius fronte, "Quid autem ego," inquam,
mali feci, si dolorem meum naturali convicio exoneravi?
Aut quid est quod in corpore humano ventri male dicere
solemus aut gulae capitique etiam, cum saepius dolet?
Quid? Non et Ulixes cum corde litigat suo, / et quidem L
tragici oculos suos tamquam audientes castigant?
14 Podagrici pedibus suis male dicunt, chiragrici manibus,
lippi oculis, et qui offenderunt saepe digitos, quicquid
doloris habent in pedes deferunt:

15 / Quid me constricta spectatis fronte Catones LO
damnatisque novae simplicitatis opus?
Sermonis puri non tristis gratia ridet,
quodque facit populus, candida lingua refert.
Nam quis concubitus, Veneris quis gaudia nescit?
Quis vetat in tepido membra calere toro?
Ipse pater veri doctos Epicurus amare
Iussit, et hoc vitam vitam dixit habere telos *

L (= lrtp), O (= BRP)
132 13 perfricta L autem *om.* L 14 offenderunt lp: offendunt rt 15 vetat *Dousa*: petat doctos *Canter*: doctus amare: *Canter*: in arte *post carmen lac. ind. codd. ordinis L*

Still, after I'd finished with this ugly scolding I began to regret my words, and I blushed in secret at having so forgotten my sense of propriety as to bandy words with a part of my body whose presence the more serious kind of people don't even acknowledge. But then, after much head scratching, "Where's the harm," I said, "in unburdening my resentment with some understandable abuse? In the bodily context we curse our stomachs or throats or heads when they are sore, as often, and what of it? Doesn't even Ulysses wrangle with his heart, and don't roles in the tragic stage reproach their eyes, as if listening? Gouty folks heap abuse on their feet, arthritics on their hands, the conjunctive on their eyes; and people who go about stubbing their toes in embarrassment blame their feet:

Why do the critics knit their brows and peer at me?
Convict a work of novel simplicity?
The graceful purity of tongue laughs merrily,
In candid speech recording all that people be.
For who of Venus' joys and couplings does not know?
And who forbids our limbs in sweaty beds to glow?
Wise Epicure himself, the father of our truth, did show
The need to love, the goal that life entire should follow *

The issue is whether Petronius emerges from his novelist's detachment just this once to defend his "work" against charges of salaciousness, in these splendid, apposite words; or whether he would really bother. The setting is a kind of diversion, pretending that Encolpius' penis-scolding is the bone of contention, a "work" surely in miniature. In other words, the defence is both pointless and far too good for such a limited, incongruous application; so I am emboldened to see the poem as applying to the *Satyrica*.

16 / "Nihil est hominum inepta persuasione falsius L
nec ficta severitate ineptius" *

133 / Hac declamatione finita Gitona voco et, "narra LO
mihi," inquam, "frater, sed tua fide: ea nocte, qua te
mihi Ascyltos subduxit, usque in iniuriam vigilavit an
2 contentus fuit vidua pudicaque nocte?" Tetigit puer
oculos suos conceptissimis iuravit verbis sibi ab
Ascylto nullam vim factam *

Positoque in limine genu sic deprecatus sum numen aversum:

3 "Nympharum Bacchi comes, quem pulchra Dione
divitibus silvis numen dedit, inclita paret
cui Lesbos viridisque Thasos, quem Lydus adorat
septifluus templumque tuis imponit Hypaepis:
huc ades, o Bacchi tutor Deryadum voluptas,
et timidas admitte preces. Non sanguine tristi
perfusus venio, non templis impiius hostis
admovi dextram, sed inops et rebus egenis
attritus facinus non toto corpore feci.
Quisquis peccat inops, minor est reus. Hac prece quaeso,

L (= lrtp), O (= BRP)

133 2 numen aversum *in Burmanno anonymus, qui Palmerius secundum Stagni*: numina versu septifluus P *cum codd. ordinis* L: semper flavius B: semperfluus R o *Scaliger*: et

"There is nothing falser in mankind than ill-founded belief, and nothing more ill-founded than puritanical posturing" *

133 When I'd got that speech off, I hailed Giton: "Tell me, little brother," I asked, "word of honour: that evening Ascyltus took you from me, did he stay awake to assault you, or was he content to spend the night in lonely celibacy?" The boy touched his eyelids and swore by all that was holy that Ascyltus had done him no violence *

I knelt at the doorstep and prayed this prayer to the hostile divinity:

"Comrade of Bacchus and the Nymphs, deity whom lovely Venus
Granted to the lush forests, and whom renowned Lesbos
Answers to, and verdant Thasos, beloved of Lydia
With her seven rivers, who raised your temple in Hypaepa:
O hear me, Bacchus' sentry and of the Dryads pleasure,
And listen to my timid prayers. Not tainted by the flow
Of sorry blood I come, at temples not the wicked foe
To raise my hand, but poor and worn and worthless though
I be, 'tis not with all my body did I go
In sin. The poor in sinning sin the less. And in my vow

exonera mentem culpae ignosce minori
et quandoque mihi fortunae arriserit hora,
non sine honore tuum patiar decus. Ibit ad aras
/ sancte, tuus hircus, pecoris pater, ibit ad aras B
/ corniger et querulae fetus suis, hostia lactens. LO
Spumabit pateris hornus liquor, et ter ovantem
circa delubrum gressum feret ebria pubes" *

4 Dum haec ago curaque sollerti deposito meo caveo, intravit delubrum anus laceratis crinibus nigraque veste deformis, extraque vestibulum me iniecta manu duxit *

134 / "Quae striges comederunt nervos tuos, aut quod L
2 purgamentum [in] nocte calcasti in trivio aut cadaver? Nec puero quidem te vindicasti, sed mollis, debilis, lassus tamquam caballus in clivo, et operam et sudorem perdidisti. Nec contentus ipse peccare, mihi deos iratos excitasti" *

L (= lrtp), O (= BRP)
133 3 quandoque L: quando O sancte … aras *versus nusquam nisi* in B *repertus, unde* p pecoris *Pithou*: docoris fetus *Junius*: festus lactens *Puteolanus*: lactans
134 *del. Goldast* 2 nec puero *Courtney*: ne puero *Buecheler*: a puero mihi <quoque> *expectavit Buecheler* excitasti *Wouweren*: extricasti

Pardon, pray, a petty crime and set my mind afree,
And at such time as fortune smiles on me,
Your glory I will celebrate: and to your altars, holy one,
A goat will come, the patriarch, indeed a horny one,
And offspring of a plaintive sow, suckling offering.
In your bowls shall foam the season's wine, and hailing
Thrice the tipsy youth take step around the shrine." *

As I was making this vow, while at the same time keeping a careful watch on my collateral, there entered the shrine the old woman, a truly ugly sight with hair in distress and soiled dress. Grabbing me by the hand, she led me out of the vestibule of the shrine *

134 "What harpies have been gnawing on your sinews? What roadside muck have you stepped in, or maybe a corpse, in the dark? You haven't even made it with the boy – soft, weak, knackered as a nag on a slope, and nothing to show for the sweat and effort! And not content to sin yourself you bring down on me the anger of the gods!" *

3 / Ac me iterum in cellam sacerdotis nihil recusantem LO
perduxit impulitque super lectum et harundinem ab ostio
4 rapuit nihilque respondentem mulcavit. Ac nisi primo ictu
harundo quassata impetum verberantis minuisset, forsitan
5 etiam bracchia mea caputque fregisset. Ingenui ego [utique
propter mascarpionem], lacrimisque ubertim manantibus
6 obscuratum dextra caput super pulvinum inclinavi. Nec
minus illa fletu confusa altera parte lectuli sedit
aetatis longae moram tremulis vocibus coepit accusare,
donec intervenit sacerdos …
7 "Quid vos," inquit, "in cellam meam meam tamquam ad
recens bustum venistis? / Utique die feriarum, quo etiam O
lugentes rident?" …
8 / "O," inquit, "Oenothea, adulescens hic, quem vides, LO
malo astro natus est; nam neque puero neque puellae
bona sua vendere potest. / Numquam tu hominem tam L
infelicem vidisti: lorum in aqua, non inguina habet.
/ Ad summam, qualem putas esse qui de Circes toro sine LO
10 voluptate surrexit?" / His auditis Oenothea inter L
utrumque consedit motoque diutius capite, "istum,"

L (= lrtp), O (= BRP)
134 3 supra O nihilque L: iterum nihil O 4 verberantis impetum impetum L 5 *damnavi ut glossema: explicatione non opus* 6 *lac. ind. Buecheler* 7 ad *Buecheler*: ante *lac. ind. Buecheler* 8 adulescens hic *ego, post Giardina et Melloni* hic adulescens: hunc adulescentem 9 tu hominem *om.* l

She led me unresisting back inside, into the priestess's room, bent me over the bed, snatched a cane from the door, and thrashed me, without result. If the reed hadn't split at first blow, softening the impact of the beating, I'm sure she would have broken my very arms along with my head. I gave out a groan, and with tears flowing copiously laid my head on a pillow, concealing it beneath my right arm. The woman was badly shaken by my weeping. She sat down on another part of the bed and began to complain in a quavering voice about being so old, at which point the priestess came in …

"What are you two up to," she asked, "coming into my bedroom as if on your way to a crematorium? And on a holiday, too, when even mourners crack a smile?" …

"Oh, Oenothea!" the old woman cried. "The young man here before you was born under an unlucky star: he can't make a sale to boy or girl! You've never seen an unluckier fellow – he's got a soaked sandal strap for a penis! I mean, can you imagine anyone rising from Circe's couch without enjoying himself? On hearing this Oenothea sat down between us and shook her head over and over. "This disorder," she said, "I'm the only

---

"… thrashed me without result" (134.3: *nihilque respondentem mulcavit*) refers to the "failed" beating of Encolpius administered by Proselenos, the elderly, low-ranking female under-servant of Oenothea, commencing the curative ceremonies for his impotence. It is customary to translate it as a simple punishment taken without resistance, which it cannot mean, for non-performance, repeating the sense of the first words in the paragraph. Why? I believe the context is surely sexual, a beating designed "sadistically," with the salacious intent of reviving Encolpius' erotic feeling, the wretched old woman assigned to the task. It is a scene of pathos; well crafted by Petronius; in her aged incompetence and lamented frailty she cannot do even that correctly, breaking the cane, and rousing in Encolpius, to her chagrin, not libido (*nihil respondentem*) but a flood of tears, a reaction inexplicable to her and a failed experiment in sexual masochism. There is an analogue nearby, priming us with a splendid metaphor (133.4: *curaque sollerti deposito meo caveo*, "… keeping a careful watch on my collateral"). In practice, one fears full comprehension of jokes in this passage will forever be marred by time and text corruption.

11 inquit, "morbum sola sum quae emendare scio. Et ne putetis perplexe agere, rogo ut adulescentulus mecum nocte dormiat ... nisi tam rigidum reddidero quam cornu:

12 / Quicquid in orbe vides, paret mihi. Florida tellus, LO
cum volo, siccatis arescit languida sucis,
cum volo, fundit opes, scopulique atque horrida saxa
Niliacas iaculantur aquas. Mihi pontus inertes
submittit fluctus, zephyrique tacentia ponunt
ante meos flabra pedes. Mihi flumina parent
Hyrcanaeque tigres et iussi stare dracones.
Quid leviora loquor? Lunae descendit imago
carminibus deducta meis, trepidusque furentes
flectere Phoebus equos revoluto cogitur orbe."
[Tantum dicta valent. Taurorum flamma quiescit
virgineis extincta sacris, Phoebeia Circe
carminibus magicis socios mutavit Ulixis,
Proteus esse solet quicquid libet. His ego callens
artibus Idaeos frutices in gurgite sistam
et rursus fluvios in summo vertice ponam.]

135 Inhorrui ego tam fabulosa pollicitatione conterritus, anumque inspicere diligentius coepi ...

L (= lrtp), O (= BRP)

134 11 ne <me> *suppl. Buecheler bene* *lac. ind. Buecheler, in qua execrationem statuit* rigidam *fortasse* 12.2 siccatis: spissatis O 12.7 dracones O: leones L 12.11–16 *versus tamquam non ad rem del. Buecheler et Wehle* 12.12 Phoebeia RP: Phoebea B: Phoebeaque L *lac. ind. Buecheler*

person who knows how to cure it. It's not complicated. Just let the young man spend the night with me and I'll send it back as hard as horn!

> All on earth you see is ruled by me. The earth in bloom
> On my command it dries and languishes, its moisture gone.
> On my command it yields its riches; rock and boulder
> Surf the Nile river. For me the ocean breaker
> By the sea is stilled, and at my feet the blasts of wind
> Are calmed and settle, for me the rivers bend,
> And tigers in Hyrcania, and the snakes, are told to stand.
> Why to speak of lighter things? The image of the moon
> Descends, by spells of mine attracted, and the nervous sun
> Is made to steer his frothing steeds the earth to turn."

135 I shuddered in abject fear at this prescription of mythic resonance, and began to watch the old woman with a good deal more care …

2 "Ergo," exclamat Oenothea, "imperio parete" …
Detersisque curiose manibus inclinavit se in lectulum
ac me semel iterumque basiavit …
3 / Oenothea mensam veteram posuit in medio altari L
quam vivis implevit carbonibus, et camellam [et]iam
4 vetustate ruptam pice temperata refecit. Tum clavum,
qui detrahentem secutus cum camella lignea fuerat,
fumoso parieti reddidit. / Mox incincta quadrato pallio LO
cucumam ingentem foco apposuit, simulque pannum de
carnario detulit furca, in quo faba erat ad usum
reposita / et sincipitis vetustissima particula mille L
5 plagis dolata. / Ut solvit ergo licio pannum, partem LO
leguminis super mensam effudit iussitque me diligenter
purgare. Servio ego imperio granaque sordidissimis
6 putaminibus vestita curiosa manu segrego. At illa
inertiam meam accusans ipsa fabas tollit, dentibusque
folliculos pariter spoliat atque in terram veluti
muscarum imagines despuit *
7 Mirabar equidem paupertatis ingenium singularumque
rerum quasdam artes:

L (= lrtp), O (= BRP)
135 2 detersis … basiavit *post* apposuit (4 *infra*) *collocat* O
lac. ind. Buecheler *lac. ind. Pithou* 3 *del. Mueller*:
etiam *del. Jahn* 4 clavum <ligneum> … camella [lignea] *prop. Mueller olim* 5 vestita *susp. Martindale* 6 ipsa fabas tollit
Buecheler: improba tollit veluti *om.* L

"So," exclaimed Oenothea, "see that you follow my instructions." She wiped her hands carefully, leaned over the bed, and kissed me several times …

She put an old tray on top of the altar, in the middle, and heaped it with live coals. Warming up some pitch, she recaulked a wooden cup that had split with age. Since with the removal of the cup its nail had come down too, she proceeded to return the latter to the smoky wall. Then she put on a square-cut shift and set a large kettle upon the fire. At the same time with a fork she lifted from a meat rack a cloth bag containing some prepared beans and a very elderly bit of heavily chipped hog's jowl. She untied the string on the bag, poured some beans onto a table, and told me to shell them carefully.

Following orders, with attentive fingers I separated the seeds from their filthy pod coverings. Growing impatient at my slowness, she grabbed the beans herself and in one movement tore open the little sacs with her teeth and spat them out onto the ground where they lay like so many dead flies *

Meanwhile I was admiring the ingenuity forced upon the poor and how the individual details showed a certain flair:

8 Non Indum fulgebat ebur, quod inhaeserat auro,
nec iam calcato radiabat marmore terra
muneribus delusa suis, sed crate saligna
impositum Cereris vacuae nemus et nova terrae …
pocula, quae facili vilis rota finxerat actu,
Hinc mollis tiliae lacus et de caudice lento
vimineae lances maculataque testa Lyaeo.
At paries circa palea satiatus inani
fortuitoque luto clavos numerabat agrestes,
et viridi iunco gracilis pendebat harundo.
Praeterea quae fumoso suspensa tigillo
conservabat opes humilis casa, mitia sorba
14 et thymbrae veteres et passis uva racemis
13 inter odoratas pendebat texta coronas …
Qualis in Actaea quondam fuit hospita terra
digna sacris Hecale, quam Musa loquentibus annis
Battiadae vatis mirandum tradidit ore *

L (= lrtp), O (= BRP)
135 8.4 *lac. ind. Buecheler* 8.5 actu *Mediolanus et* r: astu 8.6 mollis *Sambucus*: molli tiliae *Pithou*: stillae O: stilla L lacus *Scaliger*: latus 8.8 at B: et *cett.* 8.9 clavos *Sambucus*: clavus 8.12 *om. versum* L sorba *Scaliger*: sorva B: servo *cett.* 8.14,13,15 *ordinem transp. Buecheler* 8.13 pendebat RP: pendebant *cett.* exta L *lac. ind. Junius* 8.16 Hecale *Pius*: Hecates 8.16,17 *versus corrupti* 8.17 Battiadae *Pius*: Bachineas vatis *Pius* et r[m]: veteres mirandam *aliquis apud Goldast*: mirando ore *Courtney*: arte *Fuchs et Mueller*: aevo

No Indian ivory glistened, inlaid in gold,
Nor here beneath our feet did gleam the marbled ground
In artificial bounty, but grove of Ceres set upon a stand
Of cane, a harvest, and new-made earthen drinking bowl …
By rapid movement fashioned of a humble wheel.
Here a bowl of soft lime wood and plates a-woven
Of pliant bark, and jars a-stained from their wine.
The wall around with lightest straw was stuffed
And in its casual mud it counted nails, but rough,
And from which hung a slender switch, tied in green.
That lowly cottage other wealth from smoky beam
Did hang, tender rowan berries, aged savoury, raisins on
Their twining twigs, dangling in their scented wreaths …
Such in the land of Actaea once was hostess Hecale,
She of ceremony so worthy, whom the muse of Cyrene's
Poet inspired him in his song
To do his homage in those years of gifted tongue *

136 Dum illa carnis etiam paululum delibat ... et dum LO
coaequale natalium suorum sinciput in carnarium furca
reponit, fracta est putris sella, quae staturae
altitudinem adiecerat, anumque pondere suo deiectam
2 super foculum mittit. Frangitur ergo cervix cucumulae
ignemque modo convalescentem restinguit. / Vexat cubitum L
ipsa stipite ardenti / faciemque totam excitato cinere LO
3 perfundit. Consurrexi equidem turbatus anumque non sine
risu erexi ... / statimque, ne res aliqua sacrificium L
moraretur, ad reficiendum ignem in viciniam cucurrit ...
4 / Itaque ad casae ostiolum processi ... cum tres LO
anseres [sacri] / qui, ut puto, medio die solebant
ab anu diaria exigere, / impetum in me faciunt foedoque
ac veluti rabioso stridore circumsistunt trepidantem.

L (= lrtp), O (= BRP)
136 dum ... et dum *locus ab interpolatore conexus videtur, cf.* 6.1 *lac. ind. Buecheler* et coaequale L suo pondere L modo *om.* O extinguit L atque totam faciem O perfundit corr. *Scaliger*: perfudit 3 *lacunas ind. Buecheler, cui enarratio haec tota in suspicionem venit* risu meo L, *nisi* risu me r viciniam *Scaliger*: vicinia cucurrit *Schioppius*: cucurri 4 itaque ... processi *in* 3 *post* erexi *inseruit* t, O *utens*: *om.* l, *"vitium suspicio factum"* l[m] itaque O] vix L (rp, non t) processi O] processeram L (rp, non t) *ante* cum *lac. ind. Buecheler* cum ecce L: et ecce O tres *om.* O *seclusit Mueller*

136 The old woman had a taste of a bit of the meat too … and as with her fork she was returning to the meat rack her contemporary the hog's jowl, the rotten chair she'd used to extend her height broke, and she collapsed and was propelled onto the hearth by her own momentum.

The neck on the kettle was smashed, dousing the fire just as it was taking. She burnt her elbow on a blazing ember and got a face full of flying ash. I jumped to my feet in consternation, and with an ill-suppressed chuckle helped the old thing to her feet … she immediately sped off next door in search of fresh kindling, to ensure no excuse for holding up the sacrificing …

I'd barely made my way to the cottage door … when three geese, who'd been waiting to claim their customary noon rations from the old woman, I suppose, attacked me, encircling with a horrible, almost demented and altogether terrifying hissing.

Atque alius tunicam meam lacerat, alius vincula
calceamentorum resolvit ac trahit; unus etiam, dux et
magister saevitiae, non dubitavit crus meum serrato
5 vexare morsu. Oblitus itaque nugarum pedem mensulae
extorsi coepique pugnacissimum animal armata elidere
manu. Nec satiatus defunctorio ictu, morte me anseris
vindicavi:

6 Tales Herculea Stymphalidas arte coactas
ad caelum fugisse reor caenoque fluentes
Harpyas, cum Phineo maduere veneno
fallaces epulae. Tremuit perterritus aether
planctibus insolitis, confusaque regia caeli *

7 / Iam reliqui devolutam passimque per totum effusam L
pavimentum collegerunt fabam, orbatique, existimo,
duce redierant in templum, cum ego praeda simul [atque]
ac vindicta gaudens post lectum occisum anserem mitto
8 vulnusque cruris haud altum aceto diluo. Deinde convicium
verens abeundi formavi consilium, collectaque cultu meo
9 ire extra casam coepi. Necdum liberaveram cellulae limen,
cum animadverto Oenotheam cum testo ignis pleno venientem.

L (= lrtp), O (= BRP)
136 6 coactas O: volucres L caenoque Krohn: peneque
7 devolutam *Buecheler*: evolutam *Mueller*: revolutam
[atque] ac *Thielmann*: atque hac 9 liberaveram l:
libaveram tp: laboraveram r *sed in* laboveram *correctum*

One tore at my shirt, another undid the straps of my sandals and was tugging on them, and the third and ringleader in this brutal assault made no bones of hanging onto my leg with its serrated beak. This was clearly no time for half-measures. I wrenched a leg from the small table and thus armed began to batter the most aggressive animal with it. Nor was I content with a routine beating. Only the goose's demise would give me revenge:

"Such were the birds of Stymphalos, as Hercules, I trow,
Coerced in skill to flee to sky, and Harpies, slime aflow,
When feasts frustrating Phineus with their venom soaked.
The upper air in terror quaked
At unaccustomed cries: there's panic in the skies *

The survivors began to peck up the beans that had rolled away and scattered to all corners of the floor. Then, feeling exposed without their leader, I imagine, they retired to the shrine. Savouring both vengeance and my prize, I threw the slain goose behind the bed and bathed the surface wound to my leg with vinegar. But then, fearing a scolding, I decided to make off, so I picked up my stuff and started out of the cottage. I had scarcely crossed the threshold before I saw Oenothea approaching with a trayful of burning coals.

10 Reduxi igitur gradum proiectaque vesta, tamquam expectarem
11 morantem, in aditu steti. Collocavit ille ignem quassis
harundinibus collectum, ingestisque super pluribus lignis
excusare coepit moram, quod amica se non dimisisset nisi
tribus potionibus e lege siccatis. "Quid porro tu,"
12 inquit "me absente fecisti, aut ubi est faba?" Ego qui
putaveram me rem laude etiam dignam fecisse, ordine illi
totum proelium exposui, et ne diutius tristius esset,
13 iacturae pensionem anserem obtuli. Quem / anus ut vidit, LO
tam magnam acremque clamorem sustulit, ut putares iterum
14 anseres limen intrasse. Confusus itaque et novitate
facinoris attonitus quaerebam quid excanduisset aut
137 quare anseris potius quam mei miseretur. At illa
complosis manibus, "Scelerate," inquit, "etiam loqueris?
2 Nescis quam magnum flagitium admiseris: occidisti Priapi
delicias, anserem omnibus matronibus acceptissimum.
Itaque ne te putes nihil egisse, si magistratus hoc
3 scierint, ibis in crucem. Poluisti sanguine domicilium
meum ante hoc diem inviolatum, fecistique ut me quisquis
voluerit inimicus sacerdotio pellat" *

L (= lrtp), O (= BRP)
136 11 quassis l: cassis *cett.* nisi tribus *Buecheler*: tribus nisi 12 pensionem] pensationem *probat Buecheler, adsumunt Giardina et Melloni (cf.* 141.6, *sed hic diverse)* 13 quem anus L: cum protuli anserem anus O *redintegrans* acremque *Cornelissen*: aeque **137** etiam *Dousa*: et O: *om.* L 2 scierint B: scierit *cett.* 3 inimicus *an glossema?*

I therefore retracted my steps, threw down my bundle to give the impression I'd been waiting all this time, and stood in the entranceway. She placed in the hearth the lit kindling made up of split reeds, piled several logs on top, and apologized for the wait: a girlfriend hadn't let her go before she downed the customary three drinks. "Anyway," she said, "what have you been doing in my absence? Where are my beans?"

I thought I'd done something worthy of commendation so I recounted the entire battle to her, and to avoid any lingering regret on her part I offered the goose in compensation against any loss. When she saw it, the old woman raised enough of a hue and cry to make one think the geese had returned. I was surprised and confused at this unexpected definition of a crime, and asked her why she was taking such offence and feeling sorry for the goose instead of for me.

137 "Bastard!" she shrieked, with a clap of her hands. "Do you have the nerve to ask? Don't you know what a serious offence you've committed? You've killed the darling of Priapus, the favourite goose of all the women around! And don't think you've done nothing wrong. If the magistrates get to hear of this you will be crucified! You've brought blood pollution upon my home, unsullied before today, and you've ensured that any enemy who wanted could drive me from the priesthood!" *

4 / "Rogo," inquam, "noli clamare: ego tibi pro ansere L
struthocamelum reddam" *
5 Dum haec me stupente in lectulo sedet anserisque
fatum complorat, interim Proselenos cum impensa sacrificii
venit, visoque ansere occiso sciscitata causam [tristitiae]
ea ipsa flere vehementius coepit meique misereri tamquam
6 patrem meum, non publicum anserem, occidissem. Itaque taedio,
"Rogo," inquam, "expiare manus pretio liceat ... si vos
provocassem, etiam si homicidium fecissem. Ecce duos aureos
7 pono, unde possitis et deos et anseres emere." Quos ut vidit
Oenothea, "Ignosce," inquit, "adulescens, sollicita sum tua
8 causa. Amoris est hoc argumentum, non malignitatis. Itaque
dabimus operam ne quis hoc sciat. Tu modo deos roga ut illi
facto tuo ignoscant."

9 / Quisquis habet nummos, secura navigat aura LO
fortunamque suo temperat arbitrio.
Uxorem ducat Danaen ipsumque licebit
Acrisium iubeat credere quod Danaen.
Carmina componat, declamat, concrepet omnes
et peragat causas sitque Catone prior.

L (= lrtp), O (= BRP)

137 5 *del. Mueller* 6 liceat *Dousa*: licet *lac. ind. Buecheler* et deos et anseres rtp: et duos anseres l 9 navigat *Vinc. Bellov.*: naviget temperat B, *Vincentius*: temperet *cett.*

"Please don't shout," I said: "I'll replace your goose with an ostrich!" *

I continued to gape as she sat on the bed and bewailed the fate of her goose, at which point Proselenos arrived with money for the sacrifice. Seeing the dead goose, she asked what had happened and then began to cry loudly as well and to pity me as if I'd killed my father and not some unclaimed goose. I was growing tired of this. "Look," I said, "I'm sorry if I've offended you by committing what you say is murder. Allow me to offer a sum of money in atonement. I've got two gold pieces here, enough to buy more geese and the gods too!" On seeing the cash Oenothea said, "Forgive me, young man; I was worried on your account, a mark of love, not spite. We shall see to it that no one finds out. Just ask the gods to forgive you for what you did."

The man with money has plain sailing,
And tempers fate to his commanding.
He'll be able to get Danae and tell
Her dad to think the thought of her as well.
He'll be a poet or teacher, snap fingers at the great,
Prove his case in court, proud Cato to defeat,

At. *Sat.* 137.7, Oenothea selects for Encolpius a cool form of address, *adulescens,* instead of his name. Cf. Circe's *"narrabo tibi, adulescens"* at *Sat.* 129.6. According to D. Dutsch, 2000, p. 124, n.32, this expresses politeness to strangers, reproach to intimates. Here we can take our pick. The women share a line in irony. Either way, the point worth making is that *adulescens* and its near-synonym *adulescentulus* notably lack the resonance to carry information about sexual status.

Iurisconsultus "parret, non parret" habeto
atque esto quicquid Servius et Labeo.
Multa loquor: quod vis nummis praesentibus opta
et veniet. Clausum possidet arca Iovem *

10 / Infra manus meas camellam vini posuit, et cum L
digitos pariter extensos porris apioque lustrasset,
avellanas nuces cum precatione mersit in vinum. Et sive
in summam redierant sive subsederant, ex hoc coniecturam
ducebat. Nec me fallebat inanes scilicet ac sine medulla
[ventosas] nuces in summo umore consistere, graves autem
et plenas integro fructu ad ima deferri *

11 Recluso pectore extraxit fortissimum iecur et inde
12 mihi futura praedixit. Immo, ne quod vestigium sceleris
superesset, totum anserem laceratum verubus confixit
epulas etiam lautas paulo ante, ut ipsa dicebat,
perituro paravit …
13 Volabant inter haec potiones mericae *

L (= lrtp), O (= BRP)
137 9 parret non parret B: paret non paret *cett.*
quod vis O: quidvis L Iovem] *Hic desinit ultimo* B
10 hoc coniecturam ducebat *Dousa*: hac coniectura dicebat
del. Mueller, qui etiam alia delenda olim probabat
11 fartissimam *Heinze*: fortissimum 12 *lac. ind. Buecheler*

As learned in the law, "Proven," "Not Proven," will he say,
And be all of Servius and Labeo in their day.
I speak too much. Choose your liking: cash aside
Will bring it, for in your strongbox Jupiter will hide *

[At this point the manuscripts of the O class conclude.]

She placed a cup of wine below my hands, had me extend my fingers in a row for her to rub with leeks and celery, and then, saying a little prayer, dropped some filberts into the wine. She made her predictions according to whether these came up or sank, though I knew full well that the nuts that were hollow and dried out inside would stay on the surface while the heavier and fresher ones would go to the bottom *

She cut open the goose's abdomen and drew out a very plump liver with which to tell my fortune. In fact, to cover all traces of my crime she pulled the whole bird to pieces and stuck them on spits, making a rather good meal for me, whose prospects shortly before had on her own admission been very bleak …

During all this time cups of unmixed wine were flying about *

138 Profert Oenothea scorteum fascinum, quod ut oleo et minuto pipere atque urticae trito circumdedit semine paulatim coepit inserere ano meo …

2 Hoc crudelissima anus spargit subinde umore femina mea *

Nasturcii sucum cum habrotono miscet perfusisque inguinibus meis viridis urticae fascem comprehendit omniaque infra umbilicum coepit lenta manu caedere *

3 Aniculae quamvis solutae mero et libidine essent, eandem viam temptant et per aliquot vicos secutae

4 fugientem, "Prende furem," clamant. Evasi tamen omnibus digitis inter praecipitem decursum cruentatis *

5 "Chrysis, quae priorem fortunam tuam oderat, haec vel cum periculo capitis persequi destinat" *

6 "Quid huic formae aut Ariadne habuit aut Leda simile? Quid contra hanc Helene, quid Venus posset. Ipse Paris,

---

L (= lrtp)

138 *lac. ind. Buecheler, qui sic enarrationem vult restituere*: … ano meo. Nasturcii sucum cum habrotomo miscet. Hoc crudelissima anus spargit subinde [humore] feminea mea. Perfusis[que] inguinibus meis …

3 aliquot lt: aliquos rp prende l: prehende rtp

138 Oenothea picked up a leather phallus, coated it with a dressing of oil, ground pepper and powdered nettle, and began to insert it slowly into my anus …

With this concoction the sadistic old woman liberally sprinkled my thighs *

She mixed the juice of cress and southernwood and rubbed it into my genitals; then she took up a bunch of fresh nettles and began to slowly whip the entire area below my navel *

The poor old women, though much the worse for drink and arousal, attempted the same route, and kept up the chase along a succession of back lanes, crying "Stop, thief!" I managed to give them the slip, running downhill full tilt and in the process bloodying all my toes *

"The Chrysis who so despised your earlier fortune is now resolved to follow it even at risk to her life! *

"What had Ariadne or Leda to challenge such beauty? Could Helen or

dearum litigantium iudex, si hanc in comparatione vidisset tam petulantibus oculis, et Helenen huic
7 donasset et deas. Saltem si permitteretur osculum capere, si illud caeleste ac divinum pectus amplecti, forsitan rediret hoc corpus ad vires et resipiscerent partes
8 veneficio, credo, sopitae. Nec me contumeliae lassant: quod verberatus sum, nescio; quod eiectus sum, lusum puto. Modo redire in gratiam liceat" *

139 Torum frequenti tractatione vexavi, amoris mei quandam imaginem *
2 "Non solum me numen et implacabile fatum
persequitur. Prius Inachiae Tirynthius ira
exagitatus onus caeli tulit, ante profanus
5 Laomedon gemini satiavit numinis iram,
4 Iunonem Pelias sensit, tulit inscius arma
Telephus et regnum Neptuni pavit Ulixes.
Me quoque per terras, per cani Nereos aequor
Hellespontiaci sequitur gravis ira Priapi" *

L (= lrtp)
138 6 litigantium *Dousa*: libidinantium 7 reviviscerent *invenitur apud Burman* **139** iactatione *Jungermann*
2.2 Inachiae *Buecheler*: Inachia ira lt^{m} p: ora rt
2.3 profanus *Scaliger*: profanam *ordinem commutavit Buecheler*
2.4 tulit inscius arma *mendosus*; tulit *errore iteratum et nomen Bacchi requitur, ut vidit Mueller* 2.6 pavit *Dousa*: cavit

Venus compete? If Paris himself, of the saucy eyes, referee to the Contest of the Goddesses, had seen you in the competition he'd have ended Helen's candidacy and that of the two goddesses! If you'd just let me kiss you, if I could hug your heavenly divine breast, perhaps my body would regain its strength, and the parts I suppose to be slumbering from sorcery would reawaken. Ill-treatment has not discouraged me, the beatings I've already forgotten, the ejection I treat as a joke. Just give me the chance to return to your favour!" *

139 I tossed and turned in the bed, reaching for some sort of imprint of my beloved *

"Not only me does a god pursue, and destiny
Implacable. Before was Heracles, who from the Argive sea
Was driven, to bear the burden of the sky; before me
Laomedon did satiate the two gods' wrath unholy,
Pelias felt Juno's, Telephus unknowing took up arms,
And Ulysses it was who feared Neptune's kingdoms.
Me too over land and grey-haired Nereus' lea
Follows Priapus in grave iniquity!" *

References to Priapus by name in the *Satyrica* are not plentiful. Several have nothing to do with a revenge theme, but here and also much earlier in *Sat.* 17 and 21 Priapus is invoked by his priestess Quartilla against Encolpius for violating her rites to the god. Now, late in the game, Encolpius seems to have got religion, referring to Priapus several times under the rubric of *numen,* acknowledging the godhead only attributively and without name. Thus, in order, *Sat.* 133.2 *sic deprecatus sum numen aversum; Sat.* 133.3.2 *comes, quem pulchra Dione / divitibus silvis numen dedit; Sat.* 139.2.1 *non solum me numen et implacabile fatum / persequitur; Sat.* 140.11 *nec se reiciebat a blanditiis doctissimus puer, sed me numen inimicum ibi quoque invenit.* The last, a failed sexual bout with Philomela's son, as the boy spied on his sister's sexual game with Eumolpus, literally one line before Encolpius could announce his cure and provide proof to Eumolpus. But the agent and god acknowledged in gratitude isn't Priapus but Mercury, *Sat.* 140. 12–13 *Mercurius … reddidit mihi quod manus irata praeciderat.*

3 Quaerere a Gitone meo coepi num aliquis me quaesisset. "Nemo," inquit, "hodie. Sed hesterno die mulier quaedam haud inculta ianuam intravit, cumque diu mecum esset locuta et me accersito sermone lassasset, ultimo coepit dicere te noxam meruisse daturumque serviles poenas, si laesus in querellis perseverasset" *

4 Nondum querellam finieram, cum Chrysis intervenit amplexuque effusissimo me invasit et "Teneo te," inquit, "qualem speraveram: tu desiderium meum, tu voluptas mea, numquam finies hunc ignem, nisi sanguine extinxeris" *

5 Una ex noviciis servis subito accurrit et mihi dominum iratissimum esse affirmavit, quod biduo iam officio defuissem. Recte ergo me facturum, si excusationem aliquam praeparassem. Vix enim posse fieri, ut rabies irascentis sine verbere consideret *

L (= lrtp)
139 4 querellam *ex superiore versu perpere sumptum del. Fraenkel* meum lt: *om.* rp 5 praeparassem] praepararem *Buecheler*: *def. Petersmann*

I asked my dear Giton if anybody had been looking for me. "Not today," he said, "but yesterday a rather posh woman came in the door. She spoke for ages and quite tired me out with her contrived chatter. Finally she said you deserved to be punished and would pay the slave's penalty if the injured party pursued his complaint" *

Before I'd even finished, Chrysis interposed and was all over me with the fondest of embraces. "I have you now," she cooed, "just where I want you, my passion and my joy! This fire you'll never put out, short of dousing it with my blood!" *

One of the apprentice slave boys suddenly dashed in with the news that my master was furious with me for taking two days off from my duties. So I'd do well, he said, to think of a very good excuse if I hoped to calm his anger without a beating *

Philomela – our very own Wife of Bath – and her children (see ensuing *Sat.* 140 ff.), residents of Croton, are on the side of the "crows a-picking" (*Sat.* 116.9). The account that follows, at almost the end of the novel, is framed as a real-time occurrence by the observing Encolpius; and of course the participating Eumolpus is ostensibly the typical mark for Philomela's wiles: trading the prostitution of her son and daughter for the continuing flow of wealth. The story is otherwise typical of the others involving potentially underage sex, though there is not quite as much judgmentally useful guidance from Petronius/Encolpius for clear visualization. The youngsters are referred to as "*iuvenes*" and "*pueri.*" The girl's age is elided, though she is remarked by Encolpius as "*speciosissima,*" very pretty. We do better with the boy, who is an "ephebe," the designation used repeatedly of the Pergamene ephebe by Eumolpus all those years ago: a youth in his later teens. This time Eumolpus chooses the girl, for "*Pygesiaca sacra.*" Behind this jocular phrase lurks a pun linked to the famed buttocks of Aphrodite, but the exact reading is as insecure as the girl's position. We know Eumolpus was supine and the girl seated, perhaps facing away. Both youngsters were "*doctissimi*" (Encolpius again): trained sexual performers courtesy of their ineffable mother. As we expect of a Petronian character describing sex, it is a merry scene, complete with the youth admiring his sister's tricks through a keyhole: *Sat.* 140.11 *dum frater sororis suae automata per clostellum miraretur.*

140 Matrona inter primas honesta, Philomela nomine, quae
multas saepe hereditates officio aetatis extorserat, tum
anus et floris extincti, filium filiamque ingerebat orbis
senibus, et per hanc artem successionem suam perseverebat
2 extendere. Ea ergo ad Eumolpum venit et commendare liberos
suos eius prudentiam bonitatique <coepit atque> credere
se et vota sua. Illum esse solum in toto orbe terrarum, qui
praeceptis etiam salubribus instruere quotidie posset, <quae
3 sola posset hereditas iuvenibus dari>. Ad summam, relinquere
se pueros in domo Eumolpi, ut illum loquentem audirent ...
4 [quae sola posset hereditas iuvenibus dari]. Nec aliter fecit
ac dixerat, filiamque speciosissimam cum fratre ephebo in
cubiculo reliquit simulavit se in templum ire ad vota nuncupanda.
5 Eumolpus, qui tam frugi erat ut illi etiam ego puer viderer,
non distulit puellam invitare ad Pygesia sacra. Sed et
6 podagricum se esse lumborum solutorum omnibus dixerat, et si non
servasset integram simulationem, periclitebatur totam tragoediam
7 evertere. Itaque ut constaret mendacio fides, puellam quidem
exoravit ut sederet supra commendatem bonitatem, Coraci autem
imperavit ut lectum, in quo ipse iacebat, subiret positisque in
8 pavimento manibus dominum lumbis suis commoveret. Ille lente
parabat imperio puellaeque artificium pari motu renumerabat.

L (= lrtp)
140 2 *et* 3 *lac. ind. Buecheler; primam implevi: postea clausulam transposui; cf.* 86.6 *et adiunct. videas* 5 Pygesiaca *Scaliger*: pigiaca: Aphrodisiaca *Buecheler sed glossema* 8 lente *Schoppius*: lento renumerabat *ego; adiunctionem videas*: remunerabat *libri*

12
Last Days in Croton

140 A highly respectable lady called Philomela, having wangled legacies many and often courtesy of her youth, had by now aged and lost her looks, so she thrust her son and daughter upon childless old men, and by this "passing of the torch" contrived to carry on her craft. Accordingly she approached Eumolpus and set to commending her children and entrusting herself and her hopes to his "penetration and rectitude," on the grounds that in all the world he alone was capable of providing young people with daily drills of wholesome inculcation, this being the only "legacy" worth giving to the young. In short, she said, she was leaving her children at Eumolpus' home to listen at his side.

She was as good as her word, dropping off her very pretty daughter along with the girl's adolescent brother at his bedroom while she pretended to visit the temple to declare her vows. Eumolpus, thrifty to the point of counting even me as a boy, wasted no time in inviting the girl to the rites of Rumpy-Bumpy. But he'd told everybody he suffered from severe gout and bad hips, and would risk ruining almost the entire performance unless he kept up his role in every particular. So, to safeguard the deception, he prevailed on the girl to sit upon that commended "rectitude," while instructing [his man] Corax at the same time to crawl under the bed upon which he lay and with hands braced against the floor get the master moving by the action of his lumbar spine. Corax began as directed, in lento, matching the girl's practised ingenuities measure for measure;

9 Cum ergo res ad effectum spectaret, clara Eumolpus voce
exhortabatur Coraca ut spissaret officium. Sic inter
mercennarium amicamque positam senex velut oscillatione ludebat.
10 Hoc semel iterumque ingenti nisu, etiam suo, Eumolpus fecerat.
11 Itaque ego quoque, ne desidia consuetudinem perderem, dum frater
sororis suae automata per clostellum miraretur, accessi
temptaturus an pateretur iniuriam. Nec se reiciebat a blanditiis
doctissimus puer, sed me numen inimicum ibi quoque invenit *

12 "Di maiores sunt qui me restituerunt in integrum.
Mercurius enim, qui animas ducere et reducere solet, suis
beneficiis mihi reddidit quod manus irata praeciderat, ut sciam
me gratiosiorem quam Protesilaum aut quemquam alium antiquorum."
Haec locutus sustuli tunicam Eumolpoque me totum approbavi.
At ille primo exhorruit, deinde ut plurimum crederet, utraque
manu deorum beneficia tractat *

14 "Socrates, deorum hominumque <iudicio sapientissimus>,
gloriari solebat, quod numquam neque in tabernam conspexerat nec
ullius turbae frequentioris concilio oculos suos crederat. Adeo
nihil est commodius quam semper cum sapientia loqui" ...
15 "Omnia," inquam, "ista vera sunt: nec ulli enim celerius
homines incidere debent in malam fortunam, quam qui alienum

L (= lrtp)
140 10 nisu *Heinze*: risu 13 beneficia rtp: beneficium l
14 *lacunam sic replevit Rutgers, Scaligero desiderante aliquod Graece lac. ind. Buecheler*

until, the matter looking to conclude, Eumolpus called sharply for the measure in double-time.

Thus ranged between manservant and new mistress, the old man enjoyed a turn on a makeshift push swing. He had this done more than once amid considerable effort, not least his own. And so I also, to forestall the loss of habit through idleness, approached the boy while he was admiring his sister's tricks through the keyhole, to see whether he'd allow me to take advantage of him. The well-drilled child did not reject my advances, but here too the god's hostility caught up with me *

"There are greater gods, and they've made me whole! Mercury, for instance, conductor of souls back and forth, has by his kindness restored to me the thing that an angry hand foreshortened and has made me more grateful than Protesilaus, you see, or any other of the ancients." So saying I lifted my shirt and offered Eumolpus the proof of my entirety. He at first recoiled, but then wishing full confirmation he felt the gods' beneficence with both hands *

"Socrates, of men and gods the wisest, used to boast that he'd never looked into a tavern nor entrusted his eyes to any gathering at all of any size. In fact you can't do better than conducting a permanent dialogue with wisdom" …

"All that you say is true," I said. "And no one should fall upon hard times

---

So why did Eumolpus choose the girl? Because she was lighter. His "hip failure" taps into a byword among "hairy old men." See Catullus 16, *"pilosis / qui duros nequeunt movere lumbos."* With his "confirmation" of Encolpius' recovery, he lays claim to being the only successfully practising bisexual male in the *Satyrica*. For the role of Mercury, not Priapus, in the restoration of Encolpius, see above.

concupiscunt. Unde plani autem, unde levatores viverent, nisi aut locellos aut sonantes aere sacellos pro hamis in turbam mitterent? Sicut muta animalia cibo inescantur, sic homines non caperentur, nisi spei aliquid morderent" *

141 "Ex Africa navis, ut promiseras, cum pecunia tua et familia non venit. Captatores iam exhausti liberalitatem imminuerunt. Itaque aut fallor aut fortuna communis coepit redire ad paenitentiam suam" *

2 "Omnes qui in testamento meo legata habent praeter libertos meos hac condicione percipient quae dedi, si corpus meum in partes conciderint et astante populo comederint" *

3 "Apud quaedam gentes scimus adhuc legem servari, ut a propinquis suis consumantur defuncti, adeo quidem ut obiurgentur aegri frequenter, quod carnem suam faciant peiorem.

4 His admoneo amicos meos ne recusent quae iubeo,sed quibus animis devoverint spiritum meum,eisdem etiam corpus consumant" …

L (= lrtp)

140 15 nisi spei *Buecheler*: nisi spe lt: spe nisi rp

141 familia l; familia tua rtp suam] tuam *Buecheler*

2 libertos l: liberos rtp 3 suam *om.* l 4 etiam rtp: omne l *lac. ind. Scaliger*

quicker than the covetous. But how could sneak thieves and pickpockets make a living unless they circulated little boxes or purses jingling with money to hook the crowd? Non-sentient animals are lured by bait, and people also would not be taken in unless they had their hopes to nibble on" *

141 "The ship from Africa you promised would be arriving with your money and slaves, it hasn't come! The legacy hunters have now been wrung out and have curbed their giving. Unless I'm mistaken our shared fortune is about to return to its sorry state" *

"All who have a legacy in my Will, my freedmen excepted, are to obtain their bequests on the sole condition that they cut up my body into little pieces and consume it in full view of the public" *

"Among some people, as you know, the custom of the deceased being eaten by their relatives is still preserved so faithfully that the chronically ill are castigated for ruining the condition of their meat. In this vein I urge my friends not to reject my terms but simply to channel the energies they have devoted to my life into the consumption of my body in death" *

5 Excaecabat pecuniae ingens fama oculos animosque
miserorum …

Gorgias paratus erat exsequi *

6 "De stomachi tui recusatione non habeo quod timeam
Sequetur imperium, si promiseris illi pro unius horae
7 fastidio multorum bonorum pensationem. Operi modo oculos
et finge te non humana viscera sed centies sestertium
8 comesse. Accedit huc quod aliqua inveniemus blandimenta,
quibus saporem mutemus. Neque enim ulla caro per se
placet, sed arte quadam corrigitur et stomacho
9 conciliatur averso. Quod si exemplis quoque vis probari
consilium, Saguntini obsessi ab Hannibale humanas edere
10 carnes nec hereditatem expectabant. Petelini idem fecerunt
in ultima fame, nec quicquam aliud in hac epulatione
11 captabant nisi tantum ne esurirent. Cum esset Numantia a
Scipione capta, inventae sunt matres quae liberorum
suorum tenerent semesa in sinu corpora" *

* * *

L (= lrtp)

141 5 pecuniae *om.* rp fames *Boschius* *lac. ind. Buecheler* *lac. ind. Scaliger* 8 accedit *Buecheler*: accedet corrigitur *aliquis in libro Junii*: conditur *vel* convertitur *Fraenkel*: commendatur *Mueller*: corrumpitur 9 quoque vis *Bucheler*: vis quoque obsessi *Rittershusius*: oppressi 10 Petelini *Puteanus*: Peta

Eumolpus' huge reputation for wealth was blinding the eyes and hearts of those poor devils …

Gorgias was ready to comply, to the letter *

"I see no reason to be afraid of throwing up. Your stomach will cooperate if you promise it the compensation, in return for one hour's revulsion, of the many good things to follow. So just close your eyes and imagine you're swallowing ten million sesterces and not human innards. Anyway, we'll get some seasoning to modify the taste. Meat never tastes good on its own. With a modicum of skill it can be 'tamed' and 'reconciled' to a reluctant stomach. If you want confirmation of your decision from precedent, why, the people of Saguntum under blockade by Hannibal ate human flesh with no expectation of a legacy. The Petelini did the same when they were dying of hunger and got nothing more out of their meal than an end to starvation. When Scipio took Numantia he found mothers holding in their arms the half-eaten bodies of their children." *

* * *

ANNEXE: ARGUED EMENDATIONS, WITH INDEX

The aim of this section is to serve as a kind of pendant for the project – to show where and how research begun materially with the manuscripts has led to emendation lemmata for an edition. These appeared earlier in a different context and format – in *Mouseion* 7 (2007) 30–52 – because the collating text and lemmata were supplied by K. Mueller's 2003 edition. Each entry therefore had to be turned inside out; and their redrafting provided the opportunity for improvements, after fifteen years, to the text and in my arguments. Hence this annexe presents in the truest sense a new revision for the purposes of the volume. Encountering a suspect word or context, I have been guided almost formulaically by a notion of improper sense or logic, which – thanks to the clear norms set by Petronius – is a standard reasonable to apply and agreeable to follow. Then comes scrutiny under the tenets of manuscript and linguistic criticism, to produce a reading of literary and philological possibility. An index of adoptions follows.

4.2–4 eloquentiam, qua nihil esse maius confitentur, pueris induunt adhuc nascentibus. Quod si paterentur laborum gradus fieri, ut studiosi [iuvenes] lectione severa irrigarentur, ... Nunc pueri in scholis ludunt, iuvenes ridentur in foro, ...

The focus of this passage is on correcting the education of *pueri* before bad habits set in, and on the need to inculcate good habits of study and imitation early on in young boys; and the paragraph continues with reference only to young boys at this critical formative juncture, on the understanding that *nihil esse magnificum quod pueris placeret* (*Sat.* 4.3). Not learning these lessons today, boys play about in school and become tomorrow's youths mocked in court. It appears that *iuvenes,* not attested in *OLD* as a synonym for young children, has entered as a copying error from below or substantival gloss from close below, but here in the wrong context of boys.

10.6 cras autem, quia hoc libet, et <aliam> habitationem mihi prospiciam et [aliquem] fratrem.

alium *pro* aliquem *librorum Buecheler*: aliam *maturius insero, deletionem servans*

As Buecheler indicated, whereas the trio of Encolpius, Ascyltus, and Giton have been (uncomfortably) sharing lodgings for some time (*Sat.* 6.3; cf. *Sat.* 8.2), his alteration of the pronominal adjective better conveys Ascyltus' point about now seeking a separate place and boyfriend; but the implicit sense travels forward more neatly to the second noun than backward to the first.

11.3 opertum me amiculo evolvit et "Quid agebas," inquit, "frater sanctissime, qui vesticontubernium facis?"

qui vesticontubernium facis *ego*: quid verti contubernium facis *libri*: vesticontubernium *Turnebus*

The soldier's cloak, *sagum,* served as a blanket on campaign, but was also a handy privacy screen for sexual activity and a familiar symbol of the pederastic ethos. Here *amiculum* (pun?) does duty. Turnebus' emendation thus seems secure (for other examples of "parasynthetic co-valent compound" nouns in Petronius see Swanson 1963: 83–4; e.g., *Sat.* 56.8 *serisapia, Sat.* 75.6 *fulcipedia*). Encolpius is recognized as enacting a trite role with a hackneyed prop, and is fair game for the sarcasm of Ascyltus, which becomes more pointed: boy-scouting is it? *Sat.* 10.3 *turpior es tu hercule, qui ut foris cenares poetam laudasti,* and *Sat.* 134.9 *qualem putas esse, qui de Circes toro sine voluptate surrexit?*

15.2 advocati tamen iam plani [nocturni] qui volebant pallium lucri facere

iam p(a)ene *Pithou, probat Mueller*: *del. Fuchs*: iam poenae *olim Buecheler*: iam plane *Giardina*: iam bene *Schoppius*: importune *Nisbet*: iam plani [nocturni] *scribo*

The manuscript reading (Pithou) defies accurate translation, as efforts show; Branham-Kinney and Walsh simply gloss over the detail or delete with Fuchs; and Giardina's suggestion does not help. What *nocturni* accomplishes is unclear. The proposed change renders: "... but now mediators, crooks in reality (*iam*) intent on reaping a windfall from the cloak ..." For *planus* and *nocturnus* together, possibly prompting the gloss, cf. *Sat.* 82.2 *miles, sive ille planus fuit sive nocturnus grassator.*

19.4 Tres enim erant mulierculae, si quid vellent conari, infirmissimae scilicet; contra nos, si nihil aliud, virilis sexus [esset] et praecincti certe altius eramus.

scilicet; contra ***distinxit Fraenkel*** **nos, < quibus>** ***Dousa deleo***

This tricky and amusing passage has been resolved over the centuries in various ways. A further possibility is to delete *esset,* making neater sense than most by recognition of the descriptive genitive as a not inelegant zeugma initial predicate of the following *eramus*: "while we at least were of the male sex and definitely more suitably dressed." For the construction cf. Caesar *BG* 2.15.5 *Nervios esse homines feros magnaeque virtutis.*

23.3.4 Femore <o> facili, clune agili, [et] manu procaces, Molles, veteres, Deliaci ferro recisi.

add. Fraenkel om. l, del. Fraenkel **ferro recisi** ***conicio*****: manu recisi L**

One suspects second *manu* of the manuscript to have encroached from the previous line, where it occurs in same position but a different sense. Repetition under such conditions makes for poor poetry and a weak conclusion. For other usages in Petronius of cutting plus instrument cf. *Frg.* 51.12 *falce recisa Ceres.* More appropriate here too would be some instrument; and for genital cutting (circumcision, if not castration), see *Frg.* 47.3 B, 50,3 M *ferro succiderit inguinis oram.* Cf. also *Sat.* 89.1.4 *[ferro] caesi vertices,* where the O-class reading is deleted by editors. Can *ferro* now be supported metrically? Who knows? This poem is in high-resolution sotadean, a salacious, versatile measure used only once elsewhere, at *Sat.* 132.8, which shares the context of genital cutting!

24.3 "per fidem," inquam, "[nostram] Ascyltus <noster> in hoc triclinio solus ferias agit?"

del. Buecheler**:** ***transponere malo***

Cf. good *per fidem* parallels from an emotional Encolpius at *Sat.* 93.3 and *Sat.* 98.3. However, transposition and not deletion seems contextually indicated, in the ironic usage with proper name. Cf. *Sat.* 25.1 *"cur non … devirginatur Pannychis nostra?"*

24.6 "quare ergo," inquit "me non basiavit?" Vocatoque [ad se] in osculum <se> applicuit.

vocatumque *libri*: *sic tamen muto deleo suppleo*

There is awkwardness in the text that needs attention. *Applico* would appear to require the reflexive object, as also Quartilla at *Sat.* 25.4 *maioribus me pueris applicui;* and at *Sat.* 67.5 *applicat se illi toro.* The phrase *vocato in osculum* I would argue to be a humorous legal echo of *vocare in ius, vocare in iudicium, vocare in discrimen* (*OLD s.v.* 4.c); *osculum* therefore as a form of *supplicium*. The error is explained by the accusative context of *me* and the influence of *osculum*.

27.3 non quidem eas quae inter manus [lusu] expellentium vibrabant

del. *Smith*: lusu H: luxu L expellentium *scribo*: expellente HL: expellentes *Asztalos in Öberg*

Difficulty with the sense was noted by Smith, but his good deletion leaves behind the cryptic oddity of *expellente.* Friedlaender struggles to defend the phrase with not very apposite citations of the property of bounce in ancient balls (a rare one in the absence of rubber). Mueller retains, and Ehlers alongside translates "… die im Prellspiel von Hand zu Hand flogen." This is still a stretch. As the balls went the round of players (*expellentium*), the tally of catches was not scored, but rather the misses landing on the floor after discharge. *Expellentium* therefore emphasizes the chain linking throwers and catchers. *Expellentes* would almost do, but the redundancy of *lusu* remains.

29.3 Erat enim venalicium <cum> titulis pictum

enim *lego*: autem *add. Burman*

Autem here requires the sense of *enim*, more as a convention of style than semantics. Cf. *Sat.* 42.2 *fui enim*. It was in the previous sentence in the sense of mild contrast: *Sat.* 29.2 *et collegae quidem mei riserunt, ego autem … non destiti …* And it occurred twice just prior to that, at *Sat.* 28.8 and *Sat.* 28.9, in the sense of "moreover." This stylistically excessive incidence of *autem*, especially in the last sense, where the context would seem to rule it out, is suspicious. Cf. at *Sat.* 81.1 for equally excessive uses of *etiam*. For a similar cadence, cf. *Sat.* 30.3 *<erant> et duae tabulae.* I try *Erat enim venalicium* in preference to the word's deletion.

34.4 Subinde intraverunt duo Aethiopes capillati cum pusillis utribus, quales solent esse <eis> qui harenam in amphitheatro spargunt,

esse: habere *Braswell* <eis> *ego*: <eorum> *Mueller*

The Latin is seen by many as suspect, and additions are proposed that would understand the subject of the relative *qui*-clause as agent (to have people as opposed to skins spattering the sand); cf. *Sat.* 47.10 *quem … ex eis vultis.*

40.1 iuramus Hipparchum Aratumque comparandos illi [homines] non fuisse

illi homines H: homini *Heinze*: comparatos illi homines *Rohde*: *deleo*

A problem is indicated by *homines*. Delete as a glossator's note that Trimalchio's competition was at least mortal.

40.4 Circa autem [minores] porcelli ex coptoplacentis facti

deleo

The emphasis on the piglets (or petite grown pigs) as "rather small" seems uncalled-for. And Swanson (p. 88) notes that only here does Petronius use an adjective of smallness to modify a diminutive (though it occurs in Martial, principally with *parvus*). The comparative is less defensible, and *minores* should rather be taken as a leaden and reflexive glossator's reminder on the smaller size of the surrounding sucklings compared to *Sat.* 40.3 *primae magnitudinis aper.*

43.6–7 Tamen verum quod <suum> frunitus est, quam diu vixit. <Est> cui datum [est], non cui destinatum.

<suum>: <sua> *vel* <vitam> *alii suppleo deleoque*

Petronius shows a way out of the first puzzle: *Sat.* 75.3 *"Habinna, sic peculium tuum fruniscaris."* Thus: "It's what you have in hand that counts, not what you're owed."

46.5 etiam si magister eius sibi placens sit nec uno loco consistit, sed venit <it. Scit qui>dem litteras.

sed venit dem H: scit quidem *Bluemner* venit <abit. Scit qui> dem *Wehle*

There have been several efforts to repair this seeming truncation, though even *dem* of the manuscript reading has been defended as a subjunctive. Mine simplifies Wehle, with an advantage in paleography: haplography. Cf. *Sat.* 47.6 *anathimia is si in cerebrum it* H. The sense of *consistit* is literal: this *magister* will not settle into doing the time and work.

52.6 Ille dimissus circa mensam percucurrit <Trimalchionis, qui> [et] "aquam foras, vinum intro," clamavit.

sic lacunam implevi, quam maiorem indicavit Buecheler delendum

Buecheler implies a lacuna of fair size, in which there is a bathroom visit, followed by the change of subject for the witticism. But it may be as brief as a small insertion and deletion combination, as printed. Antecedent/relative of this type is common (cf. 31.8 *Trimalchionem, cui*; *Sat.* 54.5 *Trimalchionis, quo*); note at *Sat.* 40.2 another instance of running around a single table; and the *aquam* could refer not to Trimalchio's toilet but to the spilled contents of the *calix* at *Sat.* 52. 4 (though the guests never got water for handwashing; *Sat.* 34.5). The *calix* is simple, dispensable ware; cf. *Sat.* 75.10 *calicem in faciem Fortunatae immisit*; and *Sat.* 74.5 *calicesque circa fictiles* (in contrast with *vinum … sacco defluens*). Deletion is a necessary step, but one may note for the general mood *Sat.* 49.8 *Trimalchio, qui relaxato in hilaritatem vultu … inquit.*

54.1 Cum maxime haec dicente eo puer [Trimalchionis] delapsus est

eo *Mueller*: gaio H *delevi quasi scribae* H *menda lac. susp. Scheffer* baronis in bracchium *suppl. Öberg*: in bracchium eius *Wehle*; *adiunctionem videas*

Far preferable is this simple deletion. The account is beautifully paced by the narrator: the boy is introduced at *Sat.* 53.11, and his routine is described; attention is diverted by a typical Trimalchionian aside on the spectacle; the boy falls; the guests cry out at the unsavoury omen. Any expression of ownership or indication of direction at this point robs the narrative of the surprise in store: Trimalchio lets out a groan and nurses his arm (*Sat.* 54.2): he is hit; or maybe not. (In fact, of the forty occurrences of *puer* in the *Cena*, not one is qualified with "Trimalchionis.")

62.9 Gladium tamen strinxi et mataiotata umbras cecidi

mataiotata *percipio ex* mataiotatos *Kelly*: ma tan Hekatan *Heraeus*: matauitatau H: *alii alia*

There have been various adjustments of the ghost word, either emending as an expletive or bringing into line with acceptable onomatopoeia for the thwackety-thwack of the sword swipes. Following Kelly, I support the regular Greek superlative in the transliterated adverb form *mataiotata[u]* as grammatical and plausible on paleographic grounds (dittography), for the "*u*" from following *umbras* has become attached: "all too uselessly." Cf. Eccles. 1.2 *mataiotes mataioteton*: vanity of vanities. Swanson (212) cites five other Greek exclamatory adverbs: *sophos, pax, io, en, deurode*.

62.11 lupus enim villam intravit et omnia pecora <laniavit>; tamquam lanius sanguinem illis misit.

omnia pecora: o mea pecora *lac. Gronovius*: *post lac. ind. Buecheler,* lancinavit *cogitans*: laceravit *suppl. Heraeus*: laniavit *praepono, vel* necavit: *anacoluthon potius quam verbum praetermissum statuit Hofmann non male*

Melissa was badly shaken but probably not at a loss for words. My choice here is the aptest for the work of a wild beast; for the figura etymologica, cf. Suet. *Frg.* 176 p. 277 Re [*OLD*] *laniat lanius, cum membratim discerpit*; cf. *Sat.* 39.10 *laniones et unguentarii*; then comes *necavit*, with a certain paleographic justification (haplography: "*pec-a*" and "*neca-*"), but less suitable for a messy massacre.

62.14 Viderint qui de hoc aliter exopinissent

***sic scripsi*: viderint alii quid de hoc *Buecheler*: viderint quid de hoc alii *Heinze*: *viderint qui hoc de alibi* H**

Some change is needed, and mine has proximity to H and sense favouring it. People with a *different* explanation (of the soldier's neck wound) had better be watching out.

63.3 Ipsimi nostri delicatus decessit, mehercules margaritum [catamitus] et omnium nummorum

ipsimi nostri *Scheffer*: ipim mostri catamitus *coniecere Jacobs, Jahn, Buecheler*: caccitus H: *deleo* nummorum *ego*: numerum H

The first of two difficulties is a special case, in that Jacobs and others appear to have recovered by correction of H not the *Satyrica* text but a gloss on the term of endearment *margaritum*, corrupted by the Renaissance scribe until those scholar contemporaries tumbled to it. With deletion the full phrase takes on a good, colloquial balance: *mehercules margaritum et omnium nummorum* – God he was a pearl beyond price! In the second, I am not comfortable with *numerum*, accepted by Buecheler and Mueller, in the face of the very apposite *Sat.* 68.8 *esset omnium nummorum* in exactly this context (where *nummorum* is emended by the same scholars to *numerum*!). There is instance nearby at *Sat.* 8.8 of an elementary slip by the same scribe, who will prove himself capable of finding *vina* instead of the easy *vitia*; and of course *ipim mostri* above.

67.10 Mulieres si non essent, omnia pro luto haberemus; nunc hoc est caldum potare et frigidum meiere

***sic ordinem sequor*: c. m. et f. p. H**

It is not clear how this proverb of the vain outcome of a nice hot drink – and I get my cue to this sense from Dama at *Sat.* 41.11 *calda potio vestiarius est* – can be a summation of Habinnas' good-natured "without women everything would be cheap as dirt," but one detects an improvement of logic in the inversion: *caldum potare et frigidum meiere*; hence one of those proverbs of futile effort.

68.8 Nam quod strabonus est, non curo: sicut Venus spectat. Ideo nihil iacet, vix oculo mortuo umquam.

nihil iacet *scribo*: nihil latet *Delz*: mihi placet *Heinze*: nihil tacet H

Another piece of obscure folk wisdom from Habinnas leaves the application unclear. Surely the boy's attractive squint cannot be summed up (*ideo*) by the present reading – a non sequitur to finish off the sentence. On the other hand, a proposed *iacet* continues the visual metaphor well and can be reconciled with *vix oculo mortuo* (hyperactive, eyes never shut). It is also closest to H. Perhaps the scribe's own eye was caught by *Sat.* 69.3 *ideo ... tace*, just a few lines further down. In regard to syntax and sense, if *nihil tacet* can mean "he's never quiet" (Walsh), I see no difficulty in rendering *nihil iacet* as "he never lies down" or "never sits still." For indeclinable noun adverbially see *OLD s.v* 11, citing Plautus *Mil.* 625 *nihil amas.* Cf. the following entry, *Sat.* 69.2 *nihil sibi defraudat.*

69.2 " Agnosco," inquit, "Cappadocem: nihil sibi defraudat, et mehercules laudo illum"

agnosco *malo*: adcognosco H

Adcognosco (or *accognosco*), though deemed an acceptable vulgarism by Heraeus 1899, 48, is very rare, and occurs nowhere else in Petronius. *Agnosco* is the normal and frequent form; cf. *Sat.* 7.3 *cum ego negarem me agnoscere domum.* The double prepositional prefix may be due to the incorporation into H of an *"ad"* superscript offered as a correction to the *"cog-"* of *cognosco* in the exemplar.

69.7 Insecuta sunt Cydonia mala etiam spinis infixa, ut echinos effingerent

mala etiam spinis *ego*: e. m. s. H effingerent *ego post Heinze*: *efficerent* H

Two problems: the quinces themselves, presumably even Cretan ones, are not unusual; it is their arrival with thorns embedded in them that startles. Thus a transposition to *mala etiam spinis infixa* is indicated. And in this elegant narrative by Encolpius *efficerent* is suspect. It is not that the thorns produce sea-urchins; they suggest or represent them. Thus *effingerent* is to be preferred, with Heinsius. The text corruption is readily attributable to *effecisset,* a mere line beneath, in the accurate "producing" sense: *Sat.* 69.7 *ferculum longe monstrosius effecisset ut vel fame perire mallemus.* Cf. *Sat.* 4.5 *quod sentio et ipse carmine effingam.* I'd come up with emendation and rationale independently of Heinze, so now must consider it a certainty.

70.6 Consternati nos [insolentia ebriorum] intentavimus oculos

deleo* ebriorum: servorum *aliquis in Buecheler, quem refutat

Here is an oddity of logic, since it is not the slaves' insubordination of being drunk that upsets the guests, but their ignoring of their master and smashing of an amphora. One prospect is to replace *ebriorum* as a gloss that drove out the underlying *servorum*, a solution rejected by Buecheler on the rather arch ground that *ebriorum* is ironical in view of the guests' drunkenness, and therefore appropriate. An alternative solution favoured here is to delete the phrase *insolentia ebriorum*; cf. *Sat.* 60.2 *consternatus ego exsurrexi et timui, ne* ... (no reason provided). The slaves' disobedience and violence startle and upset the guests. That they are fuelled by drink seems irrelevant and beside the point. Thus the phrase smacks of a miscued explanatory gloss. *Insolentia* is, according to Encolpius, a characteristic of Trimalchio (*Sat.* 50.3 *pro reliqua insolentia*).

73.2 balneum intravimus, angustum scilicet [et cisternae frigidariae simile], in quo Trimalchio rectus stabat.

angustum scilicet et *del. George*: angustum ... simile *del. Sullivan*: *ita deleo* in quo *Buecheler*: in qua H

Modern objections register discomfort with the picture of a hot tub the size of a cold water reservoir; or else, if the *balneum* is understood as the entire indoor area, the comparison is even less workable. The text is made to stand as Encolpian sarcasm, but there is something about the use of *simile*, with its explanatory resonance, that to me suggests a gloss by someone who either never knew the ancient proportions or ratios, or mistakes the meaning of *balneum*; thus retain *angustum scilicet*, indeed as irony, but delete *et cisternae frigidariae simile*, which provides intrusive, misdirected data.

79.4 notabili candore ostenderunt [errantibus] viam

deleo

Errantibus was used with perfect application just above: *Sat.* 79.1 *quae iter aperiret errantibus.* Here it's back, not ripe for immediate repetition, inelegance apart, now that the main problem has been eliminated by chalk blazes on the columns. Cf. also *Sat.* 79.4 *cum ... timeret errorem.* It's a candidate for deletion as an imported, echoic gloss.

79.6 ni tabellarius [Trimalchionis] intervenisset <quasi> ex vehiculo divus

Trimalchionis *del. Delz* intervenisset *Fr. Daniel*: invenisset *addidi* ex vehiculo divus *Watt*: * vehiculis dives t: x vehiculis dives lp

The emendation to *ex* is well justified by the manuscripts, and the meaning of the *deus ex machina* seems established, but one wonders if the minor insertion of *<quasi> ex vehiculo divus* is needed to convert metaphor to simile. Granted there is figurative language in our author, with links to proverbs and vulgar Latin, that does not have the qualifier: cf. *Sat.* 57.8 *immo lorus in aqua;* yet *quasi* is used very commonly in Petronius (seventeen times), as perhaps here in the narrative of Encolpius, to comment ironically on a representation of reality by a substitute; cf. two apposite examples in this notion of "unreal" or impossible comparison: *Sat.*1.3 *omnia dicta factaque quasi papavere et sesamo sparsa,* and *Sat.* 2.8 *omnia quasi eodem cibo pasta.* Here too, in this supernatural evocation, *quasi* (or *velut*) is indicated to draw full attention to a clever and self-conscious metaphoric image.

79.7 stabuli ianuam effregit et nos per eandem [terram] immisit

per eandem terram *libri*: per eam tandem *Gurlitt*: per eandem tramisit *Watt, non probante Mueller deleo* immisit *ego*: admisit *libri*

Because of the choice of preposition (*per*), one has interest in *immisit* (see below); the present compound could have been prompted by an attempt to heal the corruption in *per eandem terram.* Forms of *admitto* exist elsewhere, notably with different complements: *Sat.*19. 2 *vetui hodie in hoc deversorio quemquam mortalium admitti,* and *Sat.* 51.2 *admissus ergo Caesarem.* But cf. *Sat.* 72.10 *per eandem ianuam emissus,* which I believe strengthens the case for *immisit* by its proximate use in precisely the same semantic context and construction. Thus (*pace* Mueller): *stabuli ianuam effregit et nos per eandem [terram] immisit.*

80.8 Egreditur <ergo> superbus cum praemio Ascyltos

suppleo

Egreditur <ergo> superbus would be indicated after a verb of "motion," as often, to sum up and smooth the change of subject from Encolpius to Ascyltus. Cf. at *Sat.* 67. 4 *Venit ergo galbina succincta cingillo.* Here there is a paleographic basis for its disappearance: haplography.

81.1 Nec diu tamen lacrimis indulsi, sed veritus <etiam> ne Menelaus [etiam] antescholanus inter cetera mala solum me in deversorio inveniret

transpono

No less than four occurrences of *etiam* in the first part of *Sat.* 81 signify that it is one of those chapters where light repairs to the manuscript account have been attempted, yielding an uncertain relation of grammar to sense (cf. *Sat.* 29.3 *autem*). The postponement of *etiam* to its manuscript position imports conflicting emphases; whereas it accentuates *veritus* and answers *tamen* better thus: *veritus <etiam> ne Menelaus [etiam]*: "still fearing" (i.e., though he might be considered safe in his room; *OLD s.v.* 1: "still, yet, even now"). Encolpius concedes his lingering fear of being the only one found to receive the full brunt of any chiding by Menelaus for skipping out on the dinner party, since he is apparently traceable (location known to the *tabellarius*, *Sat.* 79.6–7).

83.5 et omnes fabulae quoque <modo> habuerunt sine aemulo complexus.

et *et* fabulae quoque *del. Fraenkel* quoque: quondam *"fortasse"* Mueller, *qui "nondum sanatus" declarat suppleo*

The awkwardness can be eliminated by printing *et omnes fabulae quoque <modo> habuerunt sine aemulo complexus*: "All these stories contained in some manner (i.e., in common, though in different permutations) love with the field clear." This necessitates taking *quoque* not as a conjunction but as an ablative of the distributive pronominal adjective in the transferred attested post-classical sense of *quocumque*; see *L. & S.* II; cf. the use of *cuiusque modi*, "of every kind," *OLD s.v.* 7.

87.1 rogare coepi ephebum ut reverteretur in gratiam mecum, [id est ut] <et> pateretur satis fieri sibi

id ... sibi *del. Haley deleo suppleo*

Some special insertions in our text occur in the homoerotic environment, and appear addressed to explaining or underscoring an aspect of the pederastic code that to our minds (and presumably to those of the author's original audience) need no explaining. While Haley's full interpolation is plausible along these lines, I should like to limit the intervention to the above, for having the ability to retain sense and point, with the bonus of a *double entendre*: "I set to asking the lad to be friends with me again, and to allow me the chance to make it up to him." Cf. entries at *Sat.* 91. 3 and *Sat.* 130.8. for the pederastic code.

87.8 Et [non] plane iam <non> molestum erat munus

sic transpono* (*in Petronio* et plane *5x*, non plane *1x*): et *[non] paene "fortasse" Mueller

In prospect: full intercourse for the third time over a brief period, and Mueller's change signals growing doubt in Eumolpus at his resolve or capacity. Yet I am not in favour of disrupting an obviosly preferred usage and sense: "Well, to be sure, even now this was no disagreeable task." Cf. *Sat.* 53.1 *Et plane interpellavit*; and other uses of the postpositive negation: *Sat.* 35.3 *plane non pro expectatione*; *Sat.* 63.6 *et plane non mentiar*.

88.1 Erectus his sermonibus consulere prudentiorem coepi aetates<que> tabularum et quaedam argumenta mihi obscura simulque causam desidiae praesentis excutere.

coepi <et interrogare> aetates tabularum *complet dubitanter Buecheler*: coepi aetates<que> tabularum *solum requiro*

The sentence as it stands is ungrammatical, and a less radical solution than Buecheler's is possible: *aetates<que>*: "I commenced to take counsel from a wiser head and to interrogate [*OLD excutere* 9] him on the dates of the paintings and certain themes that were unclear to me, plus the reason for the present stagnation."

88.7 Ubi sapientia consultissima <vitae> via?

sapientia: sapientiae t^{m} cultissima R: inlustrissima "fortasse" *Mueller, qui* consultissima *librorum desperat ita suppleo*

The manuscript reading of *consultissima* has detractors, but it is a good word found in Gellius and Fronto for "highly prudent," and "most well-advised," made more credible with the proposed insertion (error through haplography) and recalling *Sat.* 84.1 *rectum iter vitae coepit insistere*, with the added benefit of interesting echoism.

91.3 Supprimere ego querellam iubeo, ne quis convicia deprehenderet

convicia *scribo*: consilia *libri*

What plans would these be? At this point the lovers are not planning flight. I believe *convicia* would fit the context better, since the protagonists frequently show concern for the confidentiality of their pederastic relationship that a typical lovers' fight would expose: a common theme in their gossip-obsessed culture. Cf. *Sat.* 10.3 *ex turpissima lite* and *Sat.* 10.5 *mille causae nos quotidie collident et per totam urbem rumoribus different*: and *Sat.* 129.2 *Veritus puer, ne in secreto deprehensus daret sermonibus locum.*

91.7 Postquam se <adhuc> amari sensit, supercilium altius sustulit

suppleo

The sense in context must be "still loved" despite Giton's betrayal of a long-standing relationship, rather than "really loved" (cf. *Sat.* 97.10 for an actual use of *se vero*), and the former is the translation choice of nine of a dozen popular versions in four languages, almost as if it were the manuscript reading already; thus Ernout: "toujours aimé," Ehlers: "noch immer geliebt," Walsh: "retained my affection," Prieto: "aun lo amaba," using the modern Spanish word derived from *adhuc*. *Sat.* 45.4 *porcos coctos ambulare*! Haplography.

91.9 Exosculatus pectus sapientia plenum inieci cervicibus manus, et ut facile intellegeret redisse me in gratiam et optima fide reviviscentem amicitiam, <eum> toto corpore adstrinxi.

suppleo* toto corpore *scribo*: toto pectore *libri

First, we are getting rather far from an object, and *eum* is indicated by the sense; second, *toto pectore*, though unexceptionable where the noun is used metonymically in the sense of *cor, animus, sensus, affectus, amor* (e.g., Verg. *Aen.* 9.276 *Te vero, venerande puer, iam pectore toto Accipio* – "wholeheartedly"; cf. Ovid. *Tr.* 1.3.66 *pectora iuncta* – "hearts knit") is unsuitable anatomically after *adstrinxi* (gripped, squeezed). It hides in the plausibility of context, but a closer look yields an inept physical picture. *Pectore* has entered from nearby *Sat.* 91.9, *pectus sapientia plenum*, with help from *Sat.* 91.6 *in hoc pectore. Toto corpore* is required, as often, for the lover's press; cf. *Sat.* 86.3 *totoque corpore citra summam voluptatem me ingurgitavi*; and *Sat.* 131.11 *Totoque corpore in amplexum eius immissus. Pectus* is unattested as a physical synonym for *corpus*.

92.3 Demum ut solum hospitem vidi, <Eumolpon> momento recepi. Ille ut se in grabatum reiecit ...

demum: deinde *Scaliger suppleo*

The manuscripts ask us to accept a missing object for *recepi* – reusing *solum hospitem*? We might link its omission to an ample supply in this little sentence of words with shared letters, especially *momento* (haplography). I accept *demum*, with Buecheler, attested reading of L sources (O is absent), though some think initial position impossible; but cf. Plaut. *Merc.* 3.2.9 *demum igitur cum senex is, tum ...* What we have here is an elegant style transposition to avoid commencing the sentence with *ut*, with the usual enclitic rhythm retained in the background. I see little wrong in reading *demum ut* (= *ut demum*) to mean "when and only when." See *OLD s.v.* 1: "at the stated time and not before" – the stronger and more pointed reflection of Encolpius' caution, and of his expectation that the intimidating Ascyltus might accompany Giton (when last seen, they had departed together at *Sat.* 80.8). Finally, without an antecedent *Ille* just dangles.

92.7 Ex altera parte iuvenis nudus, qui vestimenta perdiderat, non minore [clamoris] indignatione Gitona flagitabat.

delendum

Clamoris is a good candidate for deletion as a gloss borrowed from just above, *Sat.* 92.7 *clamitare*, since the grammar is quite doubtful – defining genitive? For a similar setting of repeated indignation, this time without characterization, cf. *Sat.* 100.4 *eadem indignatione mulier lacerata ulterius excanduit.*

93.3 totam concitabit viciniam, et nos omnes sub eodem casu obruet

sub eodem casu *ego*: sub eadem causa *libri*

The phrase *sub eadem causa* seems unexpected. On the same accusation? The suggested emendation goes better with *obruet*. Cf. *Sat.* 87.1 *cum similis nos casus in eandem fortunam rettulisset.*

94.14 Rudis enim novacula <erat> et in hoc retusa, ut pueris discentibus audaciam tonsoris daret, [instruxerat thecam].

suppleo deleoque* tonsoris *del. Fraenkel

I read *novacula <erat>* through haplography, and delete *instruxerat thecam*. First, the author's style and ear for rhythm support the inclusion of the verb. For a reason for it to slip out, see two lines above, *neque Giton ulla erat suspicione vulneris laesus.* Relatedly, the absence of the verb forces *novacula* to be the subject of *instruxerat*, for the clause to mean something like "For the practice razor was still in its sheath." This is difficult Latin and a bad choice in context, since it weakens the realism of Giton's gesture and makes the restraint of the servant and Eumolpus too obvious. This was a purposely blunted practice razor which did not require a protective sheath to ensure safety. If it were in its sheath its bluntness would be irrelevant.

97.4 ac sic ut olim Ulixes Polyphemi arieti adhaesisset, extentus infra grabatum scrutantium eluderet manus.

P[r]o<lyphemi> ***lego*****: pro** ***libri*****: Cyclopis** ***Buecheler*** **arieti** ***Buecheler*****: ariete**

Earlier interpolation hunters such as Fraenkel had a field day with this passage, which seems to owe corruption to Encolpius' elaborate imagery, especially as *pro* is unlikely in any way to describe Odysseus' position, hanging upside-down and gripping the belly-fleece of the lead ram (*Od.* 9.425–30). Buecheler initially posited a short lacuna and emendatation, *pro ... arieti adhaesisset,* with various suggestions for the filler. The error may have commenced with the *po* and *pro* resemblance. Cf. *Sat.* 101.5 *Cyclops* and *Sat.* 101.7 *antrum Cyclopis,* a citation which may later have inspired Buecheler (*in adn.*) here.

100.6 ut subter constratum [navis] occuparemus secretissimum locum

subter ***Mueller*****: super** ***libri*** **super constratum** ***del. Fraenkel*** **super constratum navis** ***del. Mueller in prima deleo***

The change to *subter* seems secure as necessary to the context, and *constratum* can hereby be preserved. I should like, however, to remove *navis* as both unnecessary and encumbering: in the fifteen other uses of forms of *navis,* the descriptive is important to the sense (see, e.g., *Sat.* 110.1 *cum ancilla Tryphaenae Gitonem in partem navis inferiorem ducit*); not here. The plausibility of the phrase is perhaps due to proximate *Sat.* 100.3 *super constratum puppis.*

101.2 comprehendi <ego> Eumolpi genua

suppleo

The modesty of this change must not prejudice its correctness, since Encolpius' rhetorical sense and style are improved by it. The graphic narrative switches from subject Giton swooning on top of him, to his sweat reviving both, to his own action here as subject. It is a favourite story-telling cadence; see, among many examples, *Sat.* 25.3 *obstupui ego* and *Sat.* 90.2 *timui ego.*

102.14 et non multa una oporteat consentiant [et non] nationi <ut> mendacium constet.

oporteat *Heinze*: oportet ut omni *Crusius*: et non ratione *Pithou*: nationi *ego*: natione *delevit supplevitque Buecheler*

"As if there shouldn't be plenty else to harmonize with a people [such as the mentioned Ethiopians, Jews, Arabs, Gauls – all *nationes*] for the deception to hold up."

103.6 silentioque <lecto> compositi reliquas noctis horas male soporati consumpsimus.

***suppleo* compositi *"nescioquis" Buecheler*: composito**

Since Buecheler, the manuscript reading has been avoided, and the anonymous emendation looks sound (see below), but the thought is not yet quite complete. I propose an insertion: *silentioque lecto compositi*: "settling down on our beds in silence." Cf. *Frg.* 48.1 *lecto compositus vix prima silentia noctis carpebam.* The zeugmatic double-ablative in separate functions ("manner" and "place") seems striking but possible.

114.3 <Nam> Sicilia[m] modo ventus flabat, saepissime tamen Italici litoris aquilo possessor convertebat huc illuc obnoxiam ratem.

***suppleo deleo* flabat *ego*: dabat tamen *ego*: in oram t, *del.* lrp**

Various measures are tried to make sense of this sailing arcanum and consequent disturbance. In my version I offer some admittedly fussy surgery: an initial *nam* to lead off the complex pattern; then read *Sicilia* out of dittography, without preposition as ablatival origin of direction; *dabat* is specious and I propose *flabat; in oram* is a miscued scribal gloss or misreading that draws the genitive to it instead of where it belongs with *aquilo possessor*; a replacing *tamen* answers *modo.* "For now the wind from Sicily would blow, but next and very often Aquilo, controller of the Italian littoral, turning the exposed ship first in one direction and then in another." The awkwardness may be the result of anacoluthon at *convertebat.* For *possessor* with genitive in a similar nautical context, see Sil. 6.687 *possessor pelagi ... captivos puppes ad litora victor agebat. Modo* is frequent with a second adverb used temporally (on the analogy of *modo ... modo*): cf. *Sat* 41.6 *modo Bromium, interdum Lyaeum Euhiumque confessus.*

115.8 Substiti ergo tristis coepique umentibus oculis maris fidem increpare

maris fidem ***susp. Fraenkel*****: maris malam fidem** ***quaerit Mueller*** **increpare** ***ego*****: inspicere**

Inspicere, making *umentibus oculis* instrument rather than circumstance after *coepi,* does not seem right, and a word of upbraiding instead, such as *increpare*, improves things; for such a locution, cf. Cic. *Q.Fr. 2.3.3 cum illius in me perfidiam increparet, auditus est magno silentio malevolorum.* The permissibility of *maris fidem* is not fully settled. It has been accepted presumably through irony, though I do not have a parallel.

117.1* Prudentior Eumolpus convertit ad novitatem rei mentem genusque divisionis sibi non displicere confessus est

divisionis ***ego*****: divinationis ltp: divitionis r: ditationis** ***Dousa***

None of our L sources has the variant right, though *r* comes close. The lacuna posted by the L editors (*) may have been encouraged by the reading *divinationis,* with its implication of an elaborate alternative strategy, perhaps from Giton (see Buecheler *app. ad loc.*, where his logic is surely fanciful). Though the comparative may imply some comment or expression of surprise or dismay now missing in a small lacuna, I posit with some confidence *divisionis* as the apt characterization of a novel situation which Eumolpus is quicker than the others to grasp, relish, and put to good use. This word arises naturally out of the circumstances at Croton just described by the encountered *vilicus,* and recapitulates the essential fact of the strict binary division of the citizens of Croton into "hunters" and "hunted" (see *OLD s.v.* 'divisio' 2). The exploitation of this dichotomous *divisio* becomes, in short order, the precise basis for Eumolpus' scam.

117.12 "Quid? Vos" inquit, "iumentum me putatis esse aut lapidariam navem?"

Quid? Vos ***punxi*****: quid vos**

An adjustment in the punctuation raises the tone of indignation and sarcasm from Corax: Cf. *Sat.* 127.4 *"Quid? Tu," inquit illa, "donas mihi eum sine quo non potes vivere … ?"*

127.5 Haec ipsa cum diceret, tanta gratia conciliabat vocem [loquentis], tam dulcis sonus pertemptatum mulcebat aera

deleo

Loquentis is strictly not needed after *cum diceret,* and though the redundancy could be minimized by some such rendering as "she imbued her voice as she spoke with such charm …," an imbalance with the second object is created. To be deleted, despite the further attention to Circe's voice.

128.4 et postquam omnes vultus temptavit, quales solent inter amantes risus fingere

quales solent *ego*: quos solet risus: lusus *Mueller* fingere *Cuperus*: frangere

The emendation of Cuperus seems secure (see below), but uncertainty clouds this charming image of Circe rehearsing funny faces for her lovers in front of a mirror. It's impossible to justify *solet.* Good sense can be reached by employing the Petronian *quales solent* (*Sat.* 33.3; *quales* is common): after Circe had tried out all the expressions that customarily produce (*OLD* "fingo" *s.v.* 7) a laugh between lovers. For this use of *fingere* as a feminine wile, cf. *Sat.* 113.7 *Omnia oscula me vulnerabant, omnes blanditiae, quascumque mulier libidinosa fingebat.* An amusing parallel evoking both passages is found in Apuleius *Met.* 10.21 *et blandissimos adfatus: "amo" et "cupio" et "solum te deligo" et "sine te iam vivere nequeo" et cetera, quis mulieres et alios inducunt et suos testantur adfectationes.*

130.8 Hinc ante somnum levissima ambulatione compositus sine Gitone cubiculum intravi. [Tanta erat placandi cura, ut timerem ne latus meum frater convelleret.] Postero die, cum sine offensa corporis animique consurrexissem, in eundem platanona descendi.

adventicia damnanda

Encolpius' going to bed without Giton (*sine Gitone cubiculum intravi*) echoes the elegant, intimate instruction of Circe, *Sat.* 129.8 *si vis sanus esse, Gitonem relega* ("If you want to get better, banish Giton"). It is followed by a piece of reflection questionable from several perspectives. It sacrifices the night-to-morning flow with a proscribed option, its unique vulgarity violates the convention of discreetly shading crude physical details, and it shunts the syntax into a back-to-front meaning. "I took such pains to appease (her), that I was afraid my lover would break my balls." One notes the "resumption" immediately after it of the high style: "I rose without detriment to body and mind." Cf. *Sat.* 134.5 *utique propter mascarpionem.*

132.2 Manifestis matrona contumeliis lacerata tandem ad ultionem decurrit

lacerata *ego*: verberata L: exacerbata *Buecheler*: vexata *Nisbet*: efferata *Mueller*

Though metaphorically plausible and attested (Cic. *De Rep.* 1.9 *contumeliarum verbera subire*), *verberata* has given pause, perhaps because it is Encolpius who will shortly be on the receiving end of an actual lashing. In support of *lacerata,* see *Sat.* 100.4 *eadem indignatione mulier lacerata ulterius excanduit.*

132.7 conditusque lectulo totum ignem furoris in eam <rem> converti, quae mihi omnium malorum causa fuerat.

suppleo*: partem *item se commendat

Something has dropped out after *eam,* and *rem* seems better than taking the antecedent to anticipate the distant *causa* or to imply something like *mentulam.* Cf. *Sat.* 132.12 *secretoque rubore perfundi, quod oblitus verecundiae meae cum ea parte corporis verba contulerim, quam ne ad cognitionem quidem admittere severioris notae homines solerent.*

134.5 Ingemui ego [utique propter mascarpionem], lacrimisque ubertim manantibus obscuratum dextra caput super pulvinum inclinavi.

deleo

Here in the context of both O and L is another sexually charged gloss uncovered by vulgarity and doubtful sense (cf. *Sat.* 130.8 above). The phrase interrupts a "sobs-and-tears" flow suited to the melodrama (cf. *Sat.* 91.8 *haec cum inter gemitus lacrimasque fudissem, detersit ille pallio vultum*). *Mascarpio* is a mystery word which divides translators on derivation and meaning. A belabouring of Encolpius' groin is indicated, though the context is doubtful, and the action seems more punitive than libidinous.

140.2 Ea ergo ad Eumolpum venit et commendare liberos suos eius prudentiae bonitatique ... <coepit, atque> credere se et vota sua.

lac. ind. Buecheler* <coepit *et altera supplet Mueller*: atque> *suppleo

Minimal surgery sets the stage and pun with great point and precision. Cf. *Sat.* 140.14 *Socrates ... nec ... oculos suos crediderat* for *credere* with object of person or thing consigned; also Ter. *An.* 272 *mihi suom animum atque omnem vitam credidit.*

140.2–3 Illum esse solum in toto orbe terrarum, qui praeceptis etiam salubribus instruere iuvenes quotidie posset, <quae sola posset hereditas iuvenibus dari>. Ad summam, relinquere se pueros in domo Eumolpi, ut illum loquentem audirent [quae sola posset hereditas iuvenibus dari].

sic ordinem sententiae mutavi, geminationes non fastiditus lacunam ind. Buecheler

A lacuna is reduced, even finessed, with better sense and logic accruing, by thus moving the relative clause *quae ... dari* up into the objective position for *posset*: the only true legacy that one can vouchsafe to one's children is hardly an audience with Eumolpus, as the manuscript has it, but a diet of daily instruction in wholesome values. This places *posset ... posset* and *iuvenes ... iuvenibus* anaphoristically, but that may be the point: Philomela's meretricious flattery cannot be controlled by the propriety of speech.

140.8 Ille lente parebat imperio puellaeque artificium pari motu renumerabat.

renumerabat *ego*: remunerabat

To *reward* the tricks or to *match* them? *Renumerabat* is a better accompaniment to *pari motu*. Corax "paid back" what was "owed," balanced the tally by repaying in kind and number. Rewarding may not be the point, for all its facetious merit.

Index of Emendations Adopted into the Text

1. Those Discussed in the Annexe:

4.3 *studiosi [iuvenes]* (deletion)

10. 6 *et <aliam> … et [aliquem]* (insertion plus deletion)

11.3 *qui v. …: quid*

15.2 *iam plani [nocturni]: iam paene*

19.4 *sexus [esset.]*

23.3.4 *ferro recisi: manu recisi*

24.3 *[nostram] Ascyltus <noster>*

24.6 *vocatoque [ad se] in osculum <se> applicuit: vocatumque*

27.3 *[lusu] expellentium: expellente*

29.3 *erat enim: autem*

34.4 *esse <eis> qui*

40.1 *illi [homines]*

40.4 *[minores] porcelli*

43.6–7 *quod <suum> … <Est> cui datum [est]*

46.5 *sed venit <it. Scit qui> dem*

52.6 *<Trimalchionis, qui> [et]*

54.1 *puer [Trimalchionis]*

62.9 *mataiotata: matauitatau*

62.11 *pecora <laniavit>; tamquam lanius*

62.14 *viderint qui de hoc aliter: v. qui hoc de alibi*

63.3 *[catamitus] et omnium nummorum: caccitus et omnium numerum*

67.10 *caldum potare et frigidum meiere: c. m. et f. p.*

68.8 *nihil iacet: nihil tacet*

69.2 *agnosco: adcognosco*

69.7 *mala etiam spinis: e. m. s. effingerent: efficerent*

70.6 *[insolentia ebriorum]*

73.2 *[et cisternae frigidariae simile]*

79.4 *[errantibus]*

79.6 *intervenisset < quasi>*

79.7 *per eandem [terram] immisit: admisit*

80.8 *egreditur <ergo> superbus*

81.1 *veritus <etiam> ne Menelaus [etiam]*

83.5 *quoque <modo>*

87.1 *[id est ut] <et>*

87.8 *et [non] plane iam <non> molestum*

88.1 *coepi aetates<que> tabularum*

88.7 *sapientia consultissima <vitae> via*

91.3 *ne quis convicia: consilia*
91.7 *se<adhuc> amari*
91.9 *<eum> toto corpore: toto pectore*
92.3 *<Eumolpon> momento recepi*
92.7 *[clamoris] indignatione*
93.3 *sub eodem casu: sub eadem causa*
94.14 *novacula <erat> … daret [instruxerat thecam]*
97.4 *Polyphemi: pro*
100.6 *constratum [navis]*
101.2 *comprehendi <ego>*
102.14 *nationi: natione*
103.6 *<lecto> compositi: composito*
114.3 *<nam> Sicilia[m] modo ventus flabat: dabat … tamen: in oram*
115.8 *increpare: inspicere*
117.1 *divisionis: divinationis*
117.12 *Quid? Vos: quid vos*
127.5 *vocem [loquentis]*
128.4 *quales solent: quos solet*
130.8 *[Tanta … convelleret]*
132.2 *lacerata: verberata*
132.7 *in eam <rem>* or *<partem>*
134.5 *[utique propter mascarpionem]*
140.2 *bonitati <coepit atque> credere*
140.2–3 *Illum esse solum in toto orbe terrarum, qui praeceptis etiam salubribus instruere iuvenes quotidie posset, <quae sola posset hereditas iuvenibus dari>. Ad summam, relinquere se pueros in domo Eumolpi, ut illum loquentem audirent [quae sola posset hereditas iuvenibus dari].*
140.8 *renumerabat: remunerabat.*

2. Those Not Discussed in the Annexe or Hitherto Published:

23.4 *<me>*
45.11 *tam: iam*
47.13 *<domini>potentiae*
54.3 *[periculo] aliquid*
56.1 *putemus: putamus*
58.7 *nenias: menias*
60.8 *quorum duo <tres> Lares*
61.2 *< inquit>*
65.2 *[pro turdis]*

68.5 *offenderet*: *offenderit*
72.7 *[ebrius]*
74.10 *[convicio]*
74.13 *se de machina?*
80.1 *incumbas*: *incumbis*
86.6 *sedere <puer>*
90.1 *<quidam>*
91.7 *amoris,"<inquam>*
99.3 *"incultis" <inquam>*
100.4 *en haec*: *et haec*
100.4 *aegre*: *paene*
108.8 *tonsoria*: *tonsor*
112.2 *partem corporis ab[sti]nuit*
114.4 *postquam <tempestas> manifesta convaluit*
114.8 *<at ego Gitoni> applicitus*
126.1 *tractas*: *captas*
127.5 *toto [mihi] caelo*

AGGREGATE BIBLIOGRAPHY OF MATERIALS CITED OR ENLISTED FOR THIS VOLUME

Anton, C.G. 1781. *Petronii Arbitri Satyricon.* (Leipzig)
Arrowsmith, W. tr. 1959. *The Satyricon of Petronius.* (Ann Arbor)
Beck, C. 1863. *The Manuscripts of the Satyricon of Petronius Arbiter Described and Collated.* (Cambridge, Mass.)
Beck, R. 1975. "Encolpius at the *Cena.*" *Phoenix* 29, 271–83
Birt, T. 1925. "Zu Petron." *Philologus* 79, 6
Bluemner, H. 1920. "... Bemerkungen zu Petrons Cena Trimalchionis." *Philologus* 76, 341
Bodel, J. 1989. "Missing Links: *thymatulum* or *tomaculum.*" *HSCP* 92, 349–66
Bouhier, J. 1737. *Poème de Petrone sur la Guerre Civile.* (Amsterdam)
Branham, R.B., and Kinney, D., tr. 1997. *Petronius, Satyrica.* (London)
Braswell, B. 1981. "Zu Petron 34.4." *Philologus* 125, 152–5
Breitenstein, N. 2009. *Petronius,* Satyrica *1–15.* (Berlin)
Browning, R. 1962. Review of Mueller 1961. *CR* ns 12, 218–21
Buecheler, F. 1862[1]. *Petronii Satirarum Reliquiae.* (Berlin, *editio maior*)
– 1922[6]. *Petronii Satirarum Reliquiae.* (Berlin) (*curavit G. Heraeus*)
Burman, P. 1709. *Titi Petronii Satyricon quae supersunt.* (Utrecht)
Busche, K. 1911. "Petroniana." *RhM* 66, 452–7
Butrica, J. 2007. "*Sat.* 109.7 *structis.*" Note to author by e-mail; see Annexe ad. loc.
Cholodniak, I. 1909. "Zu Petronius." *RhM* 64, 330
Conte, G.B. 1992. "Petronio, *Sat.* 141; una congettura e un'interpretazione." *RFIC* 120, 300–12
– 1996. *The Hidden Author:An Interpretation of Petronius's* Satyricon. (Berkeley)
Corbett, P. 1969. "More Petroniana." *CP* 64, 111–13
Courtney, E. 1970. "Some Passages of Petronius." *BICS* 17, 65–9
– 1991. *The Poems of Petronius.* (Atlanta)

de la Mare, A.C. 1976. "The Return of Petronius to Italy." *Essays to R.W. Hunt*, 220–54. (Oxford)

Delz, J. 1962. Review of Mueller 1961. *Gnomon* 34, 676–84

Dutsch, D. 2000. "Boundless Nature." (diss. McGill)

Ehlers, W. 1980? In a personal letter to K. Mueller

Ernout, A. 1950[3]. *Petrone, Le Satiricon.* (Paris)

Firebaugh, W.C., tr. 1922. *The Satyricon of Petronius Arbiter.* (New York)

Fraenkel, E. 1960? In a personal letter to K. Mueller

Friedlaender, L. 1906[2]. "Petronii Cena Trimalchionis." (Leipzig)

Fuchs, H. 1938. "Zum Petrontext." *Philologus* 93, 157–75

– 1959. In *Studien zur Textgeschichte und Textkritik*, 57–82. (Cologne)

Gaselee, S. 1915. *A Collotype Reproduction of That Portion of Cod. Paris. 7989 … Which Contains the Cena Trimalchionis of Petronius.* (Cambridge)

– 1944. "Petroniana." *CQ* 38, 77

George, P. 1967. "Petroniana." *CQ* ns 17, 130–2

Giardina, G.C., and Melloni, R.C. 1995. *Petronii Arbitri Satyricon.* (Turin)

Gifanius. 1595. *Index in T. Lucretium*, 313. (Leiden). (Giardina-Melloni XI)

Goldast, M. 1610, 1621[2]. *T. Petronii Arbitri … Satiricon …* (Frankfurt)

Gurlitt, L. 1923. *Satiricon.* (Berlin)

Haarhoff, T.J. 1944. "'*Bucca, bucca*' in South Africa." *CPh* 39, 118

Habermehl, P. 2006. *Petronius* Satyrica *79–141.* (Berlin)

Hadrianides, M. 1669. *Satyricon Cum Fragmento nuper Tragurii Reperto.* (Amsterdam)

Haley, H. 1892. "Petroniana." *HSCP* 3, 184

Haupt, M. 1876. *Opuscula III*, 377, 583. (Leipzig)

Heraeus, G. 1899. *Die Sprache des Petronius und die Glossen.* (Leipzig)

– 1939. *Kleine Schriften.* (Heidelberg)

Heseltine, M., tr. 1913. *Petronius.* (Cambridge, Mass.)

– 1969 (curavit E.H. Warmington)

Hofmann, J.B. 1951. *Lateinische Umgangsprache.* (Heidelberg)

Jacobs, F. 1877. "In Petronii *Satyricon.*" *JPh* 206–11 (there are much earlier unpublished notes)

Jahn, O. 1861. See the Introduction to Buecheler[1], xliii

Kaibel, G. 1960. Unpublished notes shared with Mueller by Fraenkel at about this time

Keller, O. 1861. "Zur Kritik der petronischen *Cena Trimalchionis.*" *RhM* 16, 532–61

Korn, M., and Reizer, S. 1986. *Concordantia Petroniana.* (Hildesheim)

Kraffert, H. 1888. *Neue Beitraege zur Kritik und Erklaerung lateinischer Autoren.* (Leipzig)

Krohn, C. 1887. "Quaestiones ad anthologiam latinam spectantes." (diss. Halle)

Lachmann, K. 1892. *Brief an Moritz Haupt* (*q.v. supra*), 181. (Berlin)

Leo, F. 1960? Handwritten ms. for Kaibel (*q.v. supra*), shared with Fraenkel, then with Mueller

Lindsay, J.-N. 1944. *The Complete Works of Gaius Petronius, Tr. and Illust.* (New York)

Luck, G. 1959. *The Latin Love Elegy.* (London)

Martindale, C.A. 1976. "Petroniana." *Latomus* 35, 857–60

Mentel, J. 1664. *Anekdoton Ex Petronii Arbitri Satirico Fragmentum* … (Paris)

Morgan, J.R. 1978. "Emendations in the *Satyricon.*" *Latomus* 37, 749–51

Mueller, K. 1961[1]. *Petronii Arbitri Satyricon.* (Munich, *editio maior*)

– with Ehlers, W. 1965[2]. *Petronius, Satyrica. Schelmengeschichten.* Lateinisch-Deutsch (Munich)

– with Ehlers, W. 1983[3]. *Petronius Satyrica. Schelmenszenen.* Lateinisch-Deutsch (Munich)

– 1995[4]. *Petronii Arbitri Satyricon Reliquiae.* (Stuttgart)

– 2003[4c]. *Petronii Arbitri Satyricon Reliquiae.* (Munich)

Nelson, H.L.W. 1971. "Bemerkungen zu einem neuen Petrontext." *Mnemosyne* 24, 60–87

Nisbet, R.G.M. 1962. "Review of Mueller 1961." *JRS* 52, 227–32

Öberg, J. 1999. *Petronius Cena Trimalchionis.* (Stockholm)

Pellegrino, C. 1986. *T. Petronio Arbitro Satyricon, Vol. 1.* (Rome)

Petersmann, H. 1977. *Petrons Urbane Prosa.* (Vienna)

Prieto, E.J. 2002. *Petronio Satiricon.* (Buenos Aires)

Reeve, M. 1971. "Eleven Notes." *CR* 21, 324–9 (on *Sat.* 111.2 only)

Richardson, T.W. 1979. "Some Shared Comic Features in Petronius and P.G. Wodehouse." *CV* 23, 64–70

– 1984. "Homosexuality in the *Satyricon.*" *C&M* 35, 105–27

– 1984. "A New Renaissance Petronius Ms.: Indiana ND 58 (I)." *Scriptorium* 38, 89–100

– 1986. "Pierre Dupuy, Petronius, and B." *RHT* 16, 319–24

– 1993. *Reading and Variant in Petronius: Studies in the French Humanists and Their Manuscript Sources.* (Toronto)

– 2007. "Petroniana." *Mouseion* s. 3 vol. 7, 27–52

– 2019. "Of a Love beyond Repair: Gender Eros and Ethos in Ovid's Narcissus (*Met.* 3.339–510)." *Mouseion* s. 3 vol. 16, 171–83

Rohde, E. 1879. "Zu Petronius." *NJPhP* 119, 845–8 (see Schmeling-Stuckey 1977)

Sage, E.T. 1929. *Petronius the Satiricon.* (New York)

Salonius, A. 1926. *Petroniana, 1.* (Helsinki)

Scheffer, J. 1665. *T. Petronii Arbitri Fragmentum Nuper Tragurii Dalmatiae Repertum.* (Uppsala)

Schmeling, G.A. 1994/5. "Confessor Gloriosus: A Role of Encolpius in the *Satyrica.*" *WJA* 20, 207–24

– 2011. *A Commentary on the Satyrica of Petronius.* (Oxford)
– 2018. "The Autobiography of Encolpius." In *Dynamics of Ancient Prose.* (Berlin)
– 2020. *Petronius Satyricon & Seneca Apocolocyntosis.* (Cambridge, Mass.)
Schmeling, G.A., and Stuckey, J. 1977. *A Bibliography of Petronius.* (Leiden)
Segebade, J. 1880. "Observationes grammaticae et criticae in Petronium." (diss. Halle)
Shackleton Bailey, D.R. 1987. "On Petronius." *AJP* 108, 458–64
Simon, J.H. 1975. Unpublished (?) emendations reported by M.S. Smith in his *Cena* edition
Smith, M.S. 1975. *Petronii Arbitri Cena Trimalchionis.* (Oxford)
Strelitz, J.P. 1879. "Emendationes Petronii Satyrarum." *JP* 119, 629 *sqq.*
Sullivan, J.P. 1968. *The Satyricon of Petronius: A Literary Study.* (London)
– 1976. "Interpolations in Petronius." *PCPhS* 22, 90–122
– 1986[2] (1965[1]). *Petronius the Satyricon & Seneca the Apocolocyntosis.* (London)
– 2012. (New introduction and notes to this edition by H. Morales)
Suringar, E. 1812. *Spicilegia Critica ad Petronium de Bello Civili.* (Lingen)
Swanson, D.C. 1963. *A Formal Analysis of Petronius' Vocabulary.* (Minneapolis)
Thielmann, P. 1884. "Zu Petronius." *Philologos* 43, 358
Thomas, P. 1893. "Ad Petronium *Sat.* 129." *Mnemosyne* 21, 179
Ullman, B.L. 1943. "'Bucca, bucca.'" *CPh* 38, 94–102
Vannini, G. 2007. *Petronius 1975–2005: bilancio critico e nuove proposte.* (Goettingen)
– 2010. *Petronii Arbitri* Satiricon *100–115.* (Berlin)
van Thiel, H. 1971. *Petron: Ueberlieferung und Rekonstruktion.* (Leiden)
Voss, I. 1684. "Observationes in Catullum." (London)
Walsh, P.G. 1996. *Petronius:* The Satyricon. (Oxford)
Warmington, E.H., ed. 1969. *Petronius.* (Cambridge, Mass.)
Watt, W.S. 1986. "Notes on Petronius." *Classica et Mediaevalia* 37, 173–84
Wehle, G. 1861. "Observationes Criticae in Petronium." (diss. Bonn)
Whittick, G.C. 1986. "Tres albi sues: Petronius Cena 47.8–50.1." *PSN* 16, 8–9
Winterbottom, M. 1972. "Six Conjectures." *CR* 22, 11–12
Zinn, E. 1961. *Festschrift fuer H. Hommel.* (Tuebingen)

INDEX PERSONARUM IN EXPOSITIONE NARRATIONIS*

a) *Aequales* — contemporaries

* Name cited at first appearance only; the binomial figure (e.g. 3.1) denotes chapter and verse in the Latin text. For sense and context of the description, where needed, refer to the English translation *ad locum,* opposite.

b) *Pristini* — forerunners in myth, history, literature, and art

PHOENIX SUPPLEMENTARY VOLUMES

1 *Studies in Honour of Gilbert Norwood* edited by Mary E. White

2 *Arbiter of Elegance: A Study of the Life and Works of C. Petronius* Gilbert Bagnani

3 *Sophocles the Playwright* S.M. Adams

4 *A Greek Critic: Demetrius on Style* G.M.A. Grube

5 *Coastal Demes of Attika: A Study of the Policy of Kleisthenes* C.W.J. Eliot

6 *Eros and Psyche: Studies in Plato, Plotinus, and Origen* John M. Rist

7 *Pythagoras and Early Pythagoreanism* J.A. Philip

8 *Plato's Psychology* T.M. Robinson

9 *Greek Fortifications* F.E. Winter

10 *Comparative Studies in Republican Latin Imagery* Elaine Fantham

11 *The Orators in Cicero's* Brutus*: Prosopography and Chronology* G.V. Sumner

12 Caput *and Colonate: Towards a History of Late Roman Taxation* Walter Goffart

13 *A Concordance to the Works of Ammianus Marcellinus* Geoffrey Archbold

14 *Fallax opus: Poet and Reader in the Elegies of Propertius* John Warden

15 *Pindar's* Olympian One*: A Commentary* Douglas E. Gerber

16 *Greek and Roman Mechanical Water-Lifting Devices: The History of a Technology* John Peter Oleson

17 *The Manuscript Tradition of Propertius* James L. Butrica

18 Parmenides of Elea *Fragments: A Text and Translation with an Introduction* edited by David Gallop

19 *The Phonological Interpretation of Ancient Greek: A Pandialectal Analysis* Vít Bubeník

20 *Studies in the Textual Tradition of Terence* John N. Grant

21 *The Nature of Early Greek Lyric: Three Preliminary Studies* R.L. Fowler

22 Heraclitus *Fragments: A Text and Translation with a Commentary* edited by T.M. Robinson

23 *The Historical Method of Herodotus* Donald Lateiner

24 *Near Eastern Royalty and Rome, 100–30 BC* Richard D. Sullivan

25 *The Mind of Aristotle: A Study in Philosophical Growth* John M. Rist

26 *Trials in the Late Roman Republic, 149 BC to 50 BC* Michael Alexander

27 *Monumental Tombs of the Hellenistic Age: A Study of Selected Tombs from the Pre-Classical to the Early Imperial Era* Janos Fedak

28 *The Local Magistrates of Roman Spain* Leonard A. Curchin

29 Empedocles *The Poem of Empedocles: A Text and Translation with an Introduction* edited by Brad Inwood

30 Xenophanes of Colophon *Fragments: A Text and Translation with a Commentary* edited by J.H. Lesher

31 *Festivals and Legends: The Formation of Greek Cities in the Light of Public Ritual* Noel Robertson

32 *Reading and Variant in Petronius: Studies in the French Humanists and Their Manuscript Sources* Wade Richardson

33 *The Excavations of San Giovanni di Ruoti, Volume I: The Villas and Their Environment* Alastair Small and Robert J. Buck

34 *Catullus Edited with a Textual and Interpretative Commentary* D.F.S. Thomson

35 *The Excavations of San Giovanni di Ruoti, Volume 2: The Small Finds* C.J. Simpson, with contributions by R. Reece and J.J. Rossiter

36 The Atomists: Leucippus and Democritus *Fragments: A Text and Translation with a Commentary* C.C.W. Taylor

37 *Imagination of a Monarchy: Studies in Ptolemaic Propaganda* R.A. Hazzard

38 *Aristotle's Theory of the Unity of Science* Malcolm Wilson

39 Empedocles *The Poem of Empedocles: A Text and Translation with an Introduction, Revised Edition* edited by Brad Inwood

40 *The Excavations of San Giovanni di Ruoti, Volume 3: The Faunal and Plant Remains* M.R. McKinnon, with contributions by A. Eastham, S.G. Monckton, D.S. Reese, and D.G. Steele

41 *Justin and Pompeius Trogus: A Study of the Language of Justin's* Epitome *of Trogus* J.C. Yardley

42 *Studies in Hellenistic Architecture* F.E. Winter

43 *Mortuary Landscapes of North Africa* edited by David L. Stone and Lea M. Stirling

44 Anaxagoras of Clazomenae *Fragments and Testimonia: A Text and Translation with Notes and Essays* by Patricia Curd

45 *Virginity Revisited: Configurations of the Unpossessed Body* edited by Bonnie MacLachlan and Judith Fletcher

46 *Roman Dress and the Fabrics of Roman Culture* edited by Jonathan Edmondson and Alison Keith

47 *Epigraphy and the Greek Historian* edited by Craig Cooper

48 *In the Image of the Ancestors: Narratives of Kinship in Flavian Epic* Neil W. Bernstein

49 *Perceptions of the Second Sophistic and Its Times – Regards sur la Seconde Sophistique et son époque* edited by Thomas Schmidt and Pascale Fleury

50 *Apuleius and Antonine Rome: Historical Essays* Keith Bradley

51 *Belonging and Isolation in the Hellenistic World* edited by Sheila L. Ager and Riemer A. Faber

52 *Roman Slavery and Roman Material Culture* edited by Michele George

53 *Thalia Delighting in Song: Essays on Ancient Greek Poetry* Emmet I. Robbins

54 *Stymphalos: The Acropolis Sanctuary, Volume 1* Gerald Schaus with contributions by Sandra Garvie-Lok, Christopher Hagerman, Monica Munaretto, Deborah Ruscillo, Peter Stone, Mary Sturgeon, Laura Surtees, Robert Weir, Hector Williams, Alexis Young

55 *Roman Literary Cultures: Domestic Politics, Revolutionary Poetics, Civic Spectacle* edited by Alison Keith and Jonathan Edmondson

56 Fides *in Flavian Literature* edited by Antony Augoustakis, Emma Buckley, and Claire Stocks

57 *Maternal Conceptions in Classical Literature and Philosophy* edited by Alison Sharrock and Alison Keith

58 *Celebrity, Fame, and Infamy in the Hellenistic World* edited by Reimer Faber

59 *Walking through Elysium: Vergil's Underworld and the Poetics of Tradition* edited by Bill Gladhill and Micah Young Myers

60 *Vergil and Elegy* edited by Alison Keith and Micah Young Myers

61 *Localism in Hellenistic Greece* edited by Sheila Ager and Hans Beck

62 *Marguerite Yourcenar's Hadrian: Writing the Life of a Roman Emperor* by Keith Bradley

63 *The* Satyrica *of Petronius* by Wade Richardson

www.ingramcontent.com/pod-product-compliance
Ingram Content Group UK Ltd.
Pitfield, Milton Keynes, MK11 3LW, UK
UKHW040026100325
455904UK00006B/7/J

9 781487 550714